*Created and Directed by Hans Höfer*

# INSIGHT GUIDES
# Hawaii

Update Editor: Scott Rutherford
Managing Editor: Martha Ellen Zenfell
Editorial Director: Brian Bell

HOUGHTON MIFFLIN COMPANY

APA PUBLICATIONS

# Hawaii

*Tenth Edition (Reprint)*
© 1995 APA PUBLICATIONS (HK) LTD
*All Rights Reserved*
Printed in Singapore by Höfer Press Pte Ltd

| Distributed in the United States by: | Distributed in Canada by: | Distributed in the UK & Ireland by: | Worldwide distribution enquiries: |
|---|---|---|---|
| **Houghton Mifflin Company** | **Thomas Allen & Son** | **GeoCenter International UK Ltd** | **Höfer Communications Pte Ltd** |
| 222 Berkeley Street | 390 Steelcase Road East | The Viables Center, Harrow Way | 38 Joo Koon Road |
| Boston, Massachusetts 02116-3764 | Markham, Ontario L3R 1G2 | Basingstoke, Hampshire RG22 4BJ | Singapore 2262 |
| ISBN: 0-395-68234-7 | ISBN: 0-395-68234-7 | ISBN: 9-62421-006-3 | ISBN: 9-62421-006-3 |

# ABOUT THIS BOOK

**a**ny contemporary writer of Hawaii follows in some weighty footsteps, including those of Somerset Maugham, Robert Louis Stevenson, Jack London, and Mark Twain. What distinguished these writers from others who wrote of Hawaii – and there were many, most of whom have faded with time – were their *insightful* words, sharing Hawaii with readers who had no access even to photographic images of the islands. Hawaii's spiritual depth required more than straightforward geographical descriptions, too. "In what other land save this one," asked London, "is the commonest form of greeting not 'Good day,' not "How d'ye do,' but 'Love'? That greeting is *Aloha* – love, I love you, my love to you… It is a positive affirmation of the warmth of one's own heart-giving."

The *Insight Guide* philosophy has always been to outfit a traveler properly with background essays on a place's history, culture, people and arts, *then* move on to describing places. One of these first efforts was *Insight Guide: Hawaii*, which became an immediate bestseller. Listed as recommended reading at the University of Hawaii, the book continues to be the top-selling book in Apa Publications' 180-strong series.

## A fresh new approach

After more than a decade of periodic updating, however, the book was ready for an overhaul, with new words, new pictures and a fresh, new approach. The task was undertaken by **Scott Rutherford**, who stayed on in Hawaii way back when after a *National Geographic* photographic assignment, "seduced by the mists and the waves, and by a woman's golden smile." Only Montana has had the same effect on him, he says. "In both places, it's the light, and the tolerant people." Rutherford had previously edited *Insight Guide: East Asia* and written Apa's *Insight Pocket Guide: Hawaii*.

Overseeing this new edition from Insight Guides' editorial office in decidedly untropical London was managing editor **Martha Ellen Zenfell**, a native of the American south now based in Europe. She and Rutherford took as their starting point the fine work done in the first edition by **Leonard Leuras**, who had also supervised *Insight Guides* to Korea, Hong Kong, Florida, and Mexico.

An *Insight Guide* is in large part defined by its superb photography. **Ron Dahlquist**, at home on Maui, is well known for his editorial and advertising photography. "In Hawaii, it's inspiring for a photographer to have such a wide variety of spectacular things to shoot," he says. No doubt the other photographers, who include **Galen Rowell** at Mountain Light, **Catherine Karnow**, **Bob Krist**, **Eric Herter**, **Jim Haas**, Apa chairman **Hans Höfer**, **Frank Salmoiraghi**, **Boone Morrison** and **Steve Wilkings**, feel the same way.

A crucial feature of this book are the many historical images by pioneer cameramen like **Ray Jerome Baker**. Apa would like to thank **Don Severson** and **Robert Van Dyke** for allowing us to delve into their historical collections, as well as **Ronn Ronck**, who not only wrote some of the original book, but kept it updated over the years and was instrumental in securing Baker's pictures.

**Susan Scott**, who came to Hawaii years ago to improve her windsurfing, turned her vacation into an endless summer and never left. With a biology degree from the Univer-

*Rutherford*

*Zenfell*

*Leuras*

*Ronck*

sity of Hawaii, she has established herself as a respected natural history writer, including a weekly newspaper column, three books, and this book's natural history essay "Towering Hills and Local Flowers." A frequent traveler, coming home to Hawaii is best. "I say to myself, 'Gee, I *live* here.' And what keeps me here is the delight of living in a truly multi-cultural society."

To know Hawaii, one must know something of the *kanaka maoli,* for whom Hawaii is a homeland. **Kekuni Blaisdell**, a professor of medicine at the University of Hawaii, has long worked to sustain traditional Hawaiian culture and restore local autonomy and sovereignty. "The kanaka maoli, the Hawaiian, is like a stranger in modern Hawaii," says Blaisdell. His essay "Spirit of the Islands" was distilled from his words in *Discovery,* a book published by the Bishop Museum Press. **Larry Lindsey Kimura**, our expert on the local language, is an instructor and former coordinator of the University of Hawaii's language section. He was assisted by **Pila Wilson**, an instructor at the Hilo campus.

Writing about Hawaii's food involves knowing many cuisines. On that criterion, Honolulu-based magazine writer **Marty Wentzel** qualified to write the food chapter. "I'm constantly amazed at the magical way that Hawaii's foods interweave with its sights, smells, and sounds." When pressed for recommendations, she confesses: "Give me a fresh mango on the beach at sunset."

**Jerry Hopkins** wrote the original *Insight Guide: Hawaii* essay on Hawaiian music and dance. His essay was as timeless as its subject – it required only one sentence change. A *Rolling Stone* editor in his younger days, Hopkins has written best-selling books on Elvis Presley and Jim Morrison.

Molokai-born and Lanai-raised **Alberta deJetley,** publisher and editor of the *Hana News,* undertook the job of rewriting essays on Molokai and Lanai. Kauai-based **Joan Conrow** brought her journalism background to a significant rewrite of the Kauai chapter – necessary after two island-changing hurricanes in a decade.

Many of the original book's contributors might not recognize their writing any more, but their efforts set down a solid foundation for this book. Dutch-born journalist **Jan W.P. TenBruggencate**, a decades-long resident of Kauai who is still there, wrote that island's chapter. Magazine and newspaper writer **Hal Glatzer** covered the Big Island. Other first-edition contributors included **Nedra Chung, Jocelyn Fujii, O.A. "Ozzie" Bushnell, Carl Lindquist** and **John Charlot.**

## The Final Touches

In *Insight Guides*' London editorial office, **Jill Anderson** chased the manuscripts and complicated Hawaiian spellings through a bank of Apple Macintoshes, and **Mary Morton** proofread and indexed the book.

On the islands, a sincere *mahalo* (thank you) goes to **Kelli McCormack, Bennett Hymer, Connie Wright, Ruth Limtiaco, Ruth Ann Becker, Julia Gajcak, Kenneth Eisley, Sonia Franzel, James Cockett, Fred Duerr, Charles Park, Nancy Daniels, Albert** and **Lorna Jeyte, Kenny Ching, Stephen Boyle, Stephanie Ackerman, Carol Zahorsky, Joyce Matsumoto, Lei-Ann Stender, Denise Anderson, Sherri Rigg, Jeanne Datz, Adi Kohler, Walter Liebetrau, Barbara Sheehan, B.J. Hughes**, and 1 million people calling Hawaii home.

*Scott*          *Wentzel*          *Hopkins*

# History

21  Aloha

25  Beginnings: Ancient Hawaii

35  The Arrival of Captain Cook

42  The Kamehameha Dynasty

52  End of a Royal Era

59  Modern Hawaii

# Features

71  Spirit of the Islands

74  *Hawaiian Gods*

81  An Ethnic Mix

85  The People of Hawaii

99  Music and Dance

105  Lei

107  The Hawaiian Language

111  Talking Local

115  Food for Thought

121   Surfing

127   Towering Hills and Local Flowers

## *Places*

135   Introduction

143   OAHU AND HONOLULU

145   Downtown and Honolulu Harbor

167   Waikiki Beach

181   Honolulu Neighborhoods

193   Windward Oahu

202   Central Oahu

207   Oahu's West Side

211   *The Leeward Islands*

217   MAUI

219   Haleakala and Upcountry

227   Central and West Maui

232   *Whale Watching*

236   The Hana Coast

**245  MOLOKAI**

**254  LANAI**

**265  HAWAII**

**267  Hilo and Central Hawaii**

**275  Kohala and Kona**

**285  Ka'u and Volcano**

**295  KAUAI**

**297  Kauai and Ni'ihau**

# *Maps*

**132**  Hawaiian Archipelago
**134**  Hawaii
**136**  Oahu
**137**  Maui
**138**  Kauai
**139**  Molokai/Lanai
**142**  Honolulu

# TRAVEL TIPS

**314** *Getting There*

**315** *Travel Essentials*

**316** *Getting Acquainted*

**319** *Communications*

**320** *Emergencies*

**321** *Getting Around*

**322** *Where to Stay*

**332** *Food Digest*

**334** *Things to Do*

**338** *Nightlife*

**339** *Shopping*

**342** *Sports*

**343** *Language*

**344** *Useful Addresses*

**345** *Further Reading*

**For detailed information see page 313**

# ALOHA

Hawaii is not only one of the world's scenic splendors, it also has one of its most harmonious gatherings of people. The islands themselves are diverse – warm beaches of white, green or black sand; cuisines, religions and languages of every persuasion; wide-open expanses and secretive, lush jungles. They encompass both Honolulu – the state's capital city of nearly a million people and the largest city between the Americas and Asia – and lonely snow-capped mountains touching the stars. There is bright and loud Waikiki, and verdant, distant Waipi'o Valley, enveloped by crystal-line silence and nights.

The most remote island chain in the world, Hawaii is a travelers' legend that succeeds. Its location midway between North America and Asia helps. In one recent year, 7 million visitors generated $9 billion for the state. Much of that revenue came from Waikiki, the beach resort near Honolulu that is electric, seductive, and often great fun – but not really Hawaii, of course.

Hawaii's social orientation is American, begun when early New England missionaries tried to change the islands into their own image of paradise. But Hawaii is actually more Asian and Polynesian than American and European. And for a few, whose seafaring ancestors arrived more than 1,000 years ago, Hawaii is a homeland – the only homeland they have.

Travelers sometimes forget that Hawaii is neither amusement park nor a big Polynesian dinner show, but rather home for over a million people. The preamble to Hawaii's Tourism Policy Act of 1976 makes a clarifying pronouncement: "Hawaii is unique in its combination of beauty in the natural physical environment, in its people and their Aloha Spirit, and in its cosmopolitan mixing of ethnic groups, cultures, religions and life styles. These facets of beauty are to be preserved and enhanced, not only because they are the basis of Hawaii's attraction to visitors but because they are the basis for Hawaii's attraction to its own people."

When translated, the word *aloha* breaks down as *alo* = to face; and *ha* = the breath of life. At times it seems to have lost texture by its overuse as a tourism slogan. But it is a word that has substantive meaning for Hawaii's people, who give it generously. Embrace aloha as warmly as it is offered.

**Preceding pages:** wings over Hawaii; a rainbow for each islander; red sails, Maui; Likelike Highway, Windward Oahu; horses and mountains, Oahu; Waikiki Beach boy. **Left**, welcome to the islands.

Dess. par S. Leroy d'après J. Arago.　　　　　　　　　　　　　Gravé par Leroy.

ÎLES SANDWICH. UN OFFICIER DU ROI EN GRAND COSTUME.

Kolea: 1. Pacific golden plover (*Pluvialis dominica fulvus*), a migratory bird which comes to Hawaii about the end of August and leaves early in May for Siberia and Alaska.
— *from Samuel Elbert and Mary Kawena Pukui's "Hawaiian Dictionary"*

The speckled plover, also referred to as the American golden plover, wends its way as far south and southwest as the Marquesas Islands, Tahiti and New Zealand. For thousands of miles, save for a stop in Hawaii and other more obscure landing strips, the plover's wings beat rhythmically through Pacific winds until the bird finds a perch in the central or south Pacific. Once there, it spends between 9 and 10 months fattening up on crustaceans, snails and insects, then flies away on an annual return journey to Alaska and Siberia when these destinations are at their warmest.

Ancient seafaring Polynesians no doubt observed the comings and goings of this bird. They knew that such a fragile, transitory bird had to be going *somewhere,* coming from *somewhere.* This curiosity was eventually to lead to the discovery of Hawaii, some 2,000-mile-plus (3,200 km) away.

In seaworthy, double-hulled canoes embellished with 'aumakua – carved spirit allies – these Polynesian islanders set out on epic ocean journeys, perhaps motivated by the plover heading north. The reasons for setting off into the unknown were probably many: seeking refuge from conquering enemies, or from persecution, or escaping the pressures of over-population. The Polynesians could, however, simply have been intrigued about the horizon.

**Hawaiian discovery:** The first European to find the Marquesas Islands, Portuguese explorer Pedro Fernandez de Quiros, stated flatly that there was no possibility of Polynesians traveling eastward very far against the prevailing trade winds. Such a journey, however long or short, would have "required instruments of navigation and ves-

sels of burthen, two things of which these people are destitute."

These "destitute" Marquesans, however, were but the last chapter of an island-hopping migration of peoples that began thousands of years earlier, probably in Southeast Asia. By AD 400, Marquesan canoes had sailed as far east as Easter Island, 2,500 miles (4,000 km) distant; in time they also reached New Zealand, and Hawaii. The British explorer and navigator Captain James Cook, who first sailed to the South Pacific in 1768 to "observe the transit of Venus," watched with a seaman's respectful gaze as Tahitians took eyeball bearings on stars and plowed ahead into uncertain seas.

**Navigating by starlight:** The Polynesians reaching Hawaii for the first time, in latitudes high above the familiar stars, had not just ventured into the unknown, but had, in the words of Kenneth Brower, literally left their universe.

They had none of Cook's navigational instruments and charts, relying instead upon an inner sense, an internal navigation system programmed by intuition, knowledge, and experience. The European explorers, too, ventured into an unknown, but it was a reasonably comfortable one referenced on a round planet consisting of magnetic poles and invisible lines of longitude and latitude. Wherever he was, however mysterious and far from home, the European navigator had a piece of paper with a direction and a mark on it for guidance.

The Polynesian navigator's view of the world, of the planet, was more limited. Not dependent on inscribed lines of latitude and longitude, he used an eclectic mix of information and clues by which to chart a steady course, making a study of birds like the plover, and of dolphins, and of the colors in water and clouds.

Most obvious, of course, were the stars. But the early Polynesians did not use just one star, or even a dozen stars. They used hundreds of stars, woven into a memorized tapestry of mnemonic chants that detailed hundreds of known course settings throughout the Pacific seas.

Based on observational and astronomical

**Preceding pages:** ancient petroglyph cave on the Big Island of Hawaii. **Left,** helmeted warrior in feather cape drawn by a French artist in 1819.

data accumulated over the years, it seems that Polynesians made the 2,000-mile-plus (3,200-km) journeys to Hawaii by fixing on two key stars – Sirius and Arcturus. Contemporary astronomers at Honolulu's Bishop Museum have written that "Sirius, the brightest star in the sky, passed almost directly over Tahiti and Raiatea (also called *Hawa'iti*). The present position of Sirius with respect to the equator has changed very little from that of the ancient days of Polynesian voyaging. Arcturus, called by the Hawaiians *Hokule'a* and noted for its bright redness off the Big Dipper's handle, presently passes over the northern end of the island of Hawaii. At the time of the great voyaging it passed over the island of Kaua'i."

Some of the most skilled Polynesian navigators did not use the stars at all. They were physically blind. Perhaps because their boats were considerably smaller and more nimble than the large European sailing ships, the Polynesians "felt" the ocean more, sensing its subtle moods and messages, just as today a sports car driver feels the road better than a bus driver. The Polynesian navigator felt the ocean, literally, in the direction of swells, and, among other things, in the subtle interference of waves that were reflected off distant islands.

**Fire and gnomes:** The first discoverers and settlers of Hawaii are believed to have arrived sometime between AD 500 and 800. Evidence of Marquesan landfalls in Hawaii has been confirmed by carbon dating, and by comparison of fishhooks and adzes found in Hawaiian and Marquesan sites dating from approximately the same period.

These new Hawaiians lived in relative isolation for several centuries after the first migrations, but about 500 or 600 years later, sometime between 1100 and 1300, Polynesians from Tahiti began arriving over a period of two centuries in the land they referred to as *Hawai'ia* – or "Burning Hawaii." This is believed to be a reference to Hawaii's volcanoes.

Scholars have speculated that this second wave of Polynesians subjugated the earlier Marquesans as slaves, or perhaps drove them farther north in the Hawaiian chain until they were completely eliminated. As with the Marquesans, the Tahitian immigration to Hawaii ended, and the settled newcomers lived in isolation for several centuries, de-

veloping into the Hawaiian culture that later greeted Captain Cook.

Conquered Marquesans may have been the *manahune,* or *menehune*, mentioned in early Hawaiian and Tahitian chants. The term *manahune* was used derisively in the Tahitian homeland to refer to slaves or plebeian castes, but its meaning changed through the centuries to mean, probably sarcastically, a group of mysterious gnomes or dwarfs who lived in the Hawaiian Islands at the time of the great Tahitian migrations.

**Offspring of Tahiti:** Both Polynesian groups brought with them a similar language, as well as foods, myths, traditions and gods. It was the Tahitians, however, who are cred-

A MAN OF THE SANDWICH ISLANDS WITH HIS MASK

ited with bequeathing the name Hawaii, which was first given to the major Big Island of Hawaii and only later to the complete chain of islands.

As the Polynesian bard Kamahualele chanted in centuries past: "Behold Hawai'i, an island, a people/The people of Hawai'i are the offspring of Tahiti."

Sir Peter Buck, the eminent half-Maori ethnologist who once served as director of the Bishop Museum, explained the origin of the word Hawai'i in his 1938 book *Vikings of the Pacific*. He noted that in ancient times "the headquarters of the Polynesian main body was established in the largest island of the leeward group of Tahiti, named Havai'i after an ancient homeland."

As Havaii-based fleets set out to settle the Society Islands, Samoa, Tonga, Fiji, Hawaii and New Zealand, they established colonies they often named after their home island. Dialectal differences resulted in today's place name variations.

An even more persuasive Hawaii-Tahiti relationship is exemplified by the ancient name of a channel located south of Maui, between the smaller Hawaiian islands of Lana'i and Kaho'olawe. The channel's Hawaiian name is *Kealaikahiki*. By substituting the *k*'s in the word with *t*'s, the word *Te-ala-i-tahiti* is formed, a term which in translation

plants unique to the Hawaiian Islands. The islands' undisturbed shoreline reefs and lagoons, fern forests, rich alluvial plains, and well-watered valleys and highlands were rich with indigenous flora and fauna. (Symbols so prominent in 20th-century tourist promotions – like coconuts, orchids, sugar cane and pineapples – were actually introduced to Hawaii.)

**Neither newts or gnats:** When the first Marquesans arrived, they found some 67 varieties of native Hawaiian birds (about 23 of which are now believed extinct). But surprisingly, neither amphibia (frogs, newts and the like), nor reptiles, nor mosquitoes, lice, fleas, flies or gnats were to be found.

A CANOE of the SANDWICH ISLANDS, the ROWERS MASKED.

means "the pathway to Tahiti," or "the pathway to foreign lands."

**Early life:** When the first Polynesian canoes landed on Hawaiian shores – probably at or near South Point on the Big Island – the islands were close to being an unspoiled paradise. At the time, much of the land was barren, dusty and largely host to scrub plants. But thriving were some 2,200 kinds of higher

**Left**, Hawaiian man in gourd mask. **Above**, similarly masked canoe rowers. Both were sketched in 1779 by John Webber, the artist who accompanied Captain James Cook on his third voyage and discovery of the Hawaiian Islands.

And for nearly 1,000 years, until mariners began arriving from the East and West, most fatal or even debilitating diseases were also absent.

The *malihini* Polynesians found only two mammals in Hawaii: a small bat, *Lasiurus cinereus*, or the hoary bat, which had somehow migrated from either North or South America; and the monk seal, *Monachus schauinslandi*, a relative of seals found in the Caribbean and the Mediterranean. The hoary bat, known as the *ope'ape'a* to Hawaiians, still haunts the nights of Big Island's Kilauea Crater area. The monk seal, nearly slaughtered into extinction for its valuable skin and oil during the 1800s, rarely ventures near populated islands although rare sightings have been known to occur.

The arriving Polynesians upset Hawaii's ecological balance with dogs, pigs, chickens and, probably unintentionally, the first stowaway rats. To supplement their diet, the first Hawaiians also introduced taro, a starchy tuber from which the grey, pasty mush called *poi* is made. Also introduced were coconuts, bananas, yams, *kukui* candlenuts, wild ginger, breadfruit and sugar cane. Then came utility plants like the *wauke*, or paper mulberry (*Broussonetia papyrifera*), which was beaten and sun-bleached to make *kapa* (bark cloth), and the *ti* (*Cordyline terminalis*), a

Other insights about early Hawaii are the initial observations made by foreign explorers – James Cook, George Vancouver and Otto von Kotzebue, for example – and the memoirs of early Hawaiian scholars, notably John Papa Ii (1800–70), Samuel Kamakau (1815–76), Kepelino Keauokalani (1830–78), and David Malo (1793–1853).

Another source has been the antiquities and folk lore collected by Abraham Fornander (1812–87), a surveyor, editor and judge. Fornander, who spoke and wrote Hawaiian fluently, was married to a local woman and wrote a history of the islands called *An Account of the Polynesian Race: Its Origins and Migrations*). He also collected and

relative of the lily whose roots and leaves are still used as wrapping and matting, and for making hula skirts and a liquor called *ti*-root *okolehao*.

Most of the information known about ancient Hawaiian life is from poetic oral traditions, known in the local language as *mele*. In these *mele*, the Hawaiians' *kupuna,* or ancestors, passed on to their descendants all they knew of their history. Various aspects of physical and spiritual life – from the trivial to the momentous – were reported in this unwritten literature, which consisted of family genealogies, myths and day-to-day accounts of human experiences.

translated many Hawaiian chants into English for posterity.

According to the information offered by these chroniclers, the people of Hawaii had developed into one of the most complex nontechnological cultures ever encountered by early Europeans.

**The *kapu* life:** Hawaiian life was simple but subtle, regulated under systematic laws known as *kapu*, a variation of the Tahitian word *tapu*, or taboo.

At the time of the first contact with Europeans, Hawaiian society was feudal and defined mostly by island, with two or three *mo'i*, or kings, struggling for control of each island. Beneath the kings were hereditary groups of *ali'i*, or noblemen. Nearly on the same level as *ali'i* were the *kahuna*, a prestigious group including priests, healers, and astrologers. Lower down was a small class of craftsmen and artists, *kanaka wale*, who made the canoes, calabashes, and lei, and who also included fishermen and hula dancers. The labor and working class, *maka'ainana* or commoners, worked the land.

At the very bottom were the social outcasts, the slaves or *kauwa-maoli*. Sometimes the unfortunate *kauwa* were marked by tattooing on their foreheads, and were often summarily conscripted as sacrificial victims by *kahuna* and executioners.

put to death for allowing his shadow to fall upon the house of a chief, or for passing through that chief's stockade or doorway, or entering the house before changing his *malo* loincloth, or by appearing there with his head smeared with mud.

Other common *kapu* declared that women could not eat pork, coconuts, bananas and shark meat, nor could they eat with men. Also, certain seasons were established – probably as conservation measures – for the gathering or catching of scarce food. Sometimes sporting chiefs made certain surfing spots *kapu* for their own exclusive use. Some *kapu* were instigated by Machiavellian chiefs, priests or influential court retainers under the

Under this hierarchy, the tightly circumscribed *kapu* and bloodlines could not be crossed. A typical penalty for a *kapu* violation was execution by stoning, clubbing, strangulation, live burial, or being burned alive. Sometimes a *kapu*-breaker was singled out as a convenient sacrificial victim for a god, but usually he was sacrificed as a lesson to others.

The Hawaiian scholar and historian David Malo has recounted that a person could be

**Left**, early engraving showing *kapa*-pounding, and the first known study of a surfboard. **Above**, temple exterior and carved gods.

guise of religion, or to tyrannically oppress a person or group of people. Many of the laws, however, were simply to protect resources and assure social stability.

*Kapu* violators, however, were provided with a place of last resort where they could seek sanctuary, whatever their crime. These places of refuge, called *pu'uhonua*, had to be reached by the *kapu* transgressor before he was caught. The odds, of course, were against the transgressor. (A good example of a *pu'uhonua* is located on a lava promontory at Pu'uhonua 'O Honaunau National Historical Park, on the Big Island's Kona coast. To see a photograph, turn to the essay called

*Spirit of the Islands* on pages 71–77.)

This intricate *kapu* system affected every aspect of Hawaiian life – from birth to death – until it was abolished in 1819 by King Kamehameha II and the queen regent, Ka'ahumanu. But until its abolition, *kapu* protected the powers of Hawaiian kings.

Hawaiians generally worshipped privately and at small shrines they built in their homes or outside, but the focal points of most major religious observances were large open-air temples known as *heiau*. Ruins of these *heiau* can be seen throughout Hawaii. In most cases, what remains today are rudimentary platforms, terraces and walls made of large lava stones. In ancient times, they

astrologer, to determine the most auspicious day to do battle.

**Warfare for fun:** Given the generally clannish and feudalistic structure of ancient Hawaiian society, wars of succession and conquest were somewhat frequent. Periodic and courtly sham-battles were held between friendly chiefs to keep young warriors prepped and alert. This system of forearming and forewarning was reminiscent of European days of chivalry.

The ritual aspects of Hawaiian wars quickly gave way to brutality. There might be some opening decorum, gladiator-style, where two renowned warriors would fight to the death in front of opposing armies. But more often

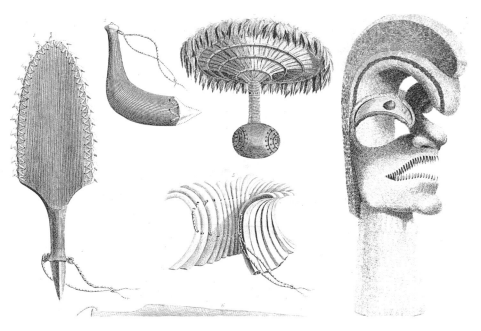

housed *kapa*-covered oracle towers, sacrificial platform-altars, carved stone and wooden sculptures, thatch and feather god images, sacred stones, rough-hewn monoliths, groupings of wood and stone sub-temple structures, and often a disposal pit for decayed human, animal or plant offerings.

The most complex temples were those built by Hawaiian chiefs to initiate a war. These *heiau waikaua* (war temples) or *luakini* temples were kept spiritually "alive," or current, by periodic human sacrifices. Once it had been decided to make war, and proper sacrifices had been made to Ku, the war god, the high chief would call for his *kilolani*, or

than not, the two armies would meet on an impromptu or chosen battleground – usually during daylight hours and following an exchange of verbal taunts and insults – and commence battle.

Common Hawaiian weapons included spears up to 18 ft (5 meters) in length, shorter javelins, assorted exotic daggers (some lined with shark teeth), stone-headed clubs, serrated shark-tooth clubs and "knuckle-dusters," a variety of sennit and stone tripping weapons, slingshots, strangling cords and any and all objects (rocks, boulders, branches and the like) that could be spontaneously introduced into the fray by the warriors.

Life in ancient times was not always an endless cycle of war-making, oppression and workaday drudgery, of course. Hawaiians developed unique forms of recreation, including such diversions as the flying of large kites (*lupe*) made of bark cloth (*kapa*); the staging of mini-dances and plays using hand puppets; numerous games of skill and chance; archery (used to kill rodents); more spectacularly, tobogganing on *holua* sleds that were raced down specially prepared hillside runways, and surfing, known as *he'e nalu*.

The Hawaiians also created the most exquisite variety of fine artwork and personal adornments found anywhere in Polynesia.

Wood and stone sculpture was extremely

It would be impossible today to duplicate one of these cloaks, because most of the birds whose feathers were plucked are now extinct. In old Hawaii, the king commissioned special groups of royal feather pluckers who stalked and snared preferred prey with nets and long sticky wands.

Hawaiian *kapa*, the soft Polynesian bark cloth fashioned from bast of the paper mulberry, also represents a major artistic achievement, but is now unfortunately extinct.

Perhaps the most diverse art practiced by the Hawaiians was adornment of the body in the form of necklaces, headbands and anklets made of flowers, nuts, seeds, shells, ivory, teeth, turtle shell, human hair, and

graphic and vigorous, and Hawaii's ancient featherwork is still considered to be the finest example of this art to be found. Captain James Cook, when first regarding the Hawaiian featherwork, observed that "the surface might be compared to the thickest and richest velvet." His lieutenant, James King, suggested that the "feathered cloak and helmet... in point of beauty and magnificence, is perhaps nearly equal to that of any nation in the world."

**Left**, articles from early Hawaii. **Above**, hand-colored engraving of a tattooed hula dancer in *kapa* (bark cloth) skirt.

other natural materials. Tattooing, too, was popular, and was often done as a sign of mourning. Both men and women tattooed their faces, limbs and torsos with a variety of favorite designs. Some were of a topical nature, but they also were of repetitious motifs resembling *kapa* patterns. The design was usually tapped and rubbed into the skin with small sharp needles of fish and bird bones or pointed shells.

Tattooing as a form of personal adornment is still practiced in other parts of Polynesia, and has long been popular in nautical circles, but on most of the Hawaiian islands it has largely disappeared.

seven o'clock A. M. a north-easterly breeze springing up, our anchors were ordered to be taken up, with a view of removing the Resolution further out. As soon as the last anchor was up, the wind veering to the east, rendered it necessary to make all the sail we could, for the purpose of clearing the shore; so that before we had good sea-room, we were driven considerably to leeward. We endeavoured to regain the road, but having a strong current against us, and very little wind, we could not accomplish that design. Our Commodore therefore dispatched Messrs. King and Williamson ashore, with three boats, to procure water and refreshments, sending at the same time, an order to Captain Clerk, to put to sea after him, if he should find that the Resolution was unable to recover the road. Having hopes of finding perhaps a harbour, at the west end of the island, we were the less anxious of regaining our former station; but boats having been sent thither, we kept as much as possible to windward, notwithstanding which, at noon, our ship was three leagues to leeward. As we approached the west end, we found that the coast rounded gradually, to the N. E. without forming a cove, or creek, wherein a vessel might be sheltered from the violence of the swell, which rolling in from the northward, broke against the shore in an amazing surf: all hopes, therefore, of meeting with a harbour here soon vanished. Many of the natives, in their canoes, followed us as we stood out to sea, bartering various articles. As we were extremely unwilling, notwithstanding the suspicious circumstances of the preceding day, to believe that these people were cannibals, we now made some further enquiries on this subject. A small instrument of wood, beset with shark's teeth, had been purchased, which, as it resembled the saw or knife made use of by the savages of New Zealand to dissect the bodies of their enemies, was suspected by us to be employed here for the same purpose. One of the islanders being questioned on this point, informed us, that the instrument above mentioned served the purpose of cutting out the fleshy part of the belly, when any person was slain. This explained and confirmed the circumstance before related, of the man's pointing to his belly. The native, however, from whom we now received this intelligence, being asked whether his countrymen eat the part thus cut out, strongly denied it; but when the question was repeated, he shewed some degree of apprehension, and swam off to his canoe. An elderly man, who sat foremost in the canoe, was then asked, whether they eat the flesh, and he answered in the affirmative. The question being put to him a second time, he again affirmed the fact; adding that it was savoury food. In the evening, about seven o'clock, the boats returned with a few hogs, some roots, plantains, and two tons of water. Mr. King reported to our Commodore, that the islanders were very numerous at the watering place, and had brought great numbers of hogs to barter; but our people had not commodities with them sufficient to purchase them all. He also mentioned, that the surf ran so very high, that it was with extreme difficulty our men landed, and afterwards got back into the boats.

On Saturday, the 24th, at day-break, we found that our ship had been carried by the currents to N. W. and N. so that the western extremity of Atooi, bore E. at the distance of one league. A northerly breeze sprung up soon after, and, expecting that this would bring the Discovery to sea, we steered for Oneeheow, a neighbouring island, which then bore S. W. with a view of anchoring there. We continued to steer for it till past eleven, when we were distant from it about six miles: but not seeing the Discovery, we were apprehensive lest some ill consequence might arise from our separating so far; we therefore relinquished the design of visiting Oneeheow for the present, and stood back to Atooi, intending to cast anchor again in the road, in order to complete our supply of water. At two o'clock, the northerly wind was succeeded by calms and variable light airs, which continued till eleven at night. We stretched to the S. E. till early in the morning of the 25th, when we tacked and stood in for Atooi road; and, not long after, we were joined by the Discovery.

We remained several days beating up, but in vain, to regain our former birth; and by the morning of Thursday the 29th, the currents had carried us to the westward within nine miles of Oneeheow. Weary with plying so unsuccessfully, we laid aside all thoughts of returning to Atooi, and resumed our intention of paying a visit to Oneeheow. With this view the master was dispatched in a boat to sound along the coast, and search for a landing place, and afterwards fresh water. In the mean time the ships followed under an easy sail. The master, at his return, reported, that there was tolerable anchorage all along the coast; and that he had landed in one place, but could not find any fresh water: but being informed by some of the natives, who had come over to the ships, that fresh water might be obtained at a village in sight, we ran down and cast anchor before it about six furlongs from the shore, the depth of water being 26 fathoms. The Discovery anchored at a greater distance from the shore, in 23 fathoms. The south eastern point of Oneeheow bore south, 65 deg. E. about one league distant; and another island which we had discovered the preceding night, named Tahoora, bore S. 61 deg. W. distant 7 leagues.

Before we anchored, several canoes had come off to us, bringing potatoes, yams, small pigs, and mats. The people resembled in their persons the inhabitants of Atooi, and, like them, were acquainted with the use of iron, which they asked for by the names of toe and hamaite, readily parting with all their commodities for pieces of that metal. Some more canoes soon reached our ships, after they had come to anchor; but the islanders who were in these had apparently no other object, than to make us a formal visit. Many of them came on board, and crouched down on the deck; nor did they quit that humble posture, till they were requested to rise. Several women, whom they had brought with them, remained along-side the canoes, behaving with much less modesty than the females of Atooi; and, at intervals, they all joined in a song, which, though not very melodious, was performed in the exactest concert, by beating time upon their breasts with their hands. The men who had come on board did not continue long with us; and before their departure, some of them desired permission to lay down locks of hair on the deck. This day we renewed the enquiry whether these islanders were cannibals, and the subject did not arise from any questions put by us, but from a circumstance that seemed to remove all doubt. One of the natives, who wished to get in at the gun-room port was refused, and he then asked, whether we should kill and eat him, if he should come in? accompanying this question with signs so expressive, that we did not entertain a doubt with respect to his meaning. We had now an opportunity of retorting the question, as to this practice; and a man behind the other, in the canoe, instantly replied, that, if we were killed on shore, they would not scruple to eat us; not that he meant they would destroy us for that purpose, but that their devouring us would be the consequence of our being at enmity with them. In the afternoon, Mr. Gore was sent with three armed boats, in search of the most commodious landing-place; being also directed to look for fresh water when he should get ashore. He returned in the evening, and reported, that he had landed at the village, and had been conducted to a well about half a mile up the country; but that the water it contained was in too small a quantity for our purpose, and the road that led to it was extremely bad.

On Friday, the 30th, Mr. Gore was sent ashore again with a guard, and a party to trade with the inhabitants for refreshments. The Captain's intention was to have followed soon afterwards; and he went from the ship with that design: but the surf had so greatly increased by this time, that he was apprehensive, if he got ashore, he should not be able to make his way back again. This circumstance really happened to our people who had landed with Mr. Gore; for the communication between them and the ships, by our own boats, was quickly stopped. They made a signal, in the evening, for the boats, which were accordingly sent; and in sho

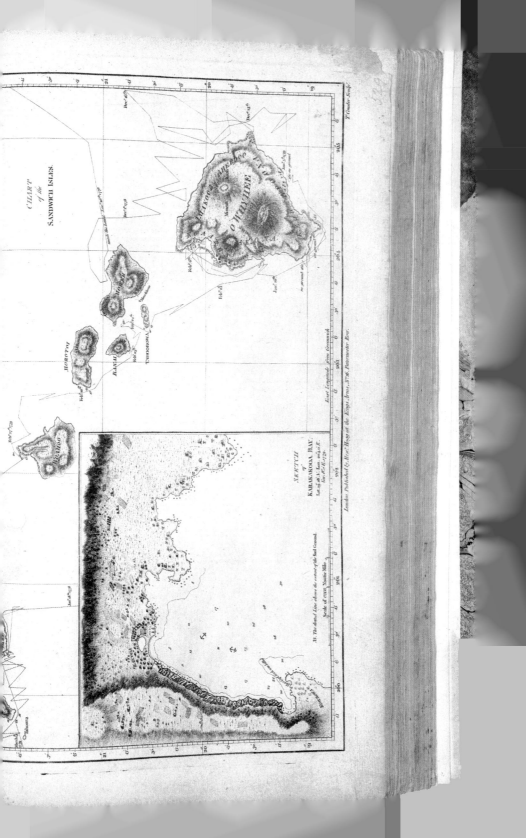

CHART
of the
SANDWICH ISLES.

MOROTOI

RANAI

TAHOOROWA

MOWEE

O WHYHEE

MOUNT WHEROO PAH

Owhyhee

SKETCH
of
KARAKAKOA BAY.
Lat. 19° 28' N. Lon. 204° E.
Var. 9° 6' 1779.

N.B. The dotted Letter shews the extent of the Fast Ground.

Scale of one Nautic Mile.

East Longitude from Greenwich

London. Published by Mess.ʳˢ Hogg at the King's Arms, N°16. Paternoster Row.

T. Conder Sculp.

# THE ARRIVAL OF CAPTAIN COOK

The ship was first sighted from Waialua and Wai'anae (on Oahu) sailing for the north. It anchored at night at Waimea, on the island of Kaua'i, that particular place being nearest at hand. A man named Moapu and his companions who were fishing with heavy lines saw this strange thing move by and saw the lights on board. Abandoning their fishing gear, they hurried ashore and hastened to tell Ka'eo and the other chiefs of Kaua'i about this strange apparition.

The next morning the ship lay outside Ka'ahe at Waimea. Chiefs and commoners saw the wonderful sight and marveled at it. Some were terrified and shrieked with fear. The valley of Waimea rang with the shouts of the excited people as they saw the boat with its masts and sails shaped like a gigantic sting ray. One asked another, "What are those branching things?" and the other answered, "They are trees moving on the sea." Still another thought, "A double canoe of the hairless ones of Mana!" A certain *kahuna* named Kuohu declared, "That can be nothing else than the *heiau* of Lono, the tower of Keolewa, and the place of sacrifice at the altar." The excitement became more intense, and louder grew the shouting – *the 19th-century Hawaiian author and historian, Samuel M. Kamakau*

**White-winged boats:** As Kamakau's report suggests, Hawaii's "modern" era began with both excitement and terror when Hawaiians on the island of Oahu saw two strange white-winged objects moving at sea in 1778. These "floating islands," as the Hawaiians were to describe them, were British ships – *HMS Resolution* and *HMS Discovery* – commanded by Captain James Cook.

En route from the South Pacific to the north – and, it was hoped, an elusive Northwest Passage – Cook and his crew (along with the astronomer and artist assigned to the *Resolution* and *Discovery* by the British Admiralty) had accidentally become the first

known non-Polynesians to land in the Hawaiian islands.

It was a formidable find, the last significant land on earth to be found by Europeans. In his ship's log, Cook later suggested that finding Hawaii was "in many respects the most important discovery made by Europeans throughout the extent of the Pacific Ocean." Cook marveled at the existence of the Polynesian settlements. "How shall we account for this Nation spreading itself so far over this Vast ocean...?" Cook named these

isles the Sandwich Islands, in honor of the Earl of Sandwich, the First Lord of the Admiralty and Cook's patron.

Oahu was the first island to be sighted, but Cook continued on to the northeast, making landfall on January 21, 1778, at Waimea on Kaua'i's west coast. After five days of replenishment and sightseeing – including a visit to impressive Waimea Valley – strong night winds blew his ships away from Kaua'i and nearer to the smaller island of Ni'ihau. There Cook's men received salt and yams and, in return, he left behind goats, pigs and the seeds of melons, pumpkins and onions. The first specimens of Western flora and fauna were also introduced at the northernmost populated island, on February 1, 1778.

Also introduced – against Cook's explicitly posted orders – were syphilis, gonorrhea, and other European diseases. All too aware of the effects of introduced diseases on indigenous peoples, Cook had told his men clearly that no Hawaiian women were to be allowed on board the ships, nor any person "having or suspected of having the venereal disease or any Symptoms thereof, shall lie with any woman" under threat of severe lashing at the ship's masthead.

Thomas Edgar, master of the *Discovery*, said his men employed every devious scheme possible to get women on board the ships,

Loa. Coming around the Big Island's southern point from the east, Cook dropped anchor on the Kona coast in a bay called Kealakekua, the "pathway of the god." It was January of 1779, exactly a year since his first landfall in Kaua'i.

If Cook was impressed a year earlier by the way Hawaiians on Kaua'i had prostrated themselves in his presence, he must have been equally if not more impressed by the second reception in Kealakekua Bay. By all accounts, Cook's second coming was monumental. He arrived at a propitious time: the *makahiki* celebration, an annual tribute for the god *Lonoikamakahiki* – and Cook's auspicious arrival was identified by the Hawai-

*An OFFERING before CAP. COOK, in the SANDWICH ISLANDS.*

even "dressing them up as Men." But he noted also that the Hawaiian women "used all arts to entice them into their Houses & even went so far as to endeavour to draw them in by force."

In February, Cook departed Hawaii to continue his search for the Northwest Passage, taking his two ships far above the Arctic Circle during the summer months. As winter once again approached, Cook returned to Hawaii, sighting Maui in November of the same year. For nearly two months, the *Discovery* and *Resolution* charted the islands – first Maui, then the Big Island with its snow-covered peaks of Mauna Kea and Mauna

ians as Lono's return. Consequently, Cook was afforded the greatest welcome ever accorded a mortal in Hawaii.

One of Cook's lieutenants estimated that some 10,000 Hawaiians turned out in canoes, on surfboards, swimming in the bay, and on shore to greet the return of Lono. Cook wrote: "I have nowhere in this sea seen such a number of people assembled in one place; besides those in the canoes, all the shore of the bay was covered with people, and hundreds were swimming about the ship like shoals of fish." John Ledyard, an American adventurer who had signed on board the *Resolution* as corporal of the marines, reported later that two officers counted from 2,500 to 3,500 canoes afloat in Kealakekua's waters. Ledyard and others also described unusual white *kapa* banners held aloft on crossbars – an ancient symbol of Lono – which resembled the British ships' masts and sails; Ledyard wrote that when Cook went onshore, the masses of Hawaiians "all bowed and covered their faces with their hands until he was passed."

During the next two weeks, there were opulent and special ceremonies held in Cook's honor, including one at a sacred temple, or *heiau*. In return, Cook and his men tried their best to please the Hawaiians with tours of their ships, a flute and violin concert,

kekua Bay by King Kalaniopu'u, the area was nearly deserted. The Hawaiians who remained were not as generous in their tribute, and in fact were surprised that a god's property could be so badly damaged within his own domain.

Increasingly the Hawaiians grew bold, taking objects from the ships that pleased their fancy, particularly things made of metal. When they took the *Discovery*'s cutter, Cook went ashore with nine marines and a lieutenant to take Kalaniopu'u hostage in exchange for return of the cutter, a strategy that had worked before on other Pacific islands. A scuffle broke out, and a large party of over 200 Hawaiian warriors attacked Cook's land-

The DEATH of CAPTAIN COOK.

and a fireworks display. All the while, Cook readied his ships for a voyage to Asia, and after two weeks, the *Discovery* and *Resolution* set sail. But three days later off the Big Island's north shore, a fierce winter storm damaged the *Resolution*'s foremast. Cook returned to Kealakekua for repairs.

**The death of Cook:** Cook found that the *makahiki* festival at Kealakekua was finished, and because of a *kapu* put on Keala-

ing party. Five of the marines escaped, but four others, as well as Cook himself, died in the shallows of Kealakekua Bay. The British ships fired on the Hawaiians, who were forced to retreat.

Two delegations of concerned Hawaiians later returned parts of Cook's body "cut to pieces & all burnt," wrote James King, Cook's second lieutenant. One bundle of Cook's bones, wrapped in fine *kapa* bark cloth and a cloak made of black and white feathers, included "the Cptns hands (which were well known from a remarkable Cut) the Scalp the Skull, wanting the lower jaw, thigh bones & Arm bone; the hands only had flesh on them,

& were cut in holes, & salt crammed in; the leg bones, lower jaw & feet, which were all that remain'd & had escaped the fire, he said were dispers'd among other Chiefs."

What remained of Cook was buried in Kealakekua Bay, and in late February of 1779, the *Discovery* and *Resolution* set sail, passing Maui, Moloka'i and Oahu before anchoring again briefly at Waimea, on Kaua'i.

Writing 80 years later – after the Hawaiian population had dropped drastically from an estimated 300,000 persons at the time of Cook's visit to about 60,000 – Hawaiian historian Kamakau wrote the following bitter (and somewhat exaggerated, perhaps) commentary on Cook:

"The seeds he planted here have sprouted and grown and grown and become the parents of others that have caused the decrease of the native population of these islands: gonorrhea and other social diseases; prostitution; the illusion of his being a god which led to worship of him; fleas and mosquitoes; epidemics; changes in the air which we breathe; the coming of things that weaken the body; changes in plant life; changes in religion, in the arts of healing, in the laws by which the land is governed...

Because he killed the people, he was killed by them without mercy and his entrails were used to rope off the arena and the palms of his hands used for fly swatters at a cockfight."

Kamakau also alleged that Cook himself received and slept with a Kauai princess, but offical British reports of the voyage deny such a liaison.

**Spanish conquest?:** Mention should also be made of the possibility that Spanish ships may have landed in Hawaii long before Cook, perhaps two centuries earlier.

Historians have offered the existence of several unexplained artifacts, including a map taken by the British in 1742 from a captured Spanish galleon, the *Nuestra Señora de Cabadongo*. The map was described as "a chart of the northern Pacific which marked the track of the round trip between the Philippines and Acapulco," showing a group of islands in approximately the same latitude as Hawaii. Pro-Spanish proponents also argue the following historical events:

• The Spanish had sustained a galleon trade between Mexico, Guam and the Philippines between 1556 and 1778, and the chances that a galleon would happen onto Hawaii at least once in 200 years were quite likely.

• That Hawaiian oral traditions speak of the coming of light-skinned people, who were given wives and became chiefs; during the 18th and early 19th centuries, Western visitors reported island residents with distinctly Caucasian features.

• That anthropologists have always been intrigued by traditional Hawaiian cloaks, helmets and daggers with a Spanish look, objects not found elsewhere in Polynesia. And Hawaiians often made their finest featherworks – the cloaks and helmets – of red and yellow feathers, which were the royal colors of Spain.

Pacific scholar Robert Langdon of the Australian National University cites "the discovery at the Bishop Museum in the 1950s of two alien items in the burial casket of a deified Hawaiian chief... who is estimated to have lived towards the end of the 17th century. The items are a piece of iron embedded in a wooden handle like a chisel, and a length of cloth 8-ft long by 1-ft wide, having the characteristics of sailcloth."

**Left**, helmeted Hawaiian warrior, *circa* 1800, resembles a Spanish grandee. **Right**, historians claim that the map captured by Commodore Anson in 1742 proves the Spanish knew about Hawaii's existence.

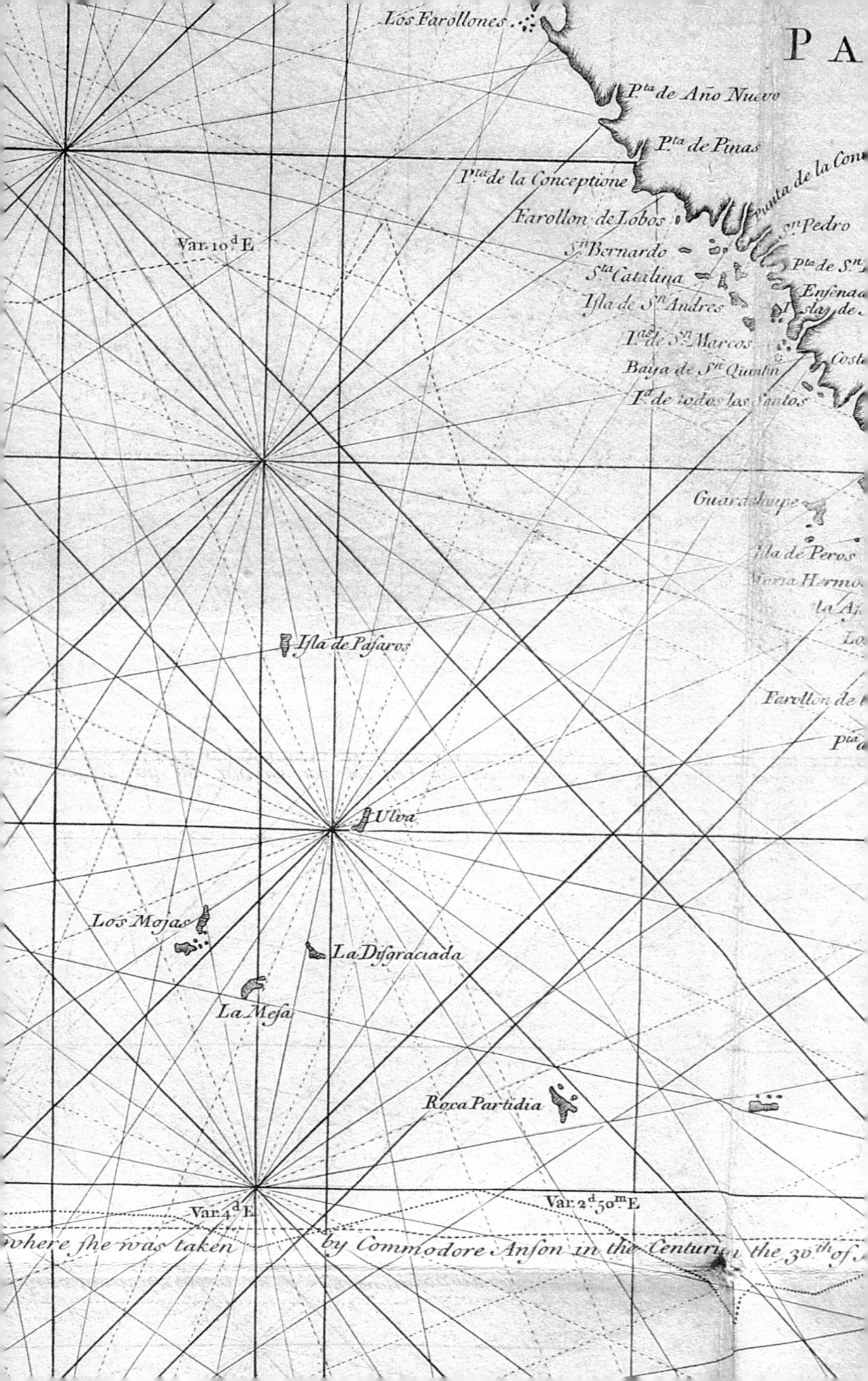

Los Farollones

P A

P.$^{ta}$ de Año Nuevo

P.$^{ta}$ de Pinas

P.$^{ta}$ de la Conceptione

punta de la Con

Farollon de Lobos

S.$^n$ Pedro

S.$^n$ Bernardo

P.$^{ta}$ de S.$^n$

S.$^{ta}$ Catalina

Ensenada

Isla de S.$^n$ Andres

slas de

Var. 10.$^d$ E.

I.$^a$ de S.$^n$ Marcos

Baya de S.$^n$ Quintin

Coste

I.$^a$ de todos los Santos

Guadalupe

Isla de Peros

Maria Hermo

la Af

Lo

Isla de Pajaros

Farollon de

p.$^{ta}$

Ulva

Los Mojas

La Disgraciada

La Mesa

Roca Partida

Var. 2.$^d$ 50.$^m$ E.

Var. 4.$^d$ E.

where she was taken            by Commodore Anson in the Centurion the 30.$^{th}$ of J

Lauvergne del

It was over five years after Cook's death before the next Europeans visited Hawaii. In 1785, a China-bound trading ship stopped for supplies, and in the following year, four ships – two each from England and France – visited the islands. They were soon followed to "Owhyee" by French, Russian, Spanish and American ships. Frigates, sloops and schooners ladened with American furs began dropping anchor in Hawaii. Most were bound for Macao, Shanghai and Canton, where the furs would be traded for silks and tea.

**Kamehameha the Great (1795–1819):** Often mentioned in the logs and diaries of visiting

ships' captains and merchants was a Hawaiian named Kamehameha, which means "the lonely one."

A distinguished warrior as a young man, Kamehameha (pronounced *ka-may-ha-may-ha*) had impressed Cook at Kealakekua Bay. Cook's lieutenant, James King, referred to *Maiha-maiha* – his phonetic interpretation of Kamehameha – as one of King Kalaniopu'u's chief subordinates. *Maiha-maiha's* hair, wrote King, "was now plaisted over with a brown dirty sort of paste or powder, & which added to as savage a looking face as I ever saw, it however by no means seemed an emblem of his disposition, which was good natur'd & humorous, although his manner shewd somewhat of an overbearing spirit, &

he seemed to be the principal director in this interview."

Kamehameha, a nephew of Kalaniopu'u, was a careful observer of the *haole* (white foreigners) and their strange objects, especially weapons. Kamehameha had been wounded by a gun on the beach when Captain Cook was killed and, despite Cook's death, it was evident to Kamehameha that one man with a small brass cannon could have a great advantage over several warriors with clubs and spears.

By 1789, Kamehameha's own large double canoe was carrying a swivel gun mounted on a platform strapped across the hulls. And not too much later, his double-hulled man-of-war was rigged as a Western-style schooner, with a jib, mainsail and foresail. On the ship's foredeck, riding between two cannon, was the feather-covered image of his war god, the fearsome *Kukailimoku* – the Snatcher of Lands.

A 10-year civil war involving Kamehameha and others erupted on the Big Island in 1782 after King Kalaniopu'u's death. When the timing seemed astrologically and militarily propitious, Kamehameha took his armies and conquered Maui and Lana'i in 1790, after a bloody battle at 'Iao Valley on Maui. He then returned to the Big Island to deal with the continuing civil war there. Keoua, his chief rival on the Big Island, was also a son of Kalaniopu'u and was distinctly displeased at how the inheritance had come to be divided.

In the meantime, Kamehameha lost Maui, whose own chief then invaded Kamehameha's Big Island domain with a war fleet of canoes. Kamehameha repelled the Maui invaders, assisted by the swivel guns and military expertise of Englishmen John Young and Isaac Davis.

**Englishmen in the court:** Young and Davis were brought together with Kamehameha by curious circumstance. Davis was serving on the schooner *Fair American,* off the Big Island near Kawaihae, when it was attacked by Hawaiians. Only Davis survived. Young was already on shore for some uncertain reason when Davis was rescued. Both were taken in by Kamehameha as advisors and later made high chiefs. During Kamehameha's conquest of the Big Island and then Oahu, Young and Davis manned the cannons on Kamehameha's war canoe. After Kamehameha's complete unification of the islands, Young and Davis were married into the Kamehameha family, thus gaining considerable land and power.

Having lived until a fine old age, Young was buried in the Royal Mausoleum. His granddaughter would become Queen Emma. The death of Davis, however, was tainted with intrigue. It's said that he was fatally poisoned after alerting Kamehameha's thorn-

volcanic explosions erupted on the southeast rim of Kilauea.

Offerings were made to the gods, but the eruptions continued unabated. Keoua ordered his men – and the accompanying women and children – to continue on in three groups at staggered intervals. The first group reached safety, but the second group, which consisted of about 400 men, women and children, was killed – probably suffocated by gases released through a rift zone vent during the eruption. In a ghostly epitaph, Keoua's expedition left footprints in the fallen volcanic ash. Some of this ash solidified, leav-

in-the-side opponent King Kaumuali'i, the holdout chief of Kaua'i, that he would be killed when he came to Honolulu to make peace with Kamehameha.

**Fire goddess:** Keoua, Kamehameha's Big Island rival, was not yielding easily. But Kamehameha had a powerful ally, perhaps, in the fire goddess Pele.

In late 1790, an expeditionary force under Keoua's command was hiking from Hilo to Ka'u through the Kilauea area when sudden

ing footprints that can still be seen today.

Hawaii's state statistician, Robert C. Schmitt, reported in an article titled "Catastrophic Mortality in Hawaii" that the 1790 volcanic devastation of Keoua's second group "was the greatest natural disaster in Island history, and ranked second only to the Pearl Harbor attack among all Hawaiian catastrophies."

A true believer in his gods, Kamehameha took no chances, despite Pele's intervention. He built an immense *heiau* to his war god near Kawaihae in Kohala – it still stands – and invited Keoua to meet him there. When Keoua arrived, Kamehameha had him killed.

Kamehameha was now king of all the Big Island. (But not of his own household, appar-

**Preceding pages:** French officers and seamen enjoy an Oahu hula extravaganza. **Left**, Kamehameha the Great. **Above**, a Big Island chief, said to be Liholiho Kamehameha II, lounges in his longhouse with his dutiful retainers.

ently. When the English captain George Vancouver visited Kamehameha the following year, he found the king at odds with his favorite wife, Ka'ahumanu. Vancouver mediated and settled the quarrel.)

His momentum regained, Kamehameha recaptured Maui, then Moloka'i. In the meantime, a small civil war had broken out on Oahu, and Kamehameha took advantage of the disorder to land with his fleet on southern Oahu in 1795. Kamehameha literally pushed Oahu's remaining army over the top of Nu'uanu Valley. With Oahu's conquest – and the ritual sacrifice of Oahu's king, Kalanikupule, to Kamehameha's war god – Kamehameha was monarch of most of Hawaii. But there remained stubborn Kaua'i and Ni'ihau.

wood proved a lucrative trade for Kamehameha. He forced commoners by the thousands to harvest it for shipment to Asia; many Hawaiians died. Kamehameha and later his son, Liholiho, continued the sandalwood exports until there was none left.

At what is now the town Kailua-Kona on the Big Island, Kamehameha the Great died of illness in 1819, near a favorite *heiau* known as *Kamaka Honu* – the Eye of the Turtle. He was about 63 years old.

A firm believer in the power of the Hawaiian gods, just before dying he nevertheless denied tradition by turning down his priests' demand for the required human sacrifice upon his death: "The men are *kapu* for the king." So that nobody could defile them – or use their powerful *mana* – Kamehameha's

In 1796 – and again in 1809 – Kamehameha assembled invasion fleets destined for Kaua'i and Ni'ihau, the most distant of the main islands. The channel from Oahu to Kaua'i is treacherous, and both invasion attempts were foiled by the elements and by outbreaks of disease. Finally, in 1810, following further threats and diplomatic overtures, Kaua'i's Kaumuali'i yielded to Kamehameha. The islands were now unified under King Kamehameha I, or more commonly, Kamehameha the Great.

Although Kamehameha retained the *kapu* system after unifying the islands and was quick to apply its punishments, he also learned the ways of the Europeans whose ships he supplied with provisions. Hawaii's sandal-

bones were hidden in a secret place somewhere on the Kona coast. No one, it seems, remembers where.

Kamehameha's death catapulted unified Hawaii into an age of mariners, merchants, missionaries, monarchs, migrants and, much later, *malihini* tourists.

**Kamehameha II (1819–24):** Kamehameha's son and successor, Liholiho, was not in his father's image of a strong and autocratic ruler. But the favorite of Kamehameha the Great's many wives, Ka'ahumanu, was strong. She made it clear to Liholiho upon Kamehameha's death that it was his father's wish that she be the *kuhina nui,* the joint ruler or queen regent of Hawaii.

One of Ka'ahumanu's first actions was to

collapse the *kapu* system. Urged on by Ka'ahumanu, Liholiho sat down with her at a feast, violating the *kapu* against men and women eating together. The ancient *kapu* system was no longer.

Ka'ahumanu and Liholiho ordered that all the *heiau* be desecrated, and that all carved wooden idols be burned. The social and cultural shock to the Hawaiian people was enormous, leaving an overwhelming spiritual vacuum.

**Missionary landing:** Congregationalist missionaries en route to Hawaii had left Boston before Kamehameha the Great died. Had the timing of the *kapu* collapse and the arrival of the missionaries not been so coincidental, the history of post-contact Hawaii could have been very different.

ing. Some of our number, with gushing tears, turned away from the spectacle. Others, with firmer nerve, continued their gaze, but were ready to exclaim, 'Can these be human beings? Can such things be civilized?' "

But missionaries by definition have a mission in mind, and although Ka'ahumanu and Liholiho had reservations about these overdressed *haole,* they let the American missionaries preach at Kailua-Kona and Honolulu for a one-year trial. The missionaries never left, and their descendants gathered land and power that still define Hawaii's politics and economics today.

**The last voyage:** The English had retained an interest in Hawaii since Cook's first contact, and in 1822 Liholiho received a gift from George IV, King of England: a small

This first party of 14 New England missionaries arrived in 1820 aboard the American brig *Thaddeus,* ready to fill the Hawaiians' spiritual void. First impressions of the local population were not favorable.

The Rev. Hiram Bingham, unofficial leader of the group, wrote: "The appearance of destitution, degradation, and barbarism, among the chattering, and almost naked savages, whose heads and feet, and much of their sunburnt skins were bare, was appall-

**Left**, the first known picture of Honolulu village, *circa* 1816, by Louis Choris. **Above**, Chief Kalanimoku is baptized by a Roman Catholic priest in 1819, aboard the ship *L'Uranie*. The painting is by Arago.

schooner named the *Prince Regent.* Delighted, Liholiho left Hawaii the next year on a British whaling ship to visit King George and negotiate a treaty.

Liholiho and his entourage were royally feted in London, but before he could meet with King George, he and his queen and consort Kamamalu caught the measles and died. Two years later, Lord George Byron, cousin of the famous poet, sailed into Honolulu Harbor with the bodies of the late king and queen.

Before setting sail for England, Liholiho had dictated a will that designated his younger brother Kauikeaouli, who was Kamehameha the Great's sole surviving son, as his logical and natural successor.

**Kamehameha III (1825–54):** The early years of Kauikeaouli – Kamehameha III – would better be called the reign of Ka'ahumanu. Kauikeaouli was only 10 years old when his brother Liholiho died. As *kuhina nui,* Ka'ahumanu exerted a strong influence on both the boy king and the Hawaiian people, most of whom were still disoriented and adrift after the end of *kapu.*

Half a year after Liholiho left on his ill-fated trip to England, Ka'ahumanu had announced a system of civil laws obviously based on the Congregationalist missionaries' teachings. And in fact, the Congregationalist had cultivated considerable spiritual and political influence with Ka'ahumanu, eventually converting her to Christianity. Ka'ahumanu became one of the

Congregationalists' most enthusiastic converts. Another convert to Christianity was an *ali'i* peer, the Big Island high chiefess Kapi'olani.

In 1824, Kapi'olani (not to be confused with her niece and namesake, the future Queen Kapi'olani) hiked up to the mouth of Halema'uma'u in the Kilauea caldera. There, at the edge of the fire goddess' domain, Kapi'olani defiantly denounced and renounced Pele. Kapi'olani lived to tell about it, and at the Hilo Congregationalist mission, 90 impressed Hawaiians became instant new converts. Ancient rites of passage were about to end.

Encouraged by the royal support, missionaries built churches and schools throughout the islands. Even more, as "messengers of Jehovah," the missionaries used their court influence to veil Hawaiians with everything Puritan. Bare skin on women in any degree – much less nudity – was condemned, and women were draped in dresses mostly ill-suited to the tropics. The ancient and sacred *hula,* a dance of communication and poetry, was denounced as a lewd and lascivious abomination, and outlawed.

Equally high on the agenda was putting the Hawaiian language into romanized script, the *palapala* of reading and writing. The missionaries' intent in doing so was evangelical, no doubt, but teaching Hawaiians to write – and read – gave them a new tool with which to communicate their own histories and thought, especially as the missionaries had suppressed traditional story-telling methods like hula.

A visiting Russian captain wrote of Ka'ahumanu: "Formerly… she could only converse with persons who were present; now, let them be ever so distant, she could whisper her thoughts softly to them alone."

Roman Catholic missionaries from France tried to upset the Protestant monopoly. But Ka'ahumanu banished the Catholics – and persecuted Hawaiian converts to Catholicism. In the end, the Catholics persevered, and today Catholics are the largest denominational group in Hawaii.

When Ka'ahumanu died in 1832, Kamehameha III took full hold of the government reins, a reign noted for a couple of frivolous early years (or perhaps a personal rebellion against Puritanism) of horse racing, gambling, drinking, and dancing the *hula.* His half-sister, Kinau, the *kuhina nui* and successor to Ka'ahumanu, managed state matters during his bouts with the bottle.

Nurturing their influence with Kinau, the missionaries continued to consolidate power, accepting government and administrative appointments. Eventually, Kamehameha III was reconciled with both his inner demons and with Kinau.

Beginning in the mid 1820s, just as the sandalwood trees had all but disappeared from Hawaii, whaling became Hawaii's most important export, placing Honolulu and Lahaina among the Pacific's most important ports.

Whaling kept Hawaii's fragile economy above water for more than 30 years, pouring hundreds of thousands of dollars into the islands. Much of that money was funneled into the interests and diversions preferred by sailors at liberty. (At whaling's peak in 1846, 429 ships were anchored in Lahaina.) Missionaries, of course, protested these activities. One visiting preacher in the early 1840s complained that Lahaina had become "one of the breathing holes of hell... a sight to make a missionary weep." Attempts by the missionaries to quench liquor and prostitution were not well received. The homes of several preachers in Lahaina were bombarded by angry sailors from aboard the safety of anchored ships.

**Land for all:** Perhaps Kamehameha III's most significant and irreversible act was an edict issued in 1848, which became known as the Great Mahele.

within a few years, the *haole* had accumulated large estates of land and the power that comes with it.

The historian Lawrence H. Fuchs writes in his book, *Hawaii Pono: A Social History:* "After the [Great] Mahele, foreigners eagerly purchased government lands at moderate prices. Even some of the missionaries found land speculation compatible with spreading the Gospel... By 1852, sixteen of the forty-six members of the Congregational mission possessed land titles, averaging 493 acres per man, some of which had come as gifts from chiefs or the King... [the] second generation of missionary families was even more active in land speculation."

So much so that by 1886, about two-thirds of all government lands sold had been bought

Under subtle pressure by missionary advisors and businessmen, Kamehameha III divided Hawaii's land ownership – previously the pleasure of the royalty – among the monarchy, the government, and the common people, thus allowing ordinary Hawaiians to own property for the first time. Two years later, foreigners – *haoles* – too were permitted land ownership.

Fortunately for the foreign business and missionary interests, land ownership was not a tradition, nor even an understandable concept, among the Hawaiian commoners and,

**Left**, King Kamehameha III and Queen Kalama posed for this picture in 1846. **Above**, a Danish artist in 1852 captured aspects of Honolulu life.

by resident *haole*. As one contemporary Hawaiian entertainer suggests, "the missionaries taught us how to bow our heads in prayer, and when we looked up again the land was gone."

By the late 1850s, whales had been hunted nearly to extinction, petroleum and coal were replacing whale oil, and the United States was sinking into a civil war. The boom days of the Hawaiian Islands were over.

**Sweet alternative:** Hawaii's business and political interests turned from whaling to a new commodity, sugar cane. During the California Gold Rush in 1849, a handful of small sugar planters in Hawaii had made great profits when gold-hungry and sugar-hungry *Kaleponi*, or California, turned to

Hawaii for its sugar supply. Sugar's potential looked sweet, especially for those with the land under the cane. Whereas whaling had been mostly a merchants' boom, sugar would be a land barons' boom.

But sugar plantations are labor intensive, and the local Hawaiian pool of laborers was almost nil; the population had been decimated by disease. And pragmatically, Hawaiians saw little merit in the low-paying, back-breaking work of harvesting sugar cane at meager wages, especially as the islands offered plenty of fish, *poi*, coconuts and other traditional foods.

For sugar to become a major industry, hundreds, then thousands, of laborers needed to be imported. The first group of 293 Chinese arrived in 1852, followed over the dec-

Foreign ways and methods were increasingly adopted into Hawaiian life and government. Kamehameha established the kingdom's first constitution which, in addition to creating a supreme court, established an upper ruling house made up of royalty and a lower house of representatives to be elected by the common people. He also ended the persecution of Catholics which had been begun by Kaʻahumanu.

Although married, Kamehameha III had no children. Before he died in 1854, he named a young nephew, Alexander Liholiho, as his successor.

**Kamehameha IV (1854–63):** Grandson of Kamehameha the Great, Alexander Liholiho had a certain dislike for America and, during his short reign, shifted Hawaii closer to the

ades by Japanese, Portuguese, Filipinos, Norwegians, Germans, Koreans, Puerto Ricans, Spaniards, and Russians. A significant percentage of Hawaii's ethnic mix today descends from those early immigrant laborers. Statistics show that their labors were productive: from sales of 1.5 million pounds (675,000 kg) of sugar in 1860, sales skyrocketed to 5.3 million pounds (2.4 million kg) in 1864, and had more than tripled to 17 million pounds (7.65 million kg) by 1872.

The 30-year reign of Kamehameha III – the longest of any Hawaiian monarch – although sometimes chaotic and autocratic, was one of considerable change and adjustment, of stability and growth, a time that would define Hawaii for what it is today.

British Empire in both spirit and policy.

Educated by Americans at an elite royal school, Kamehameha IV and a brother had visited Europe and America in 1849 and 1850. The experiences in Europe, especially England, were pleasant and enriching. But while in America, a train conductor in New York City mistook the Hawaiian prince for a Negro servant and ordered him out of the railway car. That memory of America lingered long.

Alexander Liholiho was not a shaker and a mover, but he left behind a legacy of concern for Hawaiians. One that remains today is Queen's Hospital, established by him in 1859 for sick and destitute Hawaiians, still dying from introduced European diseases.

In 1863, after the death of his four-year-old son, Kamehameha IV died at age 29 during an asthmatic attack. Some Hawaiians said he drank himself to death; others said he died of a broken heart.

**Kamehameha V (1863–72):** A believer in the strong, autocratic style of Kamehameha the Great, Lot Kamehameha, an elder brother of Kamehameha IV, refused to take an oath to uphold the liberal constitution of 1852. He believed that it weakened the powers of the Hawaiian monarchy, making it vulnerable to overthrow by non-royalists, a forethought that later turned out true.

In May of 1864, Lot declared a special convention to revise the constitution. As they often do, the convention accomplished nothing, and so Kamehameha V offered a

– mostly foreign businessmen – adding tinder to the forces that would later bring down the monarchy once and for all.

Kamehameha V was a serious monarch of little pretension and of few distractions. Hoping to keep his people tending their crops, he tried to restrain hula and other festive activities. Mark Twain wrote of Kamehameha V: "There was no trivial royal nonsense about him. He dressed plainly, poked about Honolulu, night or day, on his old horse, unattended; he was popular, greatly respected, even beloved."

A life-long bachelor, Kamehameha V left no heir and named no successor. When he died on his 42nd birthday in 1872, the 77-year-long dynasty of Kamehameha the Great came to an end.

PRECURSOR OF HAWAII'S COAT OF ARMS
*Prepared in London in 1843–44 at the order of Timothy Haalilio and the Reverend William Richards*

new constitution that abolished the matriarchal office of *kuhina nui,* established a one-chamber legislature for nobles and elected representatives, and required that persons born after 1840 pass literacy tests and meet certain property qualifications before being allowed to vote or serve in the legislature. His act was in effect a bloodless and effective *coup d'état.*

His strengthening of the monarchy sparked increasing resentment among non-royalists

**Far left, Kamehameha IV steered Hawaii through the whaling days; left, Kamehameha V was a take-charge king, who ran his kingdom as he saw fit. Above, Hawaii's first royal coat of arms; above right, a portrait of King Lunalilo.**

**Rule by election:** Under the constitution of 1864, the legislative assembly met to elect a native *ali'i,* a recognized Hawaiian chief or chiefess, to replace Kamehameha V. Lunalilo was chosen king in 1873, the year following Kamehameha V's death.

But as popular as Lunalilo – or "Prince Bill" – was with the people, he was an alcoholic, and 13 months later he died without an heir. The kingdom's representatives once again had to go about the sticky political business of electing a new sovereign. Before he died, Lunalilo composed a will which asked that his estate be used to build a home for "poor, destitute and infirm people of Hawaiian blood or extraction, giving preference to old people."

With the death of Hawaii's first elected king, Lunalilo – or "Prince Bill", as he was affectionately known – the legislative assembly met again to choose a new monarch. Only David Kalakaua, loser to Lunalilo in the previous election, and Queen Emma, widow of Kamehameha IV, vied for the throne. After a colorful campaign, the assembly handily elected Kalakaua as king of Hawaii in 1874. Although not descended from the Kamehameha dynasty, Kalakaua's ancestors had been high chiefs on the Big Island.

The disappointed backers of Queen Emma rioted in protest within minutes after

Kalakaua's selection was announced. Several people were injured, one fatally, in a free-for-all fight both inside and outside the courthouse where the election was held. Local authorities enlisted 150 American and 80 British marines stationed on visiting warships to quell the disturbance.

The disturbances were yet another cue for the sugar planters, merchants and other influential but dissatisfied businessmen – the anti-royalists – to increase their calls for annexation by the United States.

**King David Kalakaua (1874–91):** Ruling with a flourish and style that, in time, would earn him the nickname the "Merry Monarch," Kalakaua ignored the annexation calls and devoted his energy to fashioning his king-

ship in the courtly tradition of European monarchs: building himself the $350,000 'Iolani Palace; embarking on a trip around the world, distinguishing him as the first monarch to circumnavigate the globe; and presenting gala horse races, grand balls and old-style Hawaiian feasts.

Despite these excesses, Kalakaua lived a life of easy-going charm and cultivated sensibility. Robert Louis Stevenson, a friend, called Kalakaua "a very fine, intelligent man." Commoners remembered feeling comfortable in the presence of their king, who took enormous pride in being Hawaiian. During his reign, Kalakaua openly clashed with educators and the Christian community about restoring many of Hawaii's rapidly-disappearing cultural traditions.

In 1874, the same year he took the oath of office, Kalakaua traveled to Washington, DC, hoping to negotiate a reciprocity treaty with the United States. He and his entourage were grandly received by President Ulysses S. Grant and a joint session of the congress as the first reigning monarch to visit the United States. Newspaper reporters described the state banquets and other entertainment arranged for Kalakaua as the most lavish they had ever seen in the nation's capital. Kalakaua subsequently received strong personal support from Grant; by the next year, the US Senate approved a treaty giving Hawaii "favored nation" duty concessions and eliminating tariffs on sugar.

While the treaty was a diplomatic triumph for the new king, it also gave America a strategic lock on the islands; no other country could use Hawaii for its own national purposes or needs. The United States government was in effect covering its future interest in Pearl Harbor as a military base, and at the same time preventing David Kalakaua from using Hawaii's strategic location to gain political or economic concessions from Britain or France.

Perhaps most importantly for Hawaii's immediate future, the treaty gave the sugar growers increased economic confidence and security. And as would later become clear, the agreement gave the growers disproportionate political and social leverage, eventually weakening King Kalakaua's – and his successor's – power.

Perhaps inspired by the royalty encountered on his 1881 global voyage, Kalakaua crowned himself and Queen Kapi'olani (it was Hawaii's first royal coronation) at 'Iolani Palace on February 12, 1883, nine years following his election as king. Two weeks of celebrations followed, adding to his reputation as a "Merry Monarch."

He commissioned English jewelers to fashion two elaborate crowns, one for himself and one for Queen Kapi'olani at a cost of about $10,000 each, an embellishment that openly granted the exclusive use of Pearl Harbor as a coaling station, an option never exercised, however, until Hawaii was made a territory much later.

The new constitution required that voters own at least $3,000 worth of property or have an income of at least $600 a year, requirements that effectively eliminated most Hawaiians from the political franchise. Power conclusively shifted to Hawaii's land-owning and predominantly white minority.

Two years later, a fiery part-Hawaiian revolutionary named Robert Wilcox staged a counter coup against the businessmen.

only further infuriated Hawaii's non-royalist business interests.

A string of scandals began to taint Kalakaua's reign to the righteous delight of the foreign business community. In 1887, an armed insurrection led by a *haole* political group called the Hawaiian League forced Kalakaua to accept a new "Bayonet Constitution" that seriously constrained his powers. At the same time, the United States was

Wilcox, who had been educated at a military school in Turin, Italy, wore his gold braid and epauletted uniform and with about 150 armed followers loyal to the kingdom, swashbuckled his way past the King's Guards and occupied 'Iolani Palace.

But Wilcox's *coup d'état* failed miserably. Within hours, he and the other revolutionaries were flushed out with rifle fire and crude dynamite bombs laced with twenty-penny metal spikes. Wilcox finally surrendered, with seven of his men dead and another 12 wounded.

For the remainder of his reign, Kalakaua was, for the most part, a figurehead monarch. Often at the service of the sugar baron and poker partner Claus Spreckels, who had arrived in Hawaii in 1876, Kalakaua frequently dismissed cabinets when they didn't agree with his dubious money-raising schemes, which were usually concocted by Spreckels.

In 1891, while visiting California for his health, Kalakaua died in a San Francisco hotel suite. He was Hawaii's last king.

Before leaving Hawaii, Kalakaua had appointed the heir-apparent, his sister the Princess Lydia Lili'uokalani, as regent during his absence. Upon receiving her brother's body and news of his death, Lili'uokalani became Hawaii's first reigning queen.

**Queen Lili'uokalani (1891–93):** Lydia Lili'uokalani was a firm royalist. Right from the start of her two-year reign, she made it clear that she planned to restore monarchical power and the rights of native Hawaiian

waii. An ardent supporter of the pro-annexation movement, Stevens ordered the landing of US Marines from the visiting gunship *USS Boston*, ostensibly to protect American lives and property – without any authorization from Washington.

That afternoon, some 160 armed bluejackets positioned artillery pieces and Gatling guns at strategic points in Honolulu, and by the next day, "without the drawing of a sword or the firing of a shot," a self-proclaimed Provisional Government of Hawaii led by Sanford B. Dole was in power. Lili'uokalani had no choice but to abdicate her throne. As a historian wrote later, "thirty businessmen, not the 30,000 surviving Hawaiians, determined Hawaii's fate" that day.

Lili'uokalani believed that the American

people. Weary of the plodding cabinet government created by the Bayonet Constitution of 1887 – which, had she been home, she claimed, would never have been signed by her brother Kalakaua – Lili'uokalani announced in 1893 that she would issue a new constitution placing power firmly back in the hands of the monarchy.

Pro-annexation, anti-royalist forces – called the Annexation Club and led by Lorrin A. Thurston – met secretly and planned the outright overthrow of the monarchy, to be followed by the start of annexation negotiations with the United States.

In January of 1893, they launched their revolt after first enlisting the aid of John B. Stevens, the United States minister in Ha-

government, once it learned of the coup, would reinstate the monarchy. "I yield to the superior force of the United States of America," she protested to Sanford Dole, "to avoid any collision of armed forces and perhaps the loss of life.

I do this under protest, and impelled by said force, yield my authority until such time as the Government of the United States shall, upon the facts being presented to it, undo the action of its representatives and reinstate me in the authority which I claim as the constitutional sovereign of the Hawaiian Islands."

**American flags:** Unlike his predecessor, newly-elected President Grover Cleveland did not support the coup, and he dispatched a special investigator, James H. Blount, a former Georgia congressman and Confederate Army officer, to Honolulu to investigate how it had come about.

Blount arrived in Hawaii to find American flags flying above Hawaii's public buildings. He ordered the flags taken down, that the US Marines withdraw, and that the American occupation of Hawaii cease. After nearly half a year in the islands, he returned to Washington and reported to President Cleveland that "a great wrong has been done to the Hawaiians" who were "overwhelmingly opposed to annexation."

Blount's recommendation that the monarchy be restored was supported by Cleveland, who sent a message to Congress stating that the unauthorized use of American troops on Hawaii was "an act of war against a peaceful nation… A candid and thorough examination of the facts will force the conviction that the provisional government owes its existence to an armed invasion by the United States." Congress, lobbied by the sugar interests, ignored Cleveland.

In 1894, the provisional government declared the Republic of Hawaii. Sanford Dole was named president. The Cleveland administration sent a minister to Hawaii seeking reinstatement of Queen Lili'uokalani, but President Dole and his newly established cabinet refused.

Lili'uokalani and her supporters planned a counter coup for the next year – once again to be led by the indefatigable Robert Wilcox. The provisional government learned of the plans and brought the royalists before a military commission for treason. Lili'uokalani was arrested.

Lili'uokalani denied guilt, but the government's attorney pointed out some things found amidst the fruit trees and flowers of her Washington Place home: 21 bombs, 30 rifles, 38 cartridge belts, assorted pistols and swords, and about a thousand rounds of ammunition. Found guilty of high treason, she was sentenced to five years at hard labor and a fine of $5,000. The penalties, however, were never enforced.

Placed under house arrest in 'Iolani Palace, Lili'uokalani was freed late in 1896. Lili'uokalani went to Washington in an at-

tempt to rally support for her cause, but by then the American government was pursuing an expansionist policy later called the Manifest Destiny. And as a war between Spain and the United States seemed imminent – and Guam and the Philippines were Spanish colonies in the Pacific – Hawaii would become an important mid-Pacific military base.

**Yankee future:** Hawaii's future became manifest in November, 1897, when President Cleveland lost that year's presidential election to Republican William McKinley. In 1898, McKinley signed annexation papers for Hawaii. In 1900, Hawaii was made a territory, with Sanford Dole its governor.

Former President Cleveland later wrote about Hawaii's annexation: "Hawaii is ours.

As I look back upon the first steps in this miserable business and as I contemplate the means used to complete the outrage, I am ashamed of the whole affair."

No sooner had Old Glory skipped up the 'Iolani Palace flagpole than the Americans marched ashore and established a military camp just across a dirt road from Waikiki Beach, beneath the morning shadows of Diamond Head. It was named, appropriately, Camp McKinley.

Lili'uokalani and Dole publicly reconciled in 1911 at the opening of the Pearl Harbor Naval Base. Later, at the start of World War I, Lili'uokalani raised the American flag over her home, Washington Place, the first time she had done so.

**Left**, the Hawaiian flag is lowered on August 12, 1898. **Right**, US Minister Sewall accepts Hawaii from President Dole.

THIS IS IT!—These are the faces of men who've heard the war
is over. This moving moment of history was reorded by a Navy

...hotographer in downtown Honolulu late yesterday. (U. S. avy photo.)

*Honolulu Star Bulletin*, Aug. 15, 1945

SOUVENIR.

# ALOHA OE

(My love to you.)

# MARCH.

The Queen Kapiolani.    The Princess Liliuokalani.

Composed and arranged by

## J. THOMAS BALDWIN.

Incorporating the popular Song "Aloha Oe"

BY THE

## Princess Liliuokalani

And performed by

### BALDWIN'S BOSTON CADET BAND

AT THE

Grand Reception given by the City of Boston to

## Queen Kapiolani and Princess Liliuokalani

May 12th 1887.

At the start of the new century, it looked as if the schemes of the business and land barons had finally come to pass, which included political security and a favorable certainty about the islands' future.

Sugar was soon joined by a new commodity, pineapple. James Dole (a relative of Sanford Dole) successfully began marketing Hawaii-grown pineapples on the US mainland. Within a few decades, Hawaii would be the world's major supplier of pineapple.

Hawaii's usefulness in the new century, of course, depended on modern links with the world that were more dependable than ocean steamers. First came a transpacific telegraphic cable between San Francisco and Honolulu, slithering up out of the Pacific onto Waikiki Beach in 1902. Later the same year, a second cable linked Hawaii with Asia through Midway, Guam and the Philippines.

Lydia Lili'uokalani, Hawaii's last ruling monarch, lived until 1917, having reconciled with Sanford Dole six years earlier. Prince Jonah Kuhio Kalaniana'ole, Lili'uokalani's nephew and the last member of the royal family who wielded political power (as the territorial delegate to Congress), lived until 1922.

**Sugar barons:** The tenacious effort of anti-royalists, businessmen, land owners and sugar barons to bring Hawaii under the umbrella of the United States was finally consummated two years after annexation, when President William McKinley made Hawaii an American territory in 1900.

Territorial status certainly sealed the future of the monarchy – there would be no return. For better or worse, determination of local government was transferred to Washington: the territory's governor and judges were now appointed by the American president. The governor, in turn, appointed department administrators. But because the ubiquitous Sanford Dole was appointed as the territory's first governor, little would actually change until the political franchise expanded in the coming decades.

**Preceding pages:** sailors celebrate the end of World War II. **Left,** *Aloha'Oe* became Hawaii's most celebrated song.

With Dole leading the territorial government, just about all of the new territory's banking, commerce, and transportation remained under status quo control of five large *haole* corporations built largely on sugar: Castle and Cooke, Alexander and Baldwin, C. Brewer, Theo. H. Davies, and American Factors (now called Amfac). And the "Big Five," as they are still wistfully called (although they are no longer the corporate octopi of past times), by default controlled Hawaii's politics and government.

Sugar's future remained of paramount importance. Because it was now part of the US, Hawaii was classified a domestic producer and thus no longer subject to import tariffs. Greater profits could be anticipated, and the plantations could be enlarged.

But expansion of the sugar plantations required more labor. Since Hawaii had no large pool of ready local labor – Hawaiians were now too few in number and, besides, few of them saw much merit in working the hot, dusty cane fields – workers had to be imported. Before, as an independent kingdom and republic, there had been no restrictions on immigration to Hawaii, and so the sugar barons had brought in tens of thousands of workers from the Orient, first from China and then from Japan. Later, workers would come from Portugal, Puerto Rico, Korea, and the Philippines.

But now as an American territory, immigration quotas were determined in Washington, and with the American West newly opened – the transcontinental railroad was finished – immigration from the Orient was curtailed. Their labor pool in the Orient evaporating, Hawaii's sugar plantations were nevertheless in luck with a new source of labor: the Philippines, under the American flag since the 1898 war with Spain.

**Changes in attitude:** Hawaii today is a distinctly liberal Democratic Party state, with political machinery rivaling the best anywhere in its adeptness at keeping itself reelected. But a century ago, Hawaii was very much a Republican territory, governed by an entrenched oligarchy of businessmen intent on hoarding more of the power and wealth that put them on top from the start. Hawaii was a plantation society then, a place of well-defined social hierarchies. There were two political entities – white men and Hawaiians – and one had already been eliminated from contention. The first generation of immigrant laborers, mostly from Asia, buttressed this rigid plantation hierarchy. As newcomers indentured to the sugar companies, they adhered to the status quo.

But as Hawaii swaggered into the 20th century, something happened which was not at all anticipated. Those first-generation Chinese, Japanese and Filipinos who had worked hard and quietly on the plantations decided to stay on in Hawaii after their labor contracts ended. They also had children.

of immigrants, the *haole* powers at the top had been hung by their own petard.

**A new class:** In the treatment of immigrant workers, Hawaii was probably as enlightened, if not more so, as anywhere on the mainland. Indeed, the island bosses had a keen interest in keeping workers content and out of the emerging mainland unions.

From early on, plantation laborers had been identified by ethnic background. There was not a distinct "class" of laborers in Hawaii (if you weren't a white American, you existed outside of the only class that mattered). Laborers were simply Chinese and Filipinos and Japanese. Labor unrest, easily quenched by the bosses because of

Hawaiian Pineapples. District of Wahiawa. Island of Oahu.

HAWAIIAN PINEAPPLE
PICKED RIPE
PACKED RIGHT

These plantation babies were, by birth, American citizens. Unlike their parents, they were not foreigners, nor newcomers, nor strangers in a strange land. Hawaii was home.

As this second generation of Asian immigrants grew up and joined the political franchise (by 1936, 25 percent of voters in Hawaii were of Japanese ancestry), the power of the Big Five corporations, Republican politicians and missionary family land owners was challenged head on, their footing further buffeted by a growing economic depression that boosted the confidence of labor movements. By pushing Hawaii to become a territory, and by admitting tens of thousands

ethnic fragmentation, was considered a "Filipino problem," or a "Chinese problem," but not a labor problem.

In 1924, a "Filipino problem" near the town of Hanapepe, on Kaua'i, left 16 Filipinos and 4 policemen dead. The eight-month strike, sponsored by the new Filipino Higher Wages Movement, involved three thousand sugar workers and was the biggest such protest by Hawaii laborers until the late 1930s. The territorial governor had to dispatch 85 riflemen and two machine-gun squads to restore order. Arrests and convictions of the Filipinos followed.

In 1935, 10 years too late for the Hanapepe

cane laborers, an act passed by the US Congress made it legal for workers to organize into unions and engage in collective bargaining. This official support for labor initiated a slow but potent revolution in Hawaii over the next three decades.

Inter-island air transport arrived in 1929, when Inter-Island Airways – now Hawaiian Airlines – connected the islands with amphibious aircraft. Five years later, the new airline began regular inter-island mail routes.

The first flight between Hawaii and somewhere else had been completed, for the most part, four years earlier, when a navy seaplane coming from California ran out of fuel 300 miles (480 km) out at sea. Two years later,

hopping route to Manila, creating the first Pacific air connection between the US and Asia. And less than a year after that, the *Hawaii Clipper* skimmed across Pearl Harbor's waters with a cargo of seven paying passengers – tourists with money to spend.

**World War II:** Early on Sunday morning, December 7, 1941, two waves of Japanese aircraft – 360 planes in all – dropped below cloud cover and attacked every major military installation on Oahu. Japan had been expanding its control in Asia for half a century; now the Pacific was on its agenda, including Pearl Harbor, a naval station since 1908 and home of America's Pacific fleet.

The Japanese attack devastated America's

the first civilian flight to reach Hawaii ran out of fuel just off Moloka'i, crashing into an unsuspecting *kiawe* tree on the island.

A more reliable air connection with the US mainland arrived on an April morning in 1935: a 19-ton Pan Am Clipper landed at the fleet air base in Pearl Harbor, completing an "exploratory" flight from the San Francisco area that took 19 hours and 48 minutes. Seven months later, a second Pan Am aircraft, the *China Clipper,* touched down with a cargo of mail, then continued an island-

<u>Left</u>, **pineapple postcard, 1910.** <u>Above</u>, **Waikiki Beach, 1929.**

Pacific naval forces. A military board of inquiry reported at the end of the war that the "astoundingly disproportionate extent of losses" suffered by the United States on Oahu marked "the greatest military and naval disaster in our Nation's history." As the board wrote in its report, there were 3,435 American casualties, including 2,323 killed; Japanese casualties were less than 100. Continues the report: "We lost outright 188 planes; Japan, 29. We suffered severe damage to or loss of 8 battle-ships, 3 light cruisers, 3 destroyers, and 4 miscellaneous vessels; Japan lost 5 midget submarines."

Some 68 Oahu residents were killed or

injured during the attack on Oahu. Japanese submarines sank several cargo and passenger vessels in local waters. They also surfaced in order to shell Hilo, Nawiliwili, and Kahului harbors.

The same day as the attack on Oahu, President Franklin Roosevelt declared war on Japan and, later in the morning, Hawaii was placed under martial law.

The state remained under martial law until 1944, during which time military courts completely replaced all civilian jurisdiction in Hawaii – in fact, an unconstitutional jurisdiction, the US Supreme Court later ruled after the war.

At the beginning of the war, the largest

Japanese-Americans, nor in most minds of the other ethnic and racial groups in Hawaii. They were all *kama'aina,* if not *ohana,* after all. Nonetheless, Japanese-Americans in Hawaii suffered unwarranted discrimination and suppression, in large part because of outside military and civilian officials.

Eventually, AJAs of military age were permitted to enlist in the army. A volunteer group from Hawaii was assembled into a single unit called the 100th Infantry Battalion, later expanded into the 442nd Regimental Combat Team with over 1,000 volunteers. Not trusted to fight soldiers of their ancestral homeland (again, Americans of German or Italian descent had no such re-

ethnic group in Hawaii was of Japanese ancestry. On the mainland, Americans of Japanese ancestry (AJAs) were confined in desert internment camps, a policy entirely racial and not substantiated by claims of national security. (German-Americans and Italian-Americans, in contrast, were left alone.) In Hawaii, however, the AJA population was too prominent to be confined, not only because they were a significant percentage of the territory's population, but also because they were a thread in Hawaii's social and cultural fabric.

The question of loyalty was moot, for it was never a question in the minds of the

strictions), the Japanese-American soldiers were shipped to Europe. Suspicions about loyalty vanished when the 442nd became the most highly decorated unit in the American military.

Returning home to Hawaii, many of the AJAs used the GI Bill in order to pay for college, turning afterwards to law and politics, and becoming the core of yet another shift in Hawaii's power structure.

After the war, a succession of workers' strikes against local steamship companies and the sugar industry established unions as one of Hawaii's major political and economic forces. They solidified their power in

1952 with a six-month work freeze on Hawaii's docks that nearly devastated the territory's economy, almost completely dependent on shipping.

Hawaii's business and political *ancien regime,* however, were sore and sour losers. Throughout the 1950s, Hawaii's unions were closely scrutinized and accused of being revolutionary tools of an unproven Communist conspiracy in the territory.

The Republican Party, entrenched since before anyone alive could remember, was knocked out of power in 1954 by a decidedly different incoming group of territorial legislators – half were AJAs – supported by the now-powerful labor unions.

Exports to the mainland plummeted. Statehood would be necessary to sustain Hawaii as a leading sugar producer.

With World War II finished, the Big Five and other interests pushed for statehood, building momentum throughout the 1950s and eventually overcoming congressional reluctance. (It has been suggested that congressmen from southern states weren't keen on admitting a state dominated by, for heaven's sake, people of non-Caucasian persuasions.) A deal was struck linking Hawaii and Alaska for statehood and, in 1959, Hawaii became a bona-fide American state.

Statehood was ratified by Hawaii voters 17 to 1. The only precinct rejecting statehood

**Statehood push:** Between 1903 and 1957, 22 bills addressing statehood for Hawaii failed congressional votes in Washington. Unlike mainland areas annexed as territories, there had been no provisions in Hawaii's territorial legislation for eventual statehood. And in any case, territorial status had suited the sugar interests just fine.

But in 1934, Congress had given Hawaii's sugar barons a kick in the *okole* by grouping Hawaii along with foreign producers of sugar.

<u>Left</u>, **flames over Pearl Harbor, December 7, 1941.** <u>Above</u>, **the destroyer** *Shaw* **is ripped by an explosion during the Japanese attack.**

was the Kauai neighbor island of Ni'ihau, a *kapu* island owned by the rich *kama'aina* Robinson family and populated exclusively by Hawaiians.

Until this time, Hawaii had rarely been a place that people on the mainland thought about. It was, after all, a long, expensive boat journey away. Statehood was one of those historical pivots – like Cook's visit and the overthrow of Lili'uokalani – that irrevocably changed Hawaii's destiny.

At the time of statehood, the tallest building in Hawaii was Aloha Tower, and Waikiki was peppered here and there with just a few hotels. Defense and agriculture – sugar and pineapple, mostly – were Hawaii's two main sources of revenue.

That same year, a regular commercial jet service was inaugurated by Qantas between Australia, Hawaii, and San Francisco – cutting travel time from California from nine propeller hours to 4½ jet hours. A few months later Pan Am connected Honolulu with the Pacific Coast and Tokyo.

It was time for the tourists.

**The jet set:** The commercial jet's ability to maintain a constant turnover of visitors made mass tourism a promising enterprise. The jets brought increasing numbers of visitors, and the once-stately and sedate Waikiki hotels soon found themselves surrounded by

bigger and taller hotels pushing skyward.

The neighbor islands, too, got a jolt. To make room for blossoming resorts, agricultural land was shifted to development, especially on Maui and Kauai. Sugar cane workers became hotel staff. On the Big Island, resorts were built on acres of barren lava.

Hawaii's urban center since the end of whaling, Honolulu simply exploded as new mainlanders and businesses arrived. Some peripheral neighborhoods expanded in population by up to 600 percent. And in the areas where it couldn't spread out, Honolulu shot up, in wall after wall of office buildings and high-rise condos. Small, quiet rural towns –

Kailua, Kaneʻohe, Mililani, Hawaii Kai, Makakilo – turned into bedroom communities for Honolulu-bound commuters.

In the early 1980s, tourism overtook government and military spending in economic importance. Agriculture slipped to a distant third. (Some of the lost agricultural revenues, however, were replaced by the exponential growth of *pakalolo* cultivation – marijuana – which illegally flourishes in Hawaii's forests, sugar cane fields, and backyards. Some recent estimates place its value to the state's economy as greater than that of sugar and pineapples.)

**A yen for better things:** As with sandalwood, whaling, and sugar before it, tourism's fortunes were largely dependent on forces beyond Hawaii's control, including a global recession in the late 1970s. Hawaii's tourism rebounded in the 1980s, entering into a period of unparalleled expansion, fueled in part by the philosophies of using plastic money instead of cash.

Additionally, an influx of Asian capital, mostly from a superheating Japanese economy, injected the state with a building rush that would later prove to be overextended. Huge "fantasy resorts," pushed onto Hawaii by developer Chris Hemmeter, became the new resort paradigm. Designed to keep visitors, and money, on the property for their entire visit, the resorts themselves, not Hawaii, became the destination.

By the late 1980s, Japanese investors (highly leveraged by inflated stock and real estate prices) had injected $15 billion into Hawaii's economy. The Japanese bought heavily into hotels and resorts, acquiring 70 percent of hotel rooms costing over $100 a day and 30 percent of all hotel rooms in Hawaii. There was some backlash against such a concentration of foreign ownership. But the Japanese kept the hotels under American management – successfully deflecting the worries of labor unions and local residents – and spent tens of millions of dollars to upgrade tired hotel properties. Across the islands, hotel standards increased.

Thirty percent of the home purchases in 1987 and 1988 east of Diamond Head involved Japanese, who often bought at prices much higher than appraised values. One young couple sold out to a Japanese investor offering $1.1 million for their home, which the couple had bought for $275,000 four years earlier. Property assessments and taxes in some neighborhoods increased as much as 100 percent in less than a year. A number of elderly Waikiki residents were displaced by higher rents – up to $300 monthly overnight – when their apartment buildings were bought out by Japanese.

Billionaire Genshiro Kawamoto went Hawaii house-hunting in the late 1980s, saying that he was looking for a place "to keep a change of clothes in." For six months he drove around Honolulu looking for the right place. He ended up buying 160 homes for $80 million cash before he found the perfect wardrobe closet: a $40 million estate once owned by the industrialist Henry Kaiser. At around $1 billion. "I can't understand why people make such a fuss over my houses in Hawaii. It's only 160," he whined to a local newspaper reporter. Indeed. Originally he'd planned to buy between 500 and 1,000 houses.

While immense profits were made by some Hawaii residents with upscale property to sell, many others were pushed out of their homes and neighborhoods where families had lived for generations. When low-income retired people started being evicted from apartments they had long rented, Hawaii's welcome of the yen began to waver.

"I'd like to send a message back. *Enough.*" Frank Fasi, mayor of Honolulu, was not known to equivocate. "We don't want you

the time, it was the highest price ever paid – and in cash – for a US residential property.

At the peak of his house hunting, Kawamoto bought 17 homes in a single day. In the wake of his white stretch limousine, "for sale" signs sprouted throughout the fancier neighborhoods of Oahu, the signs sometimes embellished with rising suns and assurances that "we accept yen."

Kawamoto complained when a business magazine underestimated his wealth at *only*

**Left**, the city of Honolulu underwent massive expansion in the 1980s. **Above**, Texan tourists get married in paradise.

and we don't need you… I don't want Honolulu to become a suburb of Tokyo." Fasi even journeyed to Tokyo to scold the Japanese. Many disagreed with the mayor, including the governor of Hawaii, but Fasi's actions reflected a growing resentment of perceived Japanese condescension towards Hawaii, of Hawaii as a Japanese playground and a high-yield, low-risk investment for those with enough money.

The situation was compounded when the Japanese, unaccustomed to the dictates of a multi-ethnic society, purchased property and tried to exclude Americans. One Japanese investor in a planned golf course publicly blurted out that it would be exclusively for Japanese nationals. When that notion backfired with locals and the city council, it was implied that the membership fee would be so high that only Japanese – who typically pay seven figures for club memberships in Japan – could and would pay to join.

The infusion of yen into Hawaii skidded to a halt in the early 1990s, when the over-leveraged Japanese investors lost their shirts as Japan's stock and real estate markets crashed. The yen that once flowed like sweet honey was humbled now.

"The Japanese will have learned some lessons. Too much money coming in at one time will create friction and animosity," the

remaining land, three quarters is owned by a collection of less than 40 owners, mostly descended from the early Protestant missionary families with names like Bishop, Campbell, Wilcox. These private landowners collectively own 60 percent of Molokai, and 40 to 50 percent of Oahu, Maui, Hawaii, and Kauai. Nearly all of Lanai and all of Ni'ihau are privately owned. The value of land assets is astonishing. The trustees of the Bishop Estate, for example, each average a million dollars' salary annually.

Land ownership in Hawaii is unusually complex and messy. In Hawaii, land beneath a house is usually separate and often not even an option for purchase. Many of Hawaii's

Japanese consul general in Hawaii was quoted as concluding. "We can't have quick money, one-night stands. There's got to be respect for local customs and the way of life here."

The one common denominator of human history in Hawaii is the acquisition of land. The Tahitians took the land from the Marquesans. The Hawaiian kings took it from one another until only one had it all. The missionaries and sugar men took it from the Hawaiians, and now everybody wants to take it from everyone else, or at least own some of it.

About half of Hawaii is owned by the state, county, and federal governments. Of the

top hotels also sit on leased land. The home or hotel owner must make lease payments to the private estate, and at the end of the lease period renegotiate. If lease payments go up too much, tough. Once in a while, the land is offered for sale as "fee simple."

The swirl of money and resort development in the 1980s rekindled concerns about the land, and about Hawaii's priorities. The question of land, unfortunately but perhaps inevitably, has the potential to polarize and divide ethnic interests in the islands.

In January of 1993, the question of land came to the forefront over a four-day centennial remembrance of Queen Lili'uokalani's overthrow. With 'Iolani Palace covered in black bunting, it was not a time of celebration and festivities. Governor John Waihe'e, the state's first governor of Hawaiian ancestry, issued executive orders that only the Hawaiian flag, not the American, fly over state office buildings during the four days of the centennial.

There is no dispute that the overthrow of Queen Lili'uokalani was illegal under international law. In fact, the sovereignty of the islands had earlier been recognized by both the United States and the colonial European powers. The immediate events of the overthrow were orchestrated by local businessmen and a representative of the United States

nothing more than an official apology from Washington. Other groups want the total banishment of all non-Hawaiians, whether Asian or Caucasian, from the islands and complete secession from the United States.

In between somewhere is the moderate position of one of the most outspoken sovereignty groups, Ka Lahui Hawaii, which demands a "nation within a nation." It would allow Hawaiians to control their own lands and determine their own government, and establish their own laws and set their own taxes, an arrangement already guaranteed by legislation with Native American tribes on the mainland. Hawaiians, however, have never been classified as Native Americans.

whose actions – which included the dispatch of American troops from a visiting ship to sustain the coup – were done without the knowledge or authorization of the American president. Unfortunately, congressional inaction sustained the coup.

The centennial of the overthrow offered a platform for the numerous Hawaiian sovereignty groups seeking a redress of the islands' annexation. Some of the groups want

**Left**, the outspoken sovereignty group Ka Lahui Hawaii would like to establish a Hawaiian nation. **Above**, students display the Hawaiian – rather than the American – flag in solidarity.

Ka Lahui Hawaii ("the nation of Hawaii") wants the Hawaiian nation established on about 1.5 million acres (0.6 million hectares) of land – 200,000 acres (80,000 hectares) of existing Hawaiian homelands and an additional 1.2 million acres (0.48 million hectares) of land possessed by the monarchy at the time of Lili'uokalani's overthrow and ceded by Sanford Dole's republic to the US, later returned to the state in 1959.

A common theme among all the sovereignty groups, whether seeking apologies or secession, is the question of 'aina, or land. For land is crucial to making sovereignty, in any form, succeed.

# SPIRIT OF THE ISLANDS

The shapes of the clouds, the cries of birds at night, the sounds of waves on the reef – all have messages for the Hawaiian. The sheltering home, the trees outside, the earth beneath – all are alive and aware. Hawaiian tradition consisted of talking to them, listening to them, being in constant communication with people, other living beings, rocks, clouds, the sea, the spirits of ancestors.

The land is mother. The Hawaiian word for land, *'aina,* literally means "that which feeds." It doesn't belong to us; we belong to it, and are part of it. If separated from land, a people and their culture tend to drift, and are without meaning.

Today on these islands that were Hawaiian 100 years ago, *kanaka maoli* – as Hawaiians call themselves – have the shortest life expectancy of all the ethnic groups. They have the highest mortality rates for heart disease, stroke, cancer and diabetes, the highest infant mortality, the highest rates of suicide, accidents, and substance abuse.

Forty percent of the population of Oahu Prison is *kanaka maoli.* They make up less than 2 percent of the graduating class at the University of Hawaii, and have the highest drop-out rates in the school system, the lowest family median incomes, the highest rates of homelessness.

By any measure, Hawaiians are at the bottom in their own homeland, displaced by the fracturing of an intense connection with land and tradition.

**Sky father, earth mother:** *O ke au i kahuli wela ka honua. O ke au i kahuli lole ka lani.* The opening lines of "He Kumulipo," the chant describing the origins of the cosmos, literally means "at the time of the hot earth, turning against the changing sky." But the *kaona,* the hidden meaning of the words, is of the mating between the sky-father, Wakea, with the earth-mother, Papa, out of which came everything in the cosmos.

According to "He Kumulipo," the *kalo,* or the taro plant, was one of the early children of the earth-mother and the sky-father. But

**Preceding pages: traditional canoe, the Big Island. Left, Pu'uhonua 'O Honaunau (Place of Refuge) on the Big Island.**

because this kalo-child was born deformed, it was buried in the ground. Up sprouted the taro plant, later a food of traditional Hawaiian life. Clustered around the central plant – the *makua*, or parent – are *'oha* (offshoots), and around them, little *keiki* (children). Collectively, this complete plant is called *'ohana*, also the Hawaiian word for "family."

The next child born was Haloa, the first human ancestor. But since the taro plant is the *hiapo*, or eldest sibling of humans, it is the superior. It is also another form (*kinolau*) of Kane, one of the highest gods. When eating taro, one is eating the god Kane, taking in his godly *mana* (power).

Before the Westerners, Hawaiians had no

revolve around sharing and exchange.

Practically all the inhabitants of an ahupua'a were blood relatives, an extended 'ohana. Because there was no private ownership and no property to inherit, there was no need for households with one father, one mother, and their children. In the 'ohana, all the men and women in the middle generation were *makua* (parents) and one mated with whomever one desired. All youngsters were *kamali'i* (children); all elders were *kupuna* (grandparents). There was no difference between parents, aunts and uncles, and there was no word for cousin. Members of the same generation were all siblings. In the 'ohana of ordinary farmers and fishermen,

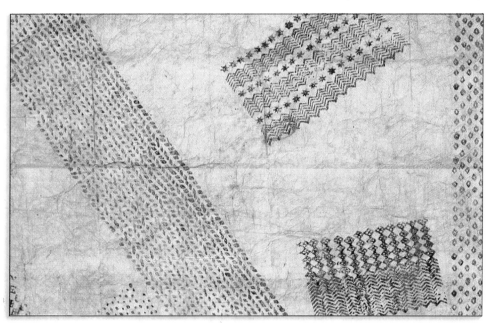

private property, no ownership of land. They had access to any and all of the natural resources except those few areas that were *kapu*, or taboo – certain fishing grounds during certain seasons, for example. Islands were divided into *ahupua'a* – large wedges of land extending inland from the coast. An ahupua'a typically contained ridges on both sides of one or several valleys, forested uplands, a length of shoreline, and the adjoining ocean. In short, self-sustaining. The fisherman fished not only for himself, but for everyone; likewise, the farmer and the woodsman. Of necessity, good interpersonal relationships were paramount; life tended to

couples certainly existed, but this was not the rule and there were no separate dwellings for them. Everyone slept in the big sleeping house (*hale noa*). Kanaka maoli children learned early about sex and childbirth.

Children were taught about the three *piko*, or centers. A *kanaka maoli* child was secure knowing that, through the three piko, she or he was firmly attached to this present life, to the ancestors back to the beginning, to the lives of generations yet unborn.

The *piko waena* is the navel, the memory of the link between mother and child in the womb. More, it is a connection with everything in this physical world. It also covers and is related to the *na'au* (the intestines), the organs of knowledge, wisdom and feeling.

The second piko – the fontanel, the opening between the bones of the child's skull that closes as the child matures – is the *piko po'o* (head center). Through this piko, the personal spirit connects with the spiritual world of the ancestors back to the beginning of time, to the natural world about us now as *'aumakua* – ancestors spirits, guardian spirits – and into the future, where they continue to live in different forms forever.

The third piko is the *piko ma'i* – the *ma'i* are the genitalia, the organs of procreation. This piko connects us with our children and their descendants into the limitless future.

loved ones – warning, guiding, informing.

Traditionally, *kanaka maoli* see sex everywhere in nature, and the link between creation and procreation is direct and obvious. In the morning, when *pali* mists are wet, the wind blows the rain in a shimmering curtain down island valleys – the rain is the semen of Wakea, the sky-father, impregnating Papa, the earth-mother. The opening lines of Queen Lili'uokalani's haunting "Aloha 'Oe" speak of the proud rain on the cliff creeping into the forest, seeking the bud of the *lehua* – the male seeking the female. There are songs about *maile* wrapped around a flower lei – male entwined with female.

Most *kanaka maoli* songs and chants are

*Kanaka maoli* are in human form right now, but have existed in many forms before, and will exist in many more in the future. Time in this human form is short; after death, *kanaka maoli* join ancestors, assume spiritual form and come back to families as *'aumakua*. Sometimes the form is of a bird, sometimes a fish, or a turtle, a shark, a tree, a rock, a breeze, a cloud, or even a new child born into the family. The *'aumakua* protects

**Left**, nature as art: a fine specimen of 19th-century *kapa* (bark cloth). **Above**, the taro plant was not only a staple food, but was thought to have played a role in the origins of the cosmos.

celebrating the same thing: the joining of the male with the female. The cosmos was created, and continues to be created, by the mating of Papa and Wakea, "the hot earth turning against the changing heaven." Hawaiians see sexuality as a central fact of nature: out of mating comes new life.

**Talking story:** What troubles most is an angry misunderstanding, a relationship that's gone out of balance. Kanaka try not to confront another kanaka, often pretending that a difference doesn't exist, or trying to resolve an imbalance by edging up to it obliquely, hoping it will resolve itself. Direct confrontation requires going through a formal process

# HAWAIIAN GODS

From their South Pacific homelands, the early Polynesian seafarers brought north with them the food that had sustained them back home. By doing so, they also brought to Hawaii the great gods of Polynesia: Kane, Ku, Lono, and Kanaloa. The gods would be essential for human achievement in the new homeland.

Polynesian gods were never distant and abstract. Rather, they moved through the waters, and on the earth, and they could take on many forms, including plants. Thus the Polynesians knew that by bringing the taro – one of the god Kane's forms – to Hawaii, they carried with them

Kane himself. With 'uala, the sweet potato, came Lono. 'Ulu, breadfruit, and niu, the coconut, bore Ku, and with mai'a, the banana, came Kanaloa.

Kane, the leading god among the gods, was the procreator, the ancestor of all chiefs and commoners, the male (kane) power who dwells in eternity – the god of sunlight, fresh water and forests. Kane was not fond of human sacrifices. An owl was one of his assumed forms.

Ku was appealed to for rain and growth, and fishing and sorcery, but was best known as a patron god of war. Resplendent images of Ku, whose combative title was "the island snatcher,"

**The Bishop Museum's Kukailimoku war god.**

were carried on the war canoes of Kamehameha the Great. According to oral traditions, these fearsome images – wrought of red i'iwi feathers embellished with mother-of-pearl eyes and mouths of jagged dog teeth – would utter fearsome cries during battle.

Lono was a god of thunder (lono means "resounding"), clouds, winds, the sea, agriculture and fertility, but his personage could assume dozens of forms, including a fish or a man-dog being. Benevolent Lono was never appealed to with human sacrifices. Most notably, he was honored during the annual makahiki harvest festivals of November, December and January, when his image was carried by chiefly retainers on their tribute-and-tax-collecting tours of the islands. (It was during makahiki that Captain Cook landed on the Big Island, a visit mistaken for the return of Lono.)

Kanaloa, lord of the ocean and ocean winds, oftentimes was embodied in the octopus and squid, but also in other natural things, such as the banana. He was a companion of Kane and, according to some, the two traveled together, "moving about the land and opening spring and water holes for the benefit of men." Kanaloa was also revered as a patron god of healing.

Coming to Polynesia from distant, unknown places, these four gods had been created before all other gods. In turn they created the universe from the earth, a calabash, by tossing the calabash's cover up, forming the sky, and the sun, and the moon. Seeds in the calabash became the stars. Also, according to one of several legends, they created the ancestors of the Pacific people.

The pantheon of Hawaiian deities is extensive, from the four great gods above to the lesser though no less notable and specialized gods, such as Pele, the volcano goddess, and Laka, the goddess of hula.

For the contemporary traveler to Hawaii, Pele is the best known of the gods because, as the fire goddess, she is responsible for the current eruptions of Kilauea, on the Big Island. A common misconception is that Pele created the Hawaiian islands. In fact, the islands were already here when Pele, driven by wanderlust, arrived in Hawaii from Tahiti in a great canoe provided by the god of sharks. From Ni'ihau, she traveled down the island chain looking for a suitable home. On the Big Island, she sought out the reigning fire god, Aila'au, hoping to settle in with him. As she approached Kilauea, he ran away, forever. Alone now, Kilauea was hers. ∎

of resolution; if this fails, violence may result.

One way of maintaining balance is by *mo'olelo*, "talking story." A visitor may simply see locals sitting and chatting. In fact, talking story is a building of trust and an emphasizing of things in common.

This is not to suggest that the traditional *kanaka maoli* world was without violence. Oral history holds that the high *kahuna* Pa'ao brought a strict new religion from Tahiti in about the 13th century, increasing the power of the ali'i, meting out harsh punishments for the breaking of new kapu, and introducing new rituals and ceremonies – including human sacrifice. Rivalry increased between chiefs for political control. But the tradi-

relationships? To some degree, one could say wars were fought to restore balance (*pono*). But the first Westerners to Hawaii may have exaggerated warfare's importance in Hawaiian society, misunderstanding its role. When Captain Cook arrived in 1778, there were indeed conflicts between Kamehameha and other high chiefs. Commoners were conscripted into their armies. Historian Samuel Kamakau later wrote of "merciless battles… in which the earth was literally covered with the innocent who were slaughtered." But in earlier times, warfare had important elements of ritual and sport, as the warrior classes tested their strength against each other, rarely disrupting the commoners.

tional culture of the *maka'ainana* (commoners – literally "the eyes of the land") continued much as it had for the centuries before the arrival of Pa'ao. In general, probably, maka'ainana didn't pay much attention to the new hierarchy or the state religious rituals, being absorbed rather with work, 'ohana and 'aumakua.

Sometimes the question of Hawaii's history arises: why warfare in a society so dedicated to maintaining harmony and proper

**Above**, phallic stone, Molokai. The link between creation and procreation was important to the ancient Hawaiians.

The arrival of Westerners intensified the bloodshed. Gunpowder tipped the balance of power. Introduced values about the acquisition of material goods – control of the sandalwood trade, for example – became war goals. The natural world was now one of 'natural resources' and no longer a sacred extension of 'ohana, of family.

**Personal power:** *Mana* (special spiritual or personal power) derives from two main sources. One is rank at birth: *ali'i* are born with more *mana* than commoners; higher-born *ali'i*, more *mana* than lesser-born. The other is training: a skilled carver, fisherman, chanter, navigator, physician or dancer developing increasingly refined abilities, gradually acquires this kind of *mana*. These skills require long apprenticeship, and one's specialized knowledge shouldn't be too readily shared with others lest its power be diminished. *Huna* (certain confidential, secret aspects of the skill) requires the understanding of how numerous forces interact, the maintenance of certain kinds of protocol, and the observance of strict kinds of behavior.

At all levels of society, *kanaka maoli* believe in balance and protocol. Preparing and consuming a meal has to be done in a certain way. Preparations for the treatment of someone who is ill, such as the gathering of *la'au lapa'au* (medicinal plants), must be done at

a certain time of day with certain rules, prayers, and thoughts. Chants and dances have to be done impeccably, as do rituals. There is a right way to do everything, and even the smallest daily activity exists in a web of belief and practice.

The chants used in ritual, prayer, and hula, if the words and songs are uttered properly, carry with them considerable power. The Hawaiian doesn't merely petition the gods and hope they'll act; Hawaiians participate by the way of the asking. The belief, the ritual, and the result all become one process. And prayers are two-way communications between humans and gods; responses are received and interpreted in whatever form they may come: patterns in the fire, images in a dream, a sudden gust of wind, a grumble of thunder, a thought that seems to come from nowhere. But of course, nothing comes from nowhere; everything has causes and exists for a reason.

This careful attention to detail and procedure led to a pursuit of excellence stretching beyond what was just necessary to survive, resulting in creations that were extraordinary by the standards of any society. *Kanaka maoli wa'a* (sailing canoes) were until very recently the swiftest sailing craft on any ocean. Dazzling feather capes and lei were admired by jaded Europeans of the time. *Kanaka maoli* agriculturists developed more than 300 varieties of taro, many of them for dyes and medicines as well as food.

Walled *loko i'a* (fishponds) extended from the shores, efficiently raising fish that fed on algae. Stone-faced terraced and irrigated pond-fields (*lo'i*) filled the valleys, growing shrimp and fish as well as prodigious amounts of taro and other crops. Hawaiians were master agriculturists, botanists, herbalists and craftsmen, fulfilling all needs and creative efforts entirely from plant materials.

**To be or not to be:** The *kanaka maoli* world view requires being in the natural environment. The depletion of fishing grounds and the loss of lands destroyed traditional sources of livelihood, which had imparted a sense of meaning to the world.

Contemporary Hawaii is promoted as one of the most ethnically diverse and harmonious societies in the world. Should the *kanaka maoli* attempt to fit in as just another ethnic group? Some advocates of Hawaiian sovereignty believe it's hard – in a sense, impossible – to be *kanaka maoli* and a part of modern America. When immigrants come here from, say, China and Portugal, and their children forget their ancestors' culture, the Chinese and Portuguese cultures still exist back in their homelands.

For the *kanaka maoli*, the Hawaiian islands *are* the homeland – the only homeland. If kanaka maoli language and culture die here, they're gone from the earth. And *kanaka maoli* vanish as a people. That is the concern.

<u>Left</u>, offerings to the gods. <u>Right</u>, communicating with nature: the late Aunty Edith Kanakaole dances in a *koa* forest.

# AN ETHNIC MIX

It is the meeting place of East and West, the very new rubs shoulders with the immeasurably old. And if you have not found the romance you expected, you have come upon something singularly intriguing. All these strange people live close to each other, with different languages and different thoughts; they believe in different gods and they have different values; two passions alone they share, love and hunger. And somehow as you watch them, you have an impression of extraordinary vitality.

—William Somerset Maugham,
*The Trembling of a Leaf,* 1921

"The meeting place of East and West... " If the writer were not Maugham, he'd be attacked for resorting to cliché. But Maugham was neither the first nor the last writer to rely on simplistic and somewhat lofty generalities about Hawaii's people. Even James Michener, in his weighty epic *Hawaii,* titled his last chapter "The Golden Men" and alluded to "a man at home in either the business councils of New York or the philosophical retreats of Kyoto."

**Ethnic medley:** Hawaii's racial and ethnic groups probably get along better than in most other places. There is, it often seems, an ethnic interdependency among Hawaii's people, an uncanny meshing of cultures and interests. Most telling, however, is that this is probably the only place in the United States, if not the world, where every single racial group is a minority. Yet Hawaii's people retain much of their ancestral identity with understated tenacity, peppering the state with a medley of languages, foods, customs and perspectives. The sense of community in Hawaii comes, in part, from a mutual understanding of one another's culture and lifestyle. Tolerance is required on an island, a small place where things said or done tend to come back around full circle.

This ethnic blending permeates Hawaii's

**Preceding pages:** this wide-eyed Hawaiian is a blend of Hawaiian, Chinese, French and German ancestry. **Left,** island fisherman inspects his catch. **Right,** Hawaii's ethnic mix is clearly shown in this slide photo of newsboys taken in 1916.

power corridors, as one would hope. In the 1990s, Hawaii's congressional delegation included two Japanese, a Caucasian and a Hawaiian. The state governor was also Hawaiian, and the lieutenant governor, Filipino.

**What's in a name:** There is an uncommonly large number of inter-racial marriages in the state and, increasingly, one's identity is based not so much on race as on group identity. Consider one's family name. The 10 most common names on 1990 birth certificates were Lee, Smith, Wong, Johnson, Williams,

Kim, Brown, Jones, Martin, and Ramos. On 1990 *death* certificates: Lee, Wong, Kim, Nakamura, Tanaka, Ching, Lum, Yamamoto, Chang, and Smith. One might conclude, correctly as it turns out, that Hawaii was shifting from a predominately Oriental background to European/North American and Filipino. But many of those Lees, Johnsons, Nakamuras, and Ramos were *hapa* (half) or even less of the nationality implied in the name. Someone named Tanaka could be as white as they are Japanese; someone with the name Ramos as Japanese as they are Filipino.

With each new generation, with each sexual shuffle of ancestry, Hawaii is creating a genetic pool of unusual and indeterminate dimensions. Ask someone their background, and the fractions involved might knot up the mathematically disinclined: a mother one-sixth this and one-fourth that, whose own mother was a third that and a half this.

And on a larger scale, Hawaii's residents of whatever name are enveloped in a distinct localism, of being *kama'aina* – an identity that somehow gives "locals" an intense kinship crossing racial boundaries, rare in other multi-racial communities.

**Facts and figures:** With less than 10 percent of the state's total land area, Oahu and Honolulu – they're one and the same with the same city/county government – are home for nearly 75 percent of Hawaii's 1,108,229 people (including military). By most accounts, Honolulu is America's 11th largest city.

Three areas dominate the job scene: the service industry (in large part directed towards tourism), retail, and government, both local and federal. Hawaii has America's highest number of state workers per capita, but the smallest number of city government workers. (In fact, Honolulu is the only incorporated city or town in Hawaii.)

Hawaii's quality of life is especially good. Its residents have the highest life expectancy in America, and are next to last in unemployment, heart disease, infant mortality, and deaths overall. In cancer deaths and violent crimes, Hawaii ranks near the bottom.

On the other hand, Hawaii's cost of living is America's highest, its median income just average, and it ranks third in the number of men per 100 women – a good deal if female, perhaps. There are 920,000 registered motor vehicles, nearly one for every resident. These are a nightmare on Honolulu's medieval road system.

In 1853, 97 percent of Hawaii's population was Hawaiian or part Hawaiian. In 1910, 20 percent were Hawaiian or part Hawaiian, 41 percent Japanese, and 23 percent Caucasian. Since the end of World War II, Caucasians, Filipinos, Koreans, and Samoans have had the greatest growth, with Caucasians becoming the largest ethnic majority.

Overall, according to recent census figures, Hawaii's population of about 1.1 million breaks down roughly as follows: Caucasians, 370,000 or 23 percent of the population; Japanese, 247,500 or 22 percent; Hawaiians and part Hawaiian, 211,000 or 20 percent (pure Hawaiian, 9,400 or about 1 percent); Filipinos, 168,500 or 15.2 percent; Chinese, 69,000 or 6.2 percent; black, 27,200 or 2.5 percent; Koreans, 24,500 or 2.2 percent; Samoans, 15,000 or 1.4 percent; other Asian/Pacific, 22,000 or 2 percent.

But statistics are never absolute, especially in Hawaii. At least a third of the population is of mixed ancestry, and how people classify themselves when asked depends on variables enigmatic even to the experts. As the *1993 Almanac of Hawaii* notes: "The subject of racial statistics is fraught with problems of definition and classification and provides employment for many academicians."

As might be expected, religion in the state is as mixed as its ethnic colors. Despite the single-mindedness of Hawaii's early Protestant missionaries, Protestantism is a minor religion, exceeded on most islands by Buddhism and Catholicism. Statewide, church membership is about 30 percent Catholic, nearly 20 percent Buddhist, 10 percent Protestant, 5 percent Shinto, 10 percent miscellaneous, and nearly 30 percent unaffiliated.

**Love and marriage:** One of the more unique statistics is that most newcomers to Hawaii since World War II have been young people less than 30 years old. Sun and surf, and Hawaii's high cost of living, are not for an aging society.

What tags Hawaii's population most definitively are love and marriage. Of approximately 18,000 marriages annually involving at least one Hawaii resident, a third are interracial, a practice that lost its social stigma – if it ever had one in Hawaii – back in the times of Kamehameha the Great.

The riddle of who is who in Hawaii, much less what the numbers might mean, didn't escape Maugham when he passed through Honolulu in 1916: "Though the air is so soft and the sky so blue," observed Maugham, "you have, I know not why, a feeling of something hotly passionate that beats like a throbbing pulse through the crowd. Though the native policeman at the corner, standing on a platform, with a white club to direct the traffic, gives the scene an air of respectability, you cannot but feel that it is a respectability only of the surface: a little below there is a darkness and mystery."

<u>Right</u>, **third-generation Korean Hawaiian.**

"What's a Hawaiian?" a *haole* reporter asked.

The young Hawaiian doctor thought for a moment, looked away, found a smile, and answered quietly.

"On the island of Molokai, local people say a Hawaiian is someone who eats *palu*." He explained that *palu* is an exotic Hawaiian condiment made of chopped fish heads and stomachs, with dashes of *kukui* nut relish, garlic and chili peppers.

"My answer wasn't meant to be facetious," he explained, wanting to point out, in a simple way, that Hawaiians are different from non-Hawaiians. *Palu* may sound unusual, but it is one of the few Hawaiian things newcomers haven't managed to change, replace or glamorize. "It's a little identity thing," he winked.

Ironically, native Hawaiians are now among the most inconspicuous people walking the streets of Hawaii, for there are few full-blooded Hawaiians left to walk the streets.

In the century following first contact with Europeans, most of Hawaii's native people died from epidemics of introduced diseases: cholera, influenza, mumps, measels, whooping cough, and smallpox. Gonorrhea caused sterility, syphilis resulted in stillbirths. The statistics astound: Hawaii's aboriginal population had shrunk from an estimated 300,000 at Captain Cook's 1778 visit to about 40,000 in 1893, when the Hawaiian monarchy was overthrown. And many of those 40,000 were *hapa* Hawaiian, or part Hawaiian.

By the mid-19th century, a hauntingly intangible but quite real disease killed many more thousands of Hawaiians: sheer psychological depression. "*Na kanaka kuu wale aku no i ka uhane* – The people freely gave up their souls and died," remembers one Hawaiian sadly.

Given the degree of inter-racial mixing over the past two centuries, it's difficult to know how many full Hawaiians still remain. According to state health department estimates, there are approximately 9,500 Ha-

waiians of unmixed ancestry, or about 0.9 percent of Hawaii's total population. Those of partial Hawaiian ancestry number between 140,000 and 210,000, depending on the source.

The most Hawaiian of islands is Ni'ihau, a privately-owned island off Kauai's west coast with a population of 230 – all Hawaiian. Only Hawaiian is spoken on the island, and visitors are not allowed. Molokai has the next-largest percentage of part Hawaiians, about 45 percent. Lanai, another mostly

privately-owned island, is next with less than 10 percent.

**Children of the soil:** The Hawaiians have made a comeback, it might be argued, by marrying into other racial groups and thus sustaining some of the blood lines. Equally if not more important is the revival of the Hawaiian culture, nearly extinquished by Protestant missionaries in the 19th century. (Despite missionary efforts to diminish everything traditionally Hawaiian, two of the most popular and important sports in Hawaii today, surfing and outrigger canoe racing, are pure Hawaiian.)

A *malihini*, or newcomer, might point out

**Left**, this helmeted Hawaiian performs in a Waikiki hula show for tourists. **Right**, spectator spotted at a Hawaiian music festival.

that part Hawaiians are also part something else, but most part Hawaiians, whatever their other ancestry, almost unanimously think of themselves as Hawaiian first. It's a thing of pride, if not of status, to be a *keiki 'aina,* a child of the soil, a Hawaiian.

The Hawaiian language, once nearly dead, is sustaining itself. Visitors will notice a plenitude of Hawaiian place and street names that can tie an unpracticed tongue into knots. Individual Hawaiian words are sprinkled into English conversation: *pau,* finished; *okole,* one's rear end; *mahalo,* thanks; *puka,* a hole or opening; *keiki,* child. Throughout the islands, by listening carefully, conversations in Hawaiian can be overheard, fluid like poetry.

Contrary to media stereotypes – the average Hawaiian as an easy-going beach boy or a kowtowing TV detective sidekick – some part Hawaiians are among the islands' most powerful people: the owner of the largest private ranch in America (Richard Smart), a US congressman (Representative Daniel K. Akaka), the state governor (John Waihe'e), one of the country's most enduring entertainers (Don Ho), and the executive director (David Trask) of the Hawaii Government Employees Union, one of the most powerful labor organizations in the state.

**On being Hawaiian:** But many Hawaiians are strangers in their own land, and alienation cultivates difficult problems. Hawaiians and part Hawaiians make up the largest number of inmates in county jails and the state prison. They account for the greatest percentage of state and federal welfare recipients, the majority of school dropouts and juvenile delinquents, and have the highest rate of illegitimate children.

Hawaiians are taking strong political and social positions for Hawaiian rights and self-government. With greater autonomy may come less alienation. The claims for autonomy and sovereignty have substantive and irrefutable historical standing.

But pragmatically, the state of Hawaii will not be turned back over *in toto* to the Hawaiians themselves. Some critics of the movement worry that the more reactionary factions could lead to an ethnocentric, if not anti-*haole,* racism. Either way, the Hawaiian has returned to Hawaii.

It's a subtle thing, this Hawaiianness, something aboriginal and abstract. It's an intangible to those who aren't. When asked the question "What is a Hawaiian?" there are many answers. George Kanahele, a local businessman: "These days, any resident of this state who considers Hawaii his home and who has an understanding of the values of Hawaiian culture ought to consider himself or herself a Hawaiian."

The late Samuel Crowningburg-Amalu, part-Hawaiian newspaper columnist: "The Hawaiians were not a middle-class society when Western man came. They were an aristocracy; because of that, of all the primitive people confronted by the white man, only the Hawaiians were accepted as equals."

Pete Thompson, Hawaiian grassroots or-

ganizer: "The biggest issue is the land question. What about the land? If you look at every Hawaiian (political) group that was formed in the past five years, every single one of them has been formed around the question of land. Every last one."

Aunty Abby Napeahi, a Hawaiian matriarch and community leader: "Being Hawaiian today is finally feeling at home after nearly a century of trying to live like foreigners told us we should live in our own land."

Edward Keliiahonui Kawananakoa, the man who one day would be King of Hawaii: "I guess, generally, I'm just trying to be a good American citizen."

**CHINESE:** "The ball at the Court House on Thursday night last, given to their majesties the King and Queen by the Chinese merchants of Honolulu and Lahaina, was the most splendid affair of its kind ever held in Honolulu... We have heard but one opinion expressed by those present (which includes all Honolulu and his wife), and that was that the Celestials have outshone the 'outside barbarians' in fete-making for the throne."

According to the above newspaper report, the party hosted by Chinese business leaders in 1856 to honor the marriage of King Kamehameha IV and Queen Emma took Honolulu by acclaim. Suggested another newspaper: "The taste displayed in getting

up this feast is a little ahead of anything we have witnessed here or elsewhere."

At the time of the ball, Hawaii's Chinese community numbered maybe 600 persons. That's a small constituency in any country, but the party meant much more to Hawaii's Chinese than mere social acceptance – it marked the entry of local Chinese into the highest of the Hawaiian kingdom's economic and political circles.

The king was so pleased that less than a year later, one of the Chinese sponsors married the foster sister of the future King

**Above**, tinted photo of traditional Chinese shop.

Kalakaua, later becoming the first and only full-blooded Chinese ever to be appointed a noble of the Hawaiian royal court.

Hawaii's Chinese didn't always have it so good. In the 1890s, jealous businessmen, in an attempt to restrict the inroads that enterprising Chinese were making into local commerce, initiated successful legislation that restricted the freedom of Chinese immigrant laborers. Nevertheless, over the decades the Chinese have become one of Hawaii's most prominent, influential, generous and financially successful ethnic groups.

**Country of the Fragrant Tree:** From the sandalwood trade of the early 1800s, the Chinese were well-acquainted with Hawaii, known to them as *Tan Heung Shan,* or the Country of the Fragrant Tree.

Opinions differ as to who were the first Chinese in Hawaii. As early as 1789, several Chinese crewmen jumped a ship captained by an infamous American trader, Simon Metcalfe. Two years later, Captain George Vancouver reported seeing a Chinese man in Hawaii who was one of three "banditti of renegadoes who had quitted different trading vessels."

The first Chinese laborers arrived in 1852, 195 workers from Kwangtung and Fukien provinces in southeastern China. Before they left China, they had signed five-year contracts promising them $36 a year, sea passage, food, clothing and housing, plus an advance of six dollars each to be deducted later from their wages.

Many of those first Chinese were intent on finishing their contracts and returning to China with money. Others, however, sought out opportunities in Hawaii. They married local women and, with their savings, set up shops in Honolulu and Lahaina, the boom towns of the mid 1800s. The Chinese often found a niche in retail, especially as they were not welcome in the sugar industry except as laborers. (But it was a Chinese who grew and milled Hawaii's first sugar, on Lanai in 1802.) In Honolulu, many settled in an area near the harbor now called Chinatown.

Most Chinese who used to live in Honolulu's so-called Chinatown left downtown long ago, taking their new-found affluence to other, ritzier sectors of the community, especially after World War II. But a few persistent old-timers stayed behind in Chinatown, where they still mind Hong Kong-style herb shops, acupuncture clinics, open-market food stalls, noodle factories and restaurants.

It was downtown Chinatown where Honolulu schoolmates Ho Fon and Dr. Sun Yatsen met to plan a Chinese revolution. That secret Honolulu society, first known by the Chinese-Hawaiian name Hsing Chung Hui (Revive China Group) was crucial to the future success of China's revolutionary movement against foreign colonial control. Dr Sun Yatsen, called the "Father of Modern China" by both Communist and Nationalist Chinese, founded his original revolutionary group in Honolulu in 1895. Because Chinese patrons in the islands contributed generous military and financial support to Dr Sun's cause, Hawaii became known in some Chinese circles as "The Cradle of the Chinese Republic."

Hawaii was also where the American writer Earl Derr Biggers found his role model for his literary creation, Charlie Chan. The "real" Charlie Chan-detective, Chang Apana, a Hawaiian-Chinese known locally as "Kana Pung," died in 1933 after 34 years service in the police force. The Royal Hawaiian Band marched in the cortege at his funeral.

**JAPANESE:** When Hirohito, the late Emperor of Japan, arrived in Hawaii in 1975, his aircraft landed at Honolulu International Airport from a southeasterly approach, rather than the standard northwesterly approach. The reason: the emperor's pilots wanted to avoid flying over Pearl Harbor and subjecting him to reminders of the war fought in his name 35 years earlier.

Meeting him at the airport was an "aloha" delegation that included three US congressmen of Japanese descent, the recently-elected Japanese-American governor of Hawaii, and an AJA (American of Japanese ancestry) president of the University of Hawaii.

Along the highway from the airport to downtown and Waikiki, Hirohito and his entourage rolled past dozens of businesses with Japanese names, fleets of fishing sampans wriggling with fresh tuna for Hawaii's *sashimi*-crazy households, and opulent Buddhist and Shinto temples and shrines.

Even local AJAs who remembered Pearl Harbor could hardly believe the changes in local social and political circles that had occurred since December 7, 1941.

To say that the Japanese have succeeded in Hawaii is an understatement. From World War II until now, their political and social power has been considerable. (It is a power, however, that may start to wane as the burgeoning Caucasian population replaces the AJAs as Hawaii's largest ethnic minority.)

This Japanese rise to prominence began with humble origins. A few Japanese survivors of nearby shipwrecks inadvertently visited Hawaii as early as 1832, but it wasn't until 1868, during the first year of Japan's reformist Meiji Era, that an "official" group of immigrants from Japan put into Hawaii. These "Gannenmono," or "First Year Men," arrived at Honolulu on board the British sailing ship *Scioto*.

Carrying three-year laborer contracts, all

were quickly assimilated into local plantations, earning about 12¢ a day or, according to one account, about twice what they could make in Japan. By 1885 that income quadrupled to about 50¢ a day, but the work remained hot, dusty and back-breaking.

Strict emigration laws in Japan, however, made it difficult for more Japanese to come to "Tenjiku," or the heavenly place, as Hawaii was called. A little diplomacy was called for on this matter.

In 1881, King Kalakaua visited Japan on the first leg of a tour around the world. He initiated treaty discussions with the Japanese, placing particular emphasis on the matter of Japanese immigration to Hawaii. As historian Ralph Kuykendall wrote, "The king let it be known that, in accordance with the policy of the government of Hawaii to increase population by inviting immigration from other countries, any Japanese who desired to settle in the Hawaiian kingdom would be permitted to do so."

Kalakaua tried to sweeten the deal, suggesting unsuccessfully that one of the imperial princes become betrothed to Princess Ka'iulani, his 6-year-old *hapa-haole* niece and heiress to the monarchy. And "to the emperor privately," reported Kuykendall, "Kalakaua suggested the formation of a federation of Asiatic nations, of which the Japa-

nese ruler would be the head and Hawaii would be one of the member nations."

While the marriage and the Asiatic federation schemes were lost somewhere in diplomatic history, Kalakaua actively pursued the Japanese immigration issue until it was given sanction. In 1885, a group of 943 immigrants – 676 men, 159 women and 108 children – arrived in Honolulu on board the Pacific mail steamer *City of Tokio*.

Life was often miserable in the plantation camps and cane fields, but Japanese from the

**Left**, Japanese orchid fancier, Honolulu. **Above**, farmer at Waipi'o Valley, the Big Island.

Yamaguchi, Hiroshima, Kumamoto, and Okinawa regions came in ever-increasing numbers. In five years, there were nearly 20,000 Japanese workers and dependents in the islands. By 1900 the number had reached 61,000 – or more than twice the number of Hawaiians, Caucasians or Chinese in Hawaii. Until the mid-1970s, the Japanese remained Hawaii's largest ethnic group.

The Japanese, like nearly all of Hawaii's non-*haole* laborers, suffered from racial and economic prejudices under Hawaii's plantation elite. And when Japan attacked Pearl Harbor, a small number of local Japanese-Americans (small compared to the numbers on the mainland) were forced into internment camps on the mainland.

In Hawaii, where AJAs made up 40 percent of the population, internment of all AJAs was out of the question. But under martial law, Japanese language schools and radio stations were shut down; Buddhist, Shinto and Zen temples were closed; Japanese newspapers were strictly censored. Historian Lawrence Fuchs notes in his social history *Hawaii Pono*: "It was not primarily the legal deprivations that demoralized the Japanese population in Hawaii. The fear and hostility of their neighbors hurt much more. *Nisei* (second generation Japanese-Americans), as well as their fathers and mothers, met discrimination in employment throughout the war."

Japanese *nisei* by the hundreds volunteered for military duty, but were turned away initially. Eventually and reluctantly, the War Department relented and, in 1942, an all-*nisei* battalion of national guardsmen and draftees was created.

A year later, when *nisei* volunteers outgrew battalion size, the 442nd Regimental Combat Team was formed. Fighting as the "Go For Broke" Infantry Regiment, *nisei* from Hawaii earned seven presidential unit citations and almost 6,000 individual awards for their performance abroad, making them the most highly-decorated American military unit in World War II. But going for broke was tough: the 442nd had a unit casualty rate three times higher than average.

Regardless of ethnic background, nearly everyone in Hawaii lives a little bit of the Japanese lifestyle, knowingly or not. Few are the homes where the shoes aren't removed shoes before entering, and few are the *kama'aina* who can't order *sushi* or *sashimi* without thinking twice.

These days, all Hawaii residents are very much at home with things Japanese – the *zori, tatami, futon* and *ofuro*. The thump of *mochi* pounding, or of drums announcing the summer Buddhist *bon odori* festivities that honor the souls of the dead, are common sounds in Hawaii's neighborhoods. And throughout the islands, even in the most remote of valleys, the Shinto shrine and Buddhist temple are as common as the New England church.

**FILIPINOS:** The first Filipinos to call Hawaii home were acrobats and musicians who swept into Honolulu after a performing tour

of China and Japan. In true Filipino spirit, they immediately set to work entertaining Oahu residents for two weeks in 1888 while waiting for their ship to San Francisco.

"The Filipino troupers pleased their Hawaiian audiences, and the spell of Hawaii upon the performers was even more potent: so much so that when sailing time came and their manager refused to pay their salaries until arrival in San Francisco, they returned to their lodgings and took up their abode in Hawaii. Four of the 12 young men found immediate employment in the Royal Hawaiian Band of King Kalakaua."

Roman Cariaga, Filipino scholar and author, wrote of the visit based on interviews with Lazaro Salamanca, one of the original 12 Filipino musicians and a 33-year member of the Royal Hawaiian Band. Salamanca. "He served through the reigns of Kalakaua and Queen Lili'uokalani, and after the revolution and establishment of the republic, and then annexation, he remained the only Filipino of the original troupe."

It was the sugar industry more than anything else that gets the credit for making Hawaii the largest Filipino community in the world outside the Philippines. In fact, Filipino immigrants comprised over half of new foreign arrivals to Hawaii in the early 1990s, and Filipino alien residents also made up over half of all foreigners in Hawaii obtaining American citizenship.

Immigration of Filipinos as laborers began in 1906 with the arrival of 15 Filipino laborers to work on a sugar plantation. For the next 40 years, Filipinos poured into Hawaii at a pace exceeded only by the Japanese. More than 125,000 Filipinos were recruited by the labor-hungry sugar companies, mostly in northern Ilocos. Of them, however, only 10,000 were women, and another 7,000 children. Not keen on being bachelors, about half of the men returned home to find wives and begin lives anew with money earned in the fields. Most who remained in Hawaii either married women from other ethnic groups or endured an extended bachelorhood.

**Collective dignity:** Tired of the plantation hierarchy and inequalities, the Filipinos organized into labor unions. The Filipino Federation and Labor Union, for example, was well-organized and actively agitating for employee benefits as early as 1919. And although some of their early labor-management confrontations ended in violence and defeat, *bum-by* (by-and-by), to use a favorite Filipino expression, their tenacity and eventual successes nurtured a collective dignity.

The Filipinos have rarely been treated as equals by the Americans and Europeans, whether in the Philippines or abroad. One writer visiting Hawaii, a certain Harry A. Franck, wrote in the 1930s:

"They are confirmed knife-toters and much given to fighting over women, who are scarce among them. It is common saying in Hawaii that the Filipino is only one pair of pants removed from the jungle." Mr. Franck was one of those unexceptional travel writers –

unlike Herman Melville, Robert Louis Stevenson and Jack London – who visited Hawaii and then slid into a literary vacuum.

Filipino food hasn't captivated island palates as decisively as have the cuisines of Korea, China, Thailand, and Japan. But for tastes à la Manila or Zamboanga, stroll into the cafés downtown and wish the proprietor a sincere *mabuhay* (hello). A complete range of Filipino food awaits, including *lechon kawali* (baked piglet), *adobo* (a stew prepared with beef, pork or chicken and green papaya chunks) and *pancit bijon* (a gourmet shrimp-pork-veggies creation with Malay, Chinese and Spanish influences).

Filipino celebrations follow Roman Catholic observances, including an exotic candlelight festival held every spring on the Feast Day of Santa Cruz. The biggest annual event is June Fiesta Filipina, which takes place at different locations throughout the islands.

Recruited in the north of the Philippines, the early immigrant laborers brought with them a passionate pastime, cockfighting. This was a "grim foreboding," a Filipino writer recounted later, which caused some local officials to worry "that this new immigration would introduce a new element of lawlessness into the 'low life' of Hawaii."

Although illegal, cockfighting still flourishes, especially in areas near the old sugar mill and plantation towns. Aficionados gather in rural arenas (Wai'anae Valley and Waimanalo on Oahu are two of the biggest) to watch groomed gamecocks fight with razorsharp blades attached to their ankles.

In years past, raiding police officers regularly arrested everyone present at these illegal gambling pits, but nowadays, following a court ruling that mass arrests are unconstitutional, only the actual bird handlers and book-keepers are nabbed when caught.

**KOREANS:** "In Hawaii you rarely ever see a group of Koreans, but you see a Korean in every group." This comment by a Honolulu-born Korean businessman isn't entirely true, but it's a contemporary comment on Hawaii's highly mobile and adaptable Korean community. Unlike the more clannish Japanese and Chinese, Hawaii's 20,000-plus Koreans have rapidly fanned out into society. Their "out-marriage" rate, for example, has been as high as 80 percent for both men and women, an inter-racial marriage statistic second only to part-Hawaiians.

In the United States, Honolulu is second only to Los Angeles in the number of native-born Korean residents. Both long-established and recently-immigrated Koreans have capitalized on their verve, ambitions and versatility to achieve business and social successes in Hawaii. Their overall education and income levels, for example, are the highest per capita of any ethnic group in Hawaii.

Although they are less than 3 percent of the local population, Koreans have introduced

considerable spice and fire to the islands. ("It's the *kim chee*," jokes a man who recently married a Korean woman, and became enamored of her country's pickled vegetables. "Once you start eating your regular food with *kim chee*, you're hooked. You've got to have more and more.") Whether in the land of Morning Calm or in Hawaii, Koreans are a down-to-earth lot, and without the communicative vagueness of their Asian neighbors. Koreans speak their minds and, as writers have suggested since the late 1880s when Korea was opened to the West, Koreans are the door-slammers and Irish of Asia.

They've adapted well to Hawaii, but many

**Left**, lantern slide taken in the early 1910s of a Filipino immigrant woman in traditional gown. **Right**, two Koreans who migrated to Hawaii – he in 1904, she in 1914.

of their traditions elude the younger generation. *Halmoni* (grandmothers) who first came to Hawaii as picture brides still try to arrange marital matches in the traditional Korean way, but second and third generation children usually have other ideas. The *haraboji* (grandfathers) still gather at community centers to spend long hours deep into clacking rounds of an ancient Korean board game, *changgi*, which they call "Korean chess."

In the Hawaiian Islands, probably the most popular nickname for Koreans is *yobo*. Literally, *yobo* means "my dear" and is a way of addressing one's husband or wife. It is also the informal equivalent of "hello" or "hey there" when used to catch one's attention.

Early Korean immigrants would address one another, "*yobo-seyo*" – or simply "*yobo*" (not quite as polite). This term stuck as an island nickname.

**Brides and revolutionaries:** Koreans first arrived in 1903, when the Pacific steamer *SS Gaelic* arrived at Honolulu with 2 interpreters, 54 men, 21 women, 13 children and 12 infants who had been recruited as laborers for the sugar plantations.

Over the next two years, more than 7,000 Koreans, most of them young men (ten for every Korean woman), signed up to work in Hawaii. But in 1905, Korea's emperor cut off all labor emigration from Korea after hearing that Korean laborers had been mistreated on hemp plantations in Mexico. Not until the Japanese annexed Korea and allowed a thousand Korean "picture brides" to join their "picture grooms" did Korean immigration to Hawaii resume.

When Japan invaded Korea in 1910, Hawaii became a source of pro-Korean revolutionary support. In fact, most of the Korean social societies still in Hawaii began as anti-Japanese and "restore the homeland" groups, some of them highly secretive.

Dr Syngman Rhee, an American-educated diplomat, turned to Koreans in Hawaii for revolutionary support against the Japanese occupation. In 1920, Dr Rhee, then a Honolulu school principal, organized a local society known as Dong Ji Hoi – the Association of Comrades – dedicated primarily to restoring Korea's sovereignty.

After Japan's defeat in World War II, Dr Rhee returned to Korea triumphant as first president of the Republic of Korea. Following a Korean military coup d'etat that deposed him in 1960 at the start of his fourth presidential term, he fled to Hawaii, dying in exile in 1965.

Brief mention should be made of the ubiquitous nightlife spots commonly referred to in Hawaii as "Korean bars," actually a catchall euphemism for the hostess bars that often have nothing to do with Koreans.

**SAMOANS:** "I wanna see some mo'a of Samoa," go the lyrics to an old *hapa-haole hula* song once popular in Hawaii, good-naturedly dedicated to Polynesian cousins far south on the island of Samoa.

Samoans, the newest of Hawaii's immigrants, come from the six isles that make up the territory of American Samoa, a 76-sq.-mile (196-sq.-km) group located about 2,600 miles (4,185 km) due southwest of Honolulu. This oceanic territory has been a part of the US since 1899 under the terms of a treaty negotiated with Great Britain and Germany. American Samoa's ruling chieftains officially ceded their islands to the US and, for the first half of this century, American Samoa was managed by the US Navy. After World War II, it was put under US Department of the Interior jurisdiction, which still appoints its governor and lieutenant governor, and oversees the election of a bicameral legislature and a delegate to Washington, DC. (American Samoa should not be confused with Western Samoa, a larger island group that is an independent nation.)

Some 500 Samoans had trickled into Hawaii after World War I, most of them to join a Mormon community at La'ie on Oahu's North Shore. In 1952, after Samoan immigration to America was liberalized, a group of 900 Samoan men, women and children boarded a navy transport ship and set off for Hawaii.

These first immigrants, about half of them Samoan-American navymen and dependents being transferred to Pearl Harbor, were seen off by some 7,000 people – "the largest gathering," a reporter wrote, "in Samoan history." Nine hundred people isn't a breathtaking wave of immigrants, but in 1952 they represented 6 percent of American Samoa's total population.

**Adjustments and aloha:** In Samoa, life is communal and sharing precedes possession. Many of these Polynesian newcomers found it extremely difficult adapting to the faster lifestyles of modern Hawaii. As a place with mostly Western inclinations regarding possession and ownership, many Hawaii residents didn't understand when a neighborly Samoan bade them *talofa* (a Samoan *aloha*) and then helped himself to the breadfruit, mangoes and bananas growing on *their* private property.

Lifestyle differences have caused Hawaii's Samoans some assimilation problems, but most have patiently stuck out this new life and adapted to American Hawaii while maintaining Samoan customs. Indeed, perhaps of all the Asian-Oceanic ethnic groups, Samoans have best retained their traditional cultural touchstones.

When a Samoan "community" problem arises, elected chiefs (some of whom represent the various expatriate Samoan clans in Hawaii) call a special *fono*. At these councils, the chiefs establish policy, mediate in the case of intra-Samoan grievances and, if they feel a Samoan problem requires government attention, draft mutually agreed-upon statements that are presented to the proper outside individual or agency.

Most Samoan gatherings, however, are of a more celebratory nature: a wedding, or the investure of a new chief, or Flag Day, an annual holiday that celebrates the raising of the American flag over Eastern Samoa. Even a regular day off warrants a gathering of the Samoan extended family. Out come the *kava* cups and the colorful *lava-lava* sarongs and *puletasi* dresses, and the finely woven *lauhala* mats to be spread out on the ground. Joined by expatriates from Tonga, Fiji, Tahiti and the Marquesas, the Samoans get together in fine *fia-fia* (feasting) fashion. *Fa'a Samoa*, the Samoan way.

American-style football was introduced to Samoa in 1968 and, in recent years, Samoan-Americans from Hawaii have become the interest of mainland university football scouts. Others have made the rather grueling

entrance into Japanese sumo, and several local Samoan-Americans are now in the top championship ranks.

**CAUCASIANS:** As some Hawaiians explain it, their ancestors called the first Europeans *haole* because they could not believe that men with such pale skins and frail bodies could be alive. *Haole,* from *ha,* which means breath or the breath of life, connects with *ole,* which connotes an absence – absence of the breath of life or, more simply, without life. Originally applied to any outsider, *haole* now refers to Caucasians.

Since the time of Captain Cook, it has been fashionable in Hawaii for both *haole* and non-*haole* to put down *haole*. Robert Louis Stevenson, himself a *haole,* was none too complimentary when he wrote that "in vile Honolulu there are too many cesspools and beastly *haoles.*"

This "thou is *haole*-er than me" attitude has taken on a mostly good-natured, or at least benign, racial connotation in recent years, though at times it's a negative moniker. For many years, the term was more a slur than a synonym for Caucasian or foreigner.

The *haole* – whether *malihini* (newcomer) or *kama'aina* (old-timer) – is now the fastest-growing ethnic group. Within a decade, they are expected to replace the Japanese as the principal political force in the state.

Since World War II, most *haole* coming to the islands more or less assimilated into the local lifestyle and rhythms, or at least attempted to. In recent years, however, new arrivals sometimes seem more interested in fashioning Hawaii into their own image of a paradise, or at least bringing a West Coast (where a good percentage come from) attitude with them.

This so-called Californication of Hawaii generates a lot of cynicism, much of it unwarranted. Since the first Polynesians arrived, every group has brought its cultural baggage with them. Times change, as do perspectives.

One distinct *haole* group that deserves special mention are the Portuguese, or "Portagee" in the local pidgin dialect, who immigrated to Hawaii in large numbers when Hawaii was still a kingdom, mostly to work in the sugar fields.

**Rough voyage:** As early as 1872, there were perhaps 400 or so Portuguese in Hawaii, most of them sailors who had left whaling ships for the landed life. These Europeans were well-received by both Hawaiians and *haole* merchants and planters, so in 1878 the Hawaiian government and sugar barons conducted an official labor recruitment campaign in Portugal's Azores and Madeira islands. Twenty years later, almost 13,000 Portuguese had made the rough voyage from their Atlantic islands to Hawaii.

Many became *lunas*, or foremen, on the sugar plantations, gaining a mid-level power foothold faster than Asian immigrants. By the 1930s, the Portuguese community boasted a territorial supreme court chief justice, a territorial secretary and acting governor, and

the Catholic vicar apostolic of the Hawaiian Islands.

The Portuguese also introduced a small four-stringed instrument – known as the *braquinho* or *cavaghindo* in Portugal – called the *'ukulele* in Hawaii. The Hawaiian word *'ukulele* literally means "leaping flea," and was said to come from the Hawaiian nickname of Edward Purvis, an English expatriate who arrived in Hawaii in 1879. Purvis made friends with newly-arrived Portuguese immigrants, and soon learned to play the *braquinho* with entertaining finesse. Purvis was small in stature and quick with his hands, so his Hawaiian friends nicknamed him *'Ukulele*, the "leaping flea."

Local Portuguese, although more than two generations removed from the "old country," still celebrate Portuguese traditions and religious festivals.

**Holy Ghost festivals:** In the spring months, there are a series of post-Easter *festas*, known as the Seven Domingas, or Holy Ghost festivals. During the seven weeks of *festa* families participate in prayer and celebration. Traditional delicacies are prepared, such as baked *pao dolce* (sweet bread), hot fried *malasadas* (a light Portuguese doughnut), spicy Portuguese bean soup, and beef and fish dishes marinated in tangy *vinha d'alhos*.

Portuguese sausage is found on breakfast menus in any worthy local coffee shop. Some cafes also serve Portuguese bean soup as a standard *soupe du jour*.

Another *haole* immigrant group with Euro-Latin origins, the Puerto Ricans, began arriving here at the turn of the century, and now number an estimated 5,000. Puerto Ricans have traditionally been classified in Hawaii's census polls as Caucasian, but their early immigrant ranks also included people of Creole blood and of mixed Spanish, American Indian and black African ancestry. The Puerto Ricans have never established a very solid cultural beachhead in the islands.

Hawaii's sugar and pineapple barons also imported Spaniards, Russians, Germans, Norwegians, Austrians, Italians, Scots, and both black and white Americans for work, but few of those laborers stayed on the islands for long. If they did stay, they blended into the local tapestry which has become the people of Hawaii.

<u>Right</u>, beach boys and buggy.

Few other types of music have girdled the earth more smoothly, more often and more completely than Hawaiian music and few have remained so popular with so many for so long. Say "Hawaiian music" to a banker in Bangkok, an army captain in Amsterdam, a housewife in Minneapolis and all get the same romantic, dreamy look. They're thinking of swaying palms and hips... the hula... the sultry slack-key guitar... a chilling, tremulous falsetto voice... the dazzling plunkyplunkiness of a ukulele... the keening accents of a steel guitar. Phrases from old songs float by: "I wanna go back to my little grass shack..." "Tiny bubbles, in the wine..." "Dreams come true, in blue Hawaii..." "To you, sweetheart, aloha..." "Lovely hula hands..." "Oh, we're going to a *hukilau*..." "*Aloha'oe*..."

**Coconut drums:** Hawaii has been described as a melting pot, historically quick to accept whatever comes to its golden shores. Nowhere is this phenomenal rate and degree of cultural assimilation more apparent than in the music. Listening to Hawaiian music today is like listening to the islands' history.

In ancient times, Hawaiian music sounded primitive, consisting of long, monotonous chants recited either without accompaniment or against a musical background of drums made from coconut trees, gourds, bamboo rattles and pipes, sticks and pebble castanets. The ritualistic aspects of the music were quite complex, on the other hand, playing a vital part of daily life and a significant role in all religious beliefs and services. The chant was the means of establishing contact between man and god. Entering a hula school was equivalent to entering a monastery.

The hula is Hawaiian folk dance. Legends say that goddesses of the dance were Laka and Hi'iaka. (If not actually worshipped, both are still well respected today.) At first, it was performed by men and women, but only men could perform the hula during temple worship services. It was believed that by pantomiming an action, that action could be controlled in the future. Thus there were many dances for wished-for events, such as a successful hunt, or fertility.

The hula later engulfed all of Hawaiian society and became many things – a teaching tool, a popular entertainment, and a basic foundation for the *lua*, an art of self-defense known only to ancient Hawaiians. As the hula became widespread, wars and governing duties kept the men too busy for the years of rigid training required to be a performer. Thus the women began to share equally in the performance of the hula.

**Missionary music:** Then an odd thing happened. After uncounted hundreds of years, King Kamehameha II overthrew the *kapu* (taboo) system in 1819 and with it the ancient religion. This left the Hawaiian people spiritually disoriented – and ripe for Christian missionaries from New England.

These devout and dedicated settlers built churches amid the Hawaiian huts, held services and sang hymns. The Hawaiians had never heard melody and four-part harmony before, and they collected by the hundreds outside the small lava rock and clapboard churches to listen to these exotic combinations of sound. Thinking that the quickest way to a Hawaiian's soul might be through his ears, the missionaries enrolled the natives in church choirs.

Progress was slow. The broader tones required by church hymns were new to Hawaiians, so the songs were learned by rote as the missionaries sang the hymns – called *himeni* by the natives – over and over and over again, and the natives copied as best they could. Finally, choirs were formed. The *himeni* remain a strong influence today. Choirs are most popular and so are several Hawaiian songs with religious themes and messages.

Hawaiian music's other most dominant influence reflected a Hawaiian king's wish to be Westernized and came in the form of a single man. King Kamehameha V decided that he wanted a royal band (like those in Europe) and the brisk, mustachio'd Heinrich Berger was imported from Germany in 1868 to be bandmaster.

Berger, who is known today as the Father

**Preceding pages: the Kodak Hula Show is one of the world's oldest tourist attractions. Left, ukulele player photographed by Theodore Kelsey at Palolo Valley, Oahu.**

of Hawaiian Music, served as director of the Royal Hawaiian Band from 1872 until 1915. During this time he conducted more than 32,000 band concerts, arranged more than 1,000 Hawaiian songs, composed 75 original Hawaiian songs (including several still popular today), while reversing the traditional order of the *mele*, or song – composing the music before the words.

Soon after, the Hawaiians were doing the same and, before the 1870s ended, they were composing lyrics and music simultaneously. Berger also served as personal inspiration and teacher for two generations of Hawaiian musicians, some of whom later went on to local, if not national, stardom.

**Jumping flea and slack key:** From other lands came other influences. The guitar, for instance, was brought by early whalers or more likely by traders from Mexico and California. (And not, as is popularly believed, by Mexican cowboys, who arrived later, in 1832.) In time the traditional style of playing was changed as the Hawaiian musicians loosened the strings, and tunings became whatever the player wished them to be. This style of playing came to be known as *ki ho'alu*, or slack key, and is as uniquely Hawaiian as flamenco is Spanish.

From Madeira, Portugal, in 1878, with laborers imported to work in the sugar cane fields, came a small, four-stringed instrument called the *braquinho,* or *cavaquinho.* As with so much else in Hawaiian musical history, there is disagreement as to how the *braquino* became *'ukulele*, Hawaiian for "jumping flea," but many believe it was named for a very small English ex-patriate who quickly mastered the instrument and was unusually quick fingered.

Scholars are also arguing about who actually invented the steel guitar. Some say a Hawaiian student discovered the sound when he dropped his pocket knife upon the strings of a guitar and holding it there with one hand, plucked the strings with the other, moving the steel knife to "slide" the sound. Others think the inventor of the steel guitar had been in India, where he could have seen an Indian stringed instrument, the *gottuvadyam*, played in a similiar fashion. While the steel guitar has lately been much identified with country-and-western music, it remains the single most identifiable part of the Hawaiian instrumental sound.

The descendants of the ancient *ali'i* ruling Hawaii in the final years before annexation to the United States were among the most talented and prolific composers of song that the island culture ever produced. The best known of these was King David Kalakaua, a plump and jovial man whose "champagne dynasty" was also an inspiration for a genuine musical renaissance.

Kalakaua was a gifted politician, world traveler and patron of the arts. He promoted the ukulele and steel guitar and formed his own musical group, entering into competitions with relatives and friends. He collected the legends and myths of Hawaii into a definitive, and literate, book and co-wrote (with Heinrich Berger) Hawaii's national anthem, "Hawaii Pono'i," a song that's still sung at ball games and public assemblies. The hula, long suppressed by the missionaries and near death, was revived under his personal direction. Much music is played today on the birthday (November 16) of this bewhiskered king.

His sister, Lili'uokalani, probably came even closer than the king to understanding and synthesizing ancient Hawaiian and Western music traditions and form. Probably the most gifted Hawaiian of her class and time, she composed a song that has appeared in at least half the Hawaiian movies ever made (even Elvis Presley sang a version) and has been a certifiable "hit" for more than 70 years: "Aloha 'Oe."

The sound of Hawaiian music changed again after Lili'uokalani's kingdom was wrenched away by aggressive sugar growers and Hawaii became a territory of the United States. This directed great interest toward Hawaii and in 1915 a group of Hawaiian musicians, singers and dancers were the runaway sensation of the Panama-Pacific International Exposition in San Francisco, sparking a craze that swept North America and soon spread to Europe. Soon after, the best (most adaptable) Tin Pan Alley song-writers were writing "Hawaiian" music, too.

traditional, more authentic Hawaiian songs with the newly popular jazz beat that they heard everywhere they went.

Hula dancers became all the rage in vaudeville. They were called "cootch" dancers because many of the performers – few of whom were actually Hawaiian – adapted the movements freely and lasciviously.

Back in Hawaii, the first hotels were going up on Waikiki and dance bands were being formed for the growing number of tourists. Ragtime, jazz, blues, Latin and foxtrot rhythms were interspersed with Hawaiian themes and, horrors! – English lyrics. The purists were appalled, as always, but by 1930 the *hapa-haole* (half Caucasian) song was an

**Doubletalk:** If most of those new songs had little to do with true Hawaiian musical tradition – and often doubletalk served as Hawaiian, as in "Yaaka Hula Hickey Dula" (a hit for Al Jolson) – the influence was immediate and significant. The craze took many authentic Hawaiian groups across America for many years, where they, in turn, accepted the phony Hawaiian songs (to satisfy requests), eventually turning them into Hawaiian "classics." At the same time, they began arranging

**Left, Don Ho has been Hawaii's major musical export. Above, the late Gabby Pahinui, a well-known folksinger on the islands.**

entrenched and accepted part of Hawaiian music and a staple on what was to become the most widely heard radio program in all the world, "Hawaii Calls."

Then Hollywood called. And when Bing Crosby introduced two *hapa-haole* classics, "Sweet Leilani" and "Blue Hawaii," in a single film (*Waikiki Wedding*) in 1937 and "Sweet Leilani" won the Oscar for the best song, movie companies began churning out languid musical romances by the score.

Again the hula was revived, and – for Hollywood – cleaned up a bit as authentic island practitioners like Hilo Hattie were featured in many films. Now and forever more the swaying hips and limbs of the grass-skirted dancer would be the foremost symbol of Hawaii's widespread image of carefree sensuality.

When one songwriter urged visitors to Hawaii to keep their eyes on the hands, in one sense it was good advice, for when the singer says, "Lovely hula hands/graceful as the birds in motion," the arms are extended and the hands move gracefully to simulate swooping birds. In "The Hukilau Song," which is about fishing, the hands throw out and pull in the net.

The 30-year period from 1930 to 1960 is regarded as Hawaiian music's "golden age," as the music of Hawaii circled the world again and again, on television as well as in radio and film. Wherever the traveling hula dancers and musicians went, they found enthusiastic audiences.

Then came the Beatles, changing Hawaiian music just as they changed so many things. In fact, they nearly killed it. For 10 years, young Hawaiians were uninterested in the traditional island sound. Hawaiian music on local radio dropped to a low 5 percent. Rock dominated and middle-of-the-road singers like Kui Lee and Don Ho emerged as the only Hawaiian stars.

In the 1970s there came another Hawaiian renaissance, as people with Hawaiian blood discovered an ethnic awareness and pride. So pervasive and energetic was this second cultural rebirth that all the traditional Hawaiian arts experienced a rich revival.

**Rhythm 'n' roots:** The music became more "contemporary" (a word used by the musicians themselves). Politically relevant lyrics were added along with new rhythms, new instruments and greater amplification, thus attracting the attention of the young Hawaiians who'd turned away from their heritage for so long. At the same time, there was renewed, fervent interest in the older, more traditional Hawaiian sounds. And some of the young composers appealed to everyone by writing new songs (and chants) about the kings and ancient gods. In the 1970s, Hawaii finally acknowledged its roots.

Young Hawaiians also began dancing in the ancient style. Not since the early 1800s, when missionaries labeled many hula dances obscene and banned them, have such powerful and erotic movements been seen in Hawaii. Indeed, suppression of hula had been so complete that by the 1850s it had nearly disappeared, and when 40 years after that King Kalakaua saved the hula, much had already been lost forever.

Today, though, the hula retains much of its serious heritage. Contemporary students heed ancient ritual religiously. (Although none is asked to give up sex to be a hula performer, as was true in ancient times.) Different *hula halau* (schools) compete fiercely to outdo one another. Hula masters, or *kumu hula*, are revered figures. And with the male hula now in a period of rich revival, the dance has become a symbol of the islander's newly rediscovered sense of Hawaiianness.

**Cha-lang-a-lang:** Music is a vital part of Hawaiian daily life and songs have been written about the most mundane subjects – for example, "The Hasegawa General Store" and "Bottles and Cans" (a song about Maui's Makawao dump). The sound of the ukulele has given birth to a raucous, backyard style of playing called *cha-lang-a-lang.*

Hawaiians believe that music is not just a means of communicating with god, but also a gift from god, so they in turn give it freely – while walking along the street or lazing at the bus stop. Professionals perform for free at dozens of benefits a week.

Music is everywhere in Hawaii. The Royal Hawaiian Band, still performing after all these years, appears in several public concerts each week, notably at noon nearly every Friday at the 'Iolani Palace Coronation Bandstand. Radio station KCCN (at 1420 on the AM dial) calls itself "the world's only all-Hawaiian music station."

Hawaii's most prestigious hula event is the Merrie Monarch Festival, which pays homage to King Kalakaua. It has been held every April since 1964 at the Edith Kanakaole Stadium in Hilo. The highlight of the week-long festival (which includes a parade and music celebrations) is the two-day competition of *kahiko*, or ancient hula, and *auwana* or modern hula. Tickets for this competition are usually sold out months in advance. Recent festivals have drawn dozens of *hula halau* and several hundred dancers from every island and the mainland. It is easy to see why Kalakaua referred to hula as "the heartbeat of the Hawaiian people."

**Right**, the late Iolani Luahine, much respected for her inimitable dancing of the ancient hula.

From the time Hiʻiaka is said to have presented the first *lehua* lei to her sister Pele, the volcano goddess, lei have been prominent in Hawaiian religion, art, custom, and ornamentation.

In ancient times, a lei was offered to the gods during sacred dances and chants, taking the form of head wreaths and necklets as well as the long circular or open-ended strands common today. A lei worn in a dance was never given away, for it belonged to the goddess of the dance.

Some forms of lei have vanished with time, among them a seaweed lei called *limu kala*, used in ancient Hawaiian rituals for the ocean deities. Nor do we now see nursing mothers wearing lei of sweet potato vines, said to increase lactation.

Lei today are less superstition and more sentiment and ornamentation, made of flowers, shells, paper, and of anything that can be fashioned by five basic techniques. If the lei-maker uses *wili paukuku*, they are winding roses and begonias in a certain style. *Humuhumu* is a lei sewn onto a backing; *wili* is a lei that is wound; *hili* is braided with greens; *haku* is braided with flowers; and *kui* is strung. In the *kui* method alone there are countless variations. *Kui* lei are the *pikake*, ginger, carnation, and other popular flower *lei* sold by vendors at the airport and in downtown Honolulu.

Before needle and thread were introduced to Hawaii, stiff grass blades from Nuʻuanu Valley were used as needles, and strands of banana bark as string. For the more elaborate feather lei reserved for the royalty of old Hawaii, strips of *olona* bark were twisted into a cord that was flexible and strong enough to invisibly secure so many feathers.

Care is exercised when lei materials are gathered. A mountain or valley is never stripped. Materials are clipped, not pulled from the stalk or root. Only mature leaves are taken; the young are left to grow. Plants are never taken whole and, in any one area, enough is left growing to allow regeneration.

**Left**, girl wearing *maile lei*, about 1908, taken by Ray Jerome Baker. **Right**, Mrs Ray Jerome Baker on "Boat Day" in the 1920s.

Only in remote areas such as Haleakala Crater can one still see the *ʻiʻiwi* and *ʻapapane*, native birds noted for their crimson feathers used in the lei, capes and ornaments reserved for the ancient *aliʻi*. Other birds, once prized for their yellow feathers, are extinct.

Today, there are two basic styles – round and flat – for feather lei, made from the feathers of peacocks, pheasants, ducks and geese. (In the old days, feathers were gathered by families for years then bundled and stored in banana leaves until needed.)

The styles of Niʻihau shell lei, considered museum pieces today, have evolved as well, but not quite so dramatically. The popular three-strand *pikake* style is a later development and, like all Niʻihau shell lei, is prohibitively expensive. The tiny, fragile lei, called *pupu Niʻihau* or *momo* by the people of this privately-owned island, cost hundreds of dollars and are not easily available.

To this day, each island has its own special material for making lei – shells for Niʻihau, *mokihana* for Kauai, *ilima* for Oahu, *kaunaoa* for Lanai, *hinahina* for Kahoʻolawe, *kukui* flowers for Molokai, *lokelani* for Maui, and *lehua* for the Big Island.

# KE KUMU HAWAII.

HE PEPA HOIKEIKE I NA MEA E PONO AI KO HAWAII NEI.

"O ka pono ka mea e pomaikai ai ka lahuikanaka; aka, o ka hewa ka mea e hoinoia'i na aina."

Buke 1.　　　　HONOLULU, OAHU, MEI 13, 1835.　　　　Pepa 14.

### HE ZEBERA.

Ua like kekahi ano o ka Zebera me ko ka Lio. Ua like ka heluna o kona mau niho, a ua poepoe ka maiuu o kona mau wawae, aole hoi i maheleia, ua like no me ko ka lio.

O ka Zebera, o ka lio, ua nui ka lio. O ka Zebera, o ka hoki, ua nui ka Zebera. Ua olenalena ke oho o ka Zebera, a he onionio elecle nae. Ua kaawale ka olenalena, a me ka elecle. Nolaila ua like me ka mea i penaia. Ua like kekahi mau helehelena ona me ko ka lio, a me ko ka hoki kekahi. O kona kino a me kona uha, ua like me ko ka lio, a o ka ai, a me ke poo, ua like me ko ka hoki. He poepoe maikai kona kino, a ikaika maikai kona mau wawae e like me ko ka lio.

Aole holoholona i oi aku kona maikai mamua o ko ka Zebera, ke nana aku. O ka onionio, oia ka maikai loa.

Pokole makalii loa kona oho, a ua hinuhinu. Ua onionio kona kino a pau, he elecle, a he olenalena, o ke kino, o ka ai, o ke poo, o ka maka, o na pepeiao, nolaila, i ka ike ana aku, ua like ia me ka mea i hoonaniia i ka ribine.

Ua loaa ia holoholona ma na ululaau nui ma Aferika; aole i loaa ma Asia, a ma Europa, a ma Amerika.

Ma na ululaau, kahi o ia lio e noho ai, ua hihiu loa ia, a no kona mama, loaa ole ia e na lio Arabia a pau.

Makemake loa lakou e noho pu a hele pu, he ohana nui, nolaila, ua nui loa lakou i ikeia ma kahi hookahi.

I ka wa e ai ai kekahi mau mea, kiai no kekahi mau mea, o hiki mai auanei ka enemi, he kanaka paha, o ka ilio paha. Ina i ike mai ka poe kiai i ke kanaka, a i ka ilio huhu paha, alaila, hoike koke aku la lakou, i ka poe e ai ana; alaila, holo nui lakou, a no ko lakou mama, aole loaa iki lakou i kekahi holoholona.

No ka hihiu o ka Zebera aole ia i hoolaka loa ia, no ka mea, ina i paa i kona wa uuku, hoowahawaha no ia i ka mea e hoohana mai ia ia.

Ina i malama pio ia oia i na makahiki he nui loa, a hanai mau ia i ka lima o ke kanaka hookahi, aole ia e oluolu ke noho ke kanaka ma kona kua. A ina hele mai ka malihini, alaila, moe koke no kona mau pepeiao ilalo, a hoomakaukau e nahu mai, a i ole ia, e huli no a kehi mai.

Ma kona wahi ua hakalia loa ka loaa ana o keia lio. No kona hihiu a me kona akamai, aole ia e loaa i ka hoowalewale, a no kona mama aole loaa i ka hahai mai. Nolaila aole i loaa pinepine ka Zebera nui. I ka wa uuku, hahai ka poe hahai, a hoomanawanui loa, a pomaikai ke loaa, no ka mea, he lio kuai nui loa ia lio.

A e kuai nui loa no hoi kona ili, no ka maikai, a no ka mea, aole i loaa pinepine. Ua manao nui loa ia ia lio, i mea hoike; a nolaila ke kuai nui, i mea hoike aku i kanaka.

O ka onionio o ka Zebera, oia kona mea like ole loa me ka lio. A he okoa no kekahi helehelena ona, okoa ko ka lio. Ua nui ka lio, a ua oi aku ka maikai o kona ai, a me kona poo, a me kona mau pepeiao mamua o ko ka Zebera.

He mama ka Zebera, he lohi ka lio. He lokomaikai nae ka lio, a oluolu ia ke lawe i ke kanaka ma kona kua. Ina i ee ke kanaka maluna o ka Zebera, o kona pii no ia, a holo ino, i haule ke kanaka.

E hoomanawanui no ka lio ma na hana a pau a ke kahu e haawi aku ai ia ia. Aka, o ka Zebera, aole hiki ke hoolaka ia ia, no kona huhu loa. Ma ka onionio maikai o kona ili, ua oi aku ka maikai o ka Zebera mamua o na holoholona a pau. He onionio like, a maikai wale no.

I noonoo kakou i ka mooolelo no na holoholona a pau, maopopo no ko ke Akua lokomaikai. Ua hooneleia kekahi holoholona i ka mea i loaa mai i kekahi. O ka Elepani, ina kiiia mai oia, aole ia i mama, aole hiki ke holo a pakele, nolaila, ua hawiia mai kona nuku i mea e pale aku ai i ka hewa. He pepeiaohao ko ka Lachaokela a me ka Bufalo a me ka Bipi, i mea e pale aku ai i ka hewa.

He maiuu oioi ko ka Liona, a me ke Tiga, a he mau kui kekahi. Oia ko laua mau mea eha, e pale aku ai i ka hewa, a oia no hoi na mea e loaa ai lana ai.

O ka Zebera, aole ona pepeiaohao, aole kui, aole oioi kona maiuu, i mea e pale aku ai i ka hewa, aka, no kona mama, e hiki ia ia ke holo, a pakele, aole loa e loaa e kekahi i lio hae.

Nolaila, e mahalo kakou i ka lokomaikai o ke Akua, i kona haawi ana ina holoholona a pau ana i hana'i i na mea e pono ai, i mea hoi e pakele ai lakou i ka hewa.

# THE HAWAIIAN LANGUAGE

*I ka ʻolelo no ke ola a me ka make.*
(In the language is life and death.)
— ancient Hawaiian proverb

To describe the Hawaiian language in English is problematical because it is very much a language of emotions, poetry and nature-related sounds and nuance.

**Animate alphabet:** For hundreds of years the alphabet of the Hawaiian language was and still is nature in its many animate and inanimate forms. And probably because the language in its oral form proved satisfactory for so long, it was never given a written, literate form until after the coming of Westerners to Hawaii in the late 18th and early 19th centuries. Instead, the Hawaiian language thrived expressively and melodically as the exclusively spoken language of a Polynesian people who were rich in unwritten literature – including complicated poetry and songs, histories, genealogies and mythologies – which were never recorded outside Hawaiian minds. All that we know of the Hawaiian language and ancient Hawaiians was memorized long ago, and passed on verbally, from mouth to ear, and generation to generation, from the earliest of Hawaiian times.

Today, through accidents of history over which the present generation had no control, few people speak the Hawaiian language. However, certain words and names are still an important part of an islander's daily vocabulary, and the language is of great symbolic importance to the people. At its very least, the language of the Hawaiian people is their most ancient possession.

Historical linguists have not determined all the intricacies of the development of the Hawaiian language, but a fairly clear picture has emerged regarding its relationship to other languages. It is known, for example, that Hawaiian belongs to the Austronesian (formerly termed Malayopolynesian) language family. These were languages spoken by seafaring peoples who spread over an area of the globe larger than that covered by any other people until the 18th and 19th centu-

ries, when Europeans began exploring various parts of the then-known world.

Hawaii is the furthest point of Austronesian expansion to the north, Easter Island to the east, and New Zealand to the south. From these points westward, Austronesian tongues are spoken throughout the Pacific to Indonesia, Malaysia, the Philippines and Taiwan, with the furthest western point being the island of Madagascar which lies in the south Indian Ocean off the east coast of Africa.

Hawaiian is classified more specifically as a Polynesian language most closely related to languages spoken in Tahiti, the Marquesas and surroundings island groups of the South Pacific. According to historical linguists, it was from these islands that people destined to be ancestors of modern Hawaiians originated. They had reached the South Pacific, and later Hawaii in the Central Pacific, by slowly following a travel route which began in Southeast or Indo-Malay Asia, then coursed around the north coast of New Guinea through the islands of Melanesia and, finally, into Polynesia.

The various Indo-Malay people continued to develop along their own linguistic paths, but their distant relationship to the Hawaiians is still reflected in certain words and verbal inflections. Instead of the Hawaiian term *iʻa*, for fish, people of South-east Asia say *ika* or *ikan*; instead of *hale*, for house, they say *fare*, *ʻare* and *vale;* and instead of *maka*, for eye, they say *mata*.

**Pathway to the soul:** By 1819, when the first Calvinist-Christian missionaries began sailing to Hawaii from Boston, they had already heard the Hawaiian language being spoken by Hawaiians who had traveled to the East Coast of America as seamen on various trading ships.

The missionaries had succeeded in converting some of these adventurous Hawaiians to Christianity, and it was due to the devotion of one ardent Hawaiian Christian, who was known by the name ʻOpukhaʻia, that the first missionaries were inspired to sail to Hawaii and establish a mission here. They knew the Hawaiian language was only a spoken language, but they were eager to set it to writing, to enable them to translate their

**Left**, page from the early Hawaiian newspaper *Ke Kumu Hawaii*, printed on May 13, 1835.

Christian teachings, and ultimately gain converts in the Hawaiian Islands.

Upon arriving in Hawaii in 1820, the missionaries immersed themselves in their work of saving souls and attempted to communicate their teachings in a faltering form of Hawaiian. By 1823, after studying the language and putting it on paper in a somewhat phonetic form, the missionaries arbitrarily established a Hawaiian alphabet. They did this by voting, because various missionaries throughout the islands differed about which sounds were to be represented by their respective phonetic letters.

For example, some missionaries argued that the K sound should be a T sound, or that the flapped R sound was really an L sound. But when a final vote was taken, the K sound was adopted over the T, and the L over the flapped R.

In the end, missionary linguistic consensus established the consonants of the Hawaiian language as H, K, L, M, N, P and W, and it was agreed that the Hawaiian vowel sounds would be the five distinctive A, E, I, O and U of Western language forms. These 12 letters have functioned as the accepted Hawaiian alphabet to this day.

The Hawaiian language continued to be the spoken and, later, written language of the land in government, business and social circles of the Hawaiian kingdom, and over the years it was used almost exclusively in newspapers. Most recently, however, this rich and expressive language is on its way to becoming extinct.

**Aloha Hawaiian language:** The last Hawaiian language newspaper, *Ka Hoku O Hawai'i, The Star of Hawaii,* printed at Hilo on the Big Island, stopped its presses in 1948. And though Hawaiian was still the language in general use on the floor of the Territorial Legislature at the beginning of this century, it was quickly replaced by English. Today, Hawaiian is rarely spoken at home or heard on the streets, and the only place where Hawaiian still exists as a daily spoken language is on the privately owned island of Ni'ihau, which has a mostly Hawaiian population of fewer than 300 residents.

Today there is little hope, except on Ni'ihau, that a child will learn Hawaiian as his mother tongue. It has been estimated that there are approximately 2,000 native speakers of Hawaiian left today. Of this number many are on Ni'ihau, with the remaining scattered throughout the islands. A few are on the West Coast of America. Most of these people are senior citizens, and they rarely speak Hawaiian to their children, so the language will probably die with them.

A dedicated group of people regularly lobby for the continued welfare of the Hawaiian language but, except for recent state legislation which recognized Hawaiian as the State of Hawaii's official language, little has been done to insure the language's continued life. Hawaiian language courses are taught in a few of the islands' private and public schools and at the University of Hawaii, but the kind of public funding which would insure that the language remains strong and alive has never so far been allocated by the state.

**Mahalo for your kokua:** Nonetheless, Hawaii is special because of its language, and it is one of the few states in America which can claim such linguistic distinction. However, where does the fast-fading Hawaiian language leave the visitor to the state?

If you are like most first-time visitors, you'll probably find yourself tripping over the pronunciation of Hawaiian place names. And to make matters worse, the first local, or *kama'aina* (oldtimer), you speak to will more likely than not compound your problems by advising you incorrectly.

As a visitor, however, you should realize that you do help to preserve the Hawaiian language in indirect ways, such as paying dollars to listen to and see Hawaiian music and dance (which of course are done with Hawaiian words and lyrics). Also, a curious sort of tourist Hawaiian has evolved in recent years, which combines snatches of Hawaiian, pidgin and English at their provocative and sing-songy best. No doubt you'll hear the song lyrics, *"Honi kaua wikiwiki"* (kiss me quickly), and your waitress will say *"mahalo"* and *"aloha"* at your cafe table (though at home she'll prefer to use "thanks" and "bye").

Anyone wishing to learn more about the Hawaiian language should turn to the language guide in the *Travel Tips* section at the back of this book.

**Right**, advertising page from the later Hawaiian newspaper, *Ke Au Hou*. This issue was published on September 28, 1910 in Honolulu.

109

# TALKING LOCAL

*Eh, brah. You guys teenk we local folks talk funny kine, eh? Well, chry wait. I going learn you why you no understan'. I like educate you 'bout da kine; dat way you folks not going experience one communication gap in Hawaii nei.*

*Da kine* communications gap indeed. While perhaps multilingual and worldly-wise, the visitor to Hawaii may find that the most common ethnic language spoken in Hawaii is not Japanese, Chinese, Korean, Filipino, Samoan nor even Hawaiian. Rather, local folks of all backgrounds will be heard carrying on in pidgin English, a hybrid island language that flits in and out of conversations like a haughty mynah bird.

Pidgin is used to describe any Creole tongue that borrows freely from two or more languages. Originally, the word "pidgin" referred to the way in which Cantonese merchants, involved in the early China trade with Europeans, spoke English. "Business" sounded like "pidgin" – most conversations in those days had to do with business – and traders began referring to how Chinese spoke all English as "pidgin," or "pidgin English."

There are extreme differences between the pidgin spoken in Hana and Wai'anae, or in Kona and Hanapepe. Subtle forms of *paniolo* (cowboy) Big Island pidgin are nearly unintelligible to speakers of fishermen's pidgin on Kauai. However, certain terms such as *da kine* – a catch-all expression that refers to anything and everything (and useful when the correct word escapes one's mind) – are understood everywhere in Hawaii.

Hawaii's pidgin diversity is a phenomenon that assures language scholars perpetual fodder for academic papers. Da truth of da matter is that there are no structural or pronunciation rules for Hawaiian-style pidgin. And the only way to become fluent in one or many of its forms is to grow up in Hawaii and absorb the language's nuances. An outsider trying to speak pidgin will *make ass,* as such buffoonery is known in pidgin. Simply put, a visitor or newcomer shouldn't try to speak pidgin at all. After living here a few years, one may feel comfortable with a

few well-timed pidgin words or maybe even a complete phrase. Anything more than a simple statement and one becomes an embarrassment.

Gavan Daws, a self-described "*haole* historian" and author of a sensitive and very readable Hawaii history book, *Shoal of Time*, once wrote that local pidgin is more than just a simplified way of talking. It is also, he said, an almost secretive "resistance movement against English" and "the great mark of the local boy, whatever his genes." Daws, an Australian well-versed in "Strine," that equally peculiar mutation of the Queen's English spoken Down Under, sees pidgin as a very effective sort of underground verbal weapon.

"The consummate pidgin speaker, in fact," wrote Daws in a book called *The Hawaiians,* "is likely to be taking a continual subtle revenge upon *haole* condescension. There are witty men and genial philosophers among the pidgin speakers, and many a *haole* loose among them never learns, even with experience, whether he is being skewered and spitted for roasting or, alternatively, graciously pardoned for existing."

**Left,** talking local. **Right,** local talk.

It's late afternoon when the *luau* table is finally set under Uncle Kimo's big banyan tree. The salmon has been chopped *lomilomi* style with onions and tomatoes, and it sits next to a big bowl of *poi,* pounded taro root, a staple of the old Hawaiian diet. Aunties chatter as they carry out the rest of the dishes: *laulau* (pork and fish steamed in *ti* leaves), *poke* (seasoned raw fish), yams, squid luau with coconut milk and taro tops, *haupia* (coconut pudding), and fresh fruit. The boys have already pulled out the pig from the *imu* (underground lava-rock oven), and now the moist, smoky meat is shredded and piled on a big platter as the centerpiece of the meal. Friends and family members lay down their ukulele and guitars to pick up a plate, and the party is in full swing.

**Luau luxury:** Now *that's* Hawaiian dining. Oddly enough, the luau experience is as obscure for visitors as it is famous. There are, of course, dozens of commercialized, slicked-up versions with watery mai tais and cellophane-skirted hula girls, but we're talking about *da kine,* the institution brought to Hawaii with the earliest Polynesian settlers. If you're lucky, you might just stumble upon the real thing at a church benefit, or be invited to one by an island friend.

But as you nibble your way from shore to shore, you're more likely to encounter Asian, European and American fare than pig and *poi.* The reason is simple: Hawaii's food represents Hawaii's people. From far off lands they brought their personal cooking styles, stirring all manners of flavors and ingredients into the cultural stew.

Island menus read like a United Nations lunch order: *sushi, penne* pasta, crispy *gau gee, kim chee,* tortillas, *tandoori* chicken, wienerschnitzel, you name it. Within a relatively small geographic area, visitors find a universe of entrees served in surroundings both down-home and *haute,* from neighborhood delis hawking lox and bagels to candle-lit lairs of steak *tartare* and chocolate mousse.

Hawaii has many to thank for its tasty diversity. Start with the Chinese, who taught

islanders that rice goes just as well with eggs at breakfast as with lunch and dinner. Supermarkets of all stripes lay in supplies of *cilantro* (Chinese parsley), lemon grass and ginger, and restaurants turn out everything from Mandarin, Szechwan and Canton to Mongolian barbecue and stir-fry.

For an energizing assault on the senses, go to a house of *dim sum,* where pushy waitresses load your table with little plates of bite-sized dumplings until you hold up your hands in surrender.

From the Japanese came the gifts of *shoyu* (soy sauce), *sashimi* (thinly-sliced raw fish) and *tempura* (batter-dipped, deep-fried vegetables and meats). Most every street has a sushi bar for swigging sake while chefs with lightning-fast hands fashion edible fantasies out of rice, seafood and *wasabi* (hot green mustard). Japanese culinary sensibilities are best summed up by the *bento,* a lunch box with tidy compartments for morsels of chicken, shrimp, pork cutlets, fishcake, pickled plums, rice and other artful taste treats.

**Garlic and grills:** Wafts of garlic and grilled specialities lure diners through the doors of Hawaii's Korean restaurants, which generally assume the form of formica-tabled eateries. Therein await *kim chee* (pickled vegetables), *kalbi* (marinated short ribs), *jun* (foods dipped in an egg batter and pan-fried) and the musical *bi bim bap,* a bowl of rice, vegetables, fried egg and a sweet sauce.

The more recent influx of people from Thailand has introduced Hawaii to spring rolls, *mee krob* (noodle salad) and a coconut milk/hot pepper-flavored dish called Evil Jungle Prince, best followed by Thai iced tea with sweetened condensed milk.

Vietnamese food – less spicy than Thai – is particularly popular for its *pho,* broth with noodles and slices of beef or chicken, garnished with fresh basil and sprouts. The influence of the Portuguese makes itself known in *pao dolce* (sweet bread), *chorizo* (sausage), *vinha d'alhos* (marinated meat) and a robust bean soup, while from the Philippines comes *lumpia* (fried spring rolls), *paella* (seafood casserole), *bagoong* (fish sauce) and tripe stew.

Add to this pot the creativity of classically-

**Preceding pages:** juicy fruits of Hawaii. **Left,** shave ice for sale.

trained chefs from France, Switzerland, Germany and Italy who have been imported to work in some of Hawaii's high-class restaurants. Their continental attitude of the 1970s has evolved into today's more health-conscious cooking, but without much looking you can still find a rather authentic veal scaloppine or a decadent slab of salmon drenched in dill sauce.

The most recent take on island food is called Hawaii regional cuisine, which begins with a sort of culinary word association. Say papaya and one thinks of the plentiful trees of Puna on the Big Island. Onions conjure up images of cool upcountry Kula on Maui, where the sweetest variety is grown. Guava

Maui's Tedeschi Vineyards, then sign off with a Kona coffee *latte*.

**Passion and pineapple:** Local products have become as intrinsically linked to Hawaii's lifestyle as the ebbing and flowing of the tides. Residents and visitors alike have easy access to an abundance of fresh fruit, and we're not just talking pineapple and coconut. Equally common are the tiny apple banana, the golden papaya, the pungent *liliko'i* (passion fruit), and the guava, a yellow lemon-sized gem with a shocking pink interior.

The elusive lychee, prized for its juicy white flesh, can be spotted hanging in grape-like clumps off trees in Manoa Valley, while *poha* (cape gooseberry) thrives on bushes

thrives in Kilauea on Kauai, Molokai is known for its potatoes, and shrimp are a major commodity on Oahu's north shore.

Enthusiastic practitioners of Hawaii regional cuisine collaborate closely with farmers of each island to get the products they need, then infuse those foods with cooking techniques from around the world. The result is a menu that reads something like this: *'ulu* (breadfruit) vichyssoise, Manoa greens with Waimea vine-ripened tomatoes and Puna goat cheese, tempura-style Kahuku shrimp and apple banana, sesame-cured boar loin with guava dressing and a big slice of *liliko'i* mint chiffon pie. Enjoy it with wines from

near Kilauea Volcano. The markets of Honolulu's Chinatown district are a good source of these and lesser-known fruits, like the tamarind, kumquat, starfruit and *cherimoya* (pinecone-shaped with tart white meat).

Visit Hawaii during the summer and you'll discover the joys of the mango. When mango trees start to blossom in May, it's as big a deal as seeing the first whales of winter. By July, the fruit is weighing down the branches, and neighbors distribute free bags of fruit.

**Ocean harvests:** What is harvested by land is matched only by what is found in the sea. And what a prize catch. The king and queen of Hawaiian fish are the *mahimahi* (dolphin fish) and *opakapaka* (pink snapper), but *ulua* (jack trevalle), *ono* (wahoo), *'ahi* (yellowfin tuna) and *onaga* (red snapper) are equally impressive, whether blackened Cajun-style or baked in phyllo pastry.

Locals have been known to scamper like crabs across shorelines, hanging on when the big waves roll in, in order to pick a bunch of quarter-sized shells off the lava rocks. Called *'opihi* (limpets), they are Hawaii's answer to French *escargots* and are rarely found on restaurant menus.

More accessible is *tako* (octopus), a chewy delicacy that often shows up raw and marinated in *poke*. In the world of aquaculture, scientists on the Big Island and north shore

whelming, start with the basics. Order a *plate lunch,* the statewide institution defined by a few simple elements. Take a paper plate, then load it with "two-scoop rice" plus a mound of heavily mayonnaised macaroni salad. Order one with teriyaki beef, breaded pork or chicken, fried fish or even Spam (a passion among locals). Plate lunches are sold at carryout diners or lunch trucks.

Then try some snacks. Maybe shave ice, a snowcone soaked in neon-colored tropical syrups like mango, guava and coconut. Those in the know order it with vanilla ice cream and sweet *azuki* beans on the bottom. Munch on some *manapua*, the tennis ball-sized Chinese dumpling filled with pork or curried

of Oahu are creating miniature oceans in tanks full of prawns, lobsters, abalone and other aquatic delicacies.

Hawaii's homegrown also arrives on four legs. *Paniolo* cowboys on Maui and the Big Island saddle up in the predawn mist to round up the beef that settles onto dinner plates. Ni'ihau is promoting its own special grade of lamb. Lanai axis deer may become an entree laced with plum sauce, and Molokai venison makes for a good stew or sausage.

If all of these choices sound a little over-

chicken. Help yourself to a bowl of *saimin,* an oriental noodle soup topped with an encyclopedia of garnishes like sliced *char siu* (roast pork), fishcake and green onions. Pick up a bag of crack seed, lip-puckering pickled plums and maybe some *pipi kaula* (beef jerky). And if you find yourself at an outdoor carnival in Hawaii, the longest lines will lead you to a bag of *malasadas,* warm Portuguese doughnuts sprinkled with sugar.

In a place with so many food options, you might think the islands would suffer a gastronomic identity crisis, but this is not the case. Diners have the best of all worlds in Hawaii, and everyone is welcome to its table.

<u>Left</u>, luau with the Dillinghams, a photo taken in 1888. <u>Above</u>, native luau, 1910.

*Ina aohe nalu, alaila kahea aku i kai, penei
e hea ai:
Ku mai! Ku mai! Ka nalu nui mai Kahiki mai,
Alo poi pu! Ku mai ka pohuehue,
Hu! Kaikoo loa*
(If there is no surf, invoke seaward in the
following manner:
Arise, arise ye great surfs from Kahiki,
The powerful curling waves. Arise with the
*pohuehue.*
Well up, long raging surf.)
     *— a "pohuehue" (surf coaxing chant),
collected by historian Abraham Fornander*

It is now called surfing, but the ancient
Hawaiians called it *he'enalu*, a term rich in
oceanic and poetic nuance. The word's first
half, *he'e*, for example, can mean to change
from a solid to a liquid substance, or to run or
flow as a liquid, or to slip or glide along, or
to melt away, or to flee through fear. And
*nalu*, the second half, implies the roaring,
surging and rolling motion of a wave as it
glides toward a beach, and the forming of a
wave, and the slimy liquid on the face of a
newborn infant.

Piece those word parts together and what
emerges is a simple definition: wave sliding.
Given the diversity of the definitions above,
the meaning of "surfing," to be sure, can be
broadened with considerable undercurrents.

Nobody's sure when Polynesians first en-
gaged in this spectacular water sport, but
Hawaiian chants dating from the 15th century recount surfing exploits, indicating that
by then surfing was so refined that special
contests were held between famous surfers.
These were widely heralded affairs, sometimes pitting high-ranking chiefs against each
other; onshore crowds of supporters would
indulge in heavy-stakes gambling by placing
property bets on a favored wave rider.

Not unlike contemporary surf fanatics
who'll drop everything to catch a good wave,
Hawaiians were easily tempted and distracted
by surfing. One particularly slack month,
according to a noted Hawaiian scholar,

**Preceding pages: riding the winter waves. <u>Left</u>,
in the tube, Banzai Pipeline, Oahu. <u>Right</u>, prize-
winning surf contestants.**

Kepelino Keauokalani, was what we call
November, known in the Hawaiian calendar
as *Ikuwa*, meaning "deafening." November,
he wrote in his manuscript, *Traditions of
Hawaii*, was the "season of the worst storms."

**Waves of history:** Hawaiians had been per-
fecting *he'enalu* in small canoes and on
boards for several centuries before the arrival of Europeans.

In 1778, Britain's Captain James Cook
marveled at the agility of men riding across
crystal combers on short or long wooden

planks, the early surfboards. Cook's lieutenant, James King, said of Hawaiian surfing:
"The boldness and address, with which we
saw them perform these difficult and dangerous manoeuvres, was altogether astonishing
and is scarce to be credited."

Nearly every early writer spending time in
Hawaii was astonished by this uniquely
Polynesian entertainment. "It did not seem
that a lightning express train could shoot
along at a more hair-lifting speed," wrote
Mark Twain in 1866. And much later, in
1907, author Jack London spun grand ro-
coco lines in "A Royal Sport: Surfing at
Waikiki" about a surfer who emerged from

an "invincible roar... not struggling frantically in that wild movement, not buried and crushed and buffeted by those mighty monsters, but standing above them all, calm and superb, poised on the giddy summit, his feet buried in the churning foam, the salt smoke rising to his knees..."

By the turn of the 20th century, however, surfing, like the people who had refined its movements, was dying, in part because Christian missionaries discouraged it as a decadent distraction, and in part because Hawaiians were becoming preoccupied with a new Western lifestyle. A few so-called "beach boys," however, still rode the mellow swells that curled over Waikiki's broad reefs.

Gone are the days when *ali'i* Hawaiians rode on *koa* boards weighing 150 lb (68 kg). Also gone are early 1900s Waikiki-style surfboards made of California redwood. And just as extinct are the balsa "pig boards" popular in the early 1950s. All have given way to high-tech boogie boards, knee machines, lightning bolts, fish, pin and swallow tails, stinger fins and other such surfing esoterica.

The modern surfer now maintains not just one surfboard, but an all-purpose "quiver" of boards. One board is shaped for country waves of medium-but-solid wall intensity, another is for hot-dog-sized town waves on sleepy south-swell summer days. Others,

London's gushy piece on surfing is often credited with renewing interest in surfing. But it was probably early tourism to Hawaii that brought surfing back into vogue. The sport was further promoted in 1908 when a group of *haole* sportsmen leased land at Waikiki Beach and started a private club called the Outrigger Canoe Club, dedicated to the preservation of outrigger canoeing and board surfing. Another, older club *Hui Nalu* (Surfing Club) was formally chartered in 1911 by a group of Hawaiian surfers. Over the past few decades, surfing has spread, first to California and Australia, and later to most other countries with an active sea shore.

depending on just how specialized the surfer's riding has become, are dart-like "guns," the largest of which are designed for big-wave breaks such as the deadly Banzai Pipeline, Sunset Beach and Waimea Bay on Oahu's North Shore.

Most major big wave surfing competitions are held during November and December, when Oahu's North Shore surfing grounds thunder with the world's most famous waves.

**Left**, *Jeux Haviens*, an 1873 engraving by the French artist E. Riou, showing women surfers at an unidentified Hawaiian beach. **Right**, early 1900s surfer on the beach at Waikiki.

# TOWERING HILLS AND LOCAL FLOWERS

The Hawaiian Islands rest at the summit of one of the tallest mountain ranges in the world, the bases beginning at depths of around 15,000 ft (4,550 meters), then rising to almost that same distance above water. Volcanoes created these mountains between 20 and 50 million years ago. During that time, lava from the earth's depths escaped through cracks – a "hot spot" – in the ocean floor, built up, and eventually created a line of mountains stretching some 1,600 miles (2,500 km) from the island of Hawaii to Kure Atoll. The islands occur in a neat row because Hawaii sits on part of the earth's crust called the Pacific Plate, moving about 2 to 3 inches (5 to 8 cm) northwest each year.

However, while this surface plate moves along like a giant conveyor belt, the hot spot in the plate stays in place. As a result, each new island begins just south of the last one.

**Fiery fountains:** Eruptions on the ocean bottom are the first stage in the process of building Hawaii's broad, shield volcanoes. Underwater, lava hardens into pumice – light rocks full of gas bubbles – and pillow lava with roundish shapes. As the lava cools, it builds steep-sided, underwater mountains called seamounts. This is happening today, about 30 miles (50 km) south of the island of Hawaii with a seamount called Lo'ihi, which will eventually (thousands or probably tens of thousands of years from now) be the newest island in the Hawaiian chain. It may even connect with Hawaii above sea level, making the "Big Island" even bigger.

When seamounts break the ocean's surface, the lava erupts in fiery fountains, flowing from craters and rifts in the mountain's sides. This lava, called basalt, is the most common rock in Hawaii.

Eventually, the tops of the volcanoes collapse, creating wide depressions called calderas. Mauna Loa and Kilauea on the Big Island are at this stage now. When lava from these still-active volcanoes reaches the sea, people get rare opportunities to see island-making in the process.

Hot lava pouring into the ocean turns shore waters into churning cauldrons, giving rise to towering steam and cloud build-up. Sulfur dioxide, a gas released by active calderas, combines with rain from these clouds, falling as dilute sulfuric acid. Chlorine gas freed from boiling seawater mixes with sulfur odors, giving the area a tangy, chemical smell. It's a primordial scene not to be missed, but it can be dangerous.

Once the volcano-building stops, other forces take over. Wind and sun eat away at

the land, surf carves the coastlines, and rain cuts valleys and ridges into the new mountains. Volcanic rocks break down and gradually turn into soil. Plants arrive, then animals. Eventually, humans take over. What was once just a hot spot on the ocean floor has been transformed into fertile, life-supporting land.

**Old age:** But like the creatures that populate them, islands become middle-aged, grow old and die. This aging process is visible in the Hawaiian Island chain. After new islands are formed, coral reefs start growing at the edges, circling the island like underwater flower lei. As the island sinks on its journey to the northwest, the coral grows upward, staying in the sunshine that is so crucial to its survival. Reefs growing along the edges of middle-aged islands like Maui, Molokai, Lanai, Oahu and Kauai are called fringing reefs. The island of Hawaii is a youngster; its fringing reef is just beginning.

As the Pacific Plate continues to sink, lagoons tend to form between the reef and its island. These are called barrier reefs and can be seen in some of the older Hawaiian islands of the northwest chain. Eventually, the island in the center vanishes underwater, creating an atoll, a coral reef that encloses a lagoon. Kure, at the northwest end of the Hawaiian chain, is such an atoll.

Consisting of 132 islands, atolls, reefs and shoals, Hawaii ranks fourth in the United States in coastline – and what a coastline it is. Forces of erosion have turned gentle slopes like those found on Mauna Loa into the breathtaking ridges of Kauai's Na Pali coast, and into Molokai's towering north shore cliffs, the tallest ocean cliffs in the world. Sandy beaches, rocky shores and crater-shaped bays line other coastal areas throughout the state.

The narrow bands around each island where land and ocean meet are called coastal vegetation zones. Here, hundreds of plant and animal species live, each adapted in its own

way to this unique environment. Humans have lived for so long in coastal zones that it's sometimes hard to find a place that hasn't been drained, dredged or filled. But there are preserves where sand dunes stand tall and native species thrive. They're worth looking for. The landscapes seen around the islands have been radically altered by humans. This isn't necessarily bad; it's just different from what was once there. Even with so much human influence, researchers recognize 150 different plant communities in Hawaii, named according to elevation, moisture and vegetation. Within each of these, the plants and animals interact with one another and their environment to form ecosystems.

**Island ecosystems:** Wetlands are one kind of ecosystem. The term wetland refers to areas where water dominates the environment and its plants and animals. Wetlands can be salty, brackish (salt and fresh), or fresh, and can be up to 6 ft (2 meters) deep. Anything deeper is a lake. Hawaii's bogs, estuaries, swamps and streams contain unique scenery, plant life and bird life well worth checking out. Most remaining wetlands in the state are now preserves.

Forests contain dozens of ecosystems. Hawaii's forests are divided into dryland, medium-wet, and rain forests. Before humans came to Hawaii, dryland forests covered the leeward side of the larger islands and nearly all of Lanai and Kaho'olawe. Ancient Hawaiians cleared much of this land for agriculture; later settlers finished the job. Today, dryland forests are rare. Researchers believe that in the past, the islands were wetter, with extensive dryland forests capturing, producing and holding moisture.

Medium-wet forests, growing from 2,000 ft (600 meters) to 9,000 ft (2,700 meters) in elevation, have the largest number of native tree species of all ecosystems in Hawaii, even the celebrated rain forests, which grow in the elevation zone just above the medium-wet forests. Hawaii's rain forests receive at least 100 inches (254 cm) of rain per year. During the winter, clouds often engulf these forests, producing thick, cool mists. The two native trees seen most often in both types of forests are *koa* and *ohia-lehua,* which support Hawaii's famous forest birds, the honeycreepers and their relatives.

Above the forests are alpine zones where few plants grow. Some desert-type plants like Hawaii's famous silverswords thrive in these high, dry, alpine areas, as well as some insects. In winter, snow falls.

**Plants and animals:** The Hawaiian Islands began their existence as barren lava rock, thousands of miles from the nearest land. Today the islands are lush with plants and laden with animals. Some of these are native; most have been introduced by people.

Hawaii's native species are the plants and animals that managed to get here without human help. Floating seeds, fish, and marine larvae drifted to the islands on ocean currents. Winds carried fern spores, tiny seeds and insects. And birds, sometimes full of fertile eggs or viable seeds, landed here, often helped by storm winds. Over millions of years, these isolated colonists changed to suit their environment, making them unique, or endemic, to Hawaii.

This colonizing of the islands was a slow process. If the islands are 27 million years old – a conservative estimate – then just one plant had to establish itself about every 100,000 years to account for all of Hawaii's native plants. The best places to see these plants and animals are in Hawaii's national parks, wildlife refuges, and the state's marine conservation districts, where all reef life is protected from fishing. Most marine life encountered is native except for several species of snappers, imported by the state from Tahiti in the 1950s as game fish. All sea turtles in Hawaii are native, and are endangered and protected by law. It is illegal to ride or chase these shy, harmless creatures.

Hawaii's only native land mammal is the Hawaiian bat. Because of their night-time habits and secretive nature, bats are extremely difficult to find, even for researchers.

Native marine mammals are whales, dolphins and monk seals. These are also protected by federal laws. With only about 1,600 creatures left, Hawaiian monk seals are in extreme danger of extinction. If you see one resting on a beach, which is normal behavior for them, back off quietly and consider it a lucky day.

Most of the flowers and trees seen while driving along Hawaii's highways are not native, but there are a few. Seven kinds of hibiscus, Hawaii's state flower, are native.

But with 200 species of hibiscus in the world, and more than 5,000 hybrids, the ones you see are often not Hawaii natives. Pandanus, also called screwpine or *hala,* are roadside native trees. *Koa* and *ohia-lehua* are native trees common to parks and preserves.

Since many of their seeds float, beach plants are often native. Common are beach morning glories, which trail their pretty pink flowers through the sand, and beach *naupaka,* thick green bushes with white flowers that look as if they've been cut in half.

**Early introductions:** Starting around AD 500 or even earlier, early Polynesian voyagers brought the plants and animals they needed with them to live in their new home. Al-

though keeping these species alive through such voyages was tricky business, the immigrants managed to shuttle at least 27 kinds of plants and several kinds of animals – some wanted, some not – to Hawaii.

Even though this happened centuries ago, these species are considered alien because humans had a hand in their introduction. As a result, a few plants and animals that many might think of as native to Hawaii are actually aliens, introduced by those early Hawaiians. Some common plants on this list are coconut palms, bananas, bamboo, *ti* plants and bottle gourds.

Candlenut trees, called *kukui* in Hawaiian,

**Left**, an ʻoʻo (*moho nobilis*), now extinct. **Right**, nene goose from the Volcano area.

were also introduced but this is still Hawaii's official state tree. *Kukui* products are common. Lei makers string the flowers together, the oil from the nuts is used in cosmetics, and the nuts themselves are polished to make necklaces and bracelets. It's easy to pick the abundant *kukui* trees out of a forest: their leaves, which look as if they've been dusted with flour, are very pale next to others.

Sugar cane is another introduced Polynesian plant. Ancient Hawaiians used sugar cane for sweetener, famine food and medicine; the leaves were used for hats and thatching. Today, sugar cane is Hawaii's leading crop. One acre of land on the islands yields over 11 tons (9,900 kg) of cane, giving

Hawaii the highest yield per acre in the agricultural world.

Ancient Hawaiians brought pigs, dogs and chickens to Hawaii as food stock. Loose in the forests, pigs and dogs wreaked havoc on native species, and continue to do so. Pigs eat native plants and transport alien pest plants in their faeces, and wild dogs kill native birds, most of which nest on the ground.

Stowaways on ancient Polynesian canoes were geckos, skinks, rats, houseflies, fleas and lice. Skinks and geckos are welcome in island homes because they eat insects, but the others are widespread pests.

Hawaii's landscape changed forever when those ancient Hawaiians landed with their plants and animals, but that was only the beginning. Since Captain Cook's arrival, plants and animals have streamed into the islands from all over the world; today, these post-contact introductions are more common than both native and Polynesian-introduced species.

Since these aliens often outcompete or eat native species, the flood of introductions is causing the extinction of many of Hawaii's plants and animals. But introduced species aren't all bad. The exotic plants provide Hawaii with stunning flower *lei*, sweet-smelling and bird-filled parks, and highways lined with color.

The masses of brilliant color common along the roadsides come from, among others, bougainvilleas and plumeria, native to tropical America. Other common aliens are ironwood and silk oaks from Australia, banyan trees from Asia, and Cook's pines from the South Pacific's Cook Islands.

Orchid growers in the state, especially on the Big Island, have made Hawaii world-famous for orchid hybrids. Hawaii has three native orchids, a piddling number compared to the almost 20,000 species of the family.

Many food plants that people associate with Hawaii are foreign. Among these are coffee (Africa), pineapples (Brazil), mangos (India), guava (Mexico to Peru), papayas (tropical America) and lychees (China).

While many alien fruits and flowers are welcome, many alien animals are not. Some, like cockroaches, mosquitoes, centipedes, goats, sheep and wild cats, have caused environmental disasters and human misery. Mongooses, for example, were imported from India via Jamaica by sugar growers to eat rats, but they preferred eating native birds and their eggs. People discovered too late that mongooses hunted during the day, while rats were active at night.

The state has recently cracked down on importing animals. While residents and visitors welcome and enjoy some alien creatures, like mynah birds and red-crested cardinals, the danger of pests like snakes (outside the zoo, there aren't any in the islands), destructive birds and insects arriving in Hawaii is a persistent worry.

**Left** and **right**, the Hawaii islands have 150 different plant communities.

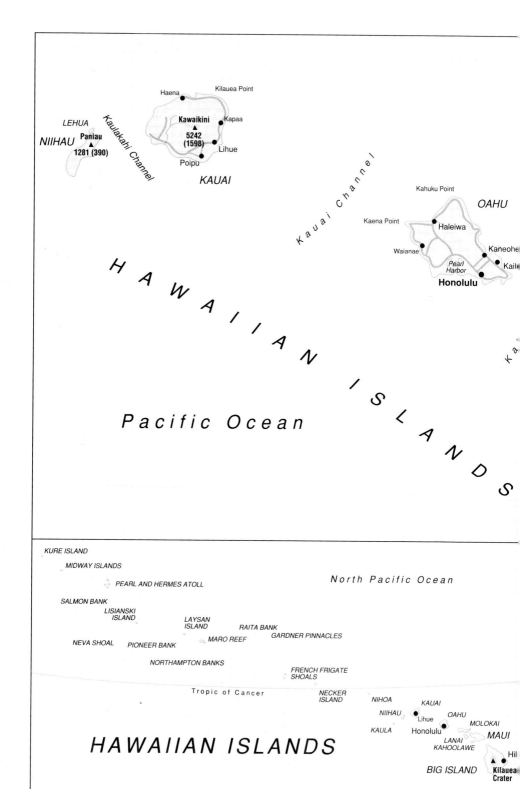

Kilauea Point

Haena

*LEHUA*

*NIIHAU* **Paniau**
**1281 (390)** ▲

Kaulakahi Channel

**Kawaikini**
▲
**5242**
**(1598)**

Kapaa

Lihue

Poipu

*KAUAI*

Kauai Channel

Kahuku Point

Kaena Point

*OAHU*

Haleiwa

Waianae

Kaneohe

*Pearl*
*Harbor*

Kail▪

**Honolulu**

H A W A I I A N   I S L A N D S

*Pacific Ocean*

Ka

KURE ISLAND

MIDWAY ISLANDS

PEARL AND HERMES ATOLL

*North Pacific Ocean*

SALMON BANK

LISIANSKI
ISLAND

LAYSAN
ISLAND

RAITA BANK

NEVA SHOAL

PIONEER BANK

MARO REEF

GARDNER PINNACLES

NORTHAMPTON BANKS

FRENCH FRIGATE
SHOALS

*Tropic of Cancer*

NECKER
ISLAND

NIHOA

KAUAI

NIIHAU

Lihue

OAHU

KAULA

Honolulu

MOLOKAI

LANAI
KAHOOLAWE

*MAUI*

Hil▪

*HAWAIIAN ISLANDS*

*BIG ISLAND*

**Kilauea**
**Crater**

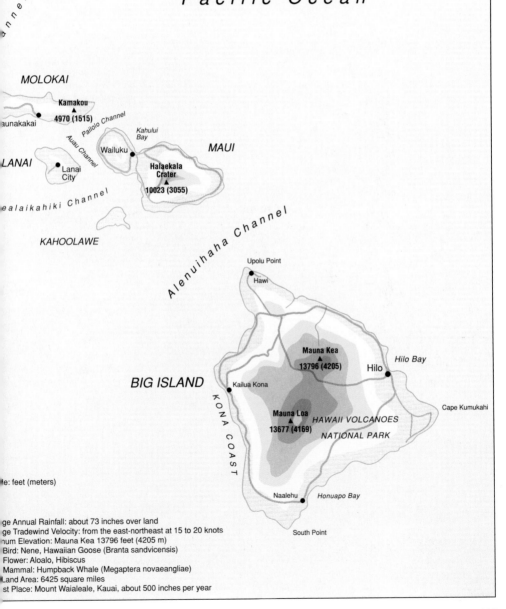

*Pacific Ocean*

MOLOKAI

Kamakou
▲
4970 (1515)

aunakakai

Pailolo Channel

Auau Channel

LANAI

Lanai City

Kahului Bay

Wailuku

MAUI

Halaekala Crater
▲
10023 (3055)

ealaikahiki Channel

KAHOOLAWE

Alenuihaha Channel

Upolu Point

Hawi

Mauna Kea
▲
13796 (4205)

Hilo Bay

Hilo

BIG ISLAND

Kailua Kona

KONA COAST

Mauna Loa
▲
13677 (4169)

HAWAII VOLCANOES

NATIONAL PARK

Cape Kumukahi

e: feet (meters)

Naalehu

Honuapo Bay

South Point

ge Annual Rainfall: about 73 inches over land
ge Tradewind Velocity: from the east-northeast at 15 to 20 knots
num Elevation: Mauna Kea 13796 feet (4205 m)
Bird: Nene, Hawaiian Goose (Branta sandvicensis)
Flower: Aloalo, Hibiscus
Mammal: Humpback Whale (Megaptera novaeangliae)
Land Area: 6425 square miles
st Place: Mount Waialeale, Kauai, about 500 inches per year

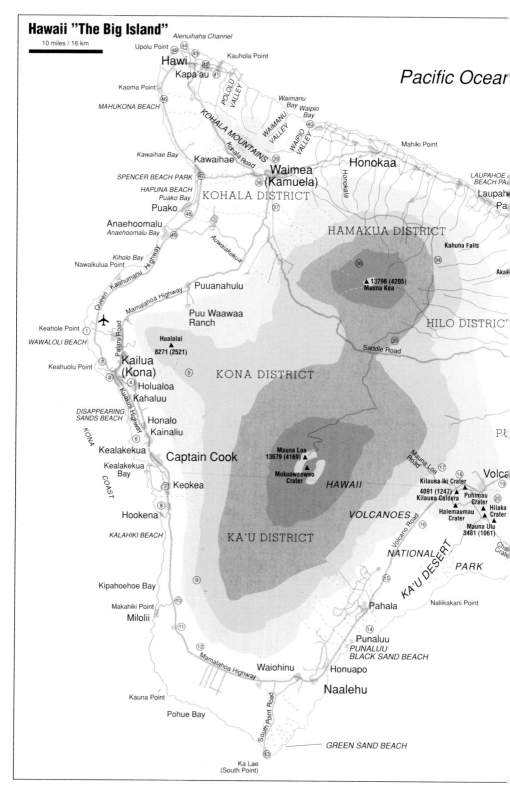

# Hawaii "The Big Island"

10 miles / 16 km

Pacific Ocean

Alenuihaha Channel
Upolu Point ④⑤ ④④
Kauhola Point
④③
Hawi ④②
Kapa'au ④①
Kaoma Point
④⑥
MAHUKONA BEACH

POLOLU VALLEY
WAIMANU VALLEY
WAIPIO VALLEY

KOHALA MOUNTAINS

Waimanu Bay Waipio Bay
④⓪

Mahiki Point

Kawaihae Bay
Kawaihae
Kohala Road
③⑨

Honokaa

LAUPAHOE
BEACH PA₂

SPENCER BEACH PARK ④⑦
HAPUNA BEACH
Puako Bay
Puako
Waimea (Kamuela)
③⑧

Honokala

Laupah₂
Pa₂

KOHALA DISTRICT
③⑦

④⑧

HAMAKUA DISTRICT

Kahuna Falls

Anaehoomalu
Anaehoomalu Bay
④⑨

Auwaiakekua

③④

Aka₂

Kiholo Bay
Nawaikulua Point

Queen Ka'ahumanu Highway

Puuanahulu
③⑥
▲ 13796 (4205)
Mauna Kea

Mamalahoa Highway

Puu Waawaa Ranch

HILO DISTRIC₂

Keahole Point ①
WAWALOLI BEACH

Palani Road

Hualalai
▲
8271 (2521)

③⑤
Saddle Road

Keahuolu Point ②
Kailua (Kona)
③

⑤

KONA DISTRICT

④
Holualoa
Kahaluu

Kuakini Highway

KONA COAST

DISAPPEARING SANDS BEACH

Honalo
Kainaliu

Kealakekua
Kealakekua Bay

⑥

Captain Cook

Mauna Loa
13679 (4169) ▲
Mokuaweoweo Crater
▲

HAWAII

Mauna Loa Road

⑰

Volca₂

Kilauea Iki Crater
⑱
4091 (1247) ▲
Kilauea Caldera
Puhimau Crater
⑲
⑳
Hiiaka Crater
▲

⑦ Keokea

⑧
Hookena

KALAHIKI BEACH

VOLCANOES

Halemaumau Crater ▲
Mauna Ulu
3481 (1061) ▲

Volcano Road

⑯

KA'U DISTRICT

NATIONAL DESERT

PARK

P₂

Cha₂
Crate₂

Kipahoehoe Bay
⑨

⑮

Naliikakani Point

Makahiki Point
Milolii

⑩

Pahala

KA'U DESERT

⑪

⑭

Punaluu
PUNALUU BLACK SAND BEACH

⑫

Mamalahoa Highway

Waiohinu

Honuapo

Naalehu

Kauna Point

South Point Road

Pohue Bay

GREEN SAND BEACH

⑬

Ka Lae (South Point)

Land Area:
4.037 square miles
93 miles long
76 miles wide

Highest Elevation:
Mauna Kea 13796 feet (4205m)

Airports:
Hilo: Hilo International Airport
Kona: Keahole Airport
Kamuela:
Waimea-Kohala Airport

Main Seaports:
Hilo Bay
Kawaihae
Kailua-Kona

KOLE
PARK

eekeo Point
eekeo

Bay

Keaau

Kaloli Point

RICT

Pahoa Road

Pahoa

Kapaho-Pahoa Road

Kipu Point

Cape Kumukahi
HALE BEACH PARK

MACKENZIE
STATE PARK

Kalapana-Kapaho

Pahoa Kalapana Road

Waipuku Point

apuki Point

**Points of Interest**
5 Ahu-a-Umi (18th. century heiau)
33 Akaka Falls State Park
16 Ancient Footprints in Lava
32 Boiling Pots
6 Coffee Farms
34 Douglas David Historical Monument
13 Heiau o Kalalea
25 Hilo Country Club
28 Hilo International Airport
29 Hilo Zoo
10 Hoopuloa Church Monument
3 Hulihee Palace (Kailua-Kona)
41 Kalahikiola Church
24 Kalamanu-old canoe shad
19 Kalani Botanical Garden
45 Kamehameha I Birthplace
42 Kamehameha I Statue
38 Kamuela Museum
14 Kane'ele 'ele Heiau
15 Kapapala
1 Keahole Airport
4 Keauhou-Kona Golf Course
17 Kipuka Puaulu Bird Park
46 Lapakahi State Historical Park

22 Lava Tree State Monument
30 Liliuokalani Gardens
26 Lyman Mission House / Museum
11 Macadamia Nut Farms
23 Mahinaakaka Heiau
12 Manuka State Park
36 Mauna Kea Observatory
44 Mookini Heiau (480A.D.)
9 Ohia Mill
27 Orchid Gardens
39 Parker Ranch Headquarters
48 Puako petroglyphs
2 Puhina o Lono Heiau
35 Puu O'o Ranch
8 Puuhonua o Honaunau National
Historical Park
47 Puukohola Heiau
21 Sea Arches
7 St. Benedict's Painted Church (1902)
31 Suisan Dock
20 Thurston Lava Tube
43 Upolu Airport
18 Volcano House
49 Waikoloa Golf Course
37 Waimea-Kohala Airport
40 Waipio Valley Lookout

Pull out the map and run a finger along the islands of Hawaii, strung across the Pacific like a series of stepping stones. The islands line up oldest to youngest, a student's oversized science project of island formation and decay. Lucky is the traveler who journeys among them, from island to neighboring island, appreciating the wind, water, and earth that conceive, nurture, and then diminish these territories.

The Hawaiian Islands' arrangement is one of chronology, and of plate tectonics, with the youngest island – the Big Island – in the southeast, and the oldest islands – or what's left of them – 1,500 miles away to the northwest. Those oldest of the islands are but atolls and shoals now, home only to sea birds and the occasional Hawaiian monk seal.

But in the southern extent of the Hawaiian chain, the islands are younger, and bigger, and more fertile, each with vital, self-sustaining and often unique ecosystems.

Kauai is the oldest of these main islands, its ancient shield volcano deeply eroded. Next is Oahu, younger, but still old, its two extinct volcanoes nearly unrecognizable as such. Younger still is Maui, a coupling of old and new, the older West Maui volcano worn down but Haleakala still looking like the powerful volcano it was, and possibly still is. Molokai and Lanai hover off Maui's west side, small volcanic siblings. Visible from Haleakala's summit is the Big Island, formed by five volcanoes and with a landscape still smoothly-contoured and pristine – and growing. And off the Big Island's South Point, several thousand feet down, is Lo'ihi, a gestating island yet to see the sun.

This well-defined and orderly progression gives each of Hawaii's seven inhabited islands distinct geographical dispositions. And since a place always imprints itself on its inhabitants, the traveler in Hawaii will notice not only distinct geographical differences, but also differences in people.

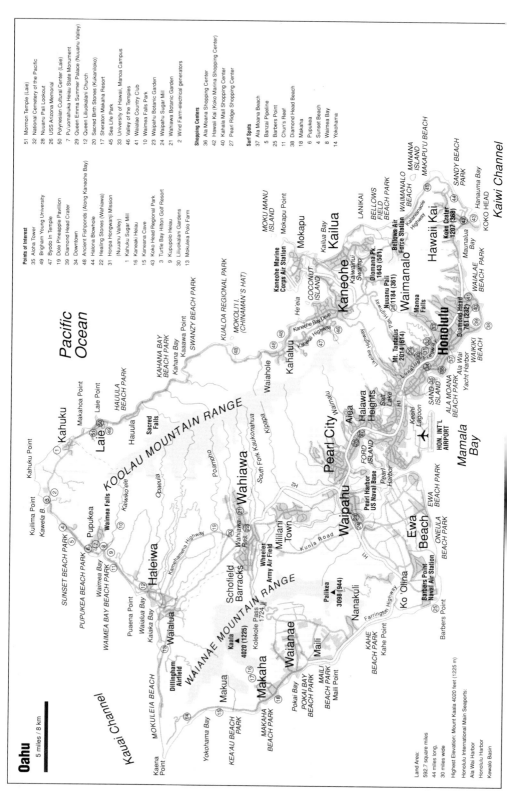

# Oahu

5 miles / 8 km

## Pacific Ocean

### Points of Interest

35 Aloha Tower
49 Brigham Young University
47 Byodo In Temple
19 Dole Pineapple Pavilion
39 Diamond Head Crater
34 Downtown
48 Ancient Fishponds (Along Kaneohe Bay)
44 Halona Blowhole
22 Healing Stones (Wahiawa)
31 Honpa Hongwanji Mission
    (Nuuanu Valley)
1 Kahuku Sugar Mill
16 Kaneaki Heiau
15 Kaneana Cave
43 Koko Head Regional Park
3 Turtle Bay Hilton Golf Resort
9 Kupupolo Heiau
30 Liliuokalani Gardens
13 Mokuleia Polo Farm
51 Mormon Temple (Laie)
32 National Cemetery of the Pacific
28 Nuuanu Pali Lookout
26 USS Arizona Memorial
50 Polynesian Cultural Center (Laie)
7 Pu'uomahuka Heiau State Monument
29 Queen Emma Summer Palace (Nuuanu Valley)
12 Queen Liliuokalani Church
20 Sacred Birth Stones (Kukaniloko)
17 Sheraton Makaha Resort
45 Sea Life Park
33 University of Hawaii, Manoa Campus
46 Valley of the Temples
41 Waialae Country Club
10 Waimea Falls Park
23 Waipahu Botanic Garden
24 Waipahu Sugar Mill
21 Wahiawa Botanic Garden
2 Wind Farm–electrical generators

### Shopping Centers

36 Ala Moana Shopping Center
42 Hawaii Kai (Koko Marina Shopping Center)
40 Kahala Mall Shopping Center
27 Pearl Ridge Shopping Center

### Surf Spots

37 Ala Moana Beach
5 Banzai Pipeline
25 Barbers Point
11 Chun's Reef
38 Diamond Head Beach
18 Makaha
6 Pupukea
4 Sunset Beach
8 Waimea Bay
14 Yokohama

Land Area:
592.7 square miles
44 miles long,
30 miles wide

Highest Elevation: Mount Kaala 4020 feet (1225 m)

Honolulu International Main Seaports:
Ala Wai Harbor
Honolulu Harbor
Kewalo Basin

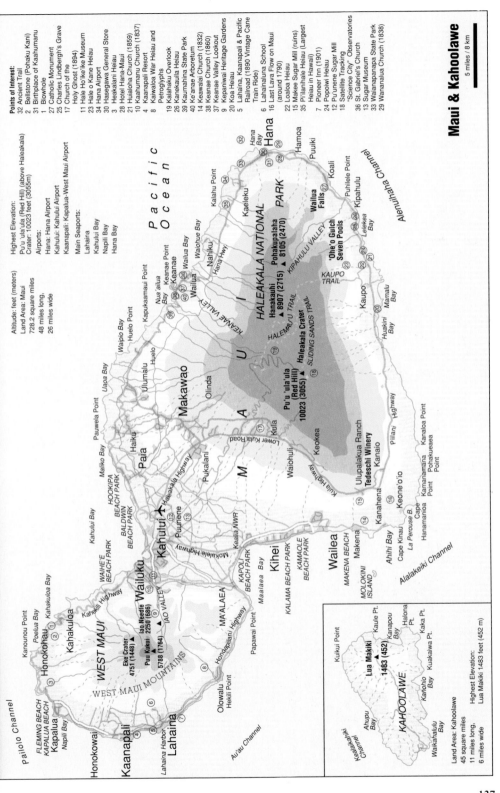

**Maui & Kahoolawe**

5 miles / 8 km

**Points of Interest:**

32  Ancient Trail
2  Bellstone (Pohaku Kani)
31  Birthplace of Kaahumanu
1  Blowhole
27  Catholic Monument
25  Charles Lindbergh's Grave
17  Church of the
    Holy Ghost (1894)
11  Hale Ho'ike'ike Museum
23  Hale o Kane Heiau
34  Hana Airport
    Hana Bay
30  Hasegawa General Store
3  Heakalani Heiau
28  Hotel Hana-Maui
21  Huaioha Church (1859)
10  Kaahumanu Church (1837)
4  Kaanapali Resort
8  Kaiwaloa War Heiau and
    Petroglyphs
19  Kalahaku Overlook
26  Kanekaulla Heiau
39  Kaumahina State Park
40  Ke'anae Arboretum
14  Ke'awaiai Church (1832)
38  Keanae Church (1860)
37  Keanae Valley Lookout
9  Kepaniwai Heritage Gardens
20  Koa Heiau
5  Lahaina, Kaanapali & Pacific
    Railroad (1890 Vintage Cane
    Train Ride)
6  Lahainaluna School
16  Last Lava Flow on Maui
    (around 1790)
22  Loaloa Heiau
15  Makee Sugar Mill (ruins)
35  Pi'ilanhale Heiau (Largest
    Heiau in Hawaii)
7  Pioneer Inn (1901)
24  Popowiwi Heiau
12  Pu'unene Sugar Mill
18  Satellite Tracking
    "Science City" Observatories
36  St. Gabriel's Church
13  Sugar Museum
33  Waianapanapa State Park
29  Wananalua Church (1838)

**Highest Elevation:**
Pu'u 'ula'ula (Red Hill) (above Haleakala)
Crater: 10023 feet (3055m)

**Airports:**
Hana: Hana Airport
Kahului: Kahului Airport
Kaanapali: Kapalua-West Maui Airport

**Main Seaports:**
Lahaina
Kahului Bay
Napili Bay
Hana Bay

Altitude: feet (meters)
Land Area:
728.2 square miles
48 miles long,
26 miles wide

**Land Area: Kahoolawe**
45 square miles
11 miles long,
6 miles wide

**Highest Elevation:**
Lua Makiki 1483 feet (452 m)

137

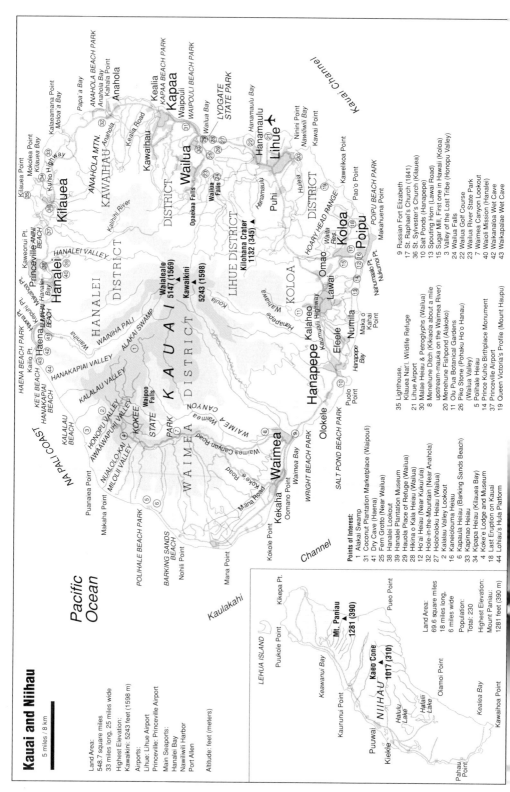

# Kauai and Niihau

5 miles / 8 km

**Land Area:**
548.7 square miles
33 miles long, 25 miles wide

**Highest Elevation:**
Kawaikini: 5243 feet (1598 m)

**Airports:**
Lihue: Lihue Airport
Princeville: Princeville Airport

**Main Seaports:**
Hanalei Bay
Nawiliwili Harbor
Port Allen

Altitude: feet (meters)

*Pacific Ocean*

**Points of Interest:**
1  Alakai Swamp
31 Coconut Plantation Marketplace (Waipouli)
41 Dry Cave (Haena)
25 Fern Grotto (Near Wailua)
38 Hanalei Lookout
39 Hanalei Plantation Museum
29 Hauola Place of Refuge (Wailua)
28 Hikina o Kala Heiau (Wailua)
12 Ho'ai Heiau (Near Kukui'ula)
32 Hole-in-the-Mountain (Near Anahola)
27 Holoholoku Heiau (Wailua)
2  Kalalau Valley Lookout
16 Kaneiolouma Heiau
6  Kapaula Heiau (Barking Sands Beach)
33 Kapinao Heiau
34 Kipapa Heiau (Kilauea Bay)
7  Koke'e Lodge and Museum
18 Last Eruption on Kauai
44 Lohiau's Hula Platform
35 Lighthouse, Kilauea Nat'l. Wildlife Refuge
21 Lihue Airport
30 Malae Heiau & Petroglyphs (Wailua)
8  Menehune Ditch (Kikiaola about a mile upstream-mauka on the Waimea River)
20 Menehune Fishpond (Alakoko)
11 Olu Pua Botanical Gardens
26 Piko Stone (Pohaku Ho o Hanau) (Wailua Valley)
5  Polihale Heiau
14 Prince Kuhio Birthplace Monument
37 Princeville Airport
19 Queen Victoria's Profile (Mount Haupu)
9  Russian Fort Elizabeth
17 St. Raphael's Church (1841)
36 St. Sylvester's Church (Kilauea)
10 Salt Ponds (Hanapepe)
13 Spouting Horn (Lawai Road)
15 Sugar Mill, First one in Hawaii (Koloa)
3  Valley of the Lost Tribe (Honopu Valley)
24 Wailua Falls
23 Wailua Golf Course
23 Wailua River State Park
40 Waioli Mission (Hanalei)
42 Waikanaloa Wet Cave
43 Waikapalae Wet Cave

**LEHUA ISLAND**

**NIIHAU**

Mt. Paniau ▲ 1281 (390)

Kaeo Cone ▲ 1017 (310)

**Land Area:**
69.6 square miles
18 miles long,
6 miles wide

**Population:**
Total: 230

**Highest Elevation:**
Mount Paniau:
1281 feet (390 m)

138

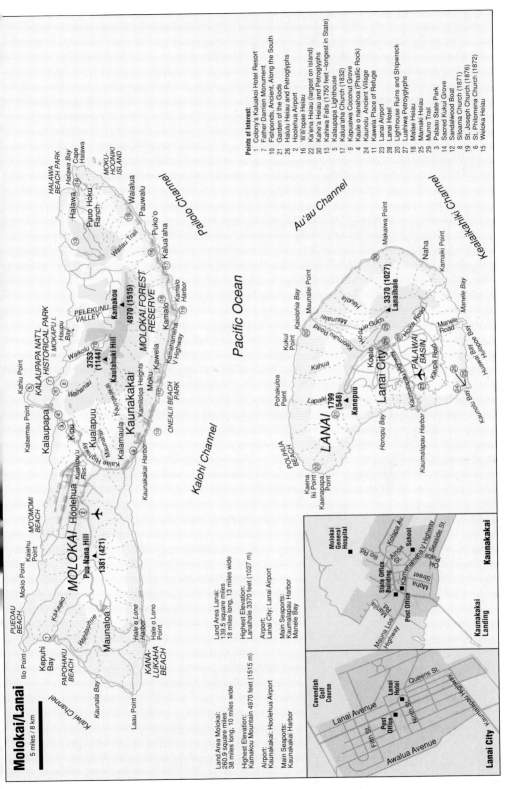

# Molokai/Lanai

5 miles / 8 km

## Points of Interest:
1 Colony's Kaluakoi Hotel Resort
7 Father Damien Monument
10 Fishponds, Ancient, Along the South
21 Garden of the Gods
26 Halulu Heiau and Petroglyphs
16 Hoolehua Airport
16 'Ili'ili'opae Heiau
22 Ka'ena Heiau (largest on island)
30 Kahe'a Heiau and Petroglyphs
13 Kahiwa Falls (1750 feet – longest in State)
5 Kalaupapa Lighthouse
17 Kalua'aha Church (1832)
9 Kapuaiwa Coconut Grove
4 Kaule o nanahoa (Phallic Rock)
24 Kaunolu Ancient Village
11 Kawela Place of Refuge
23 Lanai Airport
28 Lanai Hotel
20 Lighthouse Ruins and Shipwreck
27 Luahiwa Petroglyphs
18 Malae Heiau
25 Mamaki Heiau
29 Munro Trail
3 Palaau State Park
14 Sacred Kukui Grove
12 Sandalwood Boat
8 Siloama Church (1871)
19 St. Joseph Church (1876)
6 St. Philomena Church (1872)
15 Weloka Heiau

Land Area Molokai:
260.9 square miles
38 miles long, 10 miles wide

Highest Elevation:
Kamakou Mountain 4970 feet (1515 m)

Airport:
Kaunakakai: Hoolehua Airport

Main Seaports:
Kaunakakai Harbor

Land Area Lanai:
139.6 square miles
18 miles long, 13 miles wide

Highest Elevation:
Lanaihale 3370 feet (1027 m)

Airport:
Lanai City: Lanai Airport

Main Seaports:
Kaumalapau Harbor
Manele Bay

MOLOKAI

LANAI

Pacific Ocean

Kaunakakai

Lanai City

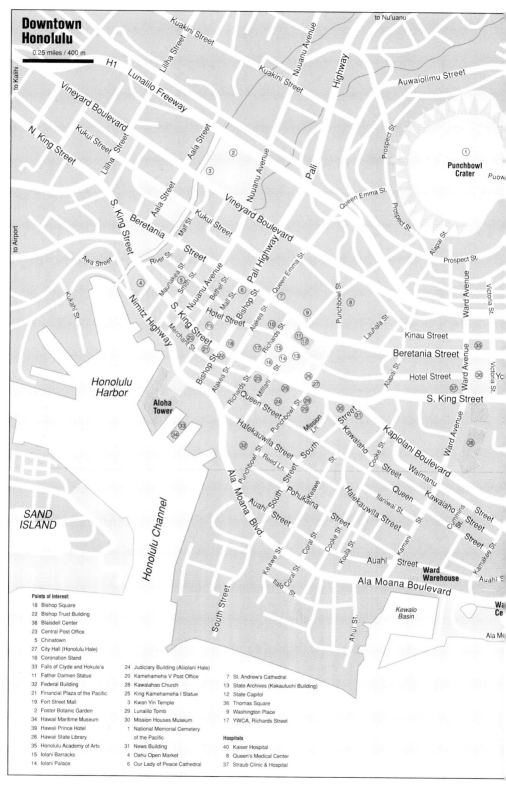

# Downtown Honolulu

0.25 miles / 400 m

to Nu'uanu

to Kalihi

to Airport

H1

Kuakini Street

Liliha Street

Lunalilo Freeway

Nuuanu Avenue

Kuakini Street

Highway

Auwaiolimu Street

Vineyard Boulevard

Aala Street

Kukui Street

Liliha Street

N. King Street

Nuuanu Avenue

Pali

Prospect St.

① Punchbowl Crater Puow

Aala Street

Vineyard Boulevard

Queen Emma St.

Prospect St.

S. King Street

Beretania Street

Kukui Street

Pali Highway

Queen Emma St.

Prospect St.

Awa Street

River St.

Maunakea St.

Smith St.

Nuuanu Avenue

Bethel St.

Punchbowl St.

Alapai St.

Kukah St.

⑤

Mail St.

⑥

Bishop St.

Queen Emma St.

⑦

⑧

Ward Avenue

Victoria St.

Nimitz Highway

Hotel Street

S. King Street

Alakea St.

⑨

Lauhala St.

Kinau Street

⑤ 35

④

Merchant St.

⑲ 19

Richards St.

⑩ 10

⑪ 11 ⑫ 12

Beretania Street

Ward Avenue

Victoria St.

Yo

⑳ 20

⑱ 18

⑰ 17 ⑮ 15

Richards St.

⑯ 16 ⑭ 14 ⑬ 13

Hotel Street

⑯ 36

⑳ 20

②① 21 ②② 22

Alapai St.

⑦ 37

Honolulu Harbor

Bishop St.

Alakea St.

②③ 23

S. King Street

Aloha Tower

Richards St.

②⑤ 25

②⑥ 26 ②⑦ 27

Kapiolani Boulevard

②④ 24

Queen Street

Punchbowl St.

②⑧ 28

③⑩ 30 ③① 31

Street

③③ 33

Mission Ln.

②⑨ 29

Kawaiaho

Ward Avenue

③④ 34

Halekauwila Street

South

Street

Waimanu

③⑧ 38

③② 32

Reed Ln.

Queen

Cooke Street

Kawaiaho

Street

SAND ISLAND

Honolulu Channel

Punchbowl St.

Pohukaina

Keawe

Ilaniwai St.

Kamani

Cummins St.

Ala Moana Blvd.

South

Street

Street

Coral St.

Cooke St.

Halekauwila Street

Koula St.

Auahi Street

Kamakee St.

Keawe St.

Coral St.

Ward Warehouse

Wa Ce

Ilalo St.

Ahui St.

Ala Moana Boulevard

Auahi St

South Street

Kewalo Basin

Ala Mo

## Points of Interest:

18 Bishop Square
22 Bishop Trust Building
38 Blaisdell Center
23 Central Post Office
5 Chinatown
27 City Hall (Honolulu Hale)
16 Coronation Stand
33 Falls of Clyde and Hokule'a
11 Father Damien Statue
32 Federal Building
21 Financial Plaza of the Pacific
19 Fort Street Mall
2 Foster Botanic Garden
34 Hawaii Maritime Museum
39 Hawaii Prince Hotel
26 Hawaii State Library
35 Honolulu Academy of Arts
15 Iolani Barracks
14 Iolani Palace

24 Judiciary Building (Aliiolani Hale)
20 Kamehameha V Post Office
28 Kawaiahao Church
25 King Kamehameha I Statue
3 Kwan Yin Temple
29 Lunalilo Tomb
30 Mission Houses Museum
1 National Memorial Cemetery
   of the Pacific
31 News Building
4 Oahu Open Market
6 Our Lady of Peace Cathedral

7 St. Andrew's Cathedral
13 State Archives (Kekauluohi Building)
12 State Capitol
36 Thomas Square
9 Washington Place
17 YWCA, Richards Street

### Hospitals

40 Kaiser Hospital
8 Queen's Medical Center
37 Straub Clinic & Hospital

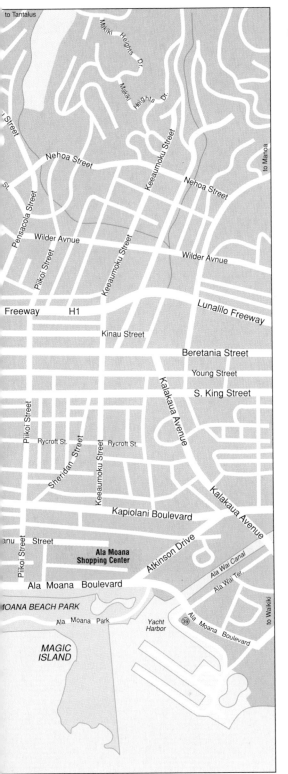

# OAHU AND HONOLULU

Like hazy Polynesian stories about the lost lands of Mu and Hawaiki, the meaning of the word *O'ahu* evaporated long ago. Nowadays, the island of Oahu is often said to mean "the gathering place," but that public relations translation is probably bogus.

Nonetheless, given that three quarters of Hawaii's population lives on Oahu, and that most tourists – 80,000 on any given day – drop anchor here, it is indeed a gathering place. Just listen to the melange of resident languages – English, Japanese, Tagalog, Chinese, Samoan, Korean, Hawaiian.

Oahu and the city, and county, of Honolulu are the same. Honolulu's jurisdiction extends 1,400 miles northwest up the Hawaiian chain to Kure Atoll, near Midway Island. In size, Honolulu is the world's largest city. In population, it is America's 11th largest city.

Honolulu is the seat of local and state government, and home to the islands' premier cultural attractions. Few trips are complete without a visit to the Bishop Museum, established in 1889 and housing the world's largest collection of Hawaiian artifacts, or stately 'Iolani Palace, the only royal palace on US soil.

Hawaiian islanders share a common vernacular for directions, which has nothing to do with cardinal directions or where the sun rises and sets. Rather, it deals with local geographical features. The two most common directional terms are *mauka* and *makai*. Mauka means upland or towards the mountains; makai means towards the sea. In Honolulu, this takes on even greater sophistication. Directions are given in relation to *'Ewa*, a plantation town just west of Pearl Harbor, and to *Diamond Head*, the famous landmark to the east of Waikiki. These orientations make eminent sense to local people. Try saying north, south, east or west in Honolulu and you'll be branded as a bewildered outsider immediately.

**Preceding pages**: Hanauma Bay, Oahu.

# DOWNTOWN AND HONOLULU HARBOR

*Honolulu* – the word rolls out like a soft Swiss yodel. There's no mystery about this word's origin: *hono,* a bay, and *lulu,* protected. It explains why Honolulu has been the business, political and cultural center of the Hawaiian Islands since the 1800s. Until Pearl Harbor was made navigable early this century, Honolulu Harbor was the only protected body of water its size within 2,000 miles (3,200 km) of Hawaii.

Downtown Honolulu – or "town" as locals prefer to call Honolulu proper – is less than a dollar and a 15-minute air-conditioned bus ride away from Waikiki. A walker's delight, downtown Honolulu can consume days, weeks or even months with its side streets, dusty or new shops of every persuasion, and oddball bars, where at least one street character will talk pidgin English into your ear and woo you back for another *aloha* beer.

As in any slow-rolling place, the key to unlocking Honolulu – where sunshine, trade winds and bikinis attract more money than stocks and bonds – is to treat it not like a city, but like the small gem that it is. Putter around serendipitously. Like the gang at Elsie's Club Polynesian on Hotel Street suggests, "Try go easy, bruddah."

**Palaces and statehouses:** Grand old 'Iolani Palace (on King Street, of course) is the only royal palace on American soil, built in the style its architects called "American Composite" or "American Florentine". Completed in 1882 during the eighth year of King Kalakaua's reign, it took three years and a little over $350,000 to finish.

King Kalakaua and his successor-sister Queen Lili'uokalani lived in the palace, holding royal court from 1882 until 1893, when a group of American businessmen staged a coup d'état and abolished the monarchy. 'Iolani, Hawaiian for "royal hawk," was renamed the Ex-

**Left**, Honolulu and the harbor as seen from Sand Island.

ecutive Building after the monarchy's overthrow, but *auwe*, or royal humiliation, did not end there. In January 1895, following a futile counter-revolution led by royalists, Lili'uokalani was convicted of high treason and returned to 'Iolani Palace, where she spent most of 1895 living on the second floor under house arrest as a prisoner of the provisional government.

**Restored splendor:** In the years since the 1893 coup, the palace has been used as a capitol for the provisional, republic, territorial, and state governments of Hawaii. In 1969, the state legislature and administration moved out of the palace and into the impressive new capitol building and grounds just *mauka* of the palace. After more than 75 years of neglect, and with the palace now unoccupied, the state and a private non-profit group began a massive effort to restore the palace to its original splendor. In 1978, after nine years of meticulous labor and some $6 million, 'Iolani Palace was officially reopened to visitors.

Original furnishings were tracked down and recovered, and the palace proper – with its Corinthian columns, etched glass door panels, chandeliered, mirrored and gilded Throne Room and spectacular three-story *koa* stairwell with carved balusters – now glows as it did when Kalakaua and Lili'uokalani hosted formal banquets and grand balls in the Dining Room and Blue Room. Also back in operation are the first flush toilets known to have been installed in any palace anywhere in the world, and Hawaii's first internal telephone and electric light systems.

In recent years, 'Iolani Palace has not been without its truly royal moments. Now and then, with little public fanfare, descendants of the Kalakaua family participate in discreet meetings on the palace's grounds with visiting Polynesian monarchs from Tahiti, Tonga or the Maori tribes of New Zealand.

On these unheralded occasions, the man who would be King of Hawaii, Edward Keliiahonui Kawananakoa, his sisters, the Princesses Poomaikelani and Kapi'olani Kawananakoa, and a cousin,

**'Iolani Palace is the only royal palace on US shores.**

Kekaulike Kawananakoa, gather on the palace's *mauka* portico to welcome and toast their royal Polynesian peers in a manner befitting such dignitaries. These private affairs, a poignant reminder of royal days past, are purely symbolic and receive no support or recognition from the state government.

Also of interest on the palace grounds are several other worthwhile sites. The **Coronation Stand**, mentioned earlier, was built in 1883 for King Kalakaua and Queen Kapi'olani's grand coronation ceremony. The stand originally stood at the foot of the palace's King Street steps, but following the coronation was moved to its present location in the *Ewa-makai* corner of the grounds. The stand's foundation was rebuilt of concrete in 1919, but the copper dome is original and now shelters the Friday noon public concerts given by the **Royal Hawaiian Band**.

The **'Iolani Barracks** is a fine, stone structure that served as headquarters and home for the Royal Household Guards from 1871 until the overthrow of the monarchy in 1893. The barracks originally stood on Hotel Street on the new state capitol grounds, but was moved piece by piece to its present location alongside Richards Street in 1965. The small building now includes a gift shop.

The **Royal Burial Ground and Tomb** is an inconspicuous grass-covered mound surrounded by *ti* plants in the *Diamond Head-makai* corner. It was the location of the first Royal Mausoleum, built in 1825 to house the remains of King Kamehameha II and Queen Kamamalu, who died in England. Later Hawaiian *ali'i* were also buried there. But in 1865, with the tomb now overcrowded with royal remains, all were moved to a new Royal Mausoleum in Nu'uanu Valley.

Also on the palace grounds, in the *mauka-Diamond Head* corner alongside the Hawaii State Library next door, are two contemporary structures – the **State Archives Building** (the Kekauluohi Building) and the **Kana'ina Building**, the original archives building. Both

**Descendants of the *ali'i* – ruling class – outside 'Iolani Palace.**

are misplaced architecturally. In front of the latter is a Captain Cook memorial plaque of little interest, and an interesting "ancient threshold rock of Liloa, an ancient king of Hawaii." This oblong lava stone, used to mark the *kapu*, or forbidden, entrance to Liloa's Big Island home, was said to have been shipped to Oahu by King Kalakaua.

**A great statue:** *Makai,* or ocean side, across King Street from 'Iolani Palace is the gilded statue of Kamehameha the Great. This heroic bronze bears little or no resemblance to the actual King Kamehameha I, better known as Kamehameha the Great, but it's a Honolulu monument photographed dozens of times a day by tourists who want to be seen in the same Kodak or Fuji frame with the warrior king who unified Hawaii. The statue is impressive on June 11 – Kamehameha Day, a state holiday – when its neck, shoulders and arms are draped with numerous 18-ft (5.5-meter) long flower lei.

The Kamehameha likeness (modeled for in the 1870s by a local fellow named John Timoteo Baker, who was mostly Anglo-Saxon but about one-fourth Tahitian) shows the king holding a barbed *polulu* (spear) in his left hand as a symbol of peace and his right arm outstretched in a gesture of *aloha*. Hanging from the king's shoulders is a huge feather cloak and on his head is a *mahiole,* or feather helmet. Around his loins and over his chest he wears a feather *malo,* loincloth, and sash.

When the Hawaiian kingdom's 1878 legislature commissioned this statue, King Kalakaua selected Baker, a local businessman and close friend, to be the main model for the statue, as he was supposed to be the handsomest man in court circles.

Photographs were taken of Baker and others wearing ancient clothing, and these pictures and copies of painted likenesses of Kamehameha were sent to Thomas B. Gould, an American sculptor in Florence, Italy. Unveiled during Kalakaua's coronation in 1883, the Honolulu statue is actually a copy of the original, which now stands in front of

**'Iolani Palace interior, main stairwell.**

the unassuming civic center in Kapaʻau, in Kohala on the Big Island, near Kamehameha's birthplace on the island's northern point.

Gould's first statue (the one now in Kohala on the Big Island) was cast in Paris in 1880 and shipped to Hawaii from Germany; the ship carrying it caught fire and sank off Port Stanley in the Falkland Islands. The statue was later recovered.

Of interest are four bas-relief plaques around the statue's white pedestal. These detailed plaques depict Kamehameha as he visits Captain James Cook aboard his flag ship HMS *Resolution*; as he demonstrates his warrior's skills by warding off five spears hurled at him simultaneously; and as he reviews a fleet of war canoes from a bluff in Kohala on the Big Island. The last plaque represents the era of peace that followed King Kamehameha's unification of the islands.

Just behind the Kamehameha statue, the **old Judiciary Building** (also known as **Aliʻiolani Hale**) has a very royal history, too. It was originally designed by an Australian architect, Thomas Rowe, to be King Kamehameha V's palace. His Majesty's household plans changed, however, and, by the time the building was completed in 1874, it was used instead as a courthouse parliament building. The building now serves as the home of the state's supreme court. *Hale* means "house," and *aliʻiolani*, one of Kamehameha V's formal Hawaiian names, means when translated "a chief of heavenly repute."

In a *Diamond Head* direction up King Street from the Judiciary Building is Hawaii's most famous Christian structure, **Kawaiahaʻo Church**. On Sunday mornings, or when the church's Hawaiian choir is in rehearsal, the royal palms and *hala* trees on its grounds swell and sway with the lyrics of *"He A-kua he mo-le-le* – God is Holy" or with *"E Ha-wai-i e kuʻu o-ne ha-nau e,"* the opening words of "Hawaii Aloha," which in translation praises, "Oh, Hawaii, my own birthplace, my own land."

For years this was the gathering place

**Roof of Hawaii's State Capitol.**

of missionaries and Christian Hawaiian *ali'i.* Even today, Kawaiaha'o often serves as a meeting place where matters of serious Hawaiian interest are discussed. Indeed, if there is an active spiritual font in Hawaii for Christian Hawaiians, it is probably this church.

**Coral church:** Designed by the Reverend Hiram Bingham, who led the first Congregationalist mission to Hawaii in 1820, the church was constructed in the late 1830s and early 1840s of some 14,000 large coral blocks cut from nearby reefs and hauled here by congregational members. (The beach was then nearby; everything *makai* has been created since then by filling in shallows.) Although the present Kawaiaha'o structure was dedicated in 1842, it was preceded by four thatched churches also built under Reverend Bingham's direction, the first in 1821.

*Kawaiaha'o,* the "water used by Ha'o," was named after an ancient sacred spring that once bubbled up in this area near the **News Building** – home of Oahu's two daily newspapers – at the corner of South Street and Kapi'olani Boulevard. Ha'o, according to oral traditions, was an ancient queen of Oahu.

It was at Kawaiaha'o Church that Kamehameha III uttered his famous words – and now the State of Hawaii's motto – *Ua mau ke ea o ka 'aina i ka pono* or "the life of the land is preserved in righteousness," following the restoration of Hawaiian sovereignty after a brief 1843 British takeover of the islands. This is also where Liholiho, Kamehameha IV, and Lunalilo formally ascended the Hawaiian throne.

On the church grounds are cemeteries for early missionary *haole* and faithful Hawaiian members of its congregation. Not too many years ago, when construction of the nearby fire station began, and again in 1988 when the adjacent streets were torn apart to improve the underground utilities, dozens of graves were found beneath.

It's estimated that as many as 2,000 Hawaiians were buried here in the 1800s, many the victims of diseases introduced by the early sailors and settlers. Mis-

**Kawaiaha'o Church; Kamehameha Statue.**

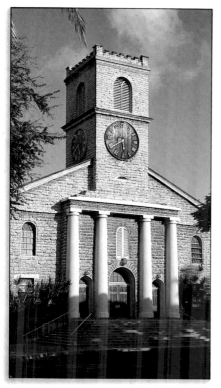

sionaries and their descendants were buried at the back of the church, while native Hawaiians and others were segregated in death on the harbor-side of Kawaiaha'o Church.

One Hawaiian, however, received special exemption from Kawaiaha'o's congregation: King William Lunalilo, the popular "Prince Bill" whose Gothic tomb, the **Mausoleum of King Lunalilo**, stands just to the right side of the main entrance to the churchyard. Lunalilo, who died in 1874 after a one-year reign, had requested that he be buried at Kawaiaha'o, away from the "clannish" Kamehameha kings and queens who rested in vaults at the Royal Mausoleum in Nu'uanu.

Lunalilo wanted to be "among his people," he said at his deathbed; so when he died, his aging father, Charles Kana'ina, respected his son's wishes. When the elder Kana'ina died later, he was also placed in this impressive burial vault that says over its *mauka* entrance, *Lunalilo Ka Moi*, Lunalilo the King.

Another edifice on Kawaiaha'o's grounds that merits closer study is **Likeke Hale**, an adobe schoolhouse built around 1836, where early Congregationalist missionaries taught Hawaiian children the *palapala*, or Bible and paper learning in general. This building of mud, limestone, and coral fragments is the only survivor of many adobe structures built in Hawaii during the early 1800s, and it's still used today for Sunday school classes and smaller church meetings.

Just over a hedge and a narrow road from the schoolhouse is the yard where the missionaries lived, prayed and printed (in 1822) the first of their many 19th-century *palapala*, or writings. These are the **Mission Houses**, now a museum complex, which are the oldest surviving Western-style structures in Hawaii. The main white **Frame House** still stands as prim, trim and true as the day it was erected in 1821 of New England timbers, which were cut and fitted in Boston and shipped around Cape Horn to Hawaii aboard the brig *Thaddeus*. It is the oldest wooden house in

**Saint Andrew's Cathedral.**

Hawaii, and for many years was home to several prominent missionaries.

The **Coral House** – where the first printing in the north Pacific was pressed and pulled from an old iron-and-mahogany press – was built in 1823. A third building, the **Chamberlain House**, also constructed of coral blocks, was completed in 1831. Chamberlain House was used as a storehouse and home for the mission's purchasing agent. All three structures belong to the Hawaiian Mission Children's Society, an exclusive *kama'aina* club made up of missionary descendants. The society also maintains, in cooperation with the Hawaiian Historical Society, a small library that is one of the finest repositories of rare and general Hawaiian history manuscripts and books. It is open to private researchers during business hours.

From the front entrance of Kawaiaha'o Church, a visual sweep *mauka* across the busy but pleasantly spaced King Street opens with the Greco-Roman **Hawaii State Library**, donated by philanthropist Andrew Carnegie and built between 1911 and 1912, and completely refurbished in the late 1980s; continues *Diamond Head* past **Honolulu Hale**, Honolulu's California-Spanish style city hall (1927); and ends in a burst of all-Americana at a red-brick structure with white pillars that a few locals facetiously call "Honolulu's Monticello" because, from a distance, it looks similar to Thomas Jefferson's historical home in Virginia. This structure, opposite the Mission Houses, was dedicated in 1916 as the **Mission Memorial Building** to honor the original New England missionaries. Since 1947, it's been used as a city hall annex.

**A capital place:** Behind 'Iolani Palace is contemporary Hawaii's center of power – the **State Capitol Building**, dedicated in 1969 and completely renovated in the early 1990s. The structure's architectural lines were designed to suggest Hawaii's volcanic and oceanic origins; its high and flaring support pillars, it has been said, represent royal palms and the obvious symbolism they stand for. Paneling made of

**Ballet is presented by both local and mainland companies.**

indigenous *koa* wood in offices and conference rooms gives the structure a Hawaiian touch, as do Hawaiian language greetings on the governor's door, *E komo mai* – Please come in.

The building is seen to best advantage during regular February through May sessions of the state legislature, when Hawaii's lawmakers *hukihuki*, or argue island-style, in the state's most eloquent parliamentary pidgin.

Dangling above the *makai* and *mauka* entrances are massive castings of the Great Seal of the State of Hawaii. This seal, an edited and embellished version of the original Royal Hawaiian coat of arms, includes images of Kamehameha the Great and the Goddess of Liberty (wearing a Phrygian cap and laurel wreath, but holding a partly unfurled Hawaiian flag in her right hand).

Other symbols are a phoenix bird with outstretched wings arising from flames; the state motto; a rising sun surrounded by the words "State of Hawaii, 1959," commemorating statehood; a quartered heraldic shield with parts of

the Hawaiian flag, *kapu* sticks and a green escutcheon with a five-pointed yellow star in the center; and lower seal engravings of taro leaves, banana foliage and sprays of maiden-hair fern. On the *makai* side of the building stands a majestic, bronze **statue of Queen Lili'uokalani**, the last monarch of Hawaii. An outstretched hand holds fresh flowers, placed there every day by her loyal supporters.

**Jack-and-stripes flag:** On the *mauka* side of the capitol fly the American and Hawaiian flags, and a blue, red and starred governor's flag. Visitors to the islands are sometimes surprised to see the British flag in the upper left corner of Hawaii's red-white-and-blue flag, designed about 1816 for Kamehameha the Great. It is thought that this flag includes the Union Jack out of consideration for the British sea Captain George Vancouver, who presented Hawaii with its first flag when Kamehameha temporarily placed his islands under the protection of Great Britain.

Other historians say Kamehameha

tripes over he city.

adopted the Jack-and-Stripes flag so that Hawaiian ships at sea would look both American and British, thereby discouraging pirates from pillaging his kingdom's vulnerable ships.

On the capitol's Beretania Street side, spend a few quiet moments studying the bronze **sculpture of Father Damien Joseph de Veuster**, the martyr-priest who lived and died among sufferers of leprosy, now called Hansen's disease, at Kalaupapa on the island of Molokai. This blockish statue of Damien, by the Venezuelan sculptress Marisol Escobar, is a duplicate of one that stands in Statuary Hall in the US Capitol building at Washington, DC.

Unveiled in 1969, it ignited controversy in local art, political and church circles because the bold and tragic likeness of Damien was based on a photograph taken of him shortly before he died of Hansen's disease in 1888. At the time, Damien was in great pain, and his former handsome features were grossly disfigured. Controversy regarding the statue has evaporated, but Marisol's

Damien remains a powerful artistic statement, and a telling memorial.

**A royal place:** Set back off Beretania Street is a tidy white mansion, **Washington Place**, since 1921 the official residence of the state's governor. Previously it was the home of Lydia Kapaʻakea Dominis, the *aliʻi* who ruled as Queen Liliʻuokalani. This gracious structure, rendered in what was called a Greek Revival form of architecture, was built in 1846 for the American sea captain John Dominis, who moved to Hawaii from New York in 1837. Dominis was lost at sea shortly after he finished building this home, but his widow and young son, John Owen Dominis, continued to live in his mansion.

One of the first things Captain Dominis's widow did was to rent several rooms in the house to Anthony Ten Eyck, then American commissioner to Hawaii. Ten Eyck established his legation in the house, and by late 1847 an American flag was fluttering over its front lawns. The following year, Commissioner Ten Eyck issued a "semi-

Controversial Father Damien sculpture, and the photo that inspired it.

official" proclamation in which he "christened the beautiful, substantial & universally admired mansion of Mrs Dominis, (as) Washington Place," after George Washington.

John Owen Dominis and Lydia Kapaʻakea – the future Liliʻuokalani – were married in 1862, taking up residence at Washington Place with Dominis's mother. Until Liliʻuokalani ascended the throne in 1891, moving into ʻIolani Palace and naming her husband the Prince Consort of Hawaii, she and Dominis continued to live here.

When Dominis died in 1891, Washington Place became the queen's property, but she didn't return there to live until her regime was overthrown in 1893. Until Liliʻuokalani's death in 1917, at age 79, Washington Place remained a center of royalty and courtly social proceedings. Many were the distinguished travelers who visited the queen here; not a few were probably treated to a private concert by the musical Liliʻuokalani, who liked to sing in her Music Room at a massive *koa* grand piano.

Washington Place is the oldest continually occupied residence in Honolulu, and, because it is now the home of Hawaii's governor, it is open to the public only on special occasions.

Down Beretania Avenue towards Diamond Head is the **Honolulu Academy of Arts**, just across the street from **Thomas Square**. Built in 1927, the academy houses galleries of Asian and Western art, plus inner courtyards rich in flora and sculpture. Paintings by Modigliani, Diego Rivera, Picasso, Miro, Gauguin, van Gogh, Mary Cassatt, Sargent and Camille Pissaro, and sculptures by Rodin, Bourdelle and Epstein vie with fine contemporary masters and one of the finest Oriental collections to be found in America, including James Michener's Japanese wood-block print collection.

Back at Washington Place, peek in next door on **St Andrew's Cathedral**, an English-Norman structure built rather slowly between 1867 and 1958 of imported English sandstone.

Only another block *Ewa* up Beretania

Washington Place was the home of Queen Liliʻuokalani.

Street – the Hawaiian form of "Britannia" – is the **Cathedral of Our Lady of Peace**, built by Roman Catholic missionaries from France. This coral building at the top of the **Fort Street Mall** was dedicated in 1843. Father Damien was ordained inside this church in 1864, the same year that Hawaiians marveled to the awe-inspiring sounds of the islands' first pipe organ.

In a quiet courtyard to the side of the cathedral is the stump of the first non-native tree planted in Hawaii. In the late 1820s, French Catholic missionaries planted on the mission grounds several seeds of mesquite, brought "from the king's garden in Paris." Seeds from this single *kiawe*, as mesquite is called in Hawaiian, eventually spread furiously throughout the islands.

Back at the capitol building, head down Richards Street to Hotel Street and the **old Armed Forces YMCA**, on the site of the original Hawaiian Hotel. This impressive 1927 building was restored in 1988 by Chris Hemmeter, highly celebrated and highly criticized for his stunning if not unrestrained contributions to Hawaii's resort industry.

After restoration, the building was briefly used as Hemmeter's corporate headquarters. Hemmeter moved to the mainland in 1990 in order to pursue other projects, selling the building and leaving behind a legacy of unmatched "fantasy resorts" across the islands. These days the building is used as office space by various state agencies and private enterprises.

Half a block further is the Richards Street **YWCA**, with its wrought iron grilling, red-tiled terrazzo flooring and courtyard swimming pool. Facing 'Iolani Palace across Richards Street, it was designed and landscaped by women, and built in 1926. This building serves as a public facility and includes a pleasant restaurant for lunch.

Historic buildings abound throughout Honolulu, as do rising glass towers. Perhaps the most interesting of the historic structures outside of the capitol district are in an area towards the harbor. This brick-rococo neighborhood is a

**Honolulu's prize-winning sake.**

pleasant four-block walk from the **Federal Post Office Building** (across from 'Iolani Palace) down **Merchant Street**, Honolulu's old "Financial Boulevard." Many of the quaint bluestone, brick and stuccoed structures in that area survived the demolition ball and have been renovated into boutiques, pubs, restaurants, design studios and offices.

One good example is the handsome **Kamehameha V Post Office**, built in 1871. This building, the first in Honolulu to be constructed entirely of concrete blocks, was used as a post office from 1884 to 1922, and then as a district court office building.

**The "Big Five":** Anchoring downtown is **Bishop Square**, a refreshing plaza with fountains at the intersection of Bishop and King streets. Named after Charles Reed Bishop, who established both the Bishop Estate and the Bishop Museum, **Bishop Street** carries both financier and fun seeker past the graciously porticoed suites and counting houses of the "Big Five" *kama'aina* corporations – conglomerates built on sugar in the last century by business and missionary families, and all clustered within whispering distance of each other. If you're in the neighborhood on "Aloha Friday," which is every Friday, nearly every man on the street – Big Five type, banker or otherwise – is wearing a crisp *aloha* shirt.

Art proliferates in Honolulu, and numerous outdoor sculptures pepper the downtown area. One favorite is the 11-ft (3.3-meters) tall brushed bronze **Sun Disc** in front of the Financial Plaza of the Pacific, at the corner of King and Bishop streets. This solar sculpture by Bernard Rosenthal weighs about 5 tons, but rotates freely on its swivel base. A few blocks *Ewa* in Chinatown, where downtown takes on funkier and less lofty proportions, old restored buildings house galleries of every persuasion.

**Into the past:** Between Bethel and Nu'uanu streets, *Ewa* of the downtown and Bishop Street area, are two immense stone lions flanking **Hotel Street** and announcing **Chinatown**, an area bounded by the waterfront, and Nu'uanu,

Beretania and River streets. In the late 1860s, Chinese plantation workers – after paying off their indentured labor contracts – gathered here and established new lives.

In 1900, a twelve-block area burned down when a fire, set by the board of health to eradicate bubonic plague, went out of control. Once the rambunctious venue for sailors on liberty and characters on the loose, if not on the lam, Hotel Street has been transformed, mostly for the better, in a long-evolving urban renewal effort. Most of the area's seedy past has been scrubbed over or pushed out, although on Hotel Street immediately beyond the stone lions, peep shows and topless/bottomless bars survive, as do long-standing watering holes like the Two Jacks Bar, Club Hubba Hubba and Elsie's Club Polynesian.

Just beyond, however, Chinatown comes into its own in a medley of Asian markets, noodle factories, shops, and art and antique galleries, the area permeated by whiffs of incense and spices. Side streets cutting across Hotel Street

and extending from King Street to Beretania tempt the curious. The **Maunakea Marketplace** is a modern open plaza nestling amidst the old – look for the clock tower with Chinese numbers – and down on King Street, towards the waterfront, the **Oahu Market** will rekindle a traveler's Asian memories with its early morning hubbub of mongering and bargaining.

Hotel Street ends at River Street, which parallels the lower **Nu'uanu Stream** descending from the Ko'olau Mountains. Wander up along the stream past old men playing chess and lovers passing time towards the mountains. On the *mauka* side of Chinatown – just past the confection, fish, flower and noodle mongers – you'll find the **Kwan Yin Temple** on Vineyard Boulevard, where both Buddhist and Taoist images gleam, and where a 10-ft (3-meter) statue of Kwan Yin, the Buddhist goddess of mercy, dominates.

A quiet respite is found beneath hardy tropical trees in the vast **Foster Botanic Gardens**, on Vineyard Boulevard just **Urban rider.**

beyond the Kwan Yin Temple. Several plants, such as the fragrant and ever-blossoming cannon ball tree indigenous to Guiana, are the only specimen of their genus and species in Hawaii.

Hidden *mauka* of the Lunalilo, or H1, Freeway are the serene **Lili'uokalani Gardens**. In this little urban vale a deep natural stream and pool are fed by two entrancing waterfalls – Makua and Waikahalulu Falls – which will erase any thoughts of the afternoon traffic in downtown paradise. Swimming is allowed in these 5 acres (2 hectares) of unspoiled nature, which was Queen Lili'uokalani's favorite cooling-off spot.

**Highways and harbors:** Towards the waterfront, Fort Street Mall empties into **Ala Moana Boulevard**, an oceanside artery that begins as the **Nimitz Highway** near the international airport, turning into Ala Moana (meaning "ocean street") downtown before continuing on into Waikiki. Near here stood the old "fort" – *Ke Ku Nohu,* circa 1816 to 1857 – that gave Fort Street its name.

Cross Ala Moana, hop on the eleva-tor to the top of the **Aloha Tower**, and watch a fabled Hawaiian sunset disappear triumphantly into Pacific waters over **Honolulu Harbor**. This pleasing 1925 structure is only 10 stories high – or 184 ft (56 meters) – but it was once the tallest building in Hawaii. Thirty-story skyscrapers across the boulevard dwarf Aloha Tower now, but it is the most well-known building in the harbor area, second in symbolic fame only to Diamond Head.

As recently as the 1940s and 1950s, the Aloha Tower's four clock faces and maritime harbor signals smiled down upon Hawaii's famous "Boat Days," when luxury Matson liners like the *Malolo* and *Lurline* would arrive and depart at Piers 10 and 11 in a hail of flowers and *hapa-haole hula-hula.* On and off the ships would go huge steamer trunks and travelers in white linen suits and ribboned hats; at pier side, local boys would dive for coins tossed into the water.

As the Royal Hawaiian Band played "Aloha 'Oe" – up-tempo if a ship were

arriving, almost funereally if it were leaving – the ships' horns would bellow a long salute. "Boat Day" is just a memory now, but the Aloha Tower still serves as the state's harbor headquarters and official maritime signals point.

Immediately adjacent to Aloha Tower is the **Hawaii Maritime Center**, a museum modeled after the boathouse of King Kalakaua. Completed in 1988, it has exhibits depicting Hawaii's 2,000-year-old seafaring heritage, from ancient Polynesian canoes to modern surfboards, sleek passenger liners, and military submarines.

Docked next to the Hawaii Maritime Center is the *Falls of Clyde*, the world's only surviving full-rigged, four-masted sailing ship. Built in Scotland in 1878, it spent 20 years in the India trade before entering the Hawaii trade routes, where its cargo was eclectic, including a locomotive in 1902 for the Hilo Railway. Its last voyage under sail was in 1921.

Next to the *Falls of Clyde,* and so small you might miss it, is the *Hokule'a,* a double-hulled, 60-ft (18-meter) modern working replica of an ancient Polynesian voyaging canoe. Several times in the 1970s and 1980s, it followed long-established Polynesian ocean routes between Hawaii and the South Pacific. Only traditional navigation techniques – stars, ocean swells, rhythm, intuition – were used to make the *Hokule'a's* modern-day voyages. In late 1992, the *Hokule'a* returned from a 5,500-mile (8,800-km) voyage to Honaunau.

Unfortunately, most of Honolulu's waterfront is inaccessible to the visitor. Proposals for reviving the area and opening it up for public recreation have surfaced and sunk over the years.

Finally, in late 1993, after the politicians had finished their banter and developers had done their song and dances, a redevelopment project got underway. Plans call for over 200 shops and kiosks, new cruise line terminals next to a renovated Aloha Tower, and entertainment and recreation areas in pier areas now dominated by warehouses. A hotel and condominium tower may follow.

**Ala Wai Yacht Harbor**

**Harbor for a king:** Honolulu Harbor – the "protected bay" – made Honolulu the most important if not the only city in the central Pacific; and it was the city, in turn, that made Hawaii more than just another island chain out in the middle of a blue nowhere.

European explorers didn't find Honolulu Harbor for more than 16 years after Captain Cook's arrival in 1778, probably because the navigable channel leading into the harbor was only about 550 ft (165 meters) wide and easily overlooked, and because in those early postcontact days the Big Island and Maui were greater centers of Hawaiian power than Oahu.

However, in late 1792 or early 1793, Captain William Brown, busy in both the Pacific Northwest-China fur trade and a new Hawaiian gun trade, accidentally found this inlet. He described it in his logbook as "a small but commodious basin with regular soundings from 7 to 3 fathoms clear and good bottom, where a few vessels may ride with the greatest safety." Brown named it "Fair Haven," a term almost synonymous with the Hawaiian name *Honolulu*.

Ironically, Brown's life ended violently two years later at the so-called Fair Haven, when he and another British skipper were killed during an attack led by Kalanikupule, Oahu's ambitious king. Kalanikupule wanted to use the two British ships, their guns and captured crewmen to attack the Big Island's well-armed and advancing King Kamehameha.

**Devastating defeats:** But the Oahu king's naval strategy was a bit late; about four months later, Kamehameha invaded Oahu and dealt Kalanikupule's soldiers a series of devastating defeats, ending in a fatal last stand at the top of Nu'uanu Valley. As for Kalanikupule, he was captured 13 months later and offered to Kamehameha's war god as a human sacrifice.

Hawaiians on Oahu had always preferred, as do tourists today, the soft sands and breezes of Waikiki. But with the coming of sailing vessels and a *haole* concept called money, *akamai*, or smart,

The Transpac Regatta.

Hawaiians, including Kamehameha the Great, began moving to Honolulu's harbor. In Kamehameha's hands, Honolulu became the most important stopover point in the mid-Pacific ocean. Within a few years, hundreds of ships yearly were lying yardarm-to-yardarm in the harbor.

Never mind that Honolulu and the surrounding plains were a backwater of fishermen's shacks and dusty slopes; what mattered was that anchored ships didn't have to worry about being swept onto jagged coral reefs and rock shores by sudden shifts in wind and sea.

Kamehameha himself was only able to tolerate the harbor's commercial chaos for about eight years, from 1803/04 to about 1812. Although he eventually moved away and finished his life at quieter Kailua-Kona on the Big Island, he closely monitored commerce at Honolulu until his death in 1819, as did his sons, Kamehameha II and Kamehameha III. Later during the whaling era, the Kamehamehas moved Hawaii's capital to the booming town of Lahaina,

on Maui. Eventually the Hawaiian elite recognized that the real long-term potential was in fact at Honolulu and, in 1845, Kamehameha III moved – lock, stock and legislature – back to Honolulu where, in 1850, he officially declared it as the capital of the Hawaiian Kingdom.

From Aloha Tower and the downtown waterfront, *Ewa* along the Nimitz Highway leads towards the airport, and *Diamond Head* on Ala Moana Boulevard leads towards Waikiki Beach. The Nimitz and Ala Moana are actually continuations of the same road; the name changes downtown.

**Along Nimitz:** The Nimitz Highway is the ugliest stretch of road anywhere in Hawaii. It's a nightmare of a tourist gateway, a tedious mess of traffic and industrial eyesores, and unfortunately visitors take this road from the airport into Waikiki. (The other option is the H1 Freeway, almost as bad.)

One very pungent all-Hawaiian assault occurs just *Ewa* of Chinatown in an area called **Iwilei** (pronounced ee-vee-lay) with the constantly fragrant

**The Dole Pineapple.**

canneries of the **Dole Pineapple Company**. A visual reminder rises high above the old canneries on Iwilei Road: the Dole Pineapple water tank, painted and enhanced with green crown and yellow-brown prickles to look like the largest pineapple around.

Long ago, this area was better known for "Horny Lulu's" notorious red light district. How the rum did flow in those sinful cribs when the visiting pirate Bully Hayes and his marine moll, Stormbird Emma, staggered past Old Chinatown's opium dens, grog shops and cat houses. An old Hawaiian folk song celebrates the "Girl of Iwilei/ sassy straying/ always eating black crabs/ sassy straying." And in his Samoa-based short story "Rain," author Somerset Maugham firmly immortalized Iwilei with Miss Sadie Thompson, a harlot Maugham met on a cruise ship from Honolulu to Pago Pago, after she had eluded a big 1916 police raid on Iwilei's resident professionals.

In those days, Maugham wrote, Iwilei was a place of row upon row of neat little green houses, each holding two women, each simply furnished with beer and gin for visitors. "When you go in the blinds are drawn down and if someone knocks, the answer is: Busy. You are at once invited to drink beer and the woman tells you how many glasses she has had that day. She asks you where you come from. The gramophone is turned on. The price is a dollar."

**Towards Waikiki:** Along Ala Moana Boulevard past the **Prince Kuhio Kalaniana'ole Federal Building**, harbor and ocean disappear behind walls and buildings. But a mile or so farther on are four "file it away" spots worth visiting. **Kewalo Basin**, where the remnants of Honolulu's fishing fleet return with the day's catch, offers fresh seafood and ambiance. Tradition has it that centuries ago, social outcasts intended for ritual sacrifice were sometimes drowned at Kewalo (meaning "the calling," as in an echo).

On the opposite or *mauka* side of Ala Moana Boulevard are two popular shopping and restaurant retreats, **Ward**

The *Falls of Clyde*.

Warehouse and **Ward Centre**. On the right just past Kewalo Basin begins the expansive **Ala Moana Beach Park**, 100 acres (40 hectares) of open space and beaches with good swimming and surfing. Along with the adjacent man-made peninsula known locally as **Magic Island** (on the map, **'Ainamoana State Recreation Area** – and with some fine romantic views of Waikiki and Diamond Head at dusk), it's probably the most popular "local" recreation site in the greater Honolulu area. Directly *mauka* from Magic Island is the large, outdoor, triple-tiered **Ala Moana Shopping Center**.

On the extreme Diamond Head end of Ala Moana Beach Park, a bridge rises over the wide **Ala Wai Canal** and into Waikiki and its concrete corridors. To the left of the **Ala Wai Bridge** is the canal itself (*ala wai,* "freshwater way"), a favorite training area for outrigger canoe paddlers. The canal was part of a Waikiki reclamation project "to reclaim a most insanitary and unsightly portion of the bay," and to turn the swamp of Waikiki into suitable land for hotels and condominiums.

Oceanside, bobbing in place and tacking hither and thither in snappy trade winds, are dozens of spindly sailing craft in **Ala Wai Yacht Harbor** and yacht basin, towered over by the **Hawaii Prince Hotel**. Many of these sailboats belong to members of the harbor's private Ala Wai and Hawaii Yacht Clubs, but nearly as many are skippered by transient live-aboards passing through on their way to and from dreams in the South Pacific.

This snug little harbor is usually a quiet place, but in summer of odd-numbered years it is the focus of the international yachting fraternity: the **Transpacific Yacht Race** from Los Angeles to Honolulu, since 1906 the world's oldest long-distance sailing competition. Upon completion of this 2,250-mile (3,600-km) race – the record is eight and a half days – the Ala Wai Harbor becomes a rich and raucous who's who of the world's yachting elite.

**Left**, silks and souvenirs.

# WAIKIKI BEACH

What is usually referred to as Waikiki Beach is actually a string of connecting beaches extending from Diamond Head to the Ala Wai Harbor: Sans Souci, Queen's Surf, Kuhio, Waikiki, Fort DeRussy, Duke Kahanamoku.

**Spouting water:** Early Hawaiians named this 1½-mile strip of coast Waikiki, or "spouting water," its inland part a swamp nurtured by descending mountain streams and gushy spring waters. As early as the 1400s, Hawaiians utilized this water and land to lay out a sophisticated irrigation system that fed aquaculture ponds and taro fields. In the 1920s, Waikiki's somewhat smelly interior was still a boggy place of fishponds, taro patches and rice paddies populated by quacking waterfowl and other damp creatures. But since ancient times Waikiki's seaside beaches, coconut groves and fish-rich reefs have made this village a favorite Hawaiian resort.

Early chants identify five important surfing breaks at Waikiki – *Aiwohi*, *Kalehuawehe*, *Kapua*, *Kapuni* and *Maihiwa*. One, Kalehuawehe, was renowned as a *kapu* surfing place reserved for royalty with their 18-ft (5.4-meter) *olo* surfboards, made of planks hewn out of *koa* and *wiliwili* trees.

During the early 1800s, the Kamehameha kings maintained a beach retreat at Waikiki. In the 1860s, a dirt road was built to comfortably link Waikiki's cool surf with hot and dusty Honolulu. In the 1880s a mule-drawn omnibus began making daily round trips to Waikiki, and by 1888 a regular tram service was initiated. Until the late 1880s and early 1890s, when a few beach cottages were converted into guest bungalows, most island visitors stayed with friends or in one of downtown Honolulu's hostelries, notably the long-gone Hawaiian Hotel on Hotel Street.

In 1884 Allen Herbert opened one of these bungalow operations at Waikiki near Diamond Head and named it **Sans Souci** (French for "without a care"). Five years later, Herbert hosted one of Waikiki's most famous early tourists, the noted Scottish author Robert Louis Stevenson.

Stevenson, who enjoyed his Waikiki vacation and some good times with the hard-drinking King Kalakaua, wrote the following endorsement into the Sans Souci's guest book: "If anyone desires such old-fashioned things as lovely scenery, quiet, pure air, clear sea water, good food, and heavenly sunsets hung out before his eyes over the Pacific and the distant hills of Wai'anae, I recommend him cordially to the 'Sans Souci'."

Even today those same heavenly sunsets take place off Sans Souci Beach, where the **New Otani Kaimana Beach Hotel** has replaced Stevenson's bungalow. One wonders if Stevenson would have approved of Waikiki even 12 years later when a group of Honolulu businessmen opened Waikiki's first real hotel, the Moana Hotel, in 1901. Certainly, chances are good that the moody Stevenson would have been infuriated by the way this gleaming structure full of steamer-set tourists would block his

**Left**, waiting for a wave. **Right**, Miss Waikiki.

view of central Waikiki's coconut groves. The inevitable development of Waikiki as a planned resort area began in earnest in the 1920s, when completion of Ala Wai Canal diverted water from the swamps and created dry land for future hotels.

**Extraterrestrial:** Many Oahu *kama'aina* consider Waikiki a kind of extraterrestrial outpost, a foreign trade zone packaged to free visitors of money. As a well-known Honolulu newspaper columnist once reasoned: "Yes, we enjoy the economic benefits of the tourist industry, and the military industry for that matter, but we stay the hell out of both. The point is, you eat the chicken, but you don't necessarily walk into the chicken coop."

Chickens and their coops aside, Waikiki is undeniably Oahu's cash cow. Consider the statistics. At 500 acres (200 hectares) in size, it covers just 0.0013 percent of Oahu's land area. Yet Waikiki recently pumped $4 billion tourism dollars into Hawaii's economy, 45 percent of the state's total tourism in-

come. It provides nearly 40,000 jobs tending to most of Oahu's daily 80,000 tourists, while remaining home for 20,000 people.

**Wizards of Waikiki:** Whether you look at Waikiki through the windows of an air-conditioned tour bus or while breaking in new flip-flop slippers on flashy **Kalakaua Avenue** – or on its *mauka* (opposite) parallel artery, **Kuhio Avenue** – Waikiki is a place with surprises and merit, local cynics and their views notwithstanding.

Take, for example, the **Wizard Stones**, or **Stones of Kapaemahu**, four large boulders at **Kuhio Beach** in the middle of Waikiki. Approach the stones with respect, because according to Hawaiian oral traditions they possess the *mana*, or spiritual powers, of four *kahuna* priests, wizards if you will, who were renowned throughout Polynesia for their wisdom and healing abilities. These four wizards – Kapaemahu, Kahaloa, Kapuni and Kinohi – came to Oahu from Tahiti in the 16th century, then left. A metal plaque on the first stone notes that "be- **Miss Bikini contest.**

fore vanishing, the wizards transferred their powers to these stones."

A smaller stone's throw away is a bronze **statue of Duke Paoa Kahanamoku** (1890–1968). In 1912, at the Stockholm Summer Olympics, Kahanamoku – a local boy who learned to swim in Waikiki – took gold medals in the 100- and 400-meter free-style events. In the years following, Duke became something of a surfing and canoeing legend not only in Hawaii, but elsewhere, as he introduced surfing to the world at large (*see pic on page 183*). A beach fixture in Waikiki, he also served as sheriff of Honolulu for a quarter century. When the Prince of Wales, accompanying Lord Mountbatten on a round-the-world voyage, visited Hawaii in 1920, he took surfing and outrigger canoe lessons from Duke.

The statue includes a bronze surfboard representing Duke's classic 24-ft (7.2-meter) *koa* long board. Short boards are the norm today, but some of the old long boards still in use can be found in storage racks wedged between the Moana Surfrider Hotel and Honolulu police substation nearby.

Duke Kahanamoku died in 1968 at the age of 78. Ten thousand people came to his funeral on Waikiki Beach, from where his ashes were carried out beyond the reef in an outrigger canoe. A local newspaper editorial concluded: "With the death of Duke Kahanamoku, Waikiki as it was, vanished."

Behind the statue, in a seaward, or *makai*, direction, are bronzed bodies drenched in coconut oil and sunburned hopefuls, and beach boys paddling oversized orange surfboards out to surf spots like Queens, Populars or Canoes, teaching those waves to middle-aged patriarchs or giggling adolescents from the mainland. Many are the local songs that have immortalized this age-old Waikiki pastime. "Coeds here, coeds there sitting 'round everywhere in short shorts and muumuus too trying to do like the Hawaiians do."

The city and state have spent millions renovating both Kalakaua Avenue and the beach facilities extending from

**Towards Diamond Head at dusk.**

Duke's statue at Kuhio Beach to Sans Souci Beach near Diamond Head. Yet even with its ongoing facelift, Waikiki retains some of its nasty but nice mystique, and, with every passing block, Waikiki gives of itself with little effort.

A block *Ewa* from the twin 40-story oceanfront towers of the **Hyatt Regency Waikiki** – imagine the top-floor ocean view – the **International Market Place** could be thought of for many years as the tropical Times Square of Waikiki. This acre or so of eateries, souvenir shops, and kiosks selling everything from shave ice to gold jewelry was once a pleasant and open place full of twittering birds, a large banyan tree, and a good share of curious local folk.

But in recent years, with Waikiki space becoming more and more dear, the Market Place has become rather overcrowded. For a while, there was talk of replacing it with a massive convention center. Fortunately, the convention center, if built, will go elsewhere.

Visiting Hawaii several years ago, the well-known Soviet poet-journalist

Yevgeni Yevtushenko wrote a poem, "The Restaurant For Two," about a small tree house office high in a banyan tree at the entrance to the International Market Place. He sang of "mermaidenly thighs... heedless brown hands... pilings of palm... baked shark's fin steeped in pineapple... the samba's throb... and flat champagne." Then, as he recalls, a man stepped up to the banyan tree, threw a switch and turned on "the bird song tape-recorded to lend the illusion of Paradise."

That's a far technological cry from Waikiki in 1913, when another poet, the Englishman Rupert Brooke, composed a sonnet, "Waikiki," which sighed about "warm perfumes" drifting "like a breath from vine and tree" and recalled hearing in the dark "hidden from eyes," the sounds of an *eukaleli* that "thrills and cries/ And stabs with pain the night's brown savagery." Brooke heard "dark scents whisper; and dim waves creep to me/ Gleam like a woman's hair, stretch out, and rise/ And new stars burn into the ancient skies/ Over the murmurous soft Hawaiian sea." Times change, but then, not.

**Rooms with a view:** Since the mid 1950s, hotels in Waikiki have sprouted like topless mushrooms in a cow paddock, in what surfers call the Great Wall of Waikiki. At last count, there were over 30,000 hotel rooms in Waikiki. However, for most of this century, three Waikiki hotels have anchored "old style Waikiki," beachfront places that are still regarded with a certain amount of respect by *kama'aina* who knew them when.

The **Sheraton Moana Surfrider Hotel**, on the beach along Kalakaua Avenue near Duke's statue, is the big white *tutu-kane* (granddaddy) of them all. At its center is Hawaii's first luxury hotel, the **Moana**. Opened in 1901 with 75 rooms, it had Hawaii's first electric elevator, and a 300-ft (90-meter) wood pier with a bandstand at its far end. (Unfortunately, the pier disappeared in 1930.) In 1918, two wings were added to the hotel, forming the **Banyan Courtyard**, still popular today for its ambiance and nightly music beneath a banyan tree planted in 1885. In 1952 another

The Sheraton Waikiki.

extension was added, and in 1969 the Surfrider tower was built.

A visit today is to visit Hawaii of 1912, for in 1989, after nearly two years and $50 million, the Moana Surfrider reopened in a meticulous and accurate restoration. On the hotel's second floor, above the open-air lobby, is a tiny museum with artifacts and photographs.

Between 1935 and 1972, the Moana's Banyan Courtyard became internationally famous as the favorite home of "Hawaii Calls," a Hawaiian music show once known as the oldest and most widely listened-to radio show on earth. Some 1,900 "Hawaii Calls" shows, sometimes carried by as many as 600 radio stations around the world, were broadcast live from Hawaii. The show's emcee, Webley Edwards, became famous with his golden-throated sign off: "All of us wish you were here with us – here in Hawaii – on this beautiful day. Come over and see us sometime! *Aloha – Aloha nui loa.*"

**Royal navigations:** When the Matson Navigation and Territorial Hotel companies unveiled the $4 million **Royal Hawaiian Hotel** in 1927, Honolulu's *kama'aina* elite shifted their focus from the 26-year-old Moana to this Moorish-Spanish style structure just down the beach. (*See picture on page 61.*)

Properly social Honolulu and San Francisco were a twitter as the Royal Hawaiian's completion date neared. An advance *Honolulu Advertiser* story promised that the Royal's opening "will be one of the greatest social events in the history of Hawaii... There will be softly thrumming music upon the air. There will be the powerful fragrance of flowers. There will be the pomp and brilliance of social glory."

And indeed there was. Some 1,200 guests turned out to witness a "semi-barbaric pageant" produced and directed by Princess Abigail Kawananakoa, the hotel's first official guest and wife of the late Prince David Kawananakoa. The princess's pageant, which began in offshore Waikiki waters, was a splendidly campy restaging of the 1795 landing at Waikiki of the conquering Kame-

Two sisters visit Hawaii.

hameha the Great. From the Royal's pink balcony, the princess hand-directed the movement of a fleet of 15 outrigger canoes and dozens of native Hawaiians outfitted in warrior regalia.

During the next 15 years, the six-story 400-room Royal Hawaiian became *the place* in Hawaii where the Hollywood likes of Mary Pickford, Douglas Fairbanks, Al Jolson and Ruby Keeler joined Duponts, Rockefellers, Fords and assorted presidents and real royalty over Green Turtle Soup Kamehameha, Medallions of Sweet Breads Wilhelmina, Gourmandise and Moka in the tapestry-filled Persian Room, now known as the Monarch Room.

With Hawaiian standards flying above its pink bell towers, and bush-jacketed beach boys and bellhops chasing after guest needs, the Royal cruised through the Depression into the 1930s. But in 1941 World War II flew into Pearl Harbor, and barbed concertina wire was rolled across the sands of Waikiki. Few of the world's big spenders could dance during blacked-out nights amidst army beach sentries carrying M-1 rifles, machine guns and hand grenades. So the Royal mothballed her tapestries and was leased to the US Navy until 1947 as a rest-and-recreation center for armed forces personnel, mainly submariners.

The Royal prospered once again in the late 1940s and into the middle 1950s, and in 1959 was purchased by Sheraton, who sold it nearly 30 years later to a Japanese investment tycoon.

The renovated Royal is easily spotted from the beach, but if you have a difficult time finding it from the mountain side, just look up in a seaward direction until you spot the massive 31-story **Sheraton Waikiki**. Walk towards the looming, curving Sheraton – which seems to block precious Waikiki views from nearly every compass point – and just to its left, on the Diamond Head side, you'll see a pink cupola peeking through floodlit palms.

The **Halekulani**, *Ewa* along the beach, too was a hotel pioneer in Waikiki, where in the early 1900s, American author Jack London drank hard, chain-

**The Royal Hawaiian Hotel.**

smoked and spun stories on his typewriter. It was here, too, that writer Earl Derr Biggers was staying when he thought up the fictional crime solver, Charlie Chan. The Halekulani's bar, "The House Without A Key," takes its name from the title of the first Charlie Chan novel, published in 1925.

Originally opened in 1907 as the Hau Inn, the Halekulani (literally, "the house befitting royalty, or heaven") was the last of the low-rise hotels on Waikiki Beach. The quaint original bungalows have been replaced with 450 modern but exquisite rooms (probably Waikiki's finest) in a cluster of reasonably low, 14-story buildings that are terraced back from the beach. At sunset, beneath the same hau tree – said to be 150 to 200 years old – that shaded London and Biggers, authentic Hawaiian music and one of the island's finest hula dancers usher in the sunset.

**Freebies by the seas:** But if classic hotels are not your cup of Kona coffee, then consider these:

● The **US Army Museum** at Fort DeRussy, on Kalia Road, where warfare artifacts include weapons of ancient Hawaii, the American Revolution period, the Spanish-American War, World Wars I and II, and the Korean and Vietnam Wars. Even for the pacifist, this is an interesting and underrated museum, located inside Battery Randolph, a massive bunker built in 1911 to protect Pearl Harbor; the walls on its seaward side are 22 ft (6.6 meters) of concrete. When the army tried to demolish the football-field-size bunker in the late 1960s, they couldn't do it, and hence the museum. The battery had two disappearing 14-inch (35-cm) shore guns, cut up in the late 1940s, that could lob a 1,600-pound shell 14 miles (22 km) out to sea.

● **Diamond Head**. Few tourists ever find out through the coconut wireless that they can actually drive into this extinct volcanic tuff cone and hike up its inside walls to its seaside rim 761 ft (231 meters) above the beach below. It's well worth the short but steep hike; the view of Waikiki and Oahu's south coast from

**Opening night at the Royal, 1927.**

up there is one of Oahu's best. And atop one of the abandoned World War II gun emplacements, it's a superb spot for a picnic. Inside the crater itself is a traffic control facility of the Federal Aviation Administration (who knows why); *mauka* outside the crater, a new film studio has been built.

"Diamond Head" is a nickname given the crater in 1825 by British sailors who found worthless calcite crystals on its slopes, thinking they were diamonds. Its original Hawaiian name was *Lae'ahi*, which means "brow" (*lae*) of the 'ahi (yellow-fin tuna). Hawaiian legends say that the fire goddess Hi'iaka, Pele's younger sister, noticed the resemblance between Diamond Head's profile and that of the 'ahi and so named it, *Lae'ahi*, which in later years was inexplicably shortened by map makers to *Leahi*. Its distinctive uplifting shape came from the trade winds 150,000 years ago that piled erupting ash higher on the ocean, or leeward, side. Its steep slopes were favored for *holua* sliding, a tropical form of tobogganing.

Long before this tuff cone became Hawaii's most famous landmark, *Lae'ahi* was the site of the Papaenaena Heiau, a significant religious site. According to historical accounts, some of the last human sacrifices ordered by Kamehameha the Great took place at this *heiau* following the decisive Battle of Nu'uanu Valley in 1795. Early descriptions indicate that the Papaenaena Heiau was located just beneath Diamond Head's jutting brow and slightly to its Waikiki side.

● **Kodak Hula Show**. Corny and campy but free and fun, this touristy hour-long performance takes place in the morning some weekday mornings on a grassy area adjacent to the **Waikiki Shell** amphitheater in Kapi'olani Park. *Hula* dancers in authentic *ti*-leaf skirts perform in front of a thatch hut to music sung and strummed by *tutu wahine* (grandmothers) in bright *holoku* dresses and flower-banded *lauhala* hats. A regular feature of this show, which has been staged since 1937, is the climbing of a coconut palm by a young Hawaiian boy.

Indoor surfing is preferred by some.

Eastman Kodak's revue is worthwhile if only to watch the tourists.

● **Kapiʻolani Park**. This vast complex of beaches, grassy picnic and play areas, amphitheaters, jogging courses, gardens, zoo, natatorium, and aquarium was dedicated on June 11, 1877 (Kamehameha Day) as Hawaii's first public park. King Kalakaua named the park after his wife, Kapiʻolani, and opening day was celebrated at a slate of high-stakes horse races held on a new track laid out just below Diamond Head.

The park's big Kamehameha Day races ended after the turn of the century, outlawed by temperance and anti-gambling forces. But since those days of the Hawaiian Jockey Club and thoroughbred runs, Kapiʻolani Park has steadily remained one of Oahu's favorite recreational areas. Whether you want cricket, soccer, kite flying, surfing or long tranquil walks under monkeypod and ironwood trees, this royal park has it.

Across the street at **Queen's Surf Beach** – named for Liliʻuokalani's beach house that once stood here – gay beach boys gather for fun and volleyball, and to listen to impromptu conga drum, guitar and flute music concerts held under a banyan, especially towards sunset.

The nearby **War Memorial Natatorium**, built to commemorate World War I veterans, is closed and in a state of inexcusable disrepair. Designed by the same architect who did the beautiful California Academy of Sciences in San Francisco, the natatorium was dedicated in 1927 as a world-class swimming stadium. There's always talk about renovating it. Talk's cheap.

At **Honolulu Zoo**, one can enjoy the typical antics of assorted monkeys, big cats, two elephants, several giraffes, hippos, and a rhinoceros. Also, and this is of great importance to island children, the zoo is the only place in Hawaii where you can observe a real live snake. As there are no wild snakes in Hawaii, strict control is maintained on their import. Not until 1971, following four years of debate in the state legislature, was a serpent allowed into Hawaii.

Except for sea birds, virtually all the

birds seen nowadays in Hawaii are introduced species. The zoo is probably the only place a visitor – and most residents – can see indigenous mountain birds, including the perky and exquisite 'apapane. Indeed, the zoo's exotic bird collection is excellent. The zoo has recently undergone significant improvements, including the opening of an expansive African savanna exhibit. At night, the shrieks of monkeys sometimes rebound, tropical enough, throughout this part of Waikiki.

In front of the zoo, seemingly out of place but then not, is a **statue of Mohandas K. Gandhi**, erected in 1990.

Probably the rarest animals in the **Waikiki Aquarium** – established in 1904, affiliated with the University of Hawaii since 1919, and the third oldest aquarium in the United States – are two monk seals. The monk seal and hoary bat are the only two mammals known to have been native to Hawaii when the first Polynesian settlers arrived. A complete renovation of the current structure in 1993 included a new habitat for the seals, and an indoor shark tank.

Kapi'olani Park has also become one of the running world's best-known marathon finishing points. The durable two-decade-old **Honolulu Marathon**, a 26 mile-, 385-yard (41.6-km) race beginning at 5.30am at Aloha Tower, draws competitors from both North America and Asia. In a recent year, 30,000 local and imported long-distance runners competed, double the number from the year before.

**Beach art:** Such an eclectic range of creations you will rarely ever see in an urban square mile anywhere, including an important 9 by 28-ft (3x8-meter) fresco mural ("Early Contacts of Hawaii with Outer World") at the Waikiki branch of First Hawaiian Bank (2189 Kalakaua Avenue) by the late internationally renowned French artist – and resident of Hawaii – Jean Charlot. Those in the know also recommend a peek at Edward M. Brownlee's 28-ft (8-meter) sculpture in the lobby of the Bank of Hawaii (2220 Kalakaua Avenue). Here too is a five-panel tapestry by Ruthadell Anderson made of natural materials.

Like your art big? Stand on Duke Kahanamoku Beach next to the Hilton Lagoon and crane your neck up at mosaic rainbows arching up the 30-story high **Rainbow Tower** of the **Hilton Hawaiian Village**, at the *Ewa* end of Waikiki. These vertical murals, made of 16,000 ceramic tiles and designed to be seen several miles out at sea, are billed as "the world's tallest murals." The Hilton Hawaiian Village – one of a dozen Waikiki hotels to get a multi-million-dollar facelift in recent years – has a collection of marble statues from China displayed on its beautifully landscaped and expansive grounds.

But perhaps the most touching work of art in Waikiki is a wall mural at the **Statewide Center for Students with Hearing and Visual Impairments** (3440 Leahi Avenue), which ceramist Kay Mura and students at the school created for people who cannot see art. Its tactile theme is Hawaiiana, and includes canoes, fishes, birds, flowers and other Hawaii symbols in its sculpted and glazed expanse.

**Left, beach art. Right, catamaran cruises are available.**

# HONOLULU NEIGHBORHOODS

Nestled against the Koʻolau Mountains that rise behind, the neighborhoods of Honolulu skirt around the hullabaloo of Waikiki and downtown Honolulu, weaving through valleys, ridges, and flats. They range from working class to million-dollar class. They extend from Kalihi, then shift east towards Koko Head, into the tropical wetness of Nuʻuanu, over the heights of Tantalus, into the valley lushness of Manoa, through the money of Kahala, and into the commute of Hawaii Kai.

**Kalihi:** A tour of Kalihi, just up from downtown heading towards the airport, would be a good way to start any Oahu day, especially if preceded by some *ono* (delicious) Hawaiian *kaukau* (food) at one of the area's many Hawaiian or Asian cafés.

Proceed *Ewa* up North King Street from downtown to the venerable old **Kaumakapili Church**, across Palama

**Preceding pages:**
**Kaneohe Bay,**
**North Shore.**
**Left**, seaside
estate in
Kahala.
**Below**, island
transportation.

Street from the locally famous **Tamashiro's** fresh seafood market. This Congregational church was originally built in 1837 at the corner of Beretania and Smith streets downtown, but after that one burned down in 1900 during a big Chinatown fire, it was relocated to this busy Kalihi corner. Kaumakapili was the common man's counterpart to Kawaiahaʻo Church, near ʻIolani Palace, which was used mostly by royalty and Honolulu's social elite. Kaumakapili Church, in contrast, was a more comfortable place of worship, and closer to the working class neighborhoods.

Further along N. King Street, then *mauka* up Kalihi Street and across the H1 freeway is the world's greatest repository of Pacific and Polynesian research and artifacts: the **Bernice Pauahi Bishop Museum**. Established in 1889 by Charles Reed Bishop, it was a memorial to his wife Bernice, a princess and the last of the Kamehameha family.

In academic centers, the Bishop Museum is considered one of America's four most important multi-disciplinary museums, in some ways on a par with the Smithsonian Institution, the American Museum of Natural History and the Field Museum of Natural History. Besides housing the largest and most comprehensive Hawaiian and Polynesian collection anywhere, the museum maintains natural history collections of nearly 20 million animal and plant specimens. It also manages and maintains a planetarium and astronomical observatory, and the *Falls of Clyde* four-masted sailing ship in Honolulu Harbor.

In the museum's cavernous *koa*-paneled **Hawaiian Hall** (1903) are carved and feathered gods, caps and other remnants of pre-contact Hawaii; brilliant regalia from the time of Kamehameha the Great; the monarchical crowns, thrones, royal orders and court costumes used in ʻIolani Palace by King Kalakaua and his sister, Queen Liliʻuokalani; and important pieces reflecting the experiences of Hawaii's many immigrant groups. The stone **Bishop Hall**, built in 1891, was the boys' department of the Kamehameha Schools until 1941.

Appropriately, the most *Hawaiian*

center of learning in Hawaii sits in **Kamehameha Heights**, just above the Bishop Museum: **Kamehameha Schools**, a private complex of elementary and secondary schools supported by income earned by the vast estate of the Princess Bernice Pauahi Bishop. The largest private estate in Hawaii, Bishop Estate's holdings – at 337,000 acres (135,000 hectares) nearly a tenth of Hawaii's land area, including much of the land under urban hotels, homes and apartment buildings – can be used solely to support and improve the Kamehameha Schools, which in turn can be attended only by students of Hawaiian ancestry. A visit to the sprawling campus offers a spectacular view of the west side of Honolulu.

**Nu'uanu:** Even the name is beautiful – *Nu'uanu*, meaning the cool height. More than a hundred years ago, the author of a guide book to Hawaii said Nu'uanu was the "most beautiful among the valleys of O'ahu."

Although residents of other valleys – Manoa comes to mind – might differ, there was no doubt among early *haole* settlers that this valley was the best place to live. Nu'uanu was the first suburb in which they built their Victorian mansions with broad *lanai*, and where they planted the monkeypods, banyans, Norfolk Island pines, bamboo, eucalyptus, African tulips and golden trees that now tower over the valley's indigenous ferns, hibiscus, *koa* and ginger. Many of these estates are still occupied by wealthy missionary descendants, but most have been sold or leased to institutions, churches or consulates of Asian nations.

Before stalking through the valley's lush rain forest, listen for the *oms* vibrating out of the **Soto Zen Mission of Hawaii** (1708 Nu'uanu Avenue), a duplicate of a major Buddhist stupa at Bodhgaya, India, the holy place where Gautama Buddha gave his first sermon. This temple's Indianesque towers would appear most at home on a Himalayan crag, but a few Japanese influences – gardens of tinkling water, sand and *bonsai* plants – give its authenticity

**Nu'uanu-style tea party, 1908.**

away. This stupa, built in 1952, is somewhat similar to an even larger one, the nearby and hard-to-miss **Honpa Hongwanji Mission** (1727 Pali Highway), which was built in 1918 to commemorate the 700th anniversary of the Shin Buddhist sect.

**Father of baseball:** Just *mauka* is the old **Oahu Cemetery**, where many names of rich or famous *haole* residents can be seen on tombstones. One in particular receives the attention of serious American sports fans: the layered, pink granite tomb with the inscription, "Alexander Joy Cartwright Jr. Born in New York City April 17, 1820. Died in Honolulu July 12, 1892."

This austere monument under a royal palm in the center of Oahu Cemetery marks the remains of the man who invented baseball. Although few people know that Cartwright lived much of his life in Honolulu before dying here, millions in the baseball-crazy United States know him as the man who dreamed up the baseball game and its sometimes odd rules. The first baseball game played under Cartwright's rules took place in 1846, at Hoboken, New Jersey.

Cartwright drifted west and eventually ended up in Hawaii, later founding Honolulu's first volunteer fire department and serving as its fire chief from 1850 to 1859.

Only a few hundred yards farther up Nu'uanu Avenue is the **Royal Mausoleum**, where the bodies of Kamehameha II, Kamehameha III, Kamehameha IV, Kamehameha V, Kalakaua, Queen Lili'uokalani and other members or favored friends of those royal Hawaiian families were buried. The only two Hawaiian monarchs not buried here were King Lunalilo, who at his own request was buried in a private tomb on the grounds of Kawaiaha'o Church, and Kamehameha the Great, whose bones were hidden away in a secret burial place on the Big Island.

The mausoleum, which lies on a 3-acre (1-hectare) site chosen by Kamehameha V, was prepared in 1865 to replace an overcrowded royal burial tomb on the grounds of 'Iolani Palace. Its Gothic-revival chapel, built in the shape of a crucifix, was designed by Honolulu's first professional architect, Theodore Heuck, and originally contained 18 royal bodies. Later, the bodies were moved from inside this crowded chapel to separate crypts on the grounds.

Nearby, below stands of plumeria, *ti*, ginger, *kamani* and palms, is **Kapena Falls**. On the mausoleum side of the falls, below the Pali Highway that curves and buzzes overhead, are three important Oahu petroglyph sites, where ancient Hawaiians incised several primitive human and dog figures and other unexplained symbols into large stones alongside Nu'uanu Stream. The popular dog figures are thought to be images of a ghost dog, *Kaupe*, who according to oral traditions once haunted this valley.

**Royal retreat:** A logical Nu'uanu traffic flow leads back onto the **Pali Highway** – gliding past the Royal Mausoleum, "Consulates Row" and a replica of the three-tiered **Sanji Pagoda**, which stands at Nara in Japan – *mauka* up to *Hanaiakamalama*, the "foster child of the moon," known more commonly as

Duke Kahanamoku and baseball superstar Babe Ruth, 1939.

the **Queen Emma's Summer Palace**.

This royal bower with a ginger and *ti*-lined driveway was built in the late 1840s, and later sold to John Young II, an uncle of Queen Emma and son of Kamehameha the Great's chief *haole* adviser, the Englishman John Young. Queen Emma and Kamehameha IV in turn bought it from Young and named it *Hanaiakamalama* after a favorite Hawaiian demigoddess. Until Emma's death, the royal family used this home as a cool summer retreat, salon and courtly social center. In 1890, the summer palace was purchased by the Hawaiian government and since 1911 has been part of a public park. The Daughters of Hawaii have maintained it as a museum since 1915.

The palace's rooms have been restored with many of the royal family's belongings. Among the items are a spectacular triple-tiered *koa* sideboard of Gothic design presented to Emma and Kamehameha IV by Britain's Prince Albert; a heavy gold necklace strung with tiger claws and pearls, given to Emma by a visiting maharajah; and various opulent wedding and baby gifts which were given to the royal family by England's Queen Victoria, who was the Hawaiian Prince Albert's godmother. Among the most fascinating Hawaiian pieces are a stand of tall feather *kahili* (royal standards) in the Queen's master bedroom.

On the mountain side of the palace is a long reception hall that Queen Emma had built to house a lavish party for the visiting Duke of Edinburgh, who for some unexplained reason didn't make it to the actual party. Outside the antique Hawaiian-Victorian interior are a proper rose garden, stands of *kukui* and *koa* trees, assorted Hawaiian flowers of seductively fragrant beauty, chattering birds and a sleepy little stream.

Behind and around the corner from the palace, off Puiwa Road, is a lovely little retreat, **Nu'uanu Valley Park**, favored by lovers and daydreamers who like to lounge under its gigantic trees.

Continue the journey through the valley with a drive through the hanging

The Bishop Museum's interior gallery.

vines, bamboo, wild ginger, jasmine and cool of the **Nuʻuanu Pali Drive**, the old route now bypassed by the four-land Pali Highway. Along this wending way you'll spot stately *kamaʻaina* mansions hidden away in the bush, and, on rainy days, dozens of tiny waterfalls that run wherever wrinkled Koʻolau ridges let them flow. One of the larger falls, **Waipuhia Valley Falls**, on the left side of Nuʻuanu Valley just before you reach the Pali Lookout, is nicknamed "**Up-side Down Falls**" because its waters are often blown straight back up a cliff and turn into mist before they can reach a precipice below. (Waipuhia, by the way, means "blown water.")

The **Nuʻuanu Pali Lookout** lies above a well-marked road spur just off the Pali Highway, and is perhaps the most written-about scenic spot on Oahu. Tour buses and rental cars often clog the parking lot near this famous precipice, but it's still a magical spot. Gale-force winds rush up this Koʻolau palisade and literally stand one's hair on end.

The view of Oahu's windward side is magnificent: alpine-looking peaks rise behind and below like church spires, green and yellow banana groves ripple far below like breezy stands of wheat, flashy subdivisions are reduced to neat map grids, and tiny ship dots at sea seem to be steaming toward an unreachable horizon. From here, the Pali Highway continues down to the windward side and the towns of Kailua and Kaneʻohe.

Since the early 19th century, guidebooks have anointed this spot as Oahu's number one not-to-be-missed tourist attraction, and it does indeed rank among the best scenic points in Hawaii.

**Craters and correspondents:** Another relaxing Honolulu ramble is up to the two areas above town – wedged between Nuʻuanu and Manoa Valleys – commonly known as **Punchbowl** and **Tantalus-Round Top**. Once a site of human sacrifices, **Punchbowl Crater** was known to Hawaiians as *Puowaina,* or "the hill for placing (of sacrifices)." Like Diamond Head and Koko Head craters, Punchbowl – which looms just above downtown Honolulu at the top of

Ward Avenue – emerged during Oahu's most recent eruption phase about 150,000 years ago, pushed upward by volcanic action through a vast coral plain that had built up around this side of the Ko'olau Mountains.

Today Punchbowl is the location of the **National Memorial Cemetery of the Pacific**, where more than 21,000 servicemen from World Wars I and II, and the Korean and Vietnam Wars, are buried. The veterans' small flat white headstones, level with Punchbowl's expanse of grass, stretch across the crater's 112-acre (45-hectare) floor.

Annual services on Easter, Veterans' Day and Memorial Day honor the soldiers buried here and another 26,280 listed in a **Courts of the Missing** monument on Punchbowl's interior *Ewa* slope.

The most famous person buried here was not a conventional war casualty. Rather, he was a journalist whose ability to write about the average foot-slogging GI made him one of the most widely-read combat correspondents ever published. **Ernest Taylor "Ernie" Pyle**, whose remains rest at grave site number D109, was 44 when, near the end of the war in 1945, he was killed by Japanese machine gun fire on a small Pacific islet west of Okinawa. Although he was originally buried in a wartime military cemetery on Okinawa, his remains were transferred along with those of other soldiers to Punchbowl in 1949, when the National Memorial Cemetery of the Pacific was officially opened.

At the spot where Pyle died, a special tablet said: "At this spot the 77th Infantry Division lost a buddy." But in Punchbowl his marker is like any other serviceman's. His burial here was allowed because he had served in the US Navy during World War I. Cemetery officials estimate that as many as 50,000 people a month visit his grave. Several large and finely-detailed ceramic mosaic maps inside the memorial building chronologically recount famous Pacific battles fought during the past century.

**To the top:** From Punchbowl's mountain-side entrance, Puowaina Drive crosses a bridge over Prospect Street and drifts along a steep valley through one of Oahu's few Hawaiian homestead communities. This is **Papakolea**, a neighborhood where persons of at least half-Hawaiian blood are allowed to lease homesites at a nominal fee established by Congress in the Hawaiian Homes Act of 1920. This neighborhood sits beside and below Makiki Heights and Tantalus, two of the island's most exclusive and expensive residential areas.

At the top of Puowaina Drive turn right onto **Tantalus Drive** – named after a Greek god by the students of Punahou School – a winding mountain road that twists through some of Oahu's largest *kama'aina* estates on **Tantalus**. Follow the road to some of the coolest and most panoramic vantage points on this side of the island. Hike one of the many marked trails near the mountain's 2,013-ft (610-meter) peak into groves of bamboo and fern. At the top, Tantalus Drive connects with **Round Top Drive**, which descends down the Diamond Head side to Makiki and Punahou.

There are at least a dozen knock-out viewpoints on Tantalus, but locals seem

Statue of Mary on the Pali Highway.

to agree that the best one – a panorama from Diamond Head to Pearl Harbor and the Wai‘anae Mountains beyond – is from **Pu‘u‘ualaka‘a State Park**, on Tantalus's *makai-Diamond Head* flank.

A few hairpin turns below this peak is a straight stretch of Round Top Drive beside a lava rock wall, with an unobstructed postcard view of Diamond Head and lush **Manoa Valley** below, famous for its rainbows and predictable curtains of cooling rain. (Advisory: the view from here is spectacular at night, but there have been theft and robbery problems at this scenic turnoff.) Down below in Makiki Heights is the **Contemporary Museum**, located in a beautiful setting with a gift shop and café.

**Manoa Valley:** Honolulu's three M's – Makiki, Mo‘ili‘ili, and Manoa – occupy areas just *mauka*, or mountain side, of Ala Moana and Waikiki. Snug against the Ko‘olau Mountains, Manoa Valley is a cool retreat favored by *kama‘aina;* Makiki and Mo‘ili‘ili lie at its mouth.

**Makiki**, named after a type of stone used as weights for octopus lures, is largely a residential neighborhood of flats and heights just below Round Top and a nice warm-up for the pleasantly cool and neighborly charms of adjacent Manoa. It's a prime example of what other parts of Honolulu may look like in a few years if property development keeps pace with the city's growing population. Condominium sprouting is at its vertical best here.

**Manoa**, meaning "vast," has long been preferred by islanders as a residential refuge from the heat and hassle of concrete Honolulu. Indeed, residents of both Manoa and Nu‘uanu consider their valleys the closest one can get to Eden – both are verdantly green, and consistently wet – and still manage to be near shopping centers and bus lines, with clear television reception.

Near the entrance to Manoa Valley, at the corner of Punahou and Beretania streets, missionary descendants built **Central Union Church** in 1924 which, like Kawaiaha‘o Church, is more Boston than Honolulu in its architecture.

Up Punahou Street, just before rising into Manoa proper, is the educational apple of every missionary descendant's eye: the private **Punahou School**, once called Oahu College, which the Rev. Hiram Bingham and his colleagues established in 1841 for the education of missionary and Hawaiian royal children; land for the school was given to the mission at the request of the powerful and Christianized Queen Ka‘ahumanu. The site of a well-known freshwater spring, the school became known as *Punahou*, or "new spring."

That same spring still bubbles fresh water into a pond that encircles a lovely memorial chapel on campus. The chapel's entrance doors, fashioned of honey-grained *koa* and embellished with copper repoussé panels created by artists Jean Charlot and Evelyn Giddings, lead into a stained glass refuge inspired, according to artist Erica Karawina, by a Eugenia Sheppard poem that sings of "trumpeting rubies, redder than fire." In all, some 20 lancets, 10 to a side, play hot and cool colors upon the *koa*, lava and plaster of this circular chapel designed by architect Vladimir Ossipoff.

Memorial
statuary in
Punchbowl.

The chapel can be visited, but arrangements should be made in advance.

If possible, pass by Punahou School's stone walls on the rare summer evening when the school's gigantic night-blooming cereus open like petaled moons. This cactus flower (*Hylocereus undatus*), a prickly climber brought from Acapulco by a visiting sea captain in the early 1800s, has foot-wide blossoms that open only at night – from about 8 pm until morning's warmth wilts them into a droopy daytime sleep.

Half a mile or so beyond Punahou is the junction of Manoa and East Manoa roads. From this point, the valley is a traveler's fancy. Branching left, **Manoa Road** leads to the back of the valley, passing through the vast **Paradise Park**, a commercially-operated retreat full of exotic birds. Beyond the park is the University of Hawaii's verdant **Lyon Arboretum**, established in 1907. Nearly 6,000 plants grow on the arboretum's 120 acres (48 hectares), rising from 300 ft (90 meters) to 1,800 ft (550meters) above sea level.

Cool **Manoa Falls** – where 160 to 200 inches of rain a year quench the wild thirsts of mountain apples, guavas, passion fruit and thimble berries – bounce rainbows at the headwaters of Manoa Stream. **East Manoa Road** leads to quiet strolls through the **Manoa Chinese Cemetery** near its end.

It was in Manoa Valley that Hawaii's powerful Queen Ka'ahumanu – favorite wife of Kamehameha the Great – died just before dawn on June 5, 1832. According to missionary accounts, as Ka'ahumanu was nearing death, she asked to be taken to her favorite valley of Manoa. There, in a small summer cottage, the queen died on a bed of fragrant *maile* and *awapuhi* (ginger), covered by velvet.

**Books and rainbows:** At the mouth of this easy-going vale is the center of higher education in Hawaii, the 300-acre (120-hectare) **University of Hawaii at Manoa** campus attended by some 19,000 full-time students. This institute has the usual academic and post-adolescent aura typical of any uni-

Hala and hala sculpture, Punahou School.

versity, except that its student body, like Hawaii, is generally more colorful, casual – T-shirts, walking shorts and sandals – and ethnically mixed than elsewhere. Lacking a mascot, they're known as the Rainbows, or 'Bows.

At the **East-West Center** – a federally-funded institute on the UH campus to promote understanding in the Pacific Basin – are a Thai pavilion personally presented and dedicated by King Bhumibol Adulyadej of Thailand in 1967; a **Center for Korean Studies** building handpainted in the busy and intricate style of Seoul-area Yi Dynasty palaces; and the center's main building, **Jefferson Hall**, which is fronted by large Chinese dog-faced lions and backed by a Japanese garden rich in sculptured grass, well-placed stones, *bonsai* trees and a lily pond full of nibbling *koi*.

On either end of Jefferson Hall are two murals. One, representing the West, is by prolific local artist Jean Charlot. (Another important Charlot mural may also be seen in **Bachman Hall**, the

University's main administration building.) The second, reflecting an Eastern perspective, is by Affandi of central Java, Indonesia.

The town of **Mo'ili'ili** – the "pebble lizard" destroyed by Hi'iaka, Pele's younger sister – is a busy place of typical university-related haunts like pubs, cheap places to eat, and a cinema showing art and high-class films.

Another area worthy of afternoon explorations is **Kaimuki** (properly though rarely pronounced kah-ee-moo-kee), adjacent to Mo'ili'ili. *Kaimuki*, the *ti* oven, is mentioned in early Hawaiian chants as a place where mysterious *menehune* toasted *ti* leaves. Its character seemingly frozen somewhere in the late 1940s, Kaimuki (locals usually say, kye-moo-kee) is a wonderful urban spot on the back side of Diamond Head, rich in red dirt, mango trees, the small and respected **Chaminade University**, and a virtual United Nations of restaurants and shops. Continuing towards Koko Head, Kaimuki – the remnants of a small shield volcano – slides down into

Affandi's mural, Jefferson Hall, East-West Center.

the high status, high priced neighborhood of Kahala.

Following Hawaii's statehood in 1959, this part of the island became increasingly residential as Honolulu proper began running out of living space. Up until then, the now-expensive Kahala and Hawaii Kai areas were noted for vegetable gardens and piggeries; the rest of this southern crescent was given over to dry scrub and sunburn. Today, this area of Oahu is a sprawling sequence of roof-to-roof housing tracts and shopping centers – most of them on land parcels which are leased from large private estates that control this side of the island.

In **Kahala**, at the end of ritzy Kahala Avenue, is the **Kahala Hilton** – part of the international, not domestic – Hilton hotel group. Built in 1959, the Kahala has become the Hawaiian escape for those with the money and position, whether Hollywood celebrity or international leader. A walk along Kahala Beach towards Diamond Head leads past rather pricey beachfront estates. In the other direction is the **Wai'alae Country Club**. Every January, the hotel and country club are the center of the golfing world when the Hawaiian Open PGA Golf Tournament is held on the club's manicured fairways and greens. Not bad, say old-timers, for the site of a dusty old Hawaiian fishing village.

Further along the **Kalaniana'ole Highway**, towards Oahu's southeastern tip, is the vast bedroom community of **Hawaii Kai**, created by the late billionaire industrialist Henry J. Kaiser during the early 1960s. This expanding spread of townhouses, condominiums, tract homes and a private inland waterway was formerly a parched expanse of *kiawe*, red earth and a shallow, neglected Hawaiian fishpond called *Kuapa*. Today, about 30,000 people make this dry coast and the connecting valleys home.

To be near his work, Kaiser built a home on Portlock Road below Koko Head. Nothing modest, **Kaiser Estate** was a flamingo pink palace (pink was his wife's favorite color), complete with a principal mansion and several other

The University of Hawaii, Manoa.

190

luxurious buildings. Kaiser's Texas buddy, President Lyndon Johnson stayed here in 1968 and exchanged war stories with fellow presidents Park Chung Hee of South Korea and Nguyen Van Thieu of the Republic of South Vietnam. Two years before that parley, Jacqueline Kennedy and her kids were tenants during a frolic-filled summer.

But even palaces, however pink, fade into memories, and in 1971 the Kaiser Estate was bought by two millionaire bachelor brothers from Oklahoma, and then again in 1988 by a Japanese tycoon for $42 million.

Hawaii Kai disappears as Kalaniana'ole Highway cuts over a saddle ridge at **Koko Head** – named either for the red earth common in the area, or for the blood (*koko*) of a man bitten by a shark long ago – and peaks above **Hanauma Bay**. The remnant of an eroded extinct volcanic tuff cone, Hanauma, "the curved bay," is now an emerald blue *cul-de-sac* chock full of protected but bold Hawaiian fish. Elvis Presley's 1961 movie *Blue Hawaii* helped make Hanauma Bay popular. Too popular, in fact. As many as 10,000 people visit the bay daily. Recent restrictions on access by taxis and tour buses, as well as car parking, have eased the congestion. Despite the crowds, worldly snorkelers still proclaim this bay as unsurpassed.

After Hanauma Bay, the feeling of a city evaporates. From along the highway on this jagged parkland's surf-pounded cliffs, other islands – Lanai, Molokai, Maui, and on clear days, the Big Island – loom out of the sea like blue ghosts.

At the next cliffside turn, *makai* of **Koko Crater**, packs of tourists wait at a parking lot lookout to hear the wheezing of the **Halona Blowhole**, a lava formation that does a brief geyser-like shtick at odd moments when the right incoming sea swell pushes up through its underwater entrance. Appropriately, *halona* means "peering place."

Just beyond, before one rounds the point to Oahu's windward side, is **Sandy Beach**, a local favorite for body surfing, kite flying, people watching, and an occasional whale-sighting in season.

Beautiful
Hanauma
Bay.

# WINDWARD OAHU

Beyond Koko Head and Sandy Beach, the highway cuts inland and upwards. At the crest, like a Panavision film, windward Oahu unfolds in one of the more beautiful Hawaiian vistas.

Directly below the lookout parking lot is **Makapu'u Beach Park**, bounded by rough open seas, sheer black cliffs, and hill-sized dunes. The rocky summit on the right is **Makapu'u Point**, where a white lighthouse is perched on the craggy black lava palisade.

Makapu'u is prized for the occasionally brutal but beautiful form of its bodysurfing waves. Lifeguards are stationed on the beach, but inexperienced bodysurfers should take extreme caution when in the water.

Off Makapu'u are two small tuff cone islands – a small, greenish-black one in the fore-ground called **Kaohikaipu Island**, and a larger, adze-shaped one properly named **Manana**, but more commonly known as **Rabbit Island**, not because of its slight rabbit's head shape, but because it was formerly a rabbit-raising farm. Rabbits no longer live on this 67-acre (27-hectare) island, which is now a state-protected and off-limits sanctuary for seabirds.

On Makapu'u's inland side, if wind conditions are amenable, brilliantly colored hang gliders may be seen floating in thermal currents that sweep up the face of sheer 1,200-ft (360-meter) cliffs. Some hang gliders have maneuvered their crafts out to Rabbit Island on "inter-island flights."

Below that neck-twisting focal point are perhaps more intelligent animals: killer whales, porpoises, penguins, seals and other such aquatic creatures at **Sea Life Park**, an arena-aquarium similar to such complexes in Florida and California. Besides being a tourism venue of aquanautics, Sea Life Park also maintains a wildlife rehabilitation and recovery unit. The professional oceanographer might be more interested in the **Makai Research Pier**, with its 700-ft (210-meter) pier and boathouse nearby.

This facility conducts undersea explorations with research submarines. Their world, however, is not open to the public.

**Misty mountains:** For the next 30 miles (50 km) or so, prepare to be dominated literally and psychologically by the peaks, *pali* and hypnotic lights and shadows that shift and play off the **Ko'olau Mountain Range**. Like a massive curtain that parts now and then to expose lone spires, fluted columns, crystal falls and little green valleys, these cliffs dwarf most other physical things in their vicinity. Meaning "windward," the Ko'olau wear mist as a lei, rainbows like jewels, and rainfall like running tears – as the Hawaiians like to poetize, *lei i ka noe.* On and on they stretch – from Makapu'u to the North Shore – like a chain of otherworldly cathedrals.

If you're looking for a beach with plenty of empty space, an awesome mountain *pali* backdrop, and warm waters to soak a jet-lagged body, **Waimanalo Beach** has few peers. It's one of those gems typically overlooked by visitors as they slice past in rental cars.

**Waimanalo** is as local a town as anywhere in Hawaii, a place where the rural Hawaiian lifestyle is sustained. In addition to its rodeo competitors, Waimanalo is noted for the deftness of its sumo wrestlers. Competing in Japan under the Japanese name Akebono ("sunrise") and that country's *yokozuna* (sumo grand champion) is Waimanalo's Chad Rowen. Also from Waimanalo was one of Hawaii's finest musicians, Gabby Pahinui.

Beyond Waimanalo and **Bellows Air Force Station** rises the peak of 1,643-ft (499-meter) **Olomana**, a mount that might look more appropriate covered with snow in the Swiss Alps. Named for a giant who jumped from Kauai to this peak, Olomana casts morning shadows at **Maunawili**, an emerald vale where two parting lovers inspired Queen Lili'uokalani to write her timeless song "Aloha 'Oe." But just minutes past Olomana, Maunawili, and their fragrant cow paddocks and banana groves, are Oahu's second and third most-populated towns – **Kailua** and **Kane'ohe** – which unfurl in a hybrid of modern suburbia and lost-in-time atmosphere.

If entering Kailua town around sunset, pause for a moment under the banyan tree on the corner of Oneawa Street and Ku'ulei Road. Scores of mynah birds will be gathering to roost for the night, kicking up a squawking fuss. A fine, swimmable beach stretches the length of **Kailua Bay**, but the most convenient access to this wide swathe of residential sand is at **Kailua Beach Park**, just before the little and nearly-obscured community of **Lanikai**. Blessed with fine winds and water, Kailua ("two seas or currents") is the site of international windsurfing competitions.

Leaving Kailua, one meets up with the **Pali Highway** from Honolulu descending down the mountains near here.

Kane'ohe town is becoming a bedroom community with residential subdivisions that hug the bay shore. Nearby, the large **Kane'ohe Marine Corps Air Station** dominates scenic **Mokapu Peninsula**. A small island, **Mokuolo'e (Coconut Island)**, is the site of the **Kualoa Beach.**

**Hawaii Institute of Marine Biology**, run by the University of Hawaii. Once polluted, **Kane'ohe Bay** is now a popular recreation area, protected by outlying reefs and good for most water sports, especially for snorkeling and diving. (Kane'ohe is an unusual name, meaning "bamboo husband." One interpretation says that a woman of ancient times compared the cruelty of her husband with the cutting edge of a bamboo knife.)

Area cultural attractions include a masterly ceramic tile mural by senior island artist Juliette May Fraser at the **Benjamin Parker Elementary School** (on Waikalua Road), and a serene **Byodo-In Temple** that glows under 2,000-ft (600-meter) Ko'olau cliffs in 'Ahuimanu Valley. This temple is a termite-proof cement replica of Kyoto's famous Byodo-In Temple of Equality, and is the major structure in the **Valley of the Temples Memorial Park**. A 7-ton bronze bell, great golden Buddha of the Western Paradise, 2-acre reflecting lake, peacocks, swans, ducks, meditation niches and dangling water-falls enhance its imported architecture.

**Ancient aquaculture:** Important culturally and historically are a series of **ancient fishponds** that pepper Windward shores north of Kane'ohe. Oahu once had some 97 such fishponds used by Hawaiians to grow seafood, but now only five are left intact. Four are on this windward coast, and a fifth is at Oki'okiolepe, at Pearl Harbor. The four are to be found at He'eia (just north of Kane'ohe), Kahalu'u, Moli'i (off Kualoa Point) and Huilua (at Kahana Bay).

The splendid **He'eia Fishpond**, on the Kane'ohe side of **Kealohi Point**, is Oahu's biggest. It has a wall 12 ft (3.6 meters) wide and 5,000 ft (1,500 meters) long, and once enclosed an area of 88 acres (35 hectares). In recent years land developers have proposed turning this classical example of Hawaiian engineering into a small-boat marina, but conservationists, historians, and archaeologists are fighting these plans, so far with limited but encouraging success.

North along the Kamehameha Highway, the sought-after "living on the

anikai
each.

easy" notion comes to a sleepy, believable reality as gentle waves lap against fishing boats docked under stilted homes, with sunlight skipping across taro paddies and Hawaiian place names lingering in the mind like poetry: Kahalu'u, Waiahole and Waikane.

In the **Waiahole** and **Waikane valleys** – where taro, orchid, anthurium and vegetable farms still operate – developers proposed a tract of nearly 7,000 expensive homes and commercial facilities on the fertile heights and lowlands. But valley residents managed to stop the encroachment on their rural lifestyle, and, in 1976, the state government bought 600 acres (240 hectares) of the threatened Waiahole Valley and zoned it in a secure agricultural designation, thus protecting it from speculative developments.

At **Kualoa Regional Park**, heads usually crane seaward for long, lingering looks at a small and distinct island known to Hawaiians as **Mokoli'i** (the little *mo'o*, or lizard), long ago nicknamed **Chinaman's Hat** for obvious reasons of resemblance. At low tide, one can easily wade out on the reef to this island, bask under palm trees and photograph the graceful Hawaiian stilts *(ae'o)* and frigate birds *(iwa)* that soar overhead. On shore, the previously-mentioned 124-acre (50 hectare) **Moli'i Fishpond**, easy to find with a 4,000-foot-long (1,200-meter) retaining wall, has been in cultivation for 800 years. It's also a good place to see endangered Hawaiian waterfowl.

Kualoa has long been sacred to the ancient Hawaiians and was favored as a royal residence. Inland is the sweeping **Kualoa Ranch**, the largest of the few working cattle ranches still left on Oahu. Of less interest are the crumbling remains of an old sugar mill up the road, built in the 1860s at a time when the sugar industry was experiencing tough financial times. It soon closed and hasn't been used since 1871.

**Prisoner of passion:** Beyond Ka'a'awa, a false front of another sort sits atop the green promontory **Mahie Point**, which overlooks the *hala* (pandanus or Elementary school, Waimanalo.

196

screwpine) groves, reedy lagoons and whistling ironwood that rim the silent beauty of **Kahana Bay**. There is a rock formation called **Kauhi**, better known as **Crouching Lion** after an entrepreneur renamed it to give his nearby restaurant a romantic name.

From a certain angle, the rock does look somewhat like a lion. According to Hawaiian tradition, Kauhi was a demigod from Tahiti who was imprisoned up there by followers of the fire goddess Pele. One day Kauhi saw Pele's sister, Hi'iaka, and fell in love with her. Trying to break out of his prison to get her, he was frozen in place in his present crouching position. He remains there, a *haole*-misnamed prisoner of passion.

Straw baskets bulging with plump papayas, "alligator pears" (avocados), and Chinese bananas hanging inside weathered wooden stands compete with hanging shell chandeliers for the traveler's dollar along this stretch to **Hau'ula**. Nearby **Sacred Falls**, a not-so-sacred waterfall except for the entry price, is known as **Kaliuwa'a Falls** in Hawaiian. *Kaliuwa'a,* the "canoe leak," was said to be an ancient hangout of the legendary pig god Kamapua'a, who in mythological times assumed the form of a man or pig, depending upon his intentions of the moment.

The half-hour hike to these falls along **Kaluanui Stream** is a bit treacherous at times and prone to flash flooding during the winter rainy season, but it does offer the fragrances and fruits of Java plum, guava, *kukui* and apple trees. The murmuring stream and trail end at a shockingly cool pool deep enough for diving.

North is **La'ie**, a predominantly Mormon community with the chaste-looking **Mormon Temple**, built in 1919 by descendants of missionary Mormons living in this area since 1864. This temple of the Church of Jesus Christ of Latter-Day Saints is closed to non-Mormons.

Also in La'ie are the Hawaii campus of **Brigham Young University**, and a vast "south seas modern" **Polynesian Cultural Center**. This successful tourist complex has been staging tours, shows and luau dinners since 1964. In

Replica of Kyoto's famous Byodo-In Temple of Equality.

show business circles it's considered one of the longest-running sold-out spectaculars in the world. The center's main shows – performed nightly by young Mormon students from Fiji, Samoa, Tahiti, Tonga, Maori New Zealand and Hawaii – are designed, according to brochures, to give visitors a "pure cultural view of Polynesia." That's a lofty goal. Its high ticket prices, its many Hollywood moments and a decidedly Disneyland veneer in its reconstructed Polynesian villages often bring it down to plain show-biz level.

A totally non-commercial but marvelously choreographed show can be enjoyed just off Kamehameha Highway, slightly north of the cultural center. This is scenic **La'ie Point**, at the end of Anemoku and Naupaka streets, where windward waters running hard from the north pound two little offshore isles – **Kukuiho'olua Islet** (on the left) and **Mokualai Islet** (directly off the point's fingertip) – with a frightening and beautiful force, especially in winter.

A floundering tourist attraction sits at the north side of Kahuku town: the **Kahuku Sugar Mill**, until 1971 an operating mill that converted sugar cane into molasses. For several years the mill was open as a 14-acre (5.6-hectare) theme park. All the mill's former flywheels, gears, centrifuges, crusher rollers and steam gauges were color-coded and marked to show mill operations. The park closed in 1982, but has reopened as a small shopping center.

Even more interesting is **Kahuku town** itself, where workers' cafes, grocery stores, *karate dojo* and tiny homes survive much as they did when residents awoke to the mill's morning steam whistle. A walk around this village, where ferns, orchids, succulent jades and donkey's tails hang out of cutaway bleach-bottle planters, is rewarding.

Aquaculture is big business in the Kahuku area. Shrimp, lobsters, and shellfish are cultivated in large ponds. Roadside stands offer the freshest of the best.

**Sunworshippers and surfers:** Where Oahu reverses itself at northernmost Kahuku Point, a few meadow-framed

**The Polynesian Cultural Center...**

moments after Kahuku, the feel of the land changes abruptly. The veil of the Ko'olau Range ends here, and so too the wet, drippy coolness. On the *mauka* side of the highway is a wind farm with 15 wind-driven electric generators, including the world's largest and most powerful windmill, a 3,200-kilowatt turbine with blades 360 ft (109 meters) in diameter, blade tip to blade tip. Alone it generates enough electricity for over a thousand homes.

The first major landmark on the **North Shore** is a huge hotel and golf resort, the **Turtle Bay Hilton Resort and Country Club**. The hotel itself sits on a dramatic point extending into the ocean. It's a great place to watch winter storms.

A few miles farther, **the world's finest surfing waves** crash onto offshore reefs and sandbars: Sunset, Rocky Point, Gas Chambers, the Banzai Pipeline, Waimea Bay, Chun's Reef, Hale'iwa and Avalanche. During spring, summer and fall months, **Waimea Bay** is often as placid as a lake, but when winter storms in the Arctic send wave pulses across the blue Pacific, Waimea Bay and the North Shore take on a mesmerizing fury. (In December 1969, more than 30 homes between Kahuku Point and Hale'iwa were reduced to tinder as monstrous 50-ft (15-meter) waves pounded the North Shore.)

The most jaded surfer will agree that a tubing, top-to-bottom spitter off one of those reefs generates enough adrenaline to keep anybody going through at least a few nervous lifetimes, especially when Waimea Bay is breaking – waves so big that hundreds of people line the road like spectators at gladiatorial finals. The waves are so thunderous that the ground trembles a little bit underfoot. Only the best of surfers paddle out towards the 20- to 30-ft (10-meter) winter swells lifting like glossy black holes on the blue-grey horizon.

A good place to take in Waimea Bay and the North Shore and distant Wai'anae Mountains is from the **Pu'uomahuka Heiau State Monument**, on a 250-ft (75-meter) bluff above the **St Peter & Paul Church**. Turn off

..has been staging shows since 1964.

onto Pupukea Road, at the small supermarket complex. It's about seven-tenths of a mile off upper Pupukea Road.

On top is an ancient *heiau,* one of Oahu's largest, where Hawaiians still leave offerings for the gods, usually lava stones wrapped in sacred *ti* leaves. It was known as **Pu'uomahuka**, the "hill of escape," though historically not for some. In 1794, two – some accounts say three – crew members of Captain Vancouver's ship *Dedalus* were offered in sacrifice at this *heiau* after being captured while filling water barrels at the mouth of the Waimea River.

At the river's mouth into the bay, look for the entrance to **Waimea Falls Park** on the *mauka* side of the road, opposite the beach park. Located at the end of the valley, this is a commercial botanical garden with an admission fee, historical and cultural demonstrations, and a diving demonstration from 55-ft (16.5-meter) walls into the pool below Waimea Falls. It's a worthwhile place for a picnic or carefree roaming down nature trails, as well as an introduction to ancient Hawaiian life and the more traditional forms of the hula.

**Summer and shave ice:** Further down along the North Shore's surfing grounds, a small cement bridge funnels traffic over a little stream into **Hale'iwa** ("house of the frigate bird"), an artsy and funky outpost (but the biggest town on this side of Oahu) where people of all ethnic and life persuasions mingle. Cafes, galleries and shops mix with remnants of the old days, especially the **M. Matsumoto Store**, noted for shave ice.

A good time to visit Hale'iwa is in the middle of summer, at the height of the Japanese Obon season, when the **Hale'iwa Jodo Mission** has its annual festival under summer stars with a unique *Toronagashi,* or floating lanterns ritual, on the east side of **Kaiaka Bay**. The sight of dozens of flickering lanterns – each a farewell light for an ancestor's spirit – floating on the dark sea is poetic. Appropriately, perhaps, Kaiaka means "shadowed sea."

Upon leaving Hale'iwa, there are two options: continue south down Kamehameha Highway through central Oahu and back to Honolulu, or go further east past taro and banana patches to the old plantation town of **Waialua**, with Oahu's second still-operating sugar mill.

Beyond Waialua, on the *mauka* side of Farrington Highway, is the **Mokule'ia Polo Farm**, Hawaii's most-exclusive athletic facility, where visiting teams from North America, Australia, England, and Ireland battle through gentlemanly chukkers of competitive polo (most Sundays between late February and July) against local pony teams. Bring a picnic and settle in; it is a nice way to end a Sunday drive into the country.

Further down the road is the **Dillingham Air Field**, Hawaii's only soaring area, where glider pilots loop and dive in thermal air currents that rise alongside the 2,000-ft (610-meters) Wai'anae *pali* that dominate Peacock Flats.

At the end of the road at Mokule'ia, a foot trail continues on to **Ka'ena Point**. Beyond by foot is the **Wai'anae Coast**. In winter, waves as high as 50 ft (15 meters) have been witnessed off Ka'ena Point. No one has surfed them. Yet.

**Left**, polo at Mokule'ia. **Right**, winter waves.

# CENTRAL OAHU

Urbanized travelers who are so inclined will find the freeways slicing across central Oahu to their liking. Indeed, with the all the housing subdivisions going up in parts of Oahu's interior, one could feel quite at home. From Honolulu proper, it's an idea to first aim west along the **Lunalilo Freeway**, more commonly called the H1, then cut north on the H2 freeway. But before heading into central Oahu proper, there are several places of interest.

In **Moanalua Gardens**, a nice retreat owned by the S.M. Damon Estate and open to the public, huge umbrella-like monkeypod trees rock lazily just off the busy freeway. Behind this popular picnic place is **Moanalua Valley**, an even more spectacular wilderness where three-story high white hibiscus trees shade a flashing stream, ancient Hawaiian petroglyphs and an old medicinal pool surrounded by colorful morning glories, gardenias, ferns and fragrant vines. (The valley is also privately-owned by the Damon Estate, and is open to hikers who call in advance; Twice a month, the Moanalua Gardens Foundation offers guided hikes.)

The Moanalua area was probably named for two ancient encampments where travelers between Honolulu and Ewa could rest. A nearby field called Pueohulunui (meaning "much-feathered owl") was said to be a place where owls from Kaua'i and Ni'ihau came to participate in a big battle of owls.

Hard to miss on a ridge overlooking the freeway is the big **Tripler Army Medical Center**, a ripe pink structure built in 1948 and the largest military hospital in the Pacific. The 14-story hospital was named after General Charles Stuart Tripler, a major general who served as medical director of the Army of the Potomac in the Civil War. (He also wrote the army's first standard manual on the medical examination of military recruits.)

Looking like the rusting metal sta-

**Veteran and Japanese tourists, Pearl Harbor.**

dium that it actually is, the 50,000-seat **Aloha Stadium** is Oahu's prime outdoor venue for major athletic and other large events. Home of the annual Hula Bowl football game between collegiate all-stars, Aloha Stadium vendors hawk Chinese crack seed and *saimin* noodles along with the usual Yankee hot dogs and hamburgers. On weekends, when there are no games, Honolulu's largest swap meet, or flea market, is held in its parking lot.

Beyond the stadium loom the west, middle and east lochs of **Pearl Harbor** – named for the pearl oysters once found here – and the harbor towns of '**Aiea** and **Pearl City**, known mostly for their shopping centers and housing subdivisions.

**Historical harbor:** Pearl Harbor has been well-known since the morning of December 7, 1941, when Japanese dive bombers devastated the US Pacific fleet at anchor, and at ease, here. The *USS Arizona* **Memorial**, the famous monument to that "day of infamy," as President Franklin D. Roosevelt called it, is a radiant memorial that straddles the hulk of the *USS Arizona,* parts of which can be seen above the water.

Inside are the remains of 1,100 men who died when a series of Japanese torpedoes and aerial bombs sank the battleship. Designed by Honolulu architect Alfred Preis, the memorial was made possible in part by a benefit concert staged in 1961 by Elvis Presley. The concert raised over $60,000 for the memorial's fund. A museum, a bookstore, and a film occupy visitors awaiting a Navy launch to the memorial.

Adjacent to the Arizona Memorial visitors' center is the *USS Bowfin* **Submarine Museum and Park**, a privately-operated attraction well worth the visit, especially as it's but five minutes walk away. Would-be submariners and the curious can check out defused torpedoes, descend into and walk through a completely refurbished World War II diesel electric submarine – the *Bowfin,* credited with 44 ship sinkings in nine patrols – and study the interior of a Japanese one-man suicide torpedo-submarine. Exhibits trace the exploits and

*ourists nside the ISS Arizona Memorial.*

hardware of "the silent service" from World War I through the nuclear submarine age.

Another monument, considerably lower in profile and cost, is on **Ford Island** alongside the rusting hulk of the *USS Utah*. Civilian visitors, however, can visit the site only if accompanied by a member or dependent of the US military. Authorities at neighboring Hickam Air Force Base have also not made a big attraction a plaque that marks the spot where America's *Apollo 11* astronauts first touched earth after their historic walk on the moon in July 1969.

**Central plateau:** Continuing north on the H2 freeway, Oahu's central plateau rises gradually until reaching the **Schofield Barracks** army post and **Wahiawa**, the highest residential community in elevation on Oahu.

Wahiawa ("place of noise") can be bypassed altogether by staying on Highway 90, which separates the town from Schofield Barracks (home of the "Tropic Lightning" 25th Light Infantry Division"). Others might care to stop in Wahiawa to take a look at the **Healing Stones**. The stones sit on a simple small altar inside a concrete building on California Street. During the late 1920s, pilgrims regularly visited these stones, which according to one legend were two sisters from the island of Kauai who flew here and were converted by greater powers into stone.

Other myths attribute other origins to these stones but, whatever the explanations, they are still thought to emanate healing powers. Offerings in the form of flowers and *ti* leaves are regularly left by believers. Also in Wahiawa is the fine **Wahiawa Botanic Garden**.

On the north side of Wahiawa, to the left side of Kamehameha Highway and just beyond Whitmore Avenue, are sacred stones of a different sort. These are the **Birth Stones of Kukaniloko**. This eucalyptus-fringed spot in a pineapple field clearing has been venerated by Hawaiians as far back as the 12th century. Wives of high-ranking chiefs bore their children on these stones' gently curved surfaces. Attendant chiefs, high

**Aerial view of Aloha Stadium.**

204

priests and physicians would gather round the infant and, during an impressive ceremony marked by great drums, chants, and offerings, the royal child would be named and the navel cord cut and ritually hidden away.

From this open-air site, in the direction of the Wai'anae Range, you can look up the side of **Leilehua Plain** to the broad **Kolekole Pass**, which was used by low-flying Japanese bombers as a convenient cover and western approach for their sneak attacks on Schofield Barracks and adjacent **Wheeler Army Air Field**. In 1969, when the joint American-Japanese movie *Tora! Tora! Tora!* was being filmed, the sight of Japanese Zeros, Kates and Vals roaring through Kolekole and raining simulated bombs and machine-gun fire on Schofield Barracks and Wheeler Air Force Base was *déjà vu* indeed.

**Plenty pineapples:** Pineapple fields spread out across central Oahu, stretching from the Wai'anae Mountains on one side to the Ko'olau on the other. Europeans first came across pineapples in South America and the West Indies. Quickly adopted as a crop, they were transplanted throughout the world, reportedly in Hawaii as early as 1813.

However, the commercial selling of pineapple in Hawaii was not begun until 1899, when Oahu entrepreneur James D. Dole – related to Sanford Dole, one of the businessmen responsible for overthrowing the royal monarchy – planted 60 acres of Wahiawa land with pineapple. Two years later, Dole organized the Hawaiian Pineapple Company, and by 1906 he began building a cannery at Iwilei, near Honolulu Harbor.

A sample of pineapple's diversity is at the **Pineapple Variety Garden**. This garden has many pineapple varieties and other bromeliads, which early Spanish explorers called the *piña*, because its fruit was shaped like a pine cone.

Established in 1954 by Dole's number one competitor, Del Monte, this unpretentious plot of land should not to be confused with the thoroughly commercial and uneducational **Dole Pineapple Pavilion** up the road towards Hale'iwa.

Pineapple fields and the Kolekole Pass.

# OAHU'S WEST SIDE

Oahu's West Side, or **Wai'anae Coast**, is perhaps the most maligned and misunderstood area of Oahu. It is true that this 20-mile (32-km) coastline is hotter, dustier, and drier than the rest of the island, but its rugged character has much natural and cultural beauty to offer the tolerant and adventurous traveler.

This side of the island lacks the usual commercial tourist attractions, with the exception of some large commercial luau, and because many of its residents are lower middle-class working people, tourism promoters typically avoid its more subtle attractions and tougher, country character.

Yet changes are unavoidable. At its southern end, where Wai'anae meets the flat 'Ewa plains west of Honolulu, a so-called "second city" is taking form, intended to relieve urban Honolulu's congestion, and to offer Oahu a second resort area outside of Waikiki.

Question a long-time resident of **Nanakuli, Ma'ili, Wai'anae** or **Makaha** about the West Side, and they'll spend hours sharing why it's paradise to them. "It's the closest thing to an unspoiled Hawaiian place on this island," says a truck driver from Lualualei. And a Nanakuli elder states flatly that "you've never been to a real luau until you've been to a big one on this side." Indeed, big wedding and first birthday luau hosted on this side of Oahu are legendary, and – often remembered by the number of *kalua* pigs and kegs of beer consumed by friends and relatives.

**Sugar shack flash:** As island-style a place as any to prepare for a West Side tour is the town of **Waipahu**, which is just past **Pearl City** and a quick freeway-ramp dash off the H1 freeway. Waipahu is Oahu's last big town before the road hooks around the southern end of the Wai'anae Range. In fact, Waipahu is not even on the Wai'anae Coast, nor especially close. Yet it's about here that the character of Oahu shifts from urban to country.

To get into the properly Hawaiian

mood, tune the car radio to station KCCN (AM 1420, FM 100.3), probably the world's only all-Hawaiian and island music station. Listen to island folk singer Liko Martin sing "Nanakuli Blues" – "I gonna get my *ka'a/* Gonna *hele* too faah/ I'm never coming back again... Birds all along/ Sunlight at dawn/ Singing Nanakuli blues."

Waipahu, which means "bursting water" and was once home to Ka'ahupahau, the shark goddess of Pearl Harbor, is also the home of Hawaii's only country music radio station, one of Oahu's last two working sugar mills (the other is at Waialua, on the North Shore), and a large Filipino community that sustains Oahu's agriculture.

A Honolulu newspaper reporter once described Waipahu town as "an old Elia Kazan movie set run over by a truck. Or maybe two." Maybe. When the red dust kicked up by trucks hauling cane settles, Waipahu is one of the last places where you can see, smell and feel an old-time sugar company town. Nearly everywhere, the sweet-and-sour smell of processed sugar cane lingers in the air.

Until the middle 1970s, Waipahu and the neighboring townships of **'Ewa, Honouliuli** and **One'ula** were devoted to the growing and milling of sugar cane; but today these lands of green, waving and tassel-topped cane are being phased out, plowed under, paved over and carved into the checkerboard subdivisions of the planned West Oahu second city and hotel resort, stretching from Pearl City to Makakilo north of Barbers Point.

The **Ko 'Olina Resort** already has the requisite golf course and is the first of several planned hotels to be clustered around artificial lagoons.

Each beach along this blazing coast from 'Ewa into Wai'anae has its character and devotees: **'Ewa Beach Park**, for example, is famed for its abundance of *limu* (also called *ogo* in Japanese) or edible seaweed. From its shallow waters Japanese, Hawaiian and Korean women sometimes pluck bags of this green delicacy, which is rich in natural salts and iodine. Favored by surfers, **Kahe** is another beach area just north of

_eft,
**lowers for
**he visitors.**

Barbers Point, past Ko ʻOlina and opposite a Hawaiian Electric Company power plant on the main road, **Farrington Highway**. This spot is formally known as the **Kahe Point Beach Park**, but locals call it **Tracks** because remnants of the old Oahu Railway and Land Company's narrow gauge train tracks still parallel the highway northward.

**Sunny and rugged:** A little over 35,000 people live along Waiʻanae's jagged shorelines and dry, rugged mountain slopes. In ancient times the west coast of Oahu was was known as a major center of Hawaiian civilization, probably because of the rich fishing grounds in the clear offshore waters between Nanakuli and Kaʻena Point.

It was here, according to oral traditions, that the demigod Maui lived and first learned to make fire after he arrived in Hawaii. All along this coast, myths refer to the infamous man-pig Kamapuaʻa, renowned throughout Hawaii as a god who both charmed and harassed mortal worshippers with his capricious antics. As a pig, he's also noted for the valleys and springs he created while digging at roots.

The stories are many, but so too are the physical remnants of these myths. A good seaside example is the **Kuʻilioloa Heiau** on the extreme fingertip of **Kaneʻilio Point**, on the south side of **Pokaʻi Bay**. Surrounded by water on three sides, this *heiau* of coral and lava rock was built in the 15th or 16th century in honor of Kuʻilioloa, a giant dog that often protected travelers; this area reportedly was populated in ancient times by cannibals preying on passersby.

According to J. Gilbert McAllister, who wrote a Bishop Museum survey entitled *Archaeology of Oahu* (1933), these highwaymen apparently hid behind high ridges and ambushed unwary victims who came their way. The largest town on this coast, **Makaha**, meaning "fierce or savage," takes its name from these marauders.

"For many years these people preyed upon the traveler," McAllister wrote, "until at one time men from Kauaʻi, hairless men (*Olohe*) came to this beach.

**Rock formations, upper Makakilo.**

They were attacked by these cannibals, but defeated them, killing the entire colony. Since then the region has been safe for traveling."

Several reefs and points of land along this coast have long been favored as surfing spots, but perhaps the most famous of all is **Kepuhi Point** at Makaha, where since 1952 the annual Makaha International Surfing Championships were held. In recent years, however, most major big-wave surfing contests have been held on Oahu's vicious North Shore, particularly at the Banzai Pipeline and Sunset Beach surf breaks.

Nevertheless, an "oldie-but-goodie" surfing event at Makaha has caught the fancy of wave-riding old-timers: the annual **Buffalo's Longboard Contest**, begun in 1978. Makaha Beach commander Buffalo Keaulana and other local bruddahs organized it to renew interest in a cruisy style of surfing in vogue during the 1950s and 1960s.

**Royal sacrifices:** Wander into the back reaches of **Makaha Valley** to the spectacular **Kane'aki Heiau**, restored by the National Park Service, Bishop Museum and the Makaha Historical Society. This 17th-century *heiau*, one of the best-preserved on Oahu, was rebuilt entirely by hand, using *pili* grass, *ohia* timber and lava stones much as they were utilized by ancient craftsmen. Originally, this was an agricultural *heiau* dedicated to the god Lono, but archaeologists speculate that Kane'aki may have been reconditioned in 1796 by Kamehameha the Great as a *luakini heiau*, or *heiau* of human sacrifice, in honor of his war god Kukailimoku.

At the time, Kamehameha was amassing a huge fleet in the Makaha area in preparation for an invasion of Kauai. The fleet was forced back to Oahu by gale-force winds and raging seas, and perhaps people were sacrificed near here to appease the angry and unhelpful gods.

This *heiau* is tucked away in a spectacular setting alongside **Makaha Stream** in Makaha Valley. Entrance to the *heiau* is limited, from 10am to 2pm daily except Monday. Head up into Makaha Valley towards the **Sheraton**

urfing with ongboards, Makaha.

**Makaha Resort**, a popular golf retreat, and continue through the golf course to the gate for Mauna Olu Estates. The guard will direct you to the *heiau*.

Another famous site you can walk into is about 3 miles (5 km) north of Makaha. This is **Kaneana**, the **Cave of Kane**. Although this cave is 100 ft (30 meters) high in places and about 450 ft (135 meters) deep, it is not, as some people suspect, a lava tube. Rather, it was carved out by sea action some 150,000 years ago when its entrance was at or below sea level. According to an old local story, this cave was occupied by a fierce character, Kamohoali'i, who was able to alternate at will between being a human and a shark.

Kamohoali'i had a fondness for human flesh, so in his or her guise as a mortal, he or she would periodically jump people and then drag them into this cave for dinner. Eventually, this human disguise was discovered and Kamohoali'i had to flee into the sea, but was captured and destroyed later by vengeful Makua residents.

**Makua Beach** is the photogenic area where much of the epic motion picture *Hawaii*, based on James Michener's novel of the same name, was filmed in 1965. Film producers recreated an entire set on this beach representing the old Maui whaling town of Lahaina. That block-long set has since been carted away, but the same spectacular backdrop remains.

A few moments later, Farrington Highway ends and briefly becomes a road which, in turn, terminates at **Keawa'ula Bay**, a favorite board- and body-surfing spot known to old-timers as **Yokohama Bay**. This sandy playground received the Japanese name at the turn of the century, when the Oahu Railway train between 'Ewa and Hale'iwa would stop here to let off Japanese fishermen who favored the fishing at Keawa'ula. Nobody knows who actually coined the term "Yokohama Bay," but the name stuck and later became well known in surfing circles because of popular left-slide waves that leap off a shallow reef on the bay's south side.

Snaking across the ground on the *mauka* side of the road are low stone walls, built earlier this century when cattle were held here while awaiting transport by train. Follow the mountain slopes up to their summits, where the geodesic domes of the US Air Force's **Ka'ena Point Satellite Tracking Station** are perched.

Beyond Yokohama Bay, the landscape loses its sandy character and turns into a jangle of black lava, thorny scrub brush and the desolation of **Ka'ena Point**. Like a beak or an arrow, Ka'ena points slightly to the northwest and the island of Kauai, and can be traversed only on foot. Continuing further on, around Ka'ena Point would lead to the North Shore.

Said to be named for the brother or cousin of Pele, in ancient times Hawaiians were reluctant to cross it. Besides being Oahu's western frontier, Ka'ena Point, according to Hawaiian traditions, was a place from which souls departed from earth – the good to the right, and others to the left.

**Fishing at Yokohama Bay.**

# THE LEEWARD ISLANDS

For most travelers, Honolulu ends at the sharp beaky tip of Ka'ena Point. Unknown to many, however, even to most Honolulu residents, is that the city of Honolulu is the most far-flung city in the world. Officially, Honolulu's jurisdiction includes 593 sq. miles (1,542 sq. km) of land on Oahu, plus dozens of smaller points of land that stretch some 1,367 nautical miles (2,200 km) to the northwest.

These shoals, atolls and desert isles have names like Nihoa, Necker, French Frigate Shoals, Gardiner Pinnacles, Maro Reef, Laysan, Lisianski, Pearl and Hermes Reef and Kure Atoll. The better-known Midway Islands are within Honolulu's sprawling city limits, but they were put under the jurisdiction of the United States Navy just after the turn of the century.

Some 2,000 Navy personnel and dependents, and hundreds of thousands of goony birds live at Midway, but the other islets are uninhabited, save for Tern Island at French Frigate Shoals, which supports an airstrip and Loran navigation station maintained by the US Coast Guard.

Now and then cruise yachts put into a protected lagoon on one of these islands but, except for periodic inspection visits by the Coast Guard and state wildlife officials, the only land life these islets see are millions of squawking seabirds, Hawaiian monk seals and occasional green sea turtles. They are oases of peace and solitude.

Among the interesting birds that populate these islands and excite ornithologists are Hawaiian noddy terns, sooty terns, red-footed and blue-faced boobies, Laysan albatrosses, shearwaters, frigate birds, wandering tattlers, Pacific golden plovers, Laysan honey eaters, bristle-thighed curlews and Laysan teals (said to be the rarest duck – not only in Hawaii – but in the world).

These far-flung islands often are referred to as the Leeward Islands, but experts on the subject note that they should be properly called the Northwestern Hawaiian Islands. Eight of these islands and reefs have been combined to form the Hawaiian Islands National Wildlife Refuge.

The two closest of these islands, Nihoa and Necker, which are located about 250 miles (402 km) northeast of Honolulu, once supported small groups of pre-contact Hawaiians. Agricultural and temple terraces and house platforms have been discovered on both, and archaeologists from the Bishop Museum have found beautifully carved stone images, stone bowls, adzes, sinkers and other evidence of early human occupation on Necker. These objects may be seen in the Pacific Collection of the Bishop Museum at Honolulu.

Although a shortage of drinking water would make living on these two islands very difficult at best, the proper harvesting of water and food sources would not make this an impossible island fantasy. The two islands certainly are large enough: Nihoa is about a mile long, a quarter of a mile wide, and covers approximately 156 acres (62 hectares). It rises to a maximum elevation of about 900 ft (270 meters).

Necker, on the other hand, is 1,300 yards (1,100 meters) long, covers about 41 acres (16 hectares), and has a maximum elevation of 276 ft (84 meters).

Deserted island fanciers would do well to apply for planning permission now. ∎

Blue-faced boobies on Lisianski Island.

# MAUI

Like voyagers of old, contemporary visitors to Maui might well believe that a shaman has cast a spell over the island. Maui may lack Kauai's idyllic mysticism and the Big Island's primal expansiveness. But there's just something bewitchingly intangible that makes it the most popular of Hawaii's islands after Oahu.

Like Oahu, just half an hour away by jet, Maui began as two separate volcanoes that surfaced, then fused together into Hawaii's second-largest island. The extinct crater area of the older volcano – 'Iao Valley and Pu'u Kukui – is the second-rainiest place in Hawaii, drenched with about 400 inches of rainfall a year. Yet 7 miles away is sunny Ka'anapali Beach, where it hardly ever rains.

The larger part of Maui is Haleakala. This 30,000-ft mountain, measured from its base on the ocean floor, is the earth's largest dormant volcano. (It last erupted in 1790.) Lava flows from Haleakala formed the low-lying isthmus that joins Haleakala and the extinct West Maui volcano. This isthmus gave Maui its uninspired nickname, the "Valley Island."

At the northern end of this isthmus are Kahului, the commercial center and airport, and Wailuku, seat of the county government. But few tourists linger in either place, instead heading south into the rain shadow of Haleakala and the dry, sunny world-class resort of Wailea. Others head to Hana, on Haleakala's wet side at the end of 600-plus curves in the road, or else to Ka'anapali, Hawaii's first planned resort and the place that put Maui on the discerning traveler's map. In fact, Maui has an international name recognition second only to Waikiki.

On a good day, both Oahu and the Big Island are visible from Maui. And everyday, the nearby islands of Molokai and Lanai, and uninhabited Kaho'olawe, all part of Maui County, rise just offshore like close siblings. Sometime back – the number of years doesn't matter – Maui, Molokai and Lanai were one island, when the ocean was lower. Loss of a land bridge assured Molokai and Lanai the isolation that has sustained a rural life-style today. Unfettered by traffic and fastfood strips, Molokai and Lanai are unpretentious and humble counterpoints to a rapidly-changing Hawaii.

<u>Preceding pages</u>: Haleakala National Park; the Hana Coast. <u>Left</u>, catamaran sailing off Ka'anapali.

# HALEAKALA AND UPCOUNTRY

Of the sunrise from atop Maui's Haleakala, Mark Twain wrote: "It was the sublimest spectacle I ever witnessed, and I think the memory of it will remain with me always."

Travelers continue to be awed by the sunrise from the 10,023-ft (3,040 meter) summit of **Haleakala**, meaning "house (used) by the sun." But from a distance, this gently sloping shield volcano – which is dormant, not extinct – lacks pretension. The first European to sight Haleakala was Captain James Cook, sailing southwestward from the Aleutian Islands in 1778. He wrote simply of Haleakala in his diary as, "an elevated hill... whose summit rose above the clouds."

Indeed, as with the Big Island's Mauna Kea and Mauna Loa, also shield volcanoes, Haleakala simply does not look the enormous mountain whose summit is two miles above sea level, and its base another 18,000 ft (5,400 meters) below sea level.

Although some New England missionaries were the first non-Hawaiians to reach the summit in 1828, the exact dimensions of Haleakala weren't fully known until 1841, when an American expedition surveyed the summit crater: 3,000 ft (910 meters) deep and 19 sq. miles (49 sq. km) in area, with a 21-mile (34-km) circumference. As deceptive as Haleakala is from afar, so too the illusion from atop. Distance has no reference, and so Haleakala's crater has no comprehensible scale.

When Mark Twain first visited Maui in 1866, he was a correspondent for a California newspaper and not yet published as a novelist. During his travels throughout Hawaii, Twain wrote humorous and thoroughly subjective travel dispatches bearing Oahu, Big Island and Maui datelines.

The highlight of Twain's trip to Maui – his favorite island – was an excursion to the top of Haleakala. In a later travel book called *Roughing It,* published in 1873, he remembered "we climbed a thousand feet up the side of this isolated colossus one afternoon; then camped, and next day climbed the remaining nine thousand feet, and anchored on the summit, where we built a fire and froze and roasted by turns all night."

Twain and his companions looked down on the inside of the "yawning dead crater, into which we now and then tumbled rocks, half as large as a barrel, from our perch, and saw them go careening down the almost perpendicular sides, bounding three hundred feet at a jump; kicking up dust clouds wherever they struck; diminishing to our view as they sped farther into distance; growing invisible, finally, and only betraying their course by faint little puffs of dust; and coming to a halt at last in the bottom of the abyss, two thousand five hundred feet down from where they started! It was magnificent sport. We wore ourselves out at it."

**House of the sun:** The island's namesake, the demigod Maui, was a magician and mythical figure in Polynesia long before the Hawaiian Islands were

inhabited. According to legend, the sun was fond of sleeping late and then racing across the sky to make up time. With the short days, Hina, mother of Maui, had trouble drying *kapa* cloth that she pounded from the bark of the mulberry.

Noticing that the sun appeared each morning over Haleakala, Maui wove a rope of coconut fiber and climbed up to the crater's edge one night to await dawn. When the sun eventually awoke and began moving overhead, Maui lassoed its rays, tied up the sun, and prepared to kill the sun with a jawbone given to him by Hina. The sun, however, begged for mercy and explained to Maui that without its heat, his mother's *kapa* cloth would never get dry.

No dummy in the face of a mother's potential wrath, Maui spared the sun after it promised him that it would move more slowly across the sky. The lasso was cut and Maui's fiery hostage released. And to this day, the sun still keeps its promise to move slowly across the sky – just in case Maui waits in ambush. For most contemporary travelers watching the sunrise from atop Haleakala, it still moves too fast.

**Satellites and silverswords:** Over half a million people visit **Haleakala National Park** annually, many venturing down by foot or on guided horseback trips into the crater along a 30-mile (50-km) trail system. The National Park Service maintains two campgrounds and three cabins on the crater bottom for visitors. The park extends down Haleakala's southeast flank to Kipahulu and the Seven Pools, embracing along the way the **Kipahulu Valley** with a scientific research reserve of native species, closed to the public. The crater is a fragile wilderness area and hikers should keep to the marked trails.

There are good overlooks of the crater itself at several spots along the way to the summit. On cold days the two visitors' buildings offer protection from the sharp winds. (If making the predawn drive to the summit for sunrise, remember that it will be bitterly cold and windy on top.)

At the **Kalahaku Overlook** one can

*Paniolo in palaka jacket; traditional town of Pa'ia.*

see the famed Haleakala silversword, a remarkable plant of the sunflower family with dagger-shaped silvery leaves. The mature silversword (*Argyroxiphium sandwicense*) stands from 3 to 8 ft (0.9 to 2.4 meters), supporting a central stem covered with yellow and reddish-purple florets. Flowering occurs from June through October and the entire plant dies after a single blooming season, 5 to 20 years after germination.

**Pu'u 'Ula'ula** ("red hill"), the summit of Haleakala, has a space-age tenant. Here at **Science City** – a cluster of government buildings on the crater rim – military scientists track satellites across the sky and bombard the heavens with laser beams, and University of Hawaii researchers operate lunar and solar observatories. Military and civilian facilities are closed to the public.

**Upcountry:** Say that you're heading Upcountry and others will know that shortly you'll be smelling eucalyptus suspended in cool air and following rolling contours more usual in Ireland or Kentucky than by the Pacific Ocean.

Upcountry is the lower slope area of Haleakala that overlooks the narrow isthmus connecting Haleakala with West Maui. The views are spectacular. Far below one can see the white ribbons of beaches, but Upcountry, the ambiance is of farms, flowers and fireplaces. There are two gateways to Upcountry: from Kahului on the **Haleakala Highway**, or else preferably through **Pa'ia**, a small village on the coast a few miles east of the airport. Once a sugar town, Pa'ia has been changed in large part by the winds and waves at **Ho'okipa Beach**, one of the world's finest windsurfing places. Pa'ia now reflects a demographic shift from plantation worker to windsurfer and artisan. Just outside of Pa'ia is the **Mantokuji Mission**, a Japanese Buddhist temple with an oceanfront cemetery of over 600 burial markers, most of them traditional Japanese.

Higher up towards Haleakala, **Pukalani** ("heavenly gate") and **Makawao** ("forest beginning") lie at the geographical entrance to Upcountry.

Makawao and surrounding villages

The annual rodeo in Makawao; ranch country around Kula.

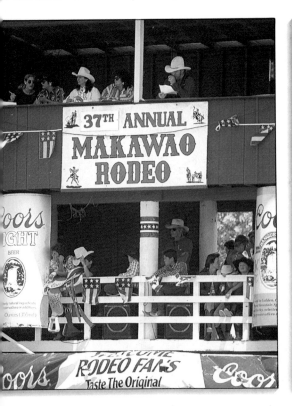

were once home for both sugar plantation laborers and cattle cowboys. Previously in decline, as are other towns once dependent on sugar, Makawao has been resuscitated by a diverse collection of newcomers ranging from upscale professionals to downscale counterculture refugees. Yet despite the influx of pesto cafes and boutiques, Makawao and Pa'ia retain a certain rough-hewn rustic feel from their days when they were Portuguese immigrant towns. On July 4th, people of all persuasions turn out for the annual **Makawao rodeo**.

**Cowboys and onions:** In the **Kula** area beyond Makawao and Pukalani, agriculture is probably the most diversified in Hawaii, in part because of climate and soil, and because of the decline in sugar and pineapple.

But even a century and a half ago, during the California Gold Rush days in the mid 1800s, Kula farmers grew potatoes, corn, and wheat for export to California. Nowadays farmers harvest lettuce, cabbage, turnips, carrots and peas. Most delectable, claim the gourmets,

are the extra-sweet Kula onions, which are said to be the best anywhere, particularly after they have been baked and stuffed with butter. Apples, peaches, plums and pears also grow well in the rich volcanic local soil.

Flowers of all colors and purposes are yet another product of Upcountry, including many of the exquisite tropical flowers like heliconias and birds of paradise. Of particular interest is the protea, a flower raised for world markets. The obscure protea – there are at least 60 varieties in assorted colors – is a tropical bloom biologically related to the macadamia nut. Increasingly it's becoming a Hawaii souvenir.

Near Waiakoa is the **Church of the Holy Ghost**. This octagonal church from the late 1890s was built by the Portuguese, who were brought to Hawaii two decades earlier as cane field workers. It was restored in 1992.

Beyond Kula and **Keokea** (a good place to stop for coffee), on a snappy and narrow two-lane road, the 20,000-acre (8,000 ha) **'Ulupalakua Ranch**

**Wind swept Huialoha Church...**

marks a terrain shift from green and cool to brown and hot. Started as a sugar plantation in the 1850s, 'Ulupalakua (which means "breadfruit ripening on backs of carriers") is a working cattle ranch of about 5,000 head, with additional sheep and elk.

'Ulupalakua ranch is also home to Hawaii's only commercial winery, **Tedeschi Winery**, which produces a rather diverse collection of wines, from pineapple wine to *méthode champenoise* (champagne), to reds and whites. A 20-acre (8-hectare) vineyard of Carnelian grapes thrives in Haleakala's rich volcanic soil as well as in the ranch's cool and arid climate.

Tourists who have done their map homework before coming Upcountry often plan to cut down from 'Ulupalakua to the beach resorts of **Makena** and **Wailea**. Virtually every map shows a road doing so, and there is one, in fact. But it is a four-wheel-drive trail, and it is private, and it is *absolutely closed* for public use. To get down to the Wailea resort coast from here, one must return

back through Kula and Makawao or Pukalani.

From the vineyards at 'Ulupalakua Ranch, the view south to the coast below and **La Pérouse Bay** is as unobstructed as one could like. A rock-strewn anchorage near the southernmost tip of Maui, the isolated bay is popular with local fishermen, who hike or drive in by four-wheel-drive vehicles. The area was populated in ancient times. The first westerner to land on Maui, La Pérouse of France (Cook had sailed past without stopping), wrote in 1786 that "during our excursion we observed four small villages of about ten or twelve houses each, built and covered with straw…"

After trading with villagers, La Pérouse sailed his two ships up along the Hawaiian island chain, where they were almost shipwrecked on what is now French Frigate Shoal. Two years later, after exploring much of the Pacific, La Pérouse and his two ships disappeared for 40 years, until it was learned that both ships had sunk in a storm.

Directly north of La Pérouse Bay is

..near the village of Kaupo.

Cape Kina'u, an outcropping of land formed by the last eruption of Haleakala in the 1790s. It is now part of the 'Ahihi-Kina'u Natural Area Reserve, a designation intended to protect its unique environmental treasures.

Beyond the 'Ulupalakua Ranch, the upcountry road begins a slow descent, rounding the southwest ridge of Haleakala and cutting across dry open range where cattle roam. Pastures are scarred by lava flows and stone foundations of old homesteads, and an incessant ocean pounds away at the rocky volcanic shore.

Despite a lack of moisture here, this is an exciting coastline drive along a rustic yet paved road. This road continues along the coast to Hana, and by continuation back to Kahului.

About 5 miles (8 km) of the road – near Kaupo, from Mamalu Bay to Lelekea Bay – are unpaved, and most rental car contracts explicitly prohibit driving the unpaved portions. The road is driveable, and many rental cars make their way every day without problems. If it has been raining at all, forget the unpaved portion entirely. Further along, the views are awesome, primal and unmatched elsewhere.

A pleasant place to stop is at the village of Kaupo, about 1½ miles (2.5 km) past pavement's end (coming from Upcountry) and just past St Joseph's Church, built in 1861. A well-defined trail winds up the southern mountain slope and through the Kaupo Gap (8,201 ft, 2,488 meters) into Haleakala Crater. It crosses through the crater and ends at the Paliku cabin area, in the crater's east side. Guided overnight horseback trips are available in Kaupo, with reservations required. (The road beyond here is covered in the Hana Coast section.)

Kaho'olawe: From the high road at 'Ulupalakua, it is impossible to miss both the small crescent which is Molokini Island, an eroded tuff cone and seabird sanctuary (its waters are popular with snorkelers), and also Kaho'olawe, the smallest of Hawaii's eight major islands and located about 7 miles (11 km) offshore from Maui.

Before Captain Cook's visit, the residents of Kaho'olawe were fishermen who probably used the island for just short periods, as the soil is too arid for much cultivation. A number of sites on Kaho'olawe have been placed on the National Register of Historic Places. During the 1800s, the island was established as a penal colony. The United States Navy was given full control of the island in 1953, and only recently has ceased using it for target practice. (Fortunately, areas near the archaeological sites were avoided.)

Kaho'olawe has been for some time the focus of the Hawaiian rights and sovereignty movement, which has included several unauthorized occupations. Hawaiians want the island returned to Hawaiian control. But the Navy argues that, with so many unexploded bombs, shells and other war material still embedded in the 45 sq. mile (117 sq. km) isle, it could not be safely returned to civilian use. The dispute between the two groups seems set to last for a long time.

Below, one of the world's rarest philatelic items. Right, penny-wise reader.

# CENTRAL AND WEST MAUI

Unlike the other more-rounded Hawaiian islands, seen from above, Maui looks pinched off to the west side. At either end of the pinched part are two extinct volcanoes: the younger, bigger and dormant Haleakala, and the older, extinct western volcano, now the **West Maui Mountains** and long eroded into steep, mist-shrouded palisades. Connecting the two is the pinched flat central isthmus of old lava flow.

Irrigated fields of sugar cane cover this fertile central plain, with pineapples on the cooler foothills. For most travelers, central Maui is a drive-through area, an intersection of highways radiating out to Haleakala, West Maui, Kihei and Wailea, and Hana.

Anchoring central Maui is the town of **Kahului**, Maui's deep-water port on the north side and the site of its major commercial airport, where most visitors (now over a million per year) arrive. Travelers don't usually tarry long in Maui's commercial center of shopping malls, a zoo, botanical gardens and a community college. Just off the highway between the airport and downtown is **Kanaha Pond**, the state's most important waterfowl sanctuary – over 50 species settle down here – and the home of several endangered species.

**Wailuku** is perched in the foothills above Kahului like an older and wiser sibling. Once centered around a now-defunct sugar mill, Wailuku is the Maui government seat, administering not only Maui, but the islands of Molokai, Lanai and the uninhabited Kaho'olawe. Wailuku has managed to sustain itself after closure of the sugar mill, in part by retaining its weathered looks despite modernization.

In Wailuku's **historic district**, in the central area of town, is **Ka'ahumanu Church**, built in 1876 of white-painted wood and plastered stone to honor Kamehameha the Great's queen, who was a potent player in establishing Christianity in the islands. An early example of island Western architecture touched with Hawaiian influences is **Hale Ho'ike'ike**, a small museum operated by the Maui Historical Society. Previously called the **Bailey House**, it was built in 1841 for Edward Bailey, headmaster of the former Wailuku Female Seminary.

Beyond Wailuku at the end of the road is the wet, lush remnants of the West Maui crater and **'Iao Valley**. At the valley's mouth is **Kepaniwai Heritage Gardens**, a country park with gardens and pavilions representing the many ethnic groups that have settled in Maui. It was established in counterpoint to a vicious Hawaiian battle that took place centuries earlier.

The valley of 'Iao, meaning "cloud supreme," was long ago a royal sacred burial area. The battle in 'Iao Valley occurred in the late 1700s, and according to some accounts, **'Iao Stream** was so full of dead bodies that its waters would not flow. Kepaniwai means "water dam," and Wailuku, the town downstream, means "water of destruction."

This scenic road ends in **'Iao Valley State Park**, a lush mountain terrain dominated by **'Iao Needle**, a cinder cone pinnacle that rises 1,200 ft (364 meters) above the stream at its base. There is a parking lot at the end of the road and a path leads down to the stream and up to various sheltered spots for a view of the valley. Surrounding this compact and spectacular valley are the walls of **Pu'u Kukui** (5,788 ft/1,756 meters), one of the wettest places in the islands with over 400 inches (1,000 cm) of rain annually. The mountains are a sponge that soaks up moisture from the trade winds before it can reach dry and sunny Lahaina ("cruel sun," referring to droughts), and the Ka'anapali beaches, 6 miles (9 km) to the west.

**Across the flats:** Backtracking to Wailuku or Kahului, one can chose to go east, towards Hana or Haleakala, south to Kihei, Makena and Wailea, or south then west, following the Honoapi'ilani Highway that hugs the West Maui slopes towards the beach resorts of West Maui.

Off the main roads in central Maui is the **Alexander & Baldwin Sugar**

eft,
aragliding
paradise.

**Museum**, in the town of **Pu'unene** ("goose hill") and next to an operating sugar mill. Once a plantation manager's residence (1902), the museum not only has working exhibits of sugar processing, but excellent exhibits on the lives of the early migrant laborers.

On the south side of the central isthmus is **Ma'alaea**, a small coastal village with a splendid view of Haleakala across **Ma'alaea Bay**. This broad bay is well-known as a calving ground for humpback whales, often seen off West Maui. The harbor is a departure point for fishing and whale-watching charters. (Advisory to the curious: the whales are protected by federal and state laws; one may not approach within 300 ft (100 meters) of whales, and violators are vigorously prosecuted with fines and jail terms.)

From Ma'alaea, the road continues around the bottom of the West Maui mountains then loops up to Lahaina and Ka'anapali. Just before Ma'alaea is the turnoff for the southwest resorts of **Kihei**, **Wailea** and **Makena**.

(Most maps show a shortcut road from Upcountry, near Tedeschi Winery, leading down to the coast. This is not much more than a jeep trail, and in fact is decidedly *not* open to the public.)

**Lahaina:** After the state capital of Honolulu, **Lahaina** is probably Hawaii's most widely-known town and a primary destination of visitors to Hawaii. Indeed, increasing numbers of visitors bypass Oahu altogether as they head for both the Ka'anapali beaches and the small, tourist-town bustle that's become a trademark of this famous old whaling port. The islands of Molokai and Lanai can be seen sharply defined in the distance, changing into rosy contours at sunset. Behind Lahaina are sugar and pineapple fields leading up the gently rounded foothills of the West Maui mountains.

Following his conquest of Maui, Kamehameha the Great established a residence in Lahaina. Several of his children, including Liholiho (Kamehameha II) and Kauikeaouli (Kamehameha III), were born in Lahaina.

Lahaina Harbor.

When Kamehameha died on the Big Island in 1819, Liholiho, the eldest son and heir to the throne, made Lahaina the capital of the Hawaiian kingdom. It remained the center of Hawaiian government until 1845.

In the same year as Kamehameha's death, the first New England whaling ships visited Hawaii. Missionaries soon followed, for where there is imagined sin there is possible salvation. In 1823, missionaries took up residence in Lahaina under the sponsorship of Keopuolani (mother of both Kamehameha II and III), who helped them build a small grass church at Waine'e.

**Lahainaluna High School**, behind the sugar mill on the hill above Lahaina, was opened by missionaries in 1831 as Lahainaluna Seminary, a general academic school. Initially its classes were for adults but eventually became a school for elementary and secondary students. During the California Gold Rush years, many Californians sent their children to school here, as it was safer than traveling to New England through hostile Indian territory. The oldest American high school west of the Rockies, it continues to be one of the most respected educational institutions in Hawaii.

Under Kamehameha III, Hawaii's first constitution was proclaimed in 1840. This constitution, which provided for representational government and a national legislature, was drafted by a group of progressive Maui Hawaiians, including David Malo, one of the first adult students at Lahainaluna Seminary and often referred to as the first modern native-Hawaiian scholar.

Malo was torn between the ancient traditions of his people and changes being brought about by westernization. He was an active yet roughly-hewn writer whose seminal work, *Hawaiian Antiquities*, is still a vital and insightful work. Near his death, Malo requested that he be taken by canoe to Lahaina to pick out the proper spot for his grave. "It would," a biographer has written, "be above and secure from the rising tide of foreign invasion, which his imagination had pictured as destined to overwhelm the whole land."

**A whaler's invasion:** Malo wasn't wrong about the invasion. By the 1840s, Hawaii had become the principal forward station of the American whaling fleet. Lahaina was a favorite port-of-call because of its protected offshore waters – the **'Au'au Channel** – that are sheltered by nearby Molokai and Lanai. Seamen took liberty from their ships and prowled the streets of Lahaina.

Over 400 ships came to Maui in 1846, when Lahaina's population was 3,557, according to the census. There were 882 grass houses, 155 adobe houses and 59 of stone or wood. Local missionaries also took a census on town dogs: 528.

The early whaling ships sailed from New England around Cape Horn in the winter, hunting whales until spring, when they stopped for supplies at Lahaina and Honolulu. After spending the summer months on the hunt, they would again visit Hawaii as they sailed back to New England.

The whalers sought the sperm whale, prized for its oil, which was found in the head cavity, and secondarily, for its

A marlin tips the scales.

large white teeth for scrimshaw. (In *Hawaiian Antiquities*, David Malo noted that in old times, the sperm whale was held to be the property of the king.)

When the sperm whale could not be found, harpooners hunted the right whale (the "right" one to catch), the bowhead, fin, gray and the humpback, which stayed close to Maui and Lanai in winter. As whaling increased, the whalers began staying year round in the Pacific, calling at Hawaii during the spring and/or autumn and leaving their oil and ivory in storage, for shipment back to New England on merchant vessels.

Herman Melville, author of the whaling epic *Moby Dick,* visited Lahaina and unsuccessfully looked for employment. He eventually found work in Honolulu as a store clerk and then as a pin setter in a downtown bowling alley. When the warship *United States* came to Hawaii, Melville enlisted as a common seaman and returned to Boston. He became a writer and never returned to the Pacific.

Pacific whaling started to decline in the late 1850s, when petroleum was discovered in Pennsylvania. Kerosene oil replaced whale oil. The American Civil War soon broke out and the Union purchased 40 whaling ships, loading them with stone and sinking them to block the strategic southern harbors of Savannah and Charleston. This loss of tonnage cut deeply into the American whaling fleet and would never be replaced. (In addition, the Confederate raiding ship *Shenandoah* captured 39 Yankee whalers in the Pacific.)

**Whaletown chic:** Although the whaling ships have long disappeared from Lahaina, this waterfront town continues to preserve the spirit and architecture of the salty 1800s, although sometimes with a decidedly Hollywood veneer.

While it's not a beach town, Lahaina is a superb walking town, compact and manageable. The heart of Lahaina lies along the **waterfront** and **Front Street**, between Shaw and Papalaua streets. The narrow streets that Mark Twain and Herman Melville walked down are now lined with gourmet cafes and restaurants (some perched out over the water

**A view of old Lahaina, *circa* 1873.**

in weathered buildings), art galleries, and trendy shops with names bordering on the cornball.

In 1962, the town was designated a National Historic District and since then the Maui County Historic Commission and the non-profit Lahaina Restoration Foundation have worked hard to encourage the preservation of older buildings and the construction of harmonious new ones. The result is a blend of seaport nostalgia and contemporary living found nowhere else in Hawaii.

Center focus of Lahaina today is the **Pioneer Inn**, facing the **yacht harbor**. Although constructed over a quarter century after the Hawaiian fleet was lost in the ice off Alaska, it is a stylistic remnant of the whaling period. Until earlier this century, it was about the only place to stay on Maui.

This all-wood structure, built in 1901 with matching additions in 1965, wraps around a large inner courtyard and is wedged between Wharf and Front streets. On its walls are fading photographs of early ships and sailors, whaling equipment and other memorabilia, including the original house rules: "Women is not allow in you room; if you burn you bed you going out; only on Sunday you can sleep all day." Despite these stringent still-posted regulations, the quaint but not-so-quiet rooms are usually always full. Downstairs is a verandah restaurant and popular bar.

Nearby are the excavated foundations for what is thought to be the first Western-style building in Hawaii, the so-called **Brick Palace**. Built of locally-produced brick around 1798, it was commissioned by Kamehameha the Great using the labor of two ex-convicts from a British penal colony in Australia. Intended for his favorite wife, Ka'ahumanu Kamehameha used the modest two-story building in 1802 while preparing his war fleet for an invasion of Kauai.

Permanently berthed in the harbor is the *Carthaginian II*, a replica of a typical 19th-century freight-carrying brig. The floating museum contains a whaling exhibit.

In a plaza next to the Pioneer Inn is the

Olmsted's 1830s whaling ketch, Pulling Teeth.

Drawn by F.A. Olmsted

Lith of Endicott N.Y.

# WHALE WATCHING

The estimated 200 to 600 humpback whales that visit Hawaii each winter spend their summers in Alaska, where the rich waters fatten the whales with krill, a type of shrimp. Around November, the whales start heading for Hawaii's warmer waters, where they mate and give birth. By the end of May, they have disappeared again, having eaten little in the nutrient-poor waters of the islands.

Although humpback whales tend to congregate in large numbers off Maui – in the protected waters between Maui, Lanai, and Molokai – they are found throughout the islands. Long endangered, the number of humpback whales wintering in Hawaii may be increasing, but no one knows for sure. In fact, only recently have researchers undertaken detailed studies of the whales' local behavior, previously spending more time studying larger Pacific migratory patterns.

Male humpbacks sing songs in a behavior possibly related to mating. (Not all whale species, however, have songs.) It is not known whether the information contained in the songs is simple or complex. What is known is that during the winter season, males repeat the song in precise sequence. And over a period of time, the whale song changes and evolves.

The songs are composed of thematic sets sung repeatedly in a specific order. The average song session lasts maybe a quarter of an hour, although they have been known to last as long as 22 hours.

When the humpbacks leave Hawaiian waters in spring, the singing stops, to resume again the following winter in almost exactly the same spot in the song as where they broke off months earlier. Humpbacks in Hawaii sing the same evolving song as humpbacks in Mexico, indicating some sort of communication between different regional whale "cultures."

Whale songs sound like creaks and groans of different lengths in many pitches. Because sound travels well underwater, it's easy to hear these enchanting tunes if the whales are singing nearby.

Humpbacks give clues regarding their moods. Slapping the long front flippers – called pectoral fins – on the water is an affectionate behavior, perhaps a whale hug or a kind of caress. A tail, or fluke, slapping the water is defensive or aggressive behavior indicating a boat, a low-flying plane or another whale that may be too close.

Each fluke is unique, a whale "fingerprint." Researchers photograph the flukes to track the animals, and to determine their life spans and patterns.

No one knows why humpback whales (as do some others) leap from the water in displays called breaches. But if a whale breaches offshore, keep watching the spot; they often do it several times before quitting. Around January, it's common to see baby whales breaching over and over next to their mothers, apparently practicing.

Humpback whales like privacy. Federal and state laws require 300 ft (100 meters) in distance for whale watchers in Hawaii. The law is strictly enforced by arrest and fines, and occasionally by imprisonment.

Whales can be seen from the shore, or from charter boats, and are easily located when they spout – inhaling and exhaling on the surface – and when they fluke, spy hop, and breach. ∎

expansive **Banyan Tree**, planted in 1873 by the town sheriff. It is the largest known banyan tree in the islands, over 60 ft (18 meters) high and covering two-thirds of an acre with its canopy.

There was a time when local Protestant preachers and visiting seamen had their differences regarding lifestyles and diversions. In one especially hotheaded period, a couple of cannonballs were fired at the preachers' houses from anchored ships. A **stone fort** was built in the 1830s as a show of the town's retaliatory potential. Reconstructed foundations of the old fort are just *makai* of the Banyan Tree.

**No furious riders:** As the threat of skirmishes between whalers and missionaries fizzled with the decline of whaling, the stone fort was pulled down in the mid 1850s and its coral blocks used to build the walls of **Hale Pa'ahao** ("stuck-in-irons house"), a prison located a few blocks *mauka* up Prison Street from the fort and the Banyan Tree. Hale Pa'ahao is a worthwhile stop, whether for its history or for its cool, quiet courtyard.

Step inside one of the whitewashed cells and imagine life in paradise. The prison had inmates convicted of the usual perfidy, including some convicted of "furious riding," 89 in 1855 but just 48 in 1857. (In that same year, one person was imprisoned for "neglect of parent to send children to school.")

Back down on Front Street, at Shaw Street south from the Pioneer Inn, is Malu'uluolele Park, a poorly-kept city park with nothing of current interest for the traveler. But there once was a pond here, with an island where Maui chiefs lived and which was later a residence for several of the Kamehameha kings. Important Maui chiefs from the 1800s were buried here, and Kamehameha III enjoyed showing visitors the ornate coffins and burial chamber, embellished with mirrors, royal feather standards, and velvet drapes.

Near the Pioneer Inn on Front Street is the **Baldwin House** and, next to it, the **Richards House**. Formerly the home of Dwight Baldwin, a Protestant missionary, it was a focus of Lahaina mission-

the
Ka'anapali
Resort area.

ary life in the mid-19th century. The house has been completely restored and is now a museum.

Half a block up Lahainaluna Road, which continues past the sugar mill to Lahainaluna School, the **Lahaina Hotel** is a beautifully restored hotel from the 1860s. Every room is exquisitely furnished with authentic antiques, and each is nearly a museum in itself.

The **Wo Hing Society Temple** is a fascinating museum of early Chinese life in the islands. Associated with the Chee Kung Tong, a global Chinese fraternal society, the early-1900s building was a cultural and social anchor for Chinese immigrants, mostly male and single. In a small building next door, old Thomas Edison movies are shown.

Farther up Front Street is the restored **Seaman's Hospital**, built in 1833 as a retreat for Kamehameha III. It was leased to the American government in 1844 as a hospital for seamen from the visiting whaling ships.

Down at the end of Front Street, beyond the commercial downtown clutter, is the seaside **Jodo Mission Buddhist Cultural Park** and the largest Buddha outside of Asia. A memorial to the arrival of laborers from Japan, it sits contemplating the Pacific Ocean.

Back in town, when the sun goes down and the night lights come up, Lahaina swells with music and night action. Quite a few top-name entertainers, from conservative ivory ticklers to heavy metal rockers, make Maui their vacation home and sometimes give surprise concerts at Lahaina bars.

**Ka'anapali and beyond:** This dry side of Maui was once an expanse of brush and scrub. Sugar fields now climb the slopes to the mountains, remaining an important contributor to the area's economy. At the top of Lahaina, on the other side of the main coastal highway, is the tall smokestack of the **Pioneer Mill**, built in the early 1870s by James Campbell.

In the 1960s, a large hunk of land was developed into a resort complex of hotels, shopping center, golf courses and condominiums called **Ka'anapali Resort**. The "world's first planned destination resort," Ka'anapali rightfully boasts one of Hawaii's finest beaches.

A rebuilt 1890s-vintage sugar cane train, the **Lahaina, Ka'anapali & Pacific Railroad**, puffs over a 6-mile (10-km) route between Lahaina and Ka'anapali, transporting tourists through cane fields. Narrow-gauge tracks follow the haul line road bed that was used by the Pioneer Mill until 1952.

The first of Ka'anapali's hotels, the **Sheraton Maui**, built in 1963, sits at the northern end of Ka'anapali Beach at a rocky point called **Black Rock**, or **Pu'u Keka'a**, "the rumble."

Ka'anapali has been a focus of Hawaiian life for nearly a millennium, especially for royalty, the *ali'i*, and was once the ancient capital of Maui. Ka'anapali was considered a powerful spiritual place. Kamehameha the Great built a *heiau*, or temple, in the area to use some of the region's spiritual power.

Pu'u Keka'a, or Black Rock, was especially rich in power, and it was one of the islands' most important *'uhane lele*, or sacred places where souls of the dead departed for ancestral spirit worlds.

Whether staying at one of the Ka'anapali deluxe resorts lining the beach – which include the **Hyatt Regency Maui**, **Westin Maui**, and **Maui Marriott** – or just passing through, a walk along Ka'anapali Beach at sunset can be unforgettable.

From Ka'anapali the road passes through the beach communities of **Honokowai, Kahana** and **Napili**, a clustering of condominiums and apartment hotels. Just beyond **Napili Bay** is **Kapalua Resort**. A golf course here embraces two luxury resort hotels, the **Kapalua Bay Hotel and Villas**, and the **Ritz-Carlton**.

Beyond Kapalua the road arcs east over the northern end of the West Maui Mountains, dipping down into the little bay of **Honokohau**, then rising into a twisting coastal road with some fine and engaging scenery. Once a dirt road considered suitable only for locals, it has now been completely paved, all the way down to Wailuku and Kahului. It's a slow drive (in places only one lane) but recommended for some of Hawaii's most rural countryside.

**A 1935 Waco biplane circles Maui.**

# THE HANA COAST

Disregard the souvenir T-shirt hyperbole about "surviving" the Hana Highway. Locals commute along it daily. It's not a treacherous road, nor is it a nightmare to drive. But there are several curves – over 600 by some counts – and the concentration needed to keep eyes on the road and off the scenery can make the trip's two to four hours seem especially long.

The gateway to the Hana Coast and the winding **Hana Highway** is the quiet community of **Huelo**, with its small 1853 Congregational **Kaulanapueo Church**, the "owl perch." Huelo is one of those rural transition points where time seems to have turned in on itself. Maui's mood and *'aina*, the land, shift here, the present slipping away amidst the tropical wetness.

**Curves and more:** One good place to unwind en route is at the **Kaumahina State Park**, a few twisting miles before **Ke'anae**. The park's carefully tended grounds, with toilets and picnic tables, include examples of plants common to this coast. A swim in a refreshing mountain pool awaits by retracing steps a few hundred yards to **Puohokamoa Falls.** Or from the Kaumahina parking lot, hike to the upper left side of the park and experience a spectacular view of the **Ke'anae Peninsula**. If you are one of the fortunate few who see the moon come up over this rugged coastal beauty, you will understand why Hawaiians named this place *Kaumahina*, which means "rising moon."

Legend has it that the god Kane thrust his spear into a rock here and that fresh water gushed forth, essential for cultivation of *taro*. Once the site of numerous fish ponds, the Ke'anae Peninsula is now host to a community of *taro* farmers, nearly all of pure or part-Hawaiian ancestry. A narrow road leaves the highway and curves a half-mile down to a scattering of houses, a tiny cemetery and a Congregationalist church, built in 1860. Crashing surf and jet-black lava

Hana Bay and Kauiki Hill from Lyon's Hill.

offer a fine spot for wine-sipping and a seaside picnic.

Decades ago, when only a horse trail connected Ke'anae and Hana, there were two country grocery stores here, and the field behind the church was a baseball diamond. The school building used to face in an opposite direction, but a tidal wave in 1946 spun it around on its foundation. Lives were lost along this coast during that disaster. Nearby is the **Ke'anae Arboretum**, pleasant for walks among tropical plants, including many unique to Hawaii.

Further along the coast, **Wailua** too has the abundant fresh water necessary for taro. Wailua's tiny **St Gabriel's Church** was one of the first to be built on this coast. The lookout on the Hana Highway above has picnic benches and more than enough in expansive vistas. Another popular roadside stop on the Hana side of Wailua is **Pua'aka'a State Park**, where toilets, picnic tables, natural waterfall and pool invite passersby to a refreshing rest and swim.

The idyllic contours of the Hana Coast

mask a past of entrepreneurial dreams. In their zeal, pioneer businessmen attempted to establish several new crops on this fertile coast, including sugar, pineapple, cotton, eucalyptus, vanilla beans and rubber. **Nahiku**, for example, gained the distinction of being the first rubber-producing plantation in America. The once-vigorous community was even serviced by a small railroad and barges.

The most impressive accomplishment along this coast, however, was intended to benefit other parts of Maui: an irrigation network of ditches, pipelines and flumes, perhaps modern Hawaii's greatest engineering accomplishment. This elaborate system transformed Maui's arid central plain into a verdant and highly productive place. A century after construction, it is still in use. Most of the small concrete bridges along the Hana Highway were built in concert with this effort, which is especially impressive considering the awesome logistics of transporting all construction materials by horse, mule and man power.

Just before **Hana Airport**, which

handles local commuter flights and celebrity charters, is the **Pi'ilanihale Heiau**, Hawaii's largest temple. Located at the bottom of 'Ula'ino Road, Pi'ilanihale dates back to the 14th century – its stones came from Hana Bay – and was possibly a retreat for *ali'i* and a place for healing. Access is gained from the **Kahanu Garden** nearby.

Beyond the Hana Airport are the water-filled caves and tide pools at **Wai'anapanapa State Park**. This overgrown lava flow is a favorite campsite with hiking trails, cabins, and good swimming on jet-black sand beaches. Water in one of the caves of Wai'anapanapa, the "glistening water," is said to run red with blood on some special nights. According to tradition, Ka'akea, a cruel chief, killed his frightened wife who was hiding in a cave after he suspected her of having an affair with her younger brother.

**Green and glimmering:** After what has probably seemed an eternity of road curves, fern grottoes, flower-studded rock walls and tinkling waterfalls, the Hana Highway unravels into the rolling hills and ranch land pastures of **Hana**.

Hawaiians say that "the sky comes close to Hana," and they tell the local legend of a deity who once stood atop **Ka'uiki Hill** (the prominent cinder cone adjacent to **Hana Bay**), and was able to throw his spear right through the sky. Ka'uiki, which stands as an omnipresent guardian of Hana and was said to be guarded by a large and fierce idol, was also the site of a large fortress where great battles were fought between Maui's army and Kamehameha the Great, during his effort to unify the islands. Big Island armies were able to establish strongholds on other parts of Maui, but Ka'uiki's strength remained intact, delaying the complete conquest of Maui. The waters along Hana, it is said, were filled with war canoes.

*Ka'uiki* – the glimmer – was a home of the demigod Maui, and also the 1768 birthplace of Queen Ka'ahumanu, the favorite and most powerful of Kamehameha the Great's many wives. Ka'ahumanu, who adopted Christianity in her later years and encouraged Kamehameha II to overthrow the ancient *kapu* system, was said to have been born in a cave at Ka'uiki.

For a magnificent view of the Hana area, hike through a pasture to the hill with a large stone cross on top, a memorial to Paul Fagan, the founder of the 3,000-acre (1,200-hectare) **Hana Ranch**, which is in charge of much of the land in these parts.

Foot access to this memorial is from the parking lot across from the **Hotel Hana-Maui**, a low profile luxury retreat frequented by the famous and the rich seeking seclusion. A meal in one of its renowned restaurants makes a fine start, or closure, to a trip to Hana. Aside from camping or bed-and-breakfast, the Hotel Hana-Maui is about the only deluxe hotel or resort around. If time permits, an overnight stay in Hana is worth the expense; tourist traffic vanishes before dinnertime and doesn't resume until well after breakfast.

There are two markets in town, but tour groups and dogmatic followers of guidebooks always want to see the well

**Banyan tree.**

known **Hasegawa General Store**. Rural Hawaii is peppered with family-owned stores like this, established a generation or two ago by descendants of Japanese immigrants. The Hasegawa store, while not unique in the islands, draws in the visitors.

This venerable establishment employs a hall closet system of inventory control, and the Hasegawa family is seldom stumped on unusual requests. The original store stood on the *mauka* side of the highway at the far end of town, but a fire destroyed the building in 1990. It was rebuilt down the road a bit towards Hana, on the *makai* side of the road.

After leaving Hana, the road passes through several country miles of scattered homes – some of them architecturally interesting, but most of them landscaped and "settled" in a comfortable Hawaiian style. Take care in these small communities: children and dogs consider the road theirs, too.

A couple miles past Hana is a spur loop road for **Hamoa Beach**, a pleasant small hideaway with good body surfing. The Hotel Hana-Maui maintains facilities for its guests here, but the beach is open to the public.

Once famous for a plenitude of ruts and potholes, the quite narrow and rustic road approaching Kipahulu has been repaved. Along the way are many deep glades and cascading waterfalls. The most popular and most accessible is **Wailua Falls**, just off the road.

A tall bridge carries the road over the fourth and fifth pools of the so-called **Seven Pools of Kipahulu**, properly known as **'Ohe'o Gulch**, the "gathering of pools." Fed by a stream descending from the Kipahulu Valley rain forests of *koa* and *'ohi'a* above – with rain up to 250 inches (635 cm) annually – the pools are natural swimming pools. The final pool drains straight into a tumultuous ocean (sharks like to gather offshore), and at times the stream and pools become raging torrents. Some of the old timers recommend dropping a flower down into the pools from atop the road bridge. If it sinks or flows downstream, reconsider a swim.

The pools are part of **Haleakala Na-**

**tional Park**, and a parking lot, campground and visitor facilities are just beyond the pools. The pools are a beautiful part of this coast, but are often congested with herds of tourists. At sunset or sunrise, the pools are quite different, even magical, both for the light and for the solitude. Near the pools and almost on the ocean are the stone foundations of an **ancient fishing village**; trails lead up into the hills to **Waimoku Falls** (400 ft/121 meters) and jungly grottoes.

Home of Laka, god of the canoe makers, **Kipahulu village** is just beyond the pools. The abandoned **Kipahulu Sugar Mill**, distinguished by a smokestack, was once overgrown with trees, but the old mill buildings have been cleared of vegetation.

About a mile from 'Ohe'o is a narrow paved road leading towards the ocean, and to tiny **Palapala Ho'omau Church** (1857), a quiet place overlooking the sea. The church is open to visitors, but respect the surrounding property and homes. Aviator Charles Lindbergh is buried behind the church. Lindbergh,

who in 1927 piloted his plane, *The Spirit of St Louis* from New York to Paris, died at his nearby home in 1974.

The church was in disrepair and unused when Samuel and Mary Taylor Pryor moved to Kipahulu in the early 1960s. A retired Pan Am executive, Sam Pryor undertook the church's restoration. The Pryors convinced Charles and Anne Morrow Lindbergh, good family friends, to build a vacation home in Hana. When they died, the Pryors were buried at their request at the edge of the consecrated cemetery grounds. Nearby on unconsecrated ground are six small marked graves: Lani, Kippy, Gungh, Keiki, Kami, and George – Sam's pet gibbon apes.

The road past Kipahulu was once dirt track, but a portion of the road beyond has been paved; only about five or so miles of the road between Kipahulu and Upcountry Maui remains rutted dirt track. Driving on the unpaved portions of the road is prohibited by most car rental companies and, as driving on the unpaved road is a violation of rental

contracts, drivers are liable for any damage incurred. When the road is dry, however, numerous rogue rental cars successfully make the loop to Upcountry every day, as do tour minivans. It's a bouncy but rewarding drive.

After skirting the ocean and cresting high ridges beyond Kipahulu, the road turns to dirt, and, when wet, can be impassable to cars. Cattle guards across the road mark the entrance to **Kaupo Ranch**, a large cattle operation since before the turn of the century.

Looking more like Scotland or Ireland than the tropics, a proverbial windswept and surf-pounded peninsula juts out below the road, embellished with a picturesque church: **Huialoha** ("meeting of compassion"), an old Congregational circuit church recently restored. The church was built in 1859, a time when Kaupo was almost totally landlocked and accessible only by sea and a primitive trail. This ancient surfing area's old name is *Mokulau*, or "many islets," for the lava islets sprinkled just offshore. The crumbling stone walls behind the church were once a school. There is an unlocked gate at the road leading down to the church.

The slopes of Haleakala rise to a deep slash at the top called the **Kaupo Gap** (8,201 ft, 2,488 meters), which opens into **Haleakala Crater**. In ancient times, the gap was the primary route taken by Hawaiians traversing Maui on foot. Horseback trips are available for the climb. Hikers can also make the climb, but the **Kipahulu Valley** on the Hana side of the gap is closed as a protected scientific reserve. Because of its unique pristine state – untouched by introduced species of flora or fauna – there are vast acres of native *koa* and *'ohi'a* sheltering endangered birds like the Maui parrotbill and Maui *nukupu'u*.

**Kaupo Store** was once the only local source of food and supplies on this part of the island, but it now caters mostly to travelers in rental cars and minivans. Memorabilia from the old days abound in this weathered store.

A few miles beyond, the road is again paved, more with the asphalt of filled potholes than original pavement.

**Left and right,** Wai'ana-panapa State Beach.

# MOLOKAI

Long overlooked by most travelers, Molokai has gained prominence, not because of its dramatic ocean cliffs, the world's tallest, but because of a former leper colony on its northern shores.

Nowhere in his Hawaiian travel letters did Mark Twain mention leprosy – now called Hansen's Disease – or the colony on Molokai. Two decades later, Robert Louis Stevenson was not so timid. In a public letter, Stevenson defended a Catholic priest, Father Damien, criticized by a Protestant minister in Honolulu as "a coarse, dirty man, headstrong and bigoted... not a pure man in his relations with women." Father Damien had died earlier of Hansen's disease while helping the patients at the Molokai exile colony.

Stevenson's tribute to Damien was circulated and published worldwide, making the "Martyr of Molokai" one of Hawaii's most beloved heroes, and putting Molokai on the map.

**"Friendly" island:** Molokai certainly wasn't the "Friendly Island" for many during those early years of Father Damien's time. Its current nickname was a public relations move to shift the island's image from leper colony to a visitor destination.

On a map, Molokai is a slender slipper, 37 miles (60 km) long and 10 miles (16 km) wide. The island has three geological anchors, each created by volcanic activity millions of years ago. **Mauna Loa** (1,381 ft/419 meters), a tableland at the western end of the island, was noted in ancient times for an adze quarry, *holua* slides, and as a source of wood for sorcery images. Later the east Molokai volcano erupted and **Mauna Kamakou** was pushed up to 4,970 ft (1,508 meters), the island's highest point. **Kalaupapa Peninsula**, sometimes called **Makanalua,** was born even more recently, when **Kauhako** (405 ft/123 meters), a small shield volcano, poured forth its lava to shape a flat tongue of land in the center of the northern coast. It is separated from the rest of

the island by a fortress-like barrier of high cliffs, perfect for a colony of exile.

Molokai's land is primarily agricultural and development has been limited. And perhaps best of all for the adventurous traveler, tourists are few.

The main **Ho'olehua Airport** is 7 miles (11 km) from the principal town of **Kaunakakai**, on the southern coast. More than half of the island's population of 6,700 people live near Kaunakakai. Ala Malama, the "main street," contains a quaint collection of wooden, false-front buildings that probably haven't changed much since the "Cockeyed Mayor of Kaunakakai," made famous in a *hapa-haole* song during the 1920s, strolled along its streets. While in Kaunakakai, stop by the **Nature Conservancy Office** for information about their hikes through the Kamakou Preserve, more than 2,000 acres (800 hectares) of pristine rain forest.

A prominent feature of Kaunakakai is the dockside wharf that extends several hundred yards out to sea. Until recently this waterfront area was congested with

*Preceding pages: anai, the Pineapple sland. Left, outhwest oast of Molokai. Right, and dunes and fresh vater pool.*

barges taking on pineapples for shipment to Honolulu canneries. But Molokai's great pineapple years are over. High labor and shipping costs have made it uneconomical to compete with growers in countries such as the Philippines and Taiwan. Both Dole and Del Monte have virtually halted pineapple-growing on Molokai. The island's farmers are now focusing on crops such as corn, watermelon, soybeans, hay, coffee and onions that rival Maui's famed Kula onions for sweetness.

Close to the wharf are the remains of Kamehameha V's old summer home. Before becoming king in 1863, Lot Kamehameha spent his summers on Molokai. In the 1860s, he planted the nearby **Kapuaiwa Coconut Grove** – originally there were 1,000 coconut trees on 10 acres (4 hectares) of land. (Kapuaiwa means "mysterious taboo, or *kapu*.")

Across the highway from the grove is Molokai's church "row," a series of churches built on property provided by the Hawaiian Homes Commission.

Churches must have at least a partly Hawaiian membership to locate here.

**Fishponds and battlefields:** Travelers will find that only a few paved roads transit Molokai. Many of Molokai's spectacular sights and archeological interests require going off the pavement; a four-wheel-drive vehicle is essential.

East from Kaunakakai, the Kamehameha V Highway runs 30 miles (48 km) to Halawa. There is much to see along this road, the second half of which is a narrow lane twisting along the coast. Plan on a long and slow drive, and remember too that, unless camping, the drive must be retraced to the hotel.

Just a few miles past Kaunakakai is **Oneali'i Park**, "royal sands," a park with campsites. For a small daily fee, campers may stay for two weeks, but must renew the permit every three days.

Along this southern coastal road are numerous **ancient fishponds** dating back as far as the 15th century, constructed to supply food for the families and retainers of chiefs. Such ponds are found on all of the Hawaiian islands, but **Halawa Bay.**

246

the largest concentration is on Molokai. The ponds were enclosed by walls of coral blocks and basalt stones, rising up to 6 ft (1.8 meters) above water. Wooden gratings allowed small fish to enter from the sea; once grown and fattened they were too large to escape. Many of the fishponds have been restored and are used to study the prospects of developing a significant aquaculture industry.

Hidden in the jungle valleys leading up the rugged southern slopes of Kamakou are enough old *heiau* and other historical sites to keep hikers busy for years. (Since many of the sites are on posted private property, check with county and state offices in Kaunakakai before striking off into the wilderness.)

Above **Kawela** is a battlefield where Kamehameha the Great won an early skirmish. It's been said that his war canoe fleet landed upon the beach in an assault wave 4 miles (6.4 km) long. In 1736, two decades before Kamehameha's birth, an invading war fleet from Oahu battled combined armies from Molokai and the Big Island here. The Oahu chief was killed, and the army defeated. Appropriately, perhaps, Kawela means "the heat."

In the same general area – and very difficult to find – are the deteriorating walls of an old *pu'uhonua*, or place of refuge. Criminals or violators of the *kapu* who reached such a walled enclosure, and stayed there for a set amount of time, were eventually able to leave without fear of punishment or capture.

Visitors should stop at **Kamalo**, where Father Damien built the second of his two churches on this side of the island. He constructed this white, wood-frame structure in 1876 and dedicated it to St Joseph. Nearby is where Ernest Smith and Emory Bronte ended the first civilian flight from California by crashing into a *kiawe* thicket, in 1927. (An earlier military attempt at flying to Hawaii from the mainland fell, literally, 300 miles (480 km) short of Hawaii.)

At **Kalua'aha** is **Our Lady of Sorrows Church**, also built by Father Damien in 1874 and recently restored. The grounds are well kept and there is a

**Ancient fishpond near Moku.**

wooden statue of the famous priest in the pavilion. Here, too, is **Kalua'aha Church**. In ruins, it was constructed by Congregationalist missionaries in 1844.

Molokai is the site of one of the largest *heiau* in the state. On private property, **'Ili'ili'opae Heiau** is 286 ft (87 meters) long and 87 ft (26 meters) wide, the largest on Molokai, and is listed in the National Register of Historic Places. A temple of human sacrifice, it's said that the stones were passed hand to hand from Wailau Valley by the legendary *menehune.* Long ago, it's also said, two sons of Kamalo, a local *kahuna,* were killed inside the *heiau.* In retaliation, Kamalo enlisted the help of Kauhuhu, the shark god, who whipped up a storm that virtually destroyed the *heiau* and took everyone, except Kamalo and his family, out to sea.

Three miles after passing **Waialua**, the road twists inland and begins winding up to **Pu'u o Hoku Ranch.** Looking back down the mountain from Pu'u o Hoku ("hill of stars"), the scenery is spectacular. Across the **Pailolo Chan-**nel is Maui and the great dome of Haleakala. Closer is tiny 10-acre (4-hectare) **Mokuho'oniki Island** ("pinch island," as a lover would pinch). Nicknamed "Elephant Rock" by inter-island pilots, it looks like an elephant lying at rest in the ocean, its trunk stretched out toward Maui.

Just past the ranch entrance is the sacred *kukui* tree grove of **Kalanikaula**, the "royal prophet." These gray-barked, silvery-leafed trees once encircled the home of Lanikaula, a local seer, a *mo'o*-killing prophet or *kahuna* who lived and was buried here. Hawaiian laborers once refused to help Del Monte clear the area because of Lanikaula's *mana,* and a non-Hawaiian grower who cut down some trees to plant pineapple here found that his crop wilted. Travelers speak of seeing torch lights moving through the grove at night, spirits returning to Kalanikaula.

The road ends in 4-mile long **Halawa Valley**. Hundreds of fishermen and farm families used to live here, but only a handful still remain. In the rear of the

**Kaunakakai.**

valley are two waterfalls that feed a stream flowing into the sea. The longest is 250-ft (76-meter) **Moa'ula Falls**, legendary home of a giant sea dragon. Before swimming in the pool beneath the falls, find out if the dragon is home by tossing a *ti* leaf into the water. If the leaf sinks, come back later. Upon Queen Emma's death in 1885, storms pushed beach sand up the valley to the pool at Moa'ula's base.

Although beautiful, the ocean at the stream's mouth can be tricky, so exercise caution. Additionally, Portuguese man-of-war jellyfish are frequently swept into the bay by offshore winds.

**Protection money:** Parking one's vehicle for a hike into Halawa Valley is problematic, with little of the *aloha* that one might hope. The parking area is public property, but posted nearby is a hand-lettered sign demanding a watch-your-car fee from a nearby homeowner. Cars have been broken into here. Read between the lines and pay the fee. Enjoy the hike into the valley rather than worrying about the car.

Beyond Halawa, the northern **Pali Coast** to Kalaupapa is as beautiful – and as rugged – as you'll find anywhere in the world, with several 1,000-ft (300-meter) waterfalls. There are meandering jeep trails through the interior, but this is a real and time-consuming adventure; it's perhaps best to see the **Wailua** and **Pelekunu** valley areas by helicopter or from an offshore boat.

Back through Kaunakakai and up past Ho'olehua Airport, the Maunaloa Highway runs through a dry landscape for about 10 miles (16 km). **Maunaloa**, itself a former plantation town, lies at the end of the road.

**Cows and giraffes:** Much of this dry leeward side of the island is grazing land owned by the 40,000-acre (16,000-hectare) **Molokai Ranch**, the largest local landowner. When Dole closed down its pineapple activities here in 1976, the company returned almost 10,000 acres (4,000 hectares) to the ranch, much of which has been planted with commercial hay. Cattle continues to be the mainstay of the ranch's opera-

All ears.

tion, which currently runs as many as 8,000 head across its arid pasture lands.

The Molokai Ranch has for years been keeping exotic animals in a high-fenced area below the former pineapple fields. Included in the **Molokai Ranch Wildlife Park** are antelope, deer, giraffes, and other creatures that have brought a touch of Africa to this end of Molokai. Tours are easily arranged.

Although axis deer are bountiful on the ranch's properties, deer hunting is no longer permitted except by special permit to the island's residents only. Molokai Ranch is also developing a recreational network whereby visitors can enjoy mountain bike treks, horseback riding, hiking and camping on ranch properties.

A number of secondary spurs branch off the main highway and wind down to the coastline. **Colony's Kaluako'i Hotel and Golf Resort**, the island's only luxury hotel, is located at **Kepuhi Bay** near the northwestern tip. The beach is good and, on clear nights, the roller-coaster lights of Oahu and Diamond Head are visible across the 26-mile (42-km) wide **Kaiwi Channel**. Only the strongest swimmers should venture into the ocean here. Nicknamed "the Oahu Express," a treacherous current and pounding waves can sweep the unwary out to sea instantly. Camping is allowed by permit at **Papohaku Beach Park**, also on the western end of the island.

Molokai's biggest social event of the year takes place at **Hale o Lono**, a rocky harbor on the southwest coast. This range of red dust and *kiawe* trees is the starting point of the annual Molokai-to-Oahu outrigger canoe race, held in October during the statewide celebration of Aloha Week. The 41-mile (66-km) race ends in Waikiki.

**Sandalwood and hula:** Another interesting Molokai side trip begins with a gravel-road turnoff just south of the junction of Maunaloa Highway and the highway to Kaunakakai.

Nine miles ahead on this bad road is the curious **sandalwood boat**, actually a hole in the ground roughly the size and shape of a 19th-century sailing ship's **Sandstone formation.**

hold. Hawaiians used the depression to measure the amount of sandalwood that these ships could carry before selling it to Western traders.

Hidden from the gaze of casual visitors is one of the most sacred spots in Hawaii. Dedicated to Laka, the goddess of hula, it is said to be the birthplace of this ancient dance form. *Halau hula* students and their *kupunas* gather at this spot to make offerings before performing at the annual Molokai Ka Hula Piko festival, held in May.

Further along this road (and off-limits to rental cars) is **Waikolu Lookout**, a sightseeing spot that gives a grand view down into a 3,000-ft (910-meter) deep valley ribboned with cascading waterfalls. This gorge is a watershed for the Kalaupapa Peninsula, and there is a tunnel at the bottom that supplies irrigation water to the dry leeward plains. It is possible to hike into the valley, but the foot trail ends at Pelekunu Valley. (As with all backcountry adventures, check in with the appropriate authorities.)

Back out on the highway, north leads to **Kualapu'u**, an old Del Monte company town, and **Pala'au State Park**. The park road passes through an attractive forested area of *koa*, paperbark, iron and cypress trees. A small arboretum with more than 40 species of trees and a picnic area await at the end of the road. From the parking lot, it's a short walk and a slight climb to **Kaule o Nanahoa** ("penis of Nanahoa," a legendary character of sexuality), a phallic rock 6-ft (1.8-meters) high visited in years gone by for curing infertility.

The **Kalaupapa Overlook** offers a spectacular view over the 1,600-ft (485-meter) cliffs to the former leper colony below. In his 1959 novel, *Hawaii*, James Michener described the peninsula as "a majestic spot, a poem of nature… In the previous history of the world no such hellish spot had ever stood in such heavenly surroundings."

**Kalaupapa:** The town of **Kalaupapa** is only a ghost of what it was during Father Damien's time. Once there were more than a thousand people living here, the Hansen's disease patients involuntarily

St Joseph's Church (1876) near Kamalo; gospel shoes.

exiled here as "lepers." There are now fewer than 100 residents.

Hansen's Disease, or leprosy, was first identified in Hawaii as early as 1830. In 1866, the year of Mark Twain's visit, the Hawaiian government began transporting victims of this disease to Molokai and literally dumping them in the waters off Kalaupapa, to swim on their own to land.

Father Damien (formerly Joseph De Veuster) arrived in the islands in 1864 from Belgium, coming to Molokai in 1873 and remaining in the colony until his death 16 years later. Under his leadership, Damien organized the colony into a community of houses (early involuntary exiles had been provided no shelter), a church and a small clinic. Land was cleared, crops were grown and a modern water system installed.

By 1883 Damien had contracted Hansen's disease himself – there was no known cure – and six years later he died, 49 years old. (Not until the late 1940s was Hansen's Disease brought under control.) Jack London traced the priest's

footsteps around Kalaupapa in 1907. He wrote a number of short stories about Hansen's disease after his visit, including a chapter about the Kalaupapa residents in *The Cruise of the "Snark"*.

Permission is required to visit **Kalaupapa Peninsula**, but this is easily obtained through airlines or tour operators. If traveling independently, contact the state department of health in Honolulu or Molokai. Children under 16 are not permitted.

There are two ways to arrive: by air to a small airport on the peninsula, or down the **steep cliff trail** that Father Damien took in the late 1800s. Popular for many years was a mule ride down the trail, but the operator of the mule ride has now suspended operations.

From the bottom of the cliff, it's only a short ride along the shore to Kalaupapa and **Kalaupapa National Historical Park**. No one is allowed to wander unattended, however. Visitors are escorted by the residents themselves, who are quite frank about their disease and lifestyles. A state law prohibits photographing the patients without their permission. Residents are no longer confined – Hansen's Disease is not highly contagious – but most residents remain because this historic peninsula has become their home.

East across the peninsula is the abandoned settlement of **Kalawao**. This beautiful spot was the site of the original colony, but after 1888, when a water pipeline was extended from Waikolu Valley, the residents moved to the rain and wind shadow of **Kauhako Crater**.

At Kalawao is **Siloama Church**, the Church of the Healing Spring, a Protestant structure built in 1871. A year later construction began on **St Philomena's Church**, completed after the arrival of Father Damien in 1873. In the adjoining cemetery there is a monument to Father Damien marking his original burial spot; in 1936, Damien's remains were returned to his native Belgium.

The Hawaii Department of Health and the National Park Service are jointly committed to maintaining the settlement until the last patient dies or willingly moves away.

**Left**, Father Damien's grave. **Right**, tranquility.

# LANAI

For almost 1,000 years after the Polynesians first arrived in Hawaii, Lanai remained uninhabited. It was considered to be a ghost island, a place of evil spirits.

According to legend, the first settler was Kaulula'au, son of an early Maui king named Ka'alaneo. A strong but mischievous boy, Kaulula'au delighted in pulling up breadfruit trees in the village of Lele, now known as Lahaina. This could not be tolerated long, as breadfruit was an important food.

Ka'alaneo finally banished the young prince to Lanai, where he figured his son would either be killed by the ghosts or forced to grow up fast. Kaulula'au had no intentions of being killed; at night he hid in a cave from the ghosts. During the days, he turned hunter and tracked down the spirits one by one. When the last was killed, he built a huge bonfire on the beach. Seeing the fire's light, Maui warriors traveled by canoe to Lanai to investigate. With all the evil spirits now dead, Kaulula'au returned to Maui a hero.

People from the neighboring islands of Maui and Molokai began settling on Lanai sometime after 1400. The first inhabitants were probably fishermen; later they discovered that the fertile inland soil was ideal for raising crops.

After Kamehameha the Great conquered and unified the islands, he kept a summer home at **Kaunolu Bay**, on Lanai's southwestern cape. There was a small village here and the king enjoyed fishing in the area. Athletic tournaments were also held at Kaunolu in his honor.

**Topographical hump:** Eight miles (13 km) west of Maui and 7 miles (11 km) south of Molokai, Lanai is the sixth largest of the Hawaiian islands. Kaho'olawe, pockmarked since World War II by gunnery practice, lies 15 miles (24 km) to the southeast.

Lanai is small, rocky and pear-shaped, buckling upward from its southern base to 3,370 ft (1,022 meters) above sea **Red earth and blue sky.**

level. From there it tapers downward, sloping gradually to the sea. This characteristic topography gives the island its sometimes-nickname, the "hump." Lanai consists of a lone volcanic crater, **Palawai**, now extinct. The surrounding **Palawai Basin** makes up much of Lanai's best farmland.

Chief Ha'alelea of Oahu offered early Mormon settlers the free use of his Lanai lands in the mid 1850s, after which they could lease land for a total of $175 per year for 15 years. Although cultivation thrived at first, three years later, drought and insects ruined their crops.

Ha'alelea offered the Mormons 10,000 acres (4,000 hectares) for $300 but no money was available and the settlement was abandoned, only to be purchased by adventurer, lecturer, and Mormon missionary Walter Murray Gibson. Using church money, he put the land in his own name. Gibson was excommunicated from the Mormon Church for his shady land dealings but went on to carve a corrupt place for himself in Hawaii's history. He left Hawaii one day ahead of a lynching.

After James Dole, a persevering businessman from Boston, purchased Lanai for $1,100,000 in 1922, mules dragged anchor chains across Palawai Basin to clear it of cactus before it could be plowed and planted with pineapple. Using boulders from Palawai Basin, Dole then created a deep-water harbor at Kaumalapau, and laid out a nearby town for the Japanese and Filipino immigrants who came to Lanai to work on his plantation.

Dole's Hawaiian Pineapple Company prospered and was later purchased by one of Hawaii's original "Big Five" *kama'aina* corporations, Castle & Cooke, which kept Dole's name and operated the plantation as the Dole Pineapple Company.

In 1987, Californian investor David Murdock bought controlling interest of Castle & Cooke. Like Dole, Murdock moved quickly and built two world-class hotels, two golf courses, new homes for the island's residents, and a recreational complex in the middle of Lanai

Pineapple fields and Norfolk pines.

City. Most stunningly of all for locals, but pragmatically given the competition of cheaper Asian pineapples, he plowed up more than 13,000 acres (5,200 hectares) of what was once the world's largest pineapple plantation.

Now less than a thousand acres (400 hectares) of pineapple remain on Lanai, token fields to provide pineapples for the island's three hotels. Other fields are being replaced by experimental crops such as citrus, onions, papayas, macadamia, coffee and grains used for cattle and other livestock feed.

For many years there was only one hotel, the 10-room **Hotel Lanai** in Lanai City; but now visitors can stay either at the country-style **Lodge at Ko'ele** located in the island's cool uplands, or the **Manele Bay Hotel**, overlooking Hulopo'e Bay on the south shore. No other hotels will be built on the island, but luxury homes are being planned around the Manele Bay's golf course.

Lanai is not an island for the package tour traveler intent on seeing sights in a brief visit. Exploring Lanai is for the hardy traveler who doesn't mind rugged hiking, brambles, rough underbrush, and dusty red earth that stains clothing a chalky rust. Although the island's population continues to grow with the influx of new workers for the hotels, there are still only about 25 miles (40 km) of paved roads on Lanai. Off the pavement, a good four-wheel-drive vehicle is essential.

Beginning at **Lanai City**, there are three paved primary roads that connect with the coast. The busiest is the southwestern highway leading down to **Kaumalapau Harbor**. When pineapple was king on Lanai, more than a million pineapples a day were loaded onto barges here for shipment to the Honolulu cannery 60 miles (96 km) away. Now, incoming barges are filled with supplies for the island.

A very rough jeep road off the highway leads down to **Kaunolu Bay**, but plan to hike over 3 miles (5 km) of rocky trails; it's off-limits for rental vehicles, four-wheel-drive or otherwise. At the hike's end are the ruins of **Kaunolu**

**Workers at Kaumalapau Harbor.**

**village**, King Kamehameha's summer residence and the most complete archaeological site of its type in Hawaii.

Excavations of Kaunolu by the Bishop Museum found the remains of 86 house platforms, 35 stone shelters, gravestones, and detached garden plots. The *heiau* of **Halulu** – named after a mythical man-eating bird – is located on the west bank overlooking the stream bed, while the king's home is thought to have been on the eastern ridge.

It is possible to walk east along the shoreline to **Hulopoʻe Bay**, but only the hardiest hikers should try it. A much easier route is down Manele Road from Lanai City. The bay, a nature conservation district, has an attractive coastal park and is the best place to swim on the island, except when pounded by south swell waves from distant ocean storms.

Spinning porpoises are frequent Hulopoʻe visitors. Shoreline fishing is permitted but spearfishing, netting, and gathering shellfish and limpets are banned. Boats are also prohibited from sailing within Hulopoʻe Bay.

Just around an easterly point from Hulopoʻe Bay and its beach is **Manele Boat Harbor**. Here sailboats can often be seen bobbing at anchor during stopovers between Maui and Oahu. Several times daily, a passenger ferry takes residents and visitors between Manele and Lahaina harbors, a short 45 minute trip.

Since nearly all of Lanai is privately owned, camping by non-residents is prohibited everywhere except for six campsites at Hulopoʻe Beach Park. Permits are available from Lanai Company for a maximum stay of seven days. Lanai residents use prime campsites under the *kiawe* trees on the beach that are reserved for their exclusive use. They guard their camping privileges zealously and will call Lanai Company rangers to evict trespassers.

Lanai's most unique touring route is surely the **Munro Trail.** This can be reached from Manele Road by taking the Hoike turnoff up to the ridge and circling around to **Lanaʻihale**, the highest elevation on Lanai at 3,370 ft (1,022 meters). On a clear day all the major

**Scuba instructions at the Manele Bay Hotel.**

Hawaiian islands except Kauai and Ni'ihau can be seen on the horizon. The four-wheel-drive trail is impassable during rainy weather.

George C. Munro was a New Zealander hired around 1910 to manage the Ko'ele Ranch. An amateur naturalist, he noticed that fog condensed on the pine needles of the old Norfolk pine tree towering over his home, spilling droplets of water onto its tin roof. Collecting seedlings from under the tree, he soon had the ranch's cowboys planting Norfolk pine trees along all of the mountain ridges to help to replenish the island's water supplies.

When James Dole laid out Lanai City, he had hundreds of pine trees planted throughout the city. Nearly a century later, a landscape architect hired by Murdock informed him that most of Lanai's famous Norfolk Island pine trees were actually Cook Island pines. Lanai is slowly readjusting to the shock.

The Munro Trail continues down past **Ho'okio Gulch**, scene of a 1778 battle involving Kamehameha the Great, to **Ko'ele** – "dark sugar cane" – and back to Lanai City.

**Windward Lanai:** Another popular excursion is to the island's convex northeast coast. It can be reached by following Keomuku Road until it forks near the shoreline. To the left is a track to Shipwreck Beach; to the right is a better road that leads to the abandoned village of Keomuku and Club Lanai, a "fantasy resort" type of day-camp. Both require at least an hour of travel time and are impassable during rainy weather.

**Shipwreck Beach** is so named because of the rusting hulk of the **Helena Pt Townsend**, a tanker that has sat impaled upon a reef in 12 ft (3.6 meters) of water for almost 50 years.

**Keomuku Village** was abandoned after the 1901 collapse of the Maunalei Sugar Company, which was owned by Walter Murray Gibson's daughter and son-in-law. An old wooden church has survived the fickle fates of both man and weather. Across from the church, in a thicket of *kiawe* trees, lies the rotting hull of an old whaling boat. Less than a **Shipwreck Beach.**

mile down the road is a large oblong stone marker, a sad memorial to the Japanese immigrant workers who died of a plague during Keomoku's sugar plantation days.

Just a few steps beyond are the bicycles, snorkel gear, hammocks, lunch and tall cool drinks of **Club Lanai**. Day visitors from Maui are shuttled across to the channel by boat in the morning and leave by mid-afternoon. Visitors who have driven the rough road are welcome to stop in for lunch.

An off-road trail continues around the eastern coast to the former Hawaiian village site at **Naha** (where Kaulula'au is said to have killed the last evil spirit roaming Lanai) but it's a dusty hot ride and there's only one way back – the same way. Further back, the traveler may have noticed the road forking off toward the mountain. Shown on the map as the '**Awehi Trail**, it's a hunting trail and deteriorates into huge ravines.

**Into the strange:** Sometimes neglected by visitors is a geologic curiosity known locally as the **Garden of the Gods**. It can be reached by driving northwest along the Polihua Road, which turns into a dirt road that passes through grasslands. This is a strange playground of strewn boulders and disfigured lava formations. Unique on Lanai, the area is good for unusual photographs at sunrise or sunset.

The route to Garden of the Gods also passes one of the largest examples of a dryland forest in Hawaii. Protected by high fences from grazing deer, the forest at **Kanepu'u** has been donated to the Nature Conservancy to preserve its native vegetation.

When exploring Lanai, leave plenty of time to get back to Lanai City before dark. Once the sun goes down, only the stars will guide you back. Despite its other-worldly appearance, the Garden of the Gods makes an interesting campsite for a night under the stars for both the stranded and the adventurous traveler. Forget the old ghosts. The name of this windswept sand canyon is proof enough that the evil spirits of ancient Lanai are never coming back.

Garden of the Gods.

# HAWAII – THE BIG ISLAND

Hawaii is the youngest of the islands – first landfall for seafaring Polynesians from the South Pacific, last landfall for the British explorer Captain Cook, and genesis of Kamehameha the Great's dream for island unification.

Properly known as "Hawaii" but rarely called such, this island has been called the Orchid Island for both the wild and cultivated purple blossoms of Puna and Hilo. It's been called the Volcano Island for the pyrotechnics of Kilauea, which make this largest of the Hawaiian islands even bigger. But most of all, it is simply called the "Big Island," the tip of the world's most voluminous mountain and twice the size of all the other Hawaiian islands combined. But no one here boasts or brags.

The Big Island is not known for its white sand beaches – there are but a few, mostly on the Kohala and Kona side – but black sand beaches abound. Much of the Big Island is draped with geologically-recent lava flows from dormant Mauna Loa, not to mention still-active flows from Kilauea. Where it hit the ocean, the lava exploded into sparkly black sand. Many of the black sand beaches are temporary – disappearing and then sometimes reappearing.

The island should be explored counterclockwise from Hilo, the state's second-largest city, often but unfortunately overlooked by visitors. Circle around Mauna Loa and Mauna Kea, themselves wonders to behold. Seen from sea level, the white-domed observatories atop Mauna Kea are so clear and crisp that one might be tempted to touch them, if they weren't actually miles away, and equally high up in the skies.

What makes the Big Island especially appealing is that its geological history, including active Kilauea, and its human history, including temples, villages, and petroglyphs, are so accessible, so new in the world, and yet so ancient.

**Preceding pages**: moon rising over Mauna Kea; fern forest at Volcano. **Left**, a wedding in paradise, the Big Island.

# HILO AND CENTRAL HAWAII

It is a tropical city, wet and warm. Unpretentious and subtle, **Hilo** can yield its charm quickly or take forever, depending on a traveler's openness. Wrote one 19th-century traveler, Isabella Bird: "I realize more fully the beauty of Hilo, as it appeared in the gloaming. The rain had ceased, cool breezes rustled through the palm groves and sighed through the foliage of the pandanus."

Named for the first night of a new moon, or possibly for an ancient Polynesian navigator, Hilo has been a place of trading since ancient Hawaiian times. At the **Wailuku River**, which spills into **Hilo Bay** at the northwest end of modern Hilo, Hawaiians shouted their bargains across the rapids, and gingerly made their exchanges. Later, foreign ships found deep anchorage between the coral heads of its wide bay, and eventually a channel was dredged so steamships could anchor. Blacksmiths, missionaries, farmers, jewelers, tailors, teachers and dentists dropped anchor in Hilo, opening their shops and churches, offices and schools. Families prospered, slowly but consistently.

The Japanese especially embody Hilo's growth. The first generation that came as sugar cane laborers raised English-speaking children – the *nisei,* or second generation – who flocked into civil service and free enterprise. Respectful of their parents, the *nisei* and *sansei* descendants have run the island with particular sensitivity to the needs of older people.

The ancestral Japanese influence is undeniable: non-Japanese join neighborhood funeral associations called *kumiai,* businessmen of all ethnic persuasions join the Japanese Chamber of Commerce, and a weekly Japanese newspaper, *The Hilo Times,* is still published here.

Like Japan, Hilo faces to the east, and the dawn. Hilo's people are soft-spoken and humble. An easy pace here doesn't encourage rapid changes. It is a daylight city. Many shops open at sunrise, and restaurants do most of their business – and serve their best food – at lunchtime.

**The crescent city:** The history of Hilo pivots around its harbor, just as does most of its life today, whether for residents or for visitors staying at one of its hotels, most of which are on the harbor. Hilo's downtown buildings are old, and many are quite beautiful; wooden awnings overhang the sidewalks as shelter from the rain. Horses were tethered to iron rings that are still imbedded in the curb along **Waianuenue Avenue**.

Downtown once stretched along the black sand harbor, and so Hilo was nicknamed the "Crescent City." But in 1946, a tidal wave, or *tsunami,* to borrow from the Japanese, swept half the town inland, then dragged the debris seaward. Hilo was rebuilt, and a stone breakwater stretched across the bay to shield the harbor. But in 1960 another *tsunami* broke through and hit the shore. This time there was no rebuilding. The city drained the lowland crescent and raised a new hill 26 ft (8 meters) above sea level, where they built a new government and commercial center, calling it **Kaiko'o**, "strong seas."

Some of the old buildings that survived the *tsunami* form an **historical downtown district** of old veneer and false fronts; the so-called Renaissance Revival style seemed popular for buildings of the early 1900s. The downtown has undergone a slow, steady restoration, and a fine walk that mixes old plantation ambiance with trendy hipness awaits in the central area – which is defined by Kino'ole Street, Furneaux Lane, Kamehameha Avenue, and Waianuenue Avenue.

A few blocks inland is the **Lyman Mission House and Museum**, a reminder of the island's early missionary days. Built in 1839, the house is the oldest frame building in Hilo and has been refurbished and refurnished to missionary-era standards. Adjacent to the mission home is a newer museum complex that features Hawaiian and other ethnic history exhibits, and upstairs, world-class shell and mineral collections.

At the other end of the harbor, to the

east, is the venerable **Banyan Drive**, a crescent of a drive lined with voluptuous banyan trees and most of Hilo's hotels. **Lili'uokalani Gardens**, off Banyan Drive, is a Japanese garden of stone bridges, lions and lanterns, and a tea ceremony pavilion. Early risers can watch Hilo's fleet of high-prowed fishing boats bring their catch to auction at the **Suisan Fish Market**.

From the **Hawaii Naniloa Hotel**, Hilo's most upscale hotel with superb harbor views, 13,796-ft (4,185 meter) **Mauna Kea** dominates the west horizon. Dark forests circle the mountain above the bright green sugar cane, thinning out as the altitude rises, finally vanishing – along with shrubs, grasses and birdlife at the alpine heights where snow in winter gave the mountain its Hawaiian name, "white mountain." A long broad saddle separates Mauna Kea, the island's older main volcano, from **Mauna Loa**, "the long mountain."

Perhaps once in a generation Mauna Loa has erupted. In 1975, after a quarter-century of dormancy, it sent a thin stream down to the northeast into the saddle. Had the flows continued their natural course, Hilo lay directly downstream. It wasn't the first time. In the late 1880s, Mauna Loa sent a flow perilously close to the city, stopping – it is said – only when Pele heard pleas and prayers from a high princess. In 1942, American aircraft dropped water and explosives on the leading edge of a similar flow with the same result.

A note if traveling to the Big Island in April, around Easter: Hilo was a favorite of King David Kalakaua, and today the city is the site of the state's most popular hula competition and performance, the annual **Merry Monarch Festival**. If you are thinking of visiting Hilo during this week, and you haven't made reservations months in advance, forget it. The city and its hotels overflow with festival goers.

Like the town itself, nearby scenic sites are quiet and contemplative places. **Rainbow Falls** in the **Wailuku River State Park** sports prismatic trim in early mornings and late afternoons, when the sun is oblique to its cascade. Further upstream are the odd **Boiling Pots**.

**Lava trees:** Often ignored by travelers is the **Puna** area, south of Hilo along Highway 130, past the turnoff for Volcano and Hawaii Volcanoes National Park, both covered in another section. There once was a loop route to both places through Puna, following the ocean then up to Volcano via the Chain of Craters Road. But part of the road has been covered by a solidified primordial flow of *pahoehoe* lava. One by one, scores of homes were destroyed over the past decade in the slow-moving flows of Kilauea, as was the entire village of Kalapana. A number of important ancient sites were also covered.

The gateway to Puna is the town of **Pahoa**, once a major supplier of *'ohi'a* wood to the railroads, which used it for ties. Its small downtown is quite funky, with raised wooden sidewalks and an unusually high number of old buildings along its main street.

In 1790, lava flows flooded a rain forest, then drained, leaving shells of solidified lava around now-vaporized **Hilo Harbor.**

trees. The lava tree mold forests of **Lava Tree State Monument**, especially when visited in early mornings before the mists have lifted, are eerie.

Further along the road is the island's westernmost point, **Cape Kumukahi**, which grew dramatically after eruptions in 1955 and 1960. Cape Kumukahi's namesake was one of two men: a chief who mocked Pele, who in turn covered him in lava flows, or else a famous migratory traveler originally from Tahiti. Either way, Kumukahi means "first beginning."

**Plantation era:** When sugar was king along the **Hamakua Coast**, north of Hilo, a railway carried sugar, freight, and commuters between the sugar mills of Hamakua and Hilo. A simple winding road between the workers' camps carried cars and horse-drawn carts, with palm trees for fence posts along the sea cliffs. After the 1946 *tsunami* undercut most of the railway bridges, the tracks were torn up. Trucks took over, clogging the old road until a new highway was built.

A traveler can return to the plantation era and enjoy an old-fashioned part of Hawaii by driving along the quiet old road, using the main highway to bridge its gaps. A turnoff leads to **Honoli'i**, a river estuary and beach park with the only reliable, year-round surfing waves in the Hilo vicinity. It's also where the demigod Maui finally came to his end while chasing a young maiden up a tree. He had turned himself into an eel during the pursuit, and a passing *kahuna* killed the eel.

After picking up the highway again, a right turn past **Papa'ikou** is marked "Scenic Drive," a beautiful 4-mile (6 km) stretch following the coast past **Onomea Bay**, once a major sugar port.

The old road rumbles over single-lane wooden bridges covered with bright red African tulip flowers in spring and squashed guavas in autumn. Plantation workers have, by and large, left the camps to buy fee-simple homes on company land. Near **Pepe'ekeo**, their fine gardens and flower beds are turning old cane fields into lush, warm neighbor-

Waipi'o Valley and the twin falls of Hi'ilawe.

hoods. At the town of **Honomu**, a spur leads to the high (400-plus ft, 120-plus meter) and thin '**Akaka Falls** and its neighbor, **Kahuna Falls**. Somewhere in the area is a special rock, a "stone of Pele," which causes the sky to cloud over and rain to fall whenever struck by a branch of the *lehua-'apane*.

Change comes so slowly to **Hamakua** that few people see it. A new house, a new car, a new storefront, perhaps, but never anything startling. Towns like **Papa'aloa, Laupahoehoe, Pa'auilo** and **Pa'auhau** look and feel much as they have for generations. On weekends Filipino families secretly pit and wager on the fighting chickens they proudly rear. Fathers and sons take their dogs into the muddy forests on pig-hunting expeditions. Children and old men play softball in the parks.

The paternal mills and the fraternal labor unions made Hamakua's plantation workers the highest-paid agricultural workers in the world. But as elsewhere in Hawaii, sugar has died in Hamakua. The largest mill and employer

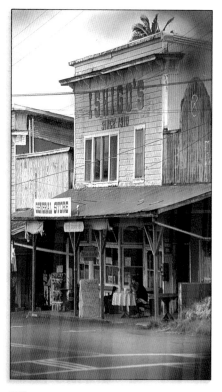

has recently closed, and the swaying fields of cane will soon vanish, if they haven't already.

What will replace the fields, and the jobs, remains to be seen. Some agribusinessmen are already hedging their bets by planting macadamia nuts (Queensland nuts, as they are called in their native Australia). The trees mature late but bear for decades, annually dropping hundreds of incredibly hard shells enclosing sweet white meats. Hawaii can't grow enough for the world's increasing markets.

**Great gulches:** Slicing through the coast are three great gulches: **Maulua, Laupahoehoe** and **Ka'awali'i**. The rivers that cut through those volcanic channels have their sources far uphill where few visitors or residents ever go.

With permission from neighboring ranchers to unlock their gates, occasional hunters and foresters ride their jeeps and horses up into the high lands of the **Laupahoehoe Natural Area Reserve**. The reserve was established to protect the watershed of the island's windward side. It is a landscape misty in summer and frosty in winter. Here the tall *koa* and '*ohi'a* trees stand; some are selectively logged, then trucked to Hilo, cut and kiln-dried to become furniture and veneer. Many others are being slowly choked by aggressive vines that the foresters desperately fight to cut back. Bluegum eucalyptus, planted as a windbreak earlier in the century, has also grown too thick, so many stands are chipped and sold to Japan to become stiff paper and wallboard.

Hidden in the forest reserve are some cold-weather trees that were planted in the 1920s by the farsighted foresters: spruce, cypress, maple, elm, redwood. When the current blight has exterminated all the elms in North America, perhaps new stock may be taken from the handful of elms untouched here at **Keanakolu**.

Beyond **Honoka'a**, a large sugar town, **Waipi'o Valley** is broad and deep, the first of many windward-side valleys in **North Kohala** and almost certainly the center of the island's cultural and political life in the century before the

Honomu on the Hamakua coast.

European arrivals. It was home to thousands of farmers who drained garden terraces and irrigated *taro* patches in the rich red earth, said to have become red when Kanaloa, one of the four primary gods, beat Maui against the rocks.

Waipi'o's **Hi'ilawe Falls** feed a broad river stocked with fish that skilled men and women would catch with their bare hands. The black alluvial beach knew the keels of dozens of canoes that crossed its treacherous currents to trade with neighboring valleys. But by the early 20th century, Waipi'o's young people had moved away from the area to work on the plantations, and rice replaced *taro* in the wet ponds. After World War II, two *tsunami* flooded the valley floor and the remaining families lost nearly all their possessions.

In the 1960s, the Peace Corps, newly initiated by President John Kennedy, trained volunteers here, preparing them for life in rural Asia by building Borneo-style longhouses and Filipino-style huts. Today, the little village is abandoned, but visitors may pitch a tent a short hike away from a swimming pool below 300-ft (100-meter) **Hi'ilawe Falls**. Many hikers cross the beach and scale the Z-trail on the far side towards **Waimanu Valley**, seven miles (11 km) north over irregular terrain.

**Central volcano country:** The older of the two largest Big Island volcanoes, **Mauna Kea** – or "white mountain" for its winter snow cap – towers over the Pacific at 13,796 ft (4,185 meters), the highest point in Hawaii and the Pacific Basin. Measured from its base below the ocean's surface, it is the tallest mountain on earth at over 30,000 ft (9,100 meters). An extinct volcano, Mauna Kea last erupted 3,500 years ago.

Those numbers are impressive on their own, but consider this: Hawaii once had a glacier on the slopes of Mauna Kea over 15,000 years ago. Nowadays, a continual layer of permafrost retains **Lake Wai'au**, close to the summit.

A goddess lived atop Mauna Kea, Poli'ahu, the snow goddess and opponent of Pele, the fire goddess. An early non-Hawaiian climber of the mountain,

ockfighting a common astime.

a missionary priest, was told that when the gods disapproved of someone's presence on the mountain, they turned him or her into stone.

It was a special type of stone that attracted Hawaiians to Mauna Kea's slopes: a dense and fine-grained basalt for use in adzes. The stone is harder than some types of steel. The **Mauna Kea adze quarry**, eternally frozen at 11,000 ft (3,337 meters) above sea level, is a national historic landmark and the only one of its type in America. It covers nearly 8 sq. miles (21 sq. km). The site contains 40 *heiau* and other shrines, and a trail leads to Lake Wai'au.

Most years, from December through March, skiers can whisk down the snow that blankets the peak. As there is no lift, four-wheel-drive vehicles must be used to reach the snow fields. Skiers have their choice of several fine runs, some over a mile long. Slalom races are often scheduled in February.

For an astronomer, no site in the Northern Hemisphere is so high, so clear, so free from light and heat, and so easily accessible as Mauna Kea's summit. The University of Hawaii and the governments of the United States, Canada, Japan, and England have built nine **giant telescopes** on summit cinder cones. The latest addition is the **Keck Observatory**, where the most powerful optical telescope in the world is located. Costing $70 million, it uses a number of mirror segments aligned by computer to create an effective light-gathering surface of 33 ft (10 meters). Two more telescopes are scheduled for the summit by the year 2000.

**The Saddle:** The Hilo and Kona sides of Hawaii have never been linked directly. The only overland road through the center of the Big Island, between the Mauna Kea and Mauna Loa, is the **Saddle Road**, which bypasses Kona and connects Hilo with Kohala and the Parker Ranch.

In 1849, a prominent *haole* doctor persuaded King Kamehameha III to let him survey and build a road over Crown lands directly from Kona, the seat of government, to Hilo, the only deep-water port. Convict laborers began at the edge of the forest and followed the nearly straight line the doctor drew on the map. In 10 years they had gone about halfway to Hilo when Mauna Loa erupted. A broad river of lava poured down the mountain and covered a part of the road. It was never completed.

A scant quarter-mile from the edge of that flow, high up in what's called **the Saddle**, stands the remains of a monument to a 16th-century king, 'Umi, the first known king of the Big Island. He completed his military unification of Hawaii here on a desolate plateau, inland behind Hualalai – where in a curious optical illusion, Mauna Kea, Mauna Loa and Hualalai appear nearly the same size. 'Umi, according to some stories, ordered a census taken. Stones were used to represent people, animals and units of land. These heaps *(ahu)* of stones were fashioned into a place of worship – Ahua 'Umi Heiau – probably decorated with artifacts and offerings.

But the high plateau, cold and waterless over a mile above sea level, proved a distant and unpleasant seat from which

**Smiles on a summer day.**

to govern the island, most of whose residents lived along the coast. The site was abandoned. Centuries later, 19th-century herdsmen built corrals with the stones, destroying many of the original walls, which have never been rebuilt. Wild goats now roam the area.

It has been 500 years since ancient armies bivouacked on the plain in the geographical center of the island. But only a few miles away in the Saddle at **Pohakuloa**, the American military practices war games. Near the Saddle's high point is the **Kipuka 'Ainahou Nene Sanctuary**, one of the places where Hawaii's native goose species is protected. (They are also protected in Haleakala National Park.)

**Eruption plus:** Unlike its northern neighbor, Mauna Kea, Hawaii's other volcano, **Mauna Loa**, is not yet considered extinct. Indeed, the Big Island districts of Kona, Ka'u, Hilo, and Puna remain vulnerable to a possible eruption of large magnitude.

Mauna Loa's last eruption was a 1984 fountain inside the summit caldera, **Moku'aweoweo**, a name referring to the *'aweoweo* fish, whose red color has obvious volcanic parallels.

In fact, Mauna Loa has erupted 36 times since European contact with Hawaii. Several times this century, it has threatened the city of Hilo, on its northeast flank, most recently during the 1984 eruption, when flows stopped just 5 miles (8 km) from the city.

Moana Loa is a classic shield dome volcano, its bulk growing through the accumulative stacking of thin lava flows of 10 to 15 ft (3 to 4.5 meters) at a time. Shorter at 13,679 ft (4,149 meters) than Mauna Kea, Mauna Loa ("long mountain") has more mass than any other mountain on the planet, with more volume (almost 10,000 cubic miles) than California's Sierra Nevada mountain range, or Mount Shasta (80 cubic miles). From the summit caldera, two prominent rift zones – fractured areas of weakness – extend deep into the ocean. The first rift zone passes through South Point, and the second, the northeast rift zone, extends towards Hilo.

Skiing on Mauna Kea in March.

# KOHALA AND KONA

Early Europeans introduced goats, sheep and cattle to the newly-united kingdom of Kamehameha the Great. But the traditional low stone walls of the Hawaiians were unable to contain these domesticated stock animals, and in less than a decade, feral herds were ravaging cultivated farmlands and gnawing down young trees.

In the early 1880s, a New England farmer named John Palmer Parker offered to round up the *haole* animals in exchange for homestead land. Kamehameha gave him two acres of land. Today, **Parker Ranch** cowboys run some 50,000 head of cattle over 210,000 acres (84,000 hectares) of pasture lands, often referred to as "the largest privately owned ranch in America." Whether this is true or not, the Parker name is nearly ubiquitous in **Kohala**, the Big Island's northern district.

As with the sugar barons during the 19th century, Parker had to import workers for his ranch, Spanish-speaking cowboys called *paniolo* (after *español*) by the Hawaiians. Today all cowboys in Hawaii are referred to as *paniolo*, and ranch lands as *paniolo* country. In later years, Portuguese joined them. Local men were trained as ranch hands, too, as were later Asian immigrants.

The Parker Ranch supplied most of the locally-produced beef in Hawaii, using a company-owned slaughterhouse in Honolulu. Until a port was constructed, cattle were herded to the surf at **Kawaihae** and forced to swim through the ocean to waiting ships, which hauled them aboard in slings onto open decks. Nowadays they are driven through gates into enclosed barges.

In the 1960s, Parker's descendant Richard Smart sold large unproductive coastal tracts in South Kohala to resort developers, who built some of the world's finest luxury resorts.

**Waimea**, sometimes called **Kamuela** (Hawaiian for Samuel, one of the Parkers), grew up alongside the family's increasing fortune. It's a cool and often misty town at nearly 3,000 ft (910 meters) in elevation. At the western edge of town, where the road to Kohala branches off, is the **Kamuela Museum**, an eclectic and completely unrelated collection of ancient Hawaiian artifacts, antique American furniture, and surprises like a Viet Cong flag and rare Chinese porcelain.

**Into the mountains:** Coming from Hilo, Waimea is the gateway both to North Kohala and South Kohala, and also to Kona beyond.

Defining **North Kohala** are the **Kohala Mountains**, what's left of a 700,000-year-old volcano which has been inactive for at least 10,000 years. From Waimea, a highway ascends to the ridge line through cool, often-misty ranch land and groves of trees planted decades ago as windbreaks. The winds – called *'apa'apa'a* – that whip across the Kohala ridge line are powerful.

At the north end of the range, the road descends down into **Hawi**, an old sugar town long suspended in the past. In **Kapa'au**, in front of the town's unas-

_eft, the North_
_Coast._ **Right**,
_Big Island_
_beauty._

suming civic center, is the **original King Kamehameha the Great statue**, lost at sea off the Falkland Islands and later recovered. Its replacement stands opposite 'Iolani Palace, in Honolulu.

In the 1880s, Kohala led the island in sugar production. Chinese laborers were hired by a businessman to construct a narrow-gauge railway from **Niuli'i**, beyond Kapa'au, to the port of **Mahukona**, on North Kohala's western coast. Formally opened by King Kalakaua, the railroad was abandoned half a century later when trucks replaced trains.

Male Chinese laborers founded the Kohala Tong Wo Society ("together in harmony") in 1886, the last of many Chinese societies established on the Big Island. In China, the Tong Wo society had emerged in 16th-century China to overthrow the Manchus, and flourished overseas wherever Chinese settled. Members identified one another by passwords, special gestures and manipulations of chopsticks. Sun Yatsen came to Hawaii in the 1880s, and again in the early 1900s, seeking help from the societies to finance his revolution in China.

The **Kohala Tong Wo Society building** was the social center of Kohala's early Chinese society. At night the men gambled at *fan tan;* there was an opium loft reached only by a rope ladder. Elderly pensioners, unable to maintain a home alone, took rooms, and as a man neared death he moved to the "death house" on the society grounds, for it was bad luck to die at home. The hillside sloping down into **Halawa Valley** is dotted with antique headstones.

The main building was restored and rededicated in 1971. Ornate but not elaborate, it has scrollwork linking the beams and posts, and plaques engraved with proverbs and phrases surrounding the doors and windows.

Beyond the Tong Wo building at the end of the road, the **Pololu Valley Lookout** offers expansive **Hamakua Coast** views of cliffs and surf. A trail leads down to the small beach which is visible from the lookout.

**Nature's wealth:** Dense forests cover the round, eroded highlands of Kohala,

**Big Island jacaranda trees.**

scarred by deep-cleft valleys and ravines. Along their eastern ocean faces, streams seep out of cracks in the cliffs and plunge a thousand feet to the sea.

At the turn of the century, a technique for tapping this mountain water was established. The **Kohala Ditch** was christened in 1906: a water course 18 miles (29 km) long that drew out the headwaters of **Waimanu Valley** and carried them to **Honokane**, terminating in an 850-ft (260-meter) man-made waterfall. Immigrant Japanese laborers bored and blasted 44 tunnels 8 ft (2.4 meters) wide and 7 ft (2 meters) high – the longest was nearly half a mile in length. At least six men died and countless others suffered from exposure and chills while working in the icy darkness of the flooded tunnels.

The northern tip of the Big Island is one of those wind-swept and expansively open places perfect for magic. At the end of the road to ʻ**Upolu Point** (named for an island in Samoa), past the small airfield, is the well-preserved **Moʻokini Heiau**, built around AD 480,

it's said, by a *kahuna* from Tahiti. A *kahuna* from the Moʻokini family of North Kohala still maintains Moʻokini, "many lineages."

Just beyond, within eyeshot, is the **birthplace of Kamehameha the Great**, *circa*1752. Signs mark both *heiau* and birthplace, both well worth the side trip.

In 1968, archaeologists excavated a 600-year-old Hawaiian fishing village, **Lapakahi**, near the highway skirting North Kohala's western coastline. The area is protected as **Lapakahi State Historical Park**. With self-guided tours, the park preserves the foundations and stone enclosures of this commoners' fishing village.

**Prairie paradise:** Hot, dusty and very dry, **South Kohala** looks like parts of the western United States – prairie and desert, with less than 9 inches (23 cm) of rain a year, but with a seacoast. Where the highways from North Kohala and Waimea meet and continue south stands the largest restored *heiau* in Hawaii: **Puʻukohola**, built in 1791 by Kamehameha the Great for his war god,

*Paniolo action at Kamuela.*

Kuka'ilimoku, in hopes of successful military conquest. To dedicate the shrine after it was finished, he invited his main Big Island rival and had him killed as a sacrificial offering. Pu'ukohola ("whale hill," no doubt for its view of the ocean during whale season) is now protected as a national historic site.

The low roads in both North and South Kohala are lined with *kiawe* (mesquite) trees and prickly-pear cacti, both of whose thorns are pests – yet the tree is burned into first-rate charcoal and the cactus blooms develop into sweet blood-red fruit. On land the Parker Ranch found too dry for cattle, Laurence Rockefeller commissioned a luxury resort, the **Mauna Kea Beach Resort**, piping water for its grounds and golf course all the way from Waimea. For over a quarter century, the Mauna Kea has been the standard by which other Hawaii resorts are measured, and is noted for its lovely crescent beach, and for its exquisite, comprehensive collection of Asian antiquities that are spread throughout the property.

Although the Mauna Kea had to import sand to widen its beautiful beach – considered one of Hawaii's best – half a mile south lies **Hapuna Beach State Park**, with the Big Island's largest white sand beach. Controversy shadowed its idyllic setting because of a proposal to build a hotel on private land at its northern end. In 1988, developers and unions barely defeated a ballot initiative that would have stopped construction. The hotel is being built.

South of Hapuna Beach is the **Mauna Lani Bay Hotel and Bungalows**. (Don't think of these bungalows as cheap – they run several thousand dollars a night and are celebrity favorites.) The hotel's regular rooms, however, are in a dramatic yet quiet six-story design. A recent addition near the Mauna Lani is the luxury **Ritz-Carlton**. In **Pauoa Bay** fronting the Ritz-Carlton is a submarine fresh water spring. The ancient Hawaiians would dive to the spring's opening and fill gourds with fresh drinking water.

In earlier days, Mauna Lani was known as **Kalahuipua'a**, a site of **ancient aquaculture ponds** that the Mauna Lani hotel has preserved. A walking trail leads from the hotel towards small Keawanui Bay ("big bay") and the ponds. There are six major ponds, the largest about 5 acres in size and 18 ft (6 meters) deep.

A spur trail heading inland past the ponds opens onto a lava field, where excavated shelter caves have yielded an ancient canoe paddle and large fishhooks, probably for catching sharks.

Kamehameha the Great maintained a **canoe landing** on the rocky coast, marked now by a replica of an old canoe shed; inside is a full-sized replica of an outrigger canoe. Uncovered at low tide, just *makai* of the shed, is a *papamu* petroglyph for playing a checkers-like game. Beyond is the **Eva Parker Woods Cottage Museum**, built in the 1920s by an early *kama'aina* family in the area and moved to its current seaside location later. Ancient Hawaiian artifacts are displayed inside.

The shoreline trail continues further south, following an ancient footpath that connected fishing villages. Along **Hotel hospitality.**

the path are ancient fishing platforms, a house site, and some **anchialine pools**, where brackish groundwater has filled natural depressions in the lava, isolated from the sea.

The west coast of the Big Island has a number of these ponds, unique in the United States. Some have been preserved, like these at Mauna Lani, where five shrimp species thrive. Just south at the sprawling Hyatt Regency Waikoloa, anchialine pools were destroyed during the resort's construction.

**Chiseled in stone:** Just north of the Ritz-Carlton is probably Polynesia's best collection of petroglyphs, the **Puako petroglyph field**. Years ago, access was through **Puako village**. Now there is a well-marked road at Mauna Lani ending in a parking lot. A guided trail leads to the field where several thousand petroglyphs have been etched into the *pahoehoe* lava. The age of these petroglyphs is indeterminate.

Most Hawaiian petroglyphs are chiseled into smooth *pahoehoe* lava along major trails. Many of the petro-glyphs are of uncertain meaning. Others, like the circles with a dot inside and called *piko* holes, are known to have been receptacles for the umbilical cords of newborn children.

Another good collection of petroglyphs is just south at the **Waikoloa Resort**, at **'Anaeho'omalu**, where ancient petroglyphs have been joined by relatively recent petroglyphs from the late 1800s: English words and initials, horses, and figures bearing rifles. Also well preserved are large ancient fishponds at the **Royal Waikoloan Hotel**.

One of Hawaii's most controversial hotels, the **Hyatt Regency Waikoloa**, bears the indelible signature of Chris Hemmeter, a developer who constructed fantasy destination resorts throughout Hawaii, of which the Hyatt is undeniably the most extravagant. Three small hotels-within-a-hotel are connected by mechanically-guided boats in an artificial canal and a sleek electric train. (There have been reports, however, of people actually walking through the hotel's spacious grounds.) Aside from

its design philosophy, most controversial was the destruction of the natural anchialine pools, replaced with artificial playground lagoons.

Unique among Hawaii's resorts is the low-profile **Kona Village Resort**, wrapped in a mystique that's in sharp contrast to the fantasy mega-resorts of the 1980s. From the main highway, a string of what look to be simple thatched huts line the ocean. In fact, they are luxury *hale*, or bungalows, sans televisions and telephones, and anything else that makes noise.

Kona Village was started in the early 1960s by Johnno and Helen Jackson, who wanted to recreate the old Hawaiian village, **Ka'upulehu**, that once stood on Kahuwai Bay. Sailing up the Kona coast on the schooner *New Moon*, the Jacksons dropped anchor in the bay and set out to clear the thick *kiawe* covering an 1801 flow from Hualalai volcano. In the early years, the resort was just a small cluster of *hale* accessible only by boat or air; no road existed. Now it is consistently chosen in traveler surveys as one of the world's most unusual resorts. Its entrance is marked by an unmarked guard shack, with one of Hawaii's worst roads leading to the resort.

**Kona:** To make matters confusing, the town of **Kailua-Kona** is known to locals usually as Kona, to the post office as Kailua-Kona, and on maps as Kailua. Generally, they're all interchangeable. Kona can also mean the Kona coast.

In the past, the only way to drive from Kohala to Kona was along a narrow road far uphill from the ocean. Today, however, a highway named for Queen Ka'ahumanu, wife of Kamehameha the Great, connects Kawaihae in Kohala with Kailua-Kona. The highway passes through some of the driest land in Hawaii, where tiny beaches and archaeological sites are strung along the coast like beads.

This open country is a gritty, broad and breezy stretch of land. Dominating **North Kona** is the 8,271-ft (2,509-meter) summit of **Hualalai**, which last erupted in 1801. The **Keahole (Kona) Airport** lies on one of its lava flows.

**Kona anglers with yellow fin tuna.**

Legend says that the 1801 eruption was initiated by Pele, the fire goddess, mostly out of jealousy for the successful Kamehameha the Great. When Kamehameha followed the advice of a *kaula,* a seer, and made offerings to Pele, the eruption stopped. Hualalai is popular with game birds, and sheep and goats wander over its dormant heights, foraging on dry shrubs and grasses.

On the flanks of Hualalai is 4,000-ft (1,200-meter) **Pu'uwa'awa'a**, a pumice cone around 100,000 years old. The typical Hawaiian lava flow is perhaps 15 ft (5 meters) thick, but flows from Pu'uwa'awa'a reach 900 ft (270 meters) in thickness. Obsidian glass, used for making sharp tools and weapons, is found here. (The only other place in the state for obsidian is the island of Kaho'olawe.)

On Hualalai's southwest flank is the village of **Holualoa**, increasingly a popular retreat for artists and others seeking refuge from the jumble of Kailua-Kona below. On the high road, it sits amidst coffee plants and lofty views.

**Old and new retreats:** The town of Kailua is one of those places noted for sun and night life, both of which are indeed ample here. **Kailua Bay**, a harbor skirted by Ali'i Drive and a seawall, is the downtown focus of Kailua.

At the north end is an *heiau,* **Ahu'ena**, used for human sacrifices and later restored by Kamehameha the Great. The site was known in the old days as **Kamakahonu**, the "turtle eye" home. This is where Kamehameha the Great retired and later died, in 1819. Loyal attendants hid his bones, lest they be defiled by his enemies or the *mana* abused. Occasionally, someone claims to have found the burial site – caves were traditional burial locations – but it has and remains undiscovered. Possibly it was sealed by a lava flow, or it may even be under water, as the island's west coast has sunk an average of 9 inches (23 cm) every 100 years, since at least AD 1200.

For years the *heiau* site was covered by a hotel. When the hotel was demolished and replaced, the new hotel, **King**

**St Peter's Church, Kona.**

**Kamehameha Hotel**, was set back from the bay and the owners restored the *heiau* to its original state.

Ali'i Drive leads along the harbor past the **Kona Hilton Hotel**, hard to miss as it juts into the ocean, and through a jungle of condominiums and apartments. The harbor area along Ali'i Drive – between the King Kamehameha and Hilton hotels – is a fine walking district, both for shopping *ad nauseam* and for history. The priceless **Hulihe'e Palace**, built in 1838 by the brother of Ka'ahumanu, sits right on the ocean just down from Ahu'ena. Restored in 1927, it is a fine museum of times when the royal family retreated to this island. The **Moku'aikaua Church**, on Ali'i Drive opposite from the palace, was built in 1837. The original church, with a pandanus roof and foundations of old *heiau* stones, was dedicated in 1823, but destroyed in 1835.

Sheltered from the prevailing trade winds, the waters off the Kona Coast contain game fish considered among the best in the world. Each summer in late July or August, the **Hawaiian International Billfish Tournament** is staged here. More than a dozen Pacific blue marlin, each weighing over 1,000 lb (454 kg), have been boated within an hour's run from the pier. *Ahi* (tuna), *ono* (bonefish), *ulua* (jack crevalle), *mahi-mahi* and swordfish are caught daily by anglers from Europe, America, Australia and Japan.

**Kona Gold:** Up above Kailua on the slopes of Mauna Loa, the climate is cooler. Moist air, clear sunshine and porous volcanic soil produce one of the world's finest gourmet coffees. Schools in Kona used to close during harvest season, when families filled burlap sacks of bright red "cherries" for delivery to the local mill. (Only one mill remains in operation now.) All along the highway south of Kailua, in the small villages clustered around the town of **Captain Cook**, Kona coffee is sold like the gold it once was, but often in blends that require only 10 percent Kona beans.

Kona has diversified, both in spirit and in economics, since the 1960s, when the area was a haven for first, self-exiled counterculture types, and later, artisans and crafts people. Other newcomers settled here to become farmers by leasing land from large estates and buying up fee-simple farmlands. Much of that new farm land went not into coffee production, but into vegetables, citrus fruits and marijuana.

The so-called "Kona Gold" – known in Hawaii as *pakalolo,* or crazy tobacco – is a cash crop far surpassing coffee (and probably sugar) in net worth. It is illegal, and even with regular police assaults in helicopters on remote pot plots, marijuana cultivation will probably continue to be a major part of Kona's economy.

Higher up Mauna Loa's slopes are forests of native trees. Around their trunks, the wild *maile* wraps itself. With the pressure of increased population, *maile* – a fragrant vine that is prized for *lei* – has become scarce and expensive.

Sandalwood once covered much of these slopes. Today, few trees remain. Whole forests of the creamy, aromatic wood were cut and sold by Kamehameha

**Bud of Kona Gold.**

the Great and his heirs for profitable shipment to China.

**Sacrifice and sanctuary:** Captain James Cook met his untimely death on a beach at **Kealakekua Bay**, a state marine conservation district. Visitors can ride a day cruise ship to this bay from Kailua-Kona, or they can drive to it on a paved road descending through lava fields. Virtually inaccessible except by water, a white 27-ft (8-meter) obelisk – on a parcel of official British territory – marks the spot where he and some of his crew died. Surveys between Kealakekua Bay and Kailua-Kona have mapped at least 40 *heiau* around here..

A traveler cruising by boat along the coast would be startled at **Honaunau Bay** to see full-sized primitive idols and an immense stone platform with walls 6-ft (2-meters) thick topped by thatched huts. In this ancient *pu'uhonua*, or place of refuge – now known as the **Pu'uhonua 'O Honaunau National Historical Park** – ancient Hawaiians pardoned *kapu* violators and war criminals who reached sanctuary here and committed themselves to the mercy of priests and vowed to do penance.

Over the centuries, the *pu'uhonua* gained importance and accumulated *mana,* or spiritual power, as more and more chiefs were buried here. Meticulously and accurately restored, it's a wonderful place for reflection amidst *heiau* and the 1,000-ft (300-meter) long **Great Wall** – 10 ft (3 meters) high and 17 ft (5 meters) wide. Towering coconut palms swing melodically above.

Near the main road, up from the historical park, the turn-of-the-century **St Benedict's "Painted" Church** is one of Hawaii's special little places. The inside is painted with biblical scenes and motifs for those unable to read. A bust of Father Damien stands outside.

Further south along this jagged Kona shore, the people of **Miloli'i** still fish for a living in a mix of old and modern boats originating from their tiny village. In few places is there a feeling of neighborliness so strong as in this little village of hand-built stone walls topped with night-blooming cereus.

St Benedict's
Church.

# KA'U AND VOLCANO

South of Kona is an increased expanse of gray and black lava, and then more of the same – the Mauna Loa lava flows of 1907, 1919, 1926, and 1950. Where the local micro-climate has permitted, lichens, grass and *'ohi'a* – usually the first tree to appear in lava flows – sprout from the new earth. This is **Ka'u**, probably the first-settled but now least-populated place in Hawaii.

In the 1950s and 1960s, unscrupulous real estate salesmen trafficked in these raw lava acres, hawking them sight-unseen as properties in paradise. Still, some have come here knowing full well the barren nature of the land.

The dead-end road to **South Point** traverses about 12 miles (19 km) of cattle range. Along the way, the road passes the *thwoosh-thwoosh-thwoosh* of three dozen immense electricity-generating windmills, spinning in the unceasing winds that have whipped this cape for eons. Privately owned, **Kamoa Wind Farm** feeds electricity into the island's main power grid.

Somewhere along South Point, the first Polynesian voyagers landed in Hawaii, calling it **Ka Lae**, the Point. Self-evident to the modern-day visitor is that this is a special place; the ancient Hawaiians built the **Kalalea Heiau**, a fishing shrine, right on the cliff's edge. The cliff at the end of the road is the southernmost place in the United States. Clear and blue waters smash against the 50-ft (15-meter) basalt cliffs. Small fishing boats often tie up below.

A 3-mile (5-km) hike east from South Point, through dry and grassy plain, leads to the unique **Green Sand Beach**. Here an entire cinder cone of olivine has collapsed into a little bay. The olivine can be set in jewelry, but none has been found much larger than buckshot. The beach is safe for swimming on a calm day, but can be reached only by scampering down the face of the cinders.

All roads on the Big Island eventually lead to **Volcano**, the highland village nestled at 3,700 ft (1,100 meters) amidst forests, morning mists and fire. There are numerous guesthouses for those wanting to stay up here, rather than returning to Hilo or Kona. The well-appointed **Kilauea Lodge** is worth a look and even an overnight stay.

The Volcano area is rich with artisans, writers and crafts people. Many of their works – paintings, photographs, sculptures – are offered for sale at the **Volcano Art Center**, next to the national park headquarters and housed in the old **Volcano House**, built in 1877.

The earliest Western visitors to Kilauea stayed in a thatched hut near the caldera's edge. In 1877, a master carpenter was hired by a steamship company to build a real hotel, Volcano House, for tourists visiting the islands. The original building was eventually moved back from the crater's edge and restored as the Volcano Art Center.

The current hotel, located in the park a short walk from the visitors center, has had its ups and downs with changes in management. In the past decade or so, the quality of facilities and service

*Left, Kilauea Crater, Hawaii Volcanoes National Park. Right, fiery feathers at sunset.*

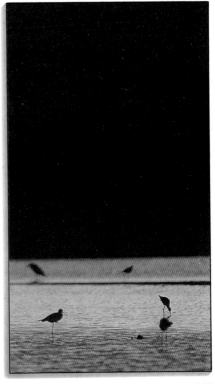

slipped considerably, but there is talk of improving standards. (Lunches, in any case, are tour bus hell and best avoided.)

**The big bang:** The Big Island's biggest draw, if not the sun and beaches of Kohala and Kona, is its volcanic activity. **Kilauea Volcano** has been erupting steadily since 1983, the longest since observations have been recorded, making it a prime draw in **Hawaii Volcanoes National Park**.

Like all Hawaiian volcanoes, Kilauea is a dome-like shield volcano with gentle slopes, rising more than 20,000 ft (6,000 meters) above its base on the ocean floor.

The summit caldera is 2½ miles (4 km) by 2 miles (3.2 km), its walls a set of step-like fault blocks that form cliffs as high as 400 ft (120 meters). At the southern edge of Kilauea is a collapsed crater, **Halema'uma'u**, the volcano's primary vent and where the principal lava conduit surfaces. From the early 1820s until 1924, Halema'uma'u was a lake of active lava.

Far from being dangerous – as are explosive volcanoes in the Mediterranean or around the Pacific rim – Hawaii's volcanoes are relatively quiet and benign, which allows visitors "drive-through" access to eruptions and lava flows. Only twice in recorded history have explosive eruptions occurred in Hawaii, the latest in 1924. Steam pressure expelled the Kilauea volcano's plug and enlarged Halema'uma'u's diameter from 1,200 ft (360 meter) to 3,000 ft (900 meters), leaving a hole 1,300 ft (400 meters) deep. An eight-ton block of basalt was tossed 3,000 ft (900 meters) from Halema'uma'u's center. Dust clouds rose to 20,000 ft (6,000 meters).

**Rifts of action:** Kilauea's eruptions have been primarily along the **Southwest Rift** and the **East Rift** zones, structural weaknesses in the shield volcano. The Southwest Rift extends through Ka'u, and the East Rift to Puna. Since 1969, a number of eruptions on the East Rift have built a new "parasitic" shield dome called **Maunaulu**, the "growing mountain." Among its achievements, Maunaulu has buried 12 miles (19 km) of park road –

**Hawaiian bird of paradise.**

some of it under 300 ft (100 meters) of lava – and added several hundred acres of land to the Big Island.

Out at sea, about 3,000 ft (900 meters) below sea level, a new island-to-be, **Lo'ihi**, gestates on the East Rift. Tens of thousands of years from now, it will probably surface, either as a new island or, if it keeps building, an extension of the Big Island itself.

At the park's **Kilauea Visitor Center**, the latest information regarding eruptions, road closures, and flow activity is displayed on maps and constantly-updated information boards.

From the visitors center, the 11-mile (17 km) **Crater Rim Road** passes over some of the Pacific's most bizarre scenery as it skirts around the active Kilauea Caldera, past wheezing steam vents at **Steaming Bluff** – where seeping groundwater hits hot rock – and several breathtaking lookouts above the caldera. Lava flows in the caldera just below the first stretch of road and the Volcano House hotel are from 1919.

The **Hawaiian Volcano Observa-**tory, operated by the US Geological Survey, is one of the world's premiere vulcanology and geophysical research centers. Next door, the **Jaggar Museum** has an exhibit open to the public.

Near the observatory, but inaccessible to visitors, is the site of one of the only two *heiau* believed to have been situated near the caldera, on the bluff of **Uwekahuna**, "the place of priestly weeping." Apparently a house was built over a pit here. A *kahuna* waited for unsuspecting visitors to enter, then yanked ropes that collapsed the floor, sending the visitor to their ends. A timely hero set the house on fire, causing the *kahuna* to cry.

The road slips into the Southwest Rift zone, crossing lava flows from 1971, 1974, and 1921 to an overlook of Halema'uma'u Crater, a collapsed depression within Kilauea Caldera. From the parking lot, whiffs of subterranean gases along the short trail are reminders that all is not finished down below. Halema'uma'u is said to be Pele's current home and, at the crater's rim, offer-

Collecting fresh lava specimens.

ings of *lei, ti*-wrapped stones, and money are left for Pele's consideration.

Kilauea is famous for its curtains of fire, walls of flaming, gushing fountains that erupt along well-known rift zones. A typical eruption begins with a change in the pressure of the underground plumbing, then a crack or rift opens on top. Fountains dozens or hundreds of feet high squirt flaming rock into the air; puddles collect and form a lake. Heat blasts from the surface, sucking up the colder air, which flings stinging cinders and sharp ashes into a whirlwind.

**Kilauea Iki Crater** was where a 2,000-ft (600-meter) volcanic geyser erupted in 1959, possibly the highest volcanic fountain ever recorded. A popular stop is the **Thurston Lava Tube** (named for the Thurston missionary family), where a short trail weaves through primal groves of fern to a short lava tube, which forms when a *pahoehoe* lava flow starts to cool on its outer edges. A channel forms, and the cooling edges meet and create a tunnel, through which flows continue to move.

**Expanding island:** The **Chain of Craters Road** cuts off the rim road and down along the East Rift, passing prehistoric pit craters and descending towards the ocean down an immense fault scarp covered with lava flows looking like black molasses. If Kilauea is erupting during one's visit, and if its flows have reached the ocean, steam plumes rise ahead at road's end. At night, a hellish yet exquisite red glow slices through the night.

It was once possible to continue along the road into Hilo via the Puna district. In the late 1980s and early 1990s, lava flows obliterated scores of homes, the **village of Kalapana**, ancient archeological sites, and the park's Waha'ula Visitor Center.

Waha'ula was a *luakini*, a *heiau* for human sacrifices. It was first established by a Tahitian priest in the 13th century, and later used by Kamehameha the Great for Kuka'ilimoku, his war god. According to one of several legends, when a young chief passed through the smoke coming from the *heiau* – a taboo as the

**Anthuriums along the Chain of Craters Road: a fern and *pahoehoe* lava.**

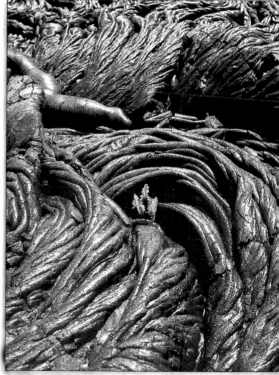

smoke was considered a shadow of the *heiau* god – he was killed. His bones were thrown in a refuse spit.

To the southwest of Kilauea is the **Ka'u Desert**, downwind from the summit where noxious gases and dehydrated breezes inhibit vegetation. In 1790, a freak eruption of gas and dust suffocated a phalanx of warriors opposing Kamehameha the Great. Those who were able to flee left footprints in the clay-like mud that fell. Today, those **Maunaiki footprints** have solidified; some are preserved under glass at the end of a trail.

From the main highway (and still inside the national park), a side road leads to the **Kipuka Puaulu**, or Bird Park, an idyllic hideaway with a nature trail circling through meadows and one of the thickest concentrations of native plants in Hawaii, including *koa, 'ohi'a, kolea,* and *mamani.*

A *kipuka* is an isolated ecosystem created when a lava flow shunts around an "island" of older growth or habitat, isolating it. These *kipuka* are important biological research areas, where native species continue to flourish independent of outside influences. Biologists often create artificial *kipuka* for research. In 1968, the National Park Service isolated an area near the coast with fences, protecting it from the wild pigs and goats that roam the Big Island. Something grew within the fenced *kipuka* that had never been seen before by modern scientists: a large bean plant with purple flowers. Until the fence was put up, island goats had eaten the bean plants before they could mature.

The 18-mile (29-km) trail to the summit of **Mauna Loa**, which is inside the national park, is a difficult and unforgettable hike. It takes a day just to reach the **Red Hill** cabin at 10,000 ft (3,030 meters), and most of the next day to attain the summit cabin. Here, from sunrise through dusk, the unspoiled colors of the lava gleam, unmelted snow glints from cracks in the rock – it is the only source of water – and the high cold air makes sturdy travelers light-headed and mystical.

Kalapana lava flows have destroyed the black beaches.

# KAUAI

Most visitors to Kauai sense it – something in the island's air nagging at the subconscious, a flickering memory of *knowing* the island, even if here for the first time. Confounding, however, is that at the same time, Kauai can be unknowable and inaccessible.

That Kauai is the oldest of the main islands might have something to do with it. Like any elder, its face is lined and shaped with time, sustaining Hawaii's proverbial Bali Ha'i image that repeatedly brings Hollywood back for more.

It's often noted that Kauai was the last of the islands to get a traffic light. Whether its reluctance was intentional or circumstantial – Kauai is a stubborn island, as Kamehameha the Great learned when trying to bring it into his unified Hawaii – Kauai now has numerous signal lights. Judging from the thick traffic around Lihu'e, its commercial center, there are either too many lights or not enough.

Unlike Hawaii's other inhabited islands, one cannot drive completely around Kauai, the most circular of the islands. Heading up along the dry and sunny west coast, the road abruptly slams into the resplendent Na Pali Coast. Drive up the often-wet eastern coast – moist trade winds from the northeast hit the island and unload on this side – and then across the North Shore past Hanalei, and again the Na Pali Coast impedes but never intrudes. In fact, Kauai's tempestuous landscape limits development, and over half of the land is reserved for conservation and preservation, a higher percentage than the other Hawaiian islands.

Inaccessible except by foot or helicopter, the Na Pali Coast leads up to the central remnants of Kauai's ancient volcano, the twin summits of Wai'ale'ale (said to be the world's rainiest place) and Kawaikini, both usually invisible beneath wet clouds.

Kauai's 50,000 people are reserved; some might say secretive. One shouldn't ask many questions. Just let things be. Even more secretive, however, is the neighboring island of Ni'ihau, a small island left dry in Kauai's rain shadow. About 230 true Hawaiians live in seclusion here, but not in isolation. Privately owned, Ni'ihau is *kapu,* off-limits to outsiders.

Kauai isn't *kapu,* but it doesn't yield easily. Then again, it does.

Preceding pages: Waimea Canyon, Kauai; rain forest on Kawaikini Peak. Left, Ke'e Beach is rich in folklore.

# KAUAI AND NI'IHAU

At the heart of the island of Kauai, at its center, is a virtual jungle of vegetation and fauna unique in the world. Here, a mile high, a long, narrow depression lies suspended amid the mountains. From its sides fall thin, jagged ridges and deep verdant valleys and canyons. The bowl, the depression, is the **Alaka'i Swamp**. At its eastern end is allegedly the wettest spot on earth, **Wai'ale'ale**, where almost 500 inches (1,270 cm) of rain fall annually. At the other end are the precipitous ridges and valleys called **Na Pali**, the cliffs.

Between them is Alaka'i, a calabash filled with rare plants and birds that exist nowhere else. The 'olapa grows here, a tree whose leaves flutter in the slightest breeze, when all else is still. And the 'ohi'a, shrouded in mists, its deep green leaves and bright red blossoms providing shelter and food for the honeycreepers and other birds of Alaka'i. There are ferns here, great, tall tree ferns and tiny fragile ones with fronds so delicate one needs a magnifying glass to pick out their parts. The environment is even more fragile than the ferns.

Many of the Alaka'i's birds are endangered. For some of them, civilization has made most of the island uninhabitable, and now only the Alaka'i remains sufficiently untouched for them to survive.

**Historic feathers:** And even here their survival is threatened. The *akialoa*, a small bird with a long, curved beak almost as long as its body, has not been seen in more than two decades, and is believed to be extinct. The 'o'o 'a'a, with its haunting, whistling call, has only been seen by man in one limited area, nesting in a single 'ohi'a tree, in the past few decades. The bird is the size of a mynah, but more slender. It has a slate-grey body with small patches of yellow feathers under its wings and on its thighs.

These feathers were used in the days before the coming of white men to make the colorful cloaks and helmets of Hawaiian royalty. The birds would be caught on sticks coated with gum, relieved of their yellow plumage, and released. The feathers, along with red ones from other birds, were worked onto a net-like backing, each carefully tied in place.

A variety of 'o'o once existed on each of the major islands, but today only the Kauai 'o'o 'a'a exists. Other bird species have declined similarly. Of all the Hawaiian islands, Kauai has lost the fewest of its native feathered creatures. Today, the final refuge of Kauai is also changing with the advance of civilization, and with the devastation wrought by Hurricane Iniki, which on September 11, 1992, stripped and opened wide portions of the native forest, making it vulnerable to invasions by alien plants and animals.

The continuing introduction and establishment of these alien species is the greatest single threat to the integrity of Kauai's native areas. Pigs, axis deer and goats, the feral descendants of domestic animals brought to Kauai by Captain James Cook and other Westerners for food and sport, are a tremendous threat because they root out native plants, making it easier for weeds to gain a foothold in the forests. Their voracious eating habits and cloven hooves also destroy the native ground cover, which hastens erosion.

Invasive weeds, such as the banana poka and blackberry, strangle native plants and create a dense canopy that inhibits sunlight from reaching low-growing vegetation. Most of these plants were brought to Kauai by Westerners who wanted attractive or familiar plants for their gardens. The plants escaped from home gardens or were deliberately planted in wild areas, where they flourished in the island's benevolent natural environment.

In much the same way, Kauai's native bird population has been decimated by the introduction of songbirds, which later escaped from their cages, and other birds brought to the island to control insect pests, as with the cattle egret. These alien birds competed with native species for food and habitat, and carried avian malaria, which continues to threaten Kauai's endemic birds. Birds that nest on the ground, such as the threatened Newell's shearwater *(a'o)*, are also extremely vulnerable to wild cats and dogs that are allowed to roam free. A federal program is seeking solutions to the problem of declining native bird populations in the forests of Hawaii, but few solutions appear to be forthcoming.

The Alaka'i is, for the most part, dense jungle. It is cut through occasionally by small streams, which splash through the vegetation. The water is the color of tea, for it is stained by pigmentation in leaves that have been steeping in Alaka'i's water for centuries. There are open spaces in the jungle: bogs, where there is virtually always standing water. A hiker sinks, sometimes to his ankles and sometimes to his waist, in the black mud.

It is so wet in the bogs that plants would drown if they sent their roots too deep, so the root systems stay on the

surface and the plants are stunted. A full-grown, flowering and seeding *'ohi'a* will be a foot high in a bog, while a few yards away another will grow to 50 ft (15 meters). In recent years, a boardwalk has been built through part of the swamp to protect its rare plants from hikers who step off the trail to avoid the bogs.

**Mountains and desert:** Outside the Alaka'i, the island changes dramatically. Trade winds, warm and wet, gather moisture from the vast Pacific, and when they breeze across Kauai are caught in a funnel formed by the **Anahola** mountain range lying to the north and the **Ha'upu** range lying to the east. The breezes are carried to Wai'ale'ale, 5,150 ft (1,562 meters) high, where the altitude and the temperature make them give up their moisture.

The rains fall all along the slopes leading to Wai'ale'ale and then over the Alaka'i, which is 10 miles (16 km) long and 2 miles (3 km) wide. By the time the winds reach the north and west side of the island, they are dry. Thus, while Wai'ale'ale tends to be drenched, Kekaha, on the far west side of the island, gets little more than 12 inches (30 cm) of rain each year.

The only populated place in the uplands is **Koke'e**, at the western end of the swamp. A road runs up from **Waimea** and **Kekaha** into the area, where residents from all over the state have vacation cabins on leased state land. Also inhabitable are a dozen state-owned cabins that anyone can rent, as long as reservations are made well in advance. The cabins are operated from the **Koke'e Lodge**, a restaurant, tourist shop, bar, convenience shopping spot and information center.

Next door is the **Koke'e Museum** with displays depicting the natural history of Kauai and the other islands. There are pictures and live examples of important native plants, as well as maps and guidebooks for sale. Also on exhibit are the birds to be found in the wild, a three-dimensional map of Kauai, a wild boar's head, and more. The lodge and museum are located in the state park, and on its grounds strut *moa*, wild Hawaiian chickens (*Galhus gallus gallus*)

Sugarcane workers spraying herbicide, Kaumakani.

which enjoy special legal protection.

There's great hiking in the Koke'e area, such as the **Iliau Nature Loop** for strolling, and, for the real hiker, the **Kukui Trail**, which drops a steep, zigzag course down the side of the remarkable **Waimea Canyon**. But if you're in the mood for less strenuous serenity, simply drive to the top of Koke'e's beauty to the **Kalalau Valley Lookout** and, on a clear day, meditate on one of the world's most wonderful views. The panorama from that 4,000-ft (1,200-meter) high lookout will more than reward the trials of your zig-zaggy ascent to Koke'e. The lookout offers a wonderful opportunity to watch and listen to many of Kauai's native birds, such as the red and black *'apapane,* and vermilion-colored *'i'iwi,* which frequents the *'ohia* tree.

Also very much worth the effort are a series of dream-like views of the Waimea Canyon. This roseate canyon's headwaters are in Alaka'i. Waterfalls tumble from this green, cool and wet swamp into deep valleys carpeted in greenery.

As the plum and guava-rich valleys converge into gorges, a change quickly occurs. Wetness of the swamp is left behind and the vegetation becomes more sparse here.

The *'ohi'a* gives way to the *kukui*, the candlenut tree. The gorges meet the main canyon, and the *kukui* yields to dry country trees, the native *wiliwili* and introduced *kiawe* and *lantana*. The weather here is hot and dry, and the stream bed holds the only moisture. Reddish dust blows from barren hillsides. By the time the **Waimea River** meets the sea, its currents carry a heavy suspension of earth. From the sky, one can see the river pour into the blue Pacific, like blood oozing from a wound.

**Barking sands:** The people of old Hawaii took advantage of the island's climate changes. The chiefs sometimes moved their courts from the warmth of Waimea to the cooler Wailua on the east side. When Captain Cook arrived at **Waimea** in January, 1778, there were no chiefs there. Historians suggest the royalty were holding court at Wailua.

Cane field workers.

Cook left before the *ali'i*, the chiefs, could return to greet him.

Cook's journal speaks of collections of grass structures all along the southern coast of Kauai. They indicated the closeness of the island's people to the sea. Kauai provided its residents with many ways to the sea; the island is ringed with sandy beaches. The largest is the stretch of nearly unbroken sand from Waimea to **Polihale**, a distance of more than 15 miles (24 km). Today, there is a state park at Polihale that offers campsites, showers and pavilions. Permits are available from the office of State Parks, located in the three-story state office building in downtown Lihu'e.

Further along the beach is the **Pacific Missile Range Facility** at **Barking Sands**, which has become the site of controversial "Star Wars" rocket launches in recent years, followed by sugar plantations, privately-owned property fronting the shore, and Waimea.

On the south bank of the Waimea River is the Russian **Fort Elizabeth**. In 1816, an agent of the Imperial Russian government came to Kauai seeking the cargo of a ship that broke up on the island's shore. The man, Dr Anton Sheffer, convinced Kauai's King Kaumuali'i that they could conquer the rest of the islands together.

Kaumuali'i helped Sheffer build a fort along the river. He used Russian design and Hawaiian construction techniques, which is why today travelers will find a star-shaped Russian-designed fort built of traditional Kauai stonework. Sheffer's Machiavellian bid for Hawaiian power failed miserably, but ruins of the fort, named after Russian Tzar Nicholas' queen, remain as a testimonial to his adventurism.

Just a few miles east of Waimea, on the ocean side of sleepy **Hanapepe** town, are a group of prehistoric **salt ponds** which have been worked by local Hawaiian salt gatherers since time immemorial. Here, along the seaside just off Highway 543, members of the Hui Hana Pa'akai 'O Hanapepe (The Hanapepe Salt Makers Group) still manufacture salt in the old Hawaiian way during **Barking Sands Beach.**

spring and summer months. These traditional saltmakers fill small, mud-lined ponds with sea water, and let the sun evaporate the water, leaving behind heavy salt crystals. Many of these Hawaiians work ponds that have been passed down through his or her family for several generations.

Also on Kauai's west side is the prestigious **Pacific Tropical Botanical Garden** in **Lawa'i Valley**. This is a congressionally-chartered botanical garden whose aims include saving endangered plants of the tropics, locating and growing plants of medicinal and economic importance and informing the public of significant findings. In recent years, the garden has begun collecting and propagating Hawaii's own endemic plants, which are found nowhere else.

A satellite garden at **Limahuli,** on the island's North Shore, is dedicated almost entirely to native plants and includes a 900-acre (360-hectare) natural area preserve that encompasses much of the striking valley. Tours of the gardens are available daily, but one should call ahead to make a reservation because walking space is limited.

Prior to Hurricane Iniki, tours normally included a visit through **Lawa'i Kai**, the verdant estate of John Gregg Allerton, who willed his gardens to the Pacific Tropical Botanical Garden on his death. Lawa'i Kai is a wonderland of vegetation and statuary at the base of **Lawa'i**, where it meets the sea in a clean, white sand beach. The estate's lovely gardens and buildings – including Queen Emma's summer home – were devastated by the 30-ft (9-meter) south swell generated by Hurricane Iniki and are not expected to be restored for some time.

As one moves further east and then north to the wet and windward sides of the island, Hawaiian names of other Kauai beaches roll off the tongue like a staccato poem: **Po'ipu, Maha'ulepu, Kalapaki, Hanama'ulu, Wailua, Kealia, Moloa'a, Kilauea, Hanalei, Wainiha, Ha'ena, Hanakapi'ai, Kalalau, Honopu, Nu'alolo, Miloli'i**. And these are only a few of the better-known

**'or the birds.**

ones. Some of Kauai's beaches are easily accessible, some require hiking, some can be reached only by boat or helicopter, and to get to some of them requires the permission of the owner of an adjacent property.

**The little people:** Theories differ as to how and when Kauai, Hawaii's oldest populated island, was first inhabited, but popular are fables regarding the *menehune*, a group of lower-class Polynesian people discussed in this book's historical section. Modern legend describes the *menehune* as a race of little people, like leprechauns. They were seldom seen and worked only after dark. In a single night, they would perform prodigious works, and accept in payment only a single shrimp per worker.

Among the construction projects attributed to these little people are the **Menehune Ditch** in Waimea, which indicated a knowledge of stonework not seen elsewhere in Hawaii, and the **Alekoko Fishpond**, also called the **Menehune Fishpond**, outside Lihu'e as well as near **Nawiliwili Harbor**.

Kauai folklore is rich in place-name romance. The volcano goddess, Pele, for example, was associated with Kauai long before she made her home at Kilauea Crater on the Big Island. One famous story about Pele places her at beautiful **Ha'ena** on Kauai's North Shore during a big hula festival. In order to join the dancing, Pele took the form of a beautiful young woman and fell in love with a young, handsome Kauai chief named Lohiau. The remnants of **Lohiau's hula platform** can still be found at the Western side of **Ke'e Beach** in the Ha'ena area.

Other Kauai legends, or oral traditions, concern the activities of *kahuna*, the Hawaiian class of trained professionals or wise men. In the realm of superstition are many visible remnants of ancient Hawaiian culture that in recent years have become popular tourist attractions. One such attraction is a large bank of rock at **Wailua**, just up the road toward the mountains from the **Coco Palms Hotel**. It is a birthstone, a place where persons of high rank were born. **Ke'e Beach.**

**Pohakuho'ohanau**, it is called or more commonly, *piko* stone, *piko* being the Hawaiian word for navel.

According to this stone's legend, the umbilical cords of the newly-born were wrapped in cloth and hidden in cracks of the stone. They were carefully hidden, because ancient chants indicate that if a rat were to steal the cord, the child would grow up to be a thief. Such superstitions – not too unlike Western fears of walking under ladders or breaking mirrors – imbued Hawaiian culture with yet other layers of respect and fantasy.

Kauai's Hawaiianness is still very obvious, but since 1835, when Hawaii's first commercial sugar plantation was started at Koloa, the island's ethnic character has gone through radical and charming changes. As in other parts of Hawaii, sugar attracted a diverse lot of people willing to work in its dusty, itchy fields and pungent mills. First, in the 1850s, came the Chinese. Then came the Japanese, and shortly after the Portuguese, Puerto Ricans, Germans, Koreans, Spaniards and last, the Filipinos.

Thus many of Kauai's communities developed as plantation towns, often with the different races separated into camps within the towns. The camp towns were spread around the island, generally as they are found now, along the sea, so sugar could easily be transported to ships for export.

Today, many of the sugar firms that started the towns are gone or have been merged with other companies, but the communities themselves persist. **Waimea, Numila** (the Hawaiian pronunciation of New Mill), **Puhi, Kealia** and **Kilauea** are some of the towns that have lost the plantations that helped build them.

There are only four sugar mills now remaining, and five sugar-growing companies. Gay & Robinson grinds its cane at Olokele Sugar Company's **Kaumakani** mill, Kekaha Sugar has its mill in **Kekaha**, McBryde Sugar Company has the **Koloa** mill, and Lihu'e Plantation Company has its mill in the Kauai county seat, **Lihu'e**.

Two museums in Lihu'e are highly

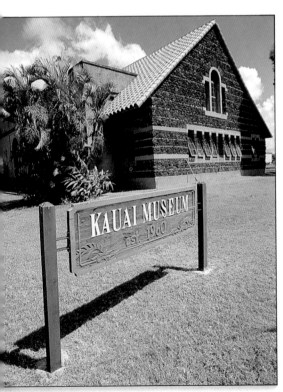

recommended. First, in the center of town, on Rice Street, is the **Kauai Museum**. It is open weekdays and Saturday mornings, and often offers half-day courses in such activities as *lauhala* weaving and lei-making. A gallery upstairs frequently displays the work of local artists, and many excellent books and maps may be found in its gift shop. Located off Nawiliwili Road (Hwy 58) in Lihu'e is the **Grove Farm Homestead**, a historical museum of plantation life in Kauai. Reservations are required in order to tour it.

Both museums offer a good introduction to the contributions made by Kauai's elite *kama'aina* families: Rice, Wilcox, Sinclair, Gay and Robinson. Many had missionary roots, but made their fortunes in the island's sugar plantations and ranches. Some, such as William Harrison Rice and his son, William Hyde Rice, had a strong affinity for the Hawaiian people and culture and did a great deal to keep the language and its legends alive.

The Kauai Museum was founded by

Rice's progeny. George N. Wilcox, whose parents were among the earliest American Protestant missionaries to the Sandwich Islands, left a legacy of land and sugar. He established Grove Farm plantation, which remains one of the largest private landowners on Kauai. With the decline of sugar, Grove Farm has branched into land development, including Kukui Grove, Kauai's only shopping mall.

The Wilcox family also still has extensive holdings on the North Shore, and recently developed a shopping center in Hanalei. The Sinclair-Robinson-Gay clan, which purchased the tiny island of Ni'ihau in 1864, continues to be active in cattle ranching and sugar cultivation.

**The good life:** The island has a substantial transient population, which grew significantly in the months following Hurricane Iniki. While the term "transient" can be used to refer to tourists, on Kauai it is more frequently used to identify people called "hippies."

They are wanderers, and sometimes backpacking college students, who generally come with little money to a place they consider paradise. Some work at odd jobs, some collect public welfare, some have personal incomes, and some make their living selling marijuana they grow in the hills and in cane fields.

In the early 1970s, there were several communities of transients on the island. The best known was **Taylor Camp**, on the far north side of the island at Ha'ena. There, the mostly-young visitors constructed houses in the trees. The structures were made of cast-off wood, bamboo and clear plastic. Sixty or more people lived there at a time. Their homes were shaded by Java plum trees and flanked by the small, clear **Limahuli Stream**. In the front yard was a magnificent white sand beach.

Taylor Camp took its name from its owner in the late 1960s and early 1970s, Howard Taylor, the brother of actress Elizabeth Taylor. In the mid 1970s, the state bought the land for part of the planned **Ha'ena State Beach Park**, but it took years of legal wrangling to move the transients, who claimed squatters' rights. Finally, the court actions com- **Po'ipu Beach.**

plete, the state burned the tree houses.

Many of the Taylor campers found other resting spots, taking their bamboo and plastic with them to more desolate parts of Kauai. Some were drawn to **Kauapea Beach** outside Kilauea, in part because of its remote location and romantic misnomer, Secret Beach. Another of the popular new places was located in the deep valleys of Kauai's **Na Pali Coast**.

The road system that circles most of the island stops at the ends of this coastline. These 13 miles (20 km) flanked by **Polihale Beach Park** on the west and **Ha'ena Beach Park**, which is popular with campers, on the north. Most of the Na Pali area itself is under state parks jurisdiction.

On their northern end, the valleys are deep and green, but toward the vast, sandy beach at Polihale, they become dry. A foot trail starts at Ha'ena – there is no vehicular access to Na Pali – then rises on a ridge and drops into lush Hanakapi'ai, which has a lovely pool and waterfall at its back and a crescent of white sand at its mouth. The ocean here is often treacherous, but the sunbathing is generally superior. And although public nudity is illegal, many visitors brown themselves in the buff when the park rangers are not around.

**Zigzagging:** From Hanakapi'ai, the Na Pali trail zigzags a heart-thumping course upwards and scurries in and out of small valleys and across a sheer cliff face to **Hanakoa**, a hanging valley. Like several other valleys here, Hanakoa sweeps from the heights in a flourish of vegetation and ends abruptly, hanging over the ocean, its stream turning into a misty waterfall that falls on the rocks and sea below.

There is a rough trail shelter well-used by hunters at Hanakoa, and from it the jungle-shaded trail wanders out and along the shallow valleys and cliffs until it drops, and ends, in **Kalalau**, which is the largest of Na Pali's valleys. You can camp at Kalalau, Hanakoa and Hanakapi'ai with a permit from the state parks office in Lihu'e; hikers who venture beyond Hanakapi'ai also need per-

Wainiha Bay near Ha'ena.

mits. Parks officials maintain portable toilets in Hanakapi'ai and Kalalau, but there's no safe drinking water. You should boil or use purification tablets if you plan to use stream water. There are no cabins and only an occasional uninhabited cave.

At Kalalau, there is a stream at one end of the valley mouth, and a waterfall at the other. A beach joins the two. And at the back of Kalalau are fruit trees, brooks and the remains of ancient house sites and stone-lined taro patches used by Hawaiians who lived here until the early years of this century.

In fact, all along Na Pali, hikers will find many reminders of the Hawaiians who inhabited the valleys. House platforms, stone walls, irrigation ditches, coffee, taro and even the trail itself were built and planted by the families that settled in what is now a wilderness.

A hardy hiker can reach **Kalalau Valley** from Ha'ena in six to eight grueling hours, but you need a kayak, motor boat or helicopter to get to most of the rest of Na Pali's valleys and beaches. The major attractions are **Honopu, Awa'awapuhi, Nu'alolo-aina, Nu'alolo-kai** and **Miloli'i.**

The people who lived here in centuries past had trails, but they are impassable today. The tree trunk that spanned a section of cliff between Honopu and Awa'awapuhi is rotted and the ladder that connected the upper and lower sections of the Nu'alolo-aina and Nu'alolo-kai trail is gone. But in the valleys, the remnants of the old civilization remain.

The extensive stonework survives that formed the taro paddies of Nu'alolo-aina (*aina* means fertile land), a hanging valley, and the remains of the fishing village at Nu'alolo-kai (*kai* means sea). The people of the former had access to the sea, and the people of the latter had little land or fresh water, so each group worked what it had, and they formed a trading relationship, a single community built of necessity in two valleys.

**Aquaculture and agronomics:** Today's Kauai is a little more complicated, but the farmers and fishermen are still here. Farmers are growing taro at Hanalei, Waimea and a few other places. They're growing papayas at Moloa'a along the main highway between Anahola and Kilauea. Kilauea Agronomics grows guava in large orchards outside Kilauea, and then processes the fruit into a frozen puree concentrate for tropical juices. Sugar is still cultivated over most of the dry and windy south and west portions of the island, but the wetter eastside fields are slowly being abandoned. Tropical flowers and crops are grown on small farms, and the fresh produce is often sold in the weekly sunshine markets held throughout the island.

There are still a few commercial fishermen left, but the majority of Kauai's fishing is done by individuals with their own small boats, who fish on days off from their regular jobs. Some of the commercial fishing docks have been taken over by sport fishing boats that take visitors out fishing for prizes like marlin, *aku, kawakawa* and *mahimahi.*

But the newest form of fishing on Kauai is a modern version of the traditional Hawaiian fishponds. In old Hawaii, large ponds were built along the

**Family-owned taro farm.**

shoreline to form enclosures in which fish for eating were raised and harvested. On Kauai, the best example of such a fishpond is a rare one built in a river instead of on the shore. The aforementioned Alekoko, or Menehune Fishpond, at Lihu'e was constructed by cutting off an elbow in the **Hule'ia River**.

It is no longer in regular use, but is a scenic spot much visited and admired by both residents and visitors who gaze upon it from an overlook or quietly paddle kayaks up the river. The modern fishponds are built inland on Kauai, and used primarily for prawns and a locally popular freshwater fish known as *tilapia*. The process is called aquaculture.

**Visitors welcome:** Kauai people are very low key and guarded about their more private and specially beautiful places, but that does not mean that tourism is shunted aside on the Garden Island. Indeed, Kauai is visited by more than a million people annually, although the numbers dropped drastically following Hurricane Iniki.

Many arrive in the morning to climb into tour buses and visit scenic areas, and leave in the evening of the same day. But many others spend several days becoming acquainted with the island. Mostly, the visitors come from the mainland United States, from Japan, and from Canada, but the lure of the islands is worldwide, and tourists come from around the globe.

They usually stay in hotels and condominiums at four major tourist destination areas, each providing something different. The big four are Po'ipu, Lihu'e, Waipouli-Wailua and Hanalei.

**Po'ipu** on Kauai's southernmost point is the sunniest of the island's resort districts. It has several large resorts, smaller hotels and many condominiums, all fronting the shore-line. There are hot, sandy beaches, generally calm, light blue water and several scenic spots, such as the **Spouting Horn**, a water spout in the shoreline rocks of an old lava flow, and "**Brennecke's Beach**," a spot renowned for its sometimes perfect bodysurfing waves.

This portion of the island suffered most from Iniki's wrath, experiencing both its strong winds and huge waves. The future of some of its hotels remains in question. Many homes, especially those along the coastline leading to Spouting Horn, were also destroyed. Some are being slowly rebuilt, but others have been razed and the empty lots put up for sale by owners who don't have the money or heart to rebuild.

**Lihu'e** is the seat of county government, the island's major business district and shopping area, and the site of Kauai's only airport capable of handling commercial jet traffic. Nearby are the Menehune Fishpond, Nawiliwili Harbor, the island's major port, and most amenities visitors crave while on this slow-paced island.

The Lihu'e area has Kauai's most talked-about hotel, the Westin Kauai, Chris Hemmeter's daring overhaul of the old Kauai Surf, on **Kalapaki Beach**. The Westin, too, took a major hit from Iniki and was foreclosed upon by the banks when Hemmeter bowed out. Its future is in question.

A string of resort hotels and condo-

Bodysurfing, Brennecke's Beach.

miniums runs along the shore from Wailua to Kapaʻa, with most of them in between at Waipouli. Here are the **Wailua Golf Course**, a municipal 18-hole facility, **Wailua Beach**, the **Wailua River**, which carries tour boats to the **Fern Grotto** (a favorite wedding site), and the modern **Coconut Plantation Marketplace**, a resort shopping center. This area suffered least during Iniki and has been largely rebuilt. Many of its hotels and condominiums remained open throughout the storm and continue to cater to visitors.

On the north shore, meanwhile, is **Princeville**, a 1,000-acre (400-hectare) resort with two 18-hole golf courses and a large clubhouse, a shopping center, homes, several luxurious condominium projects, Hanalei Bay Resort, and a luxury hotel which is managed by Sheraton. Princeville offers striking views of the bay and valleys at Hanalei, which is one of the wettest – and correspondingly greenest – parts of the island. When rains drop upon the mountains, countless waterfalls hang like strands of silk thread on the dark green cliffs.

Beginning at Princeville, to the end of the road at Haʻena, there are several valleys, each fronted by a curved sandy beach. **Hanalei Bay**, the largest on Kauai, is a favorite spot for yachtsmen in summer, and there are frequently more than two dozen yachts at anchor here. In winter, when big surf from the north makes anchorage unsafe, the bay is a challenge for the island's surfers.

Waves generated by storms in the north Pacific can reach 30 ft (9 meters) in height on the reefs of the north shore, although surf in the 10- to 20-ft range is most common The huge waves create clouds of floating sea mist, known as *ehukai,* all along the north shore from fall to spring.

Further north along this coastline is a jewel-like spot called **Lumahaʻi**, a cuticle of sand whose brightness is offset by black lava rock that protects it on both sides. There is the blue of sea beyond the sand and the green of *hala* trees behind it. Access to the beach down a dirt trail is across privately-

**Fern Grotto.**

owned property, but no one has been arrested for trespassing on this lovely spot in recent years. This is the beach where many parts of the movie **South Pacific** were filmed, where Mitzi Gaynor sang to the world that she'd wash that man right out of her hair.

**Forbidden island:** The resort areas, however, haven't cornered the market on Kauai's best places. Indeed, one part of Kauai County is completely *kapu*, or off limits, to even longtime residents of Kauai. This is the privately owned island of **Ni'ihau**, referred to by some people as "the forbidden island."

Across the **Kaulakahi Channel** from Kauai's west side, about 17 miles (27 km) distant, Ni'ihau rises dimly through sea mists like a huge prehistoric creature. It is a dry island, denied rain because it falls in the lee of Kauai, whose mountains collect most of the moisture. Ni'ihau was bought from King Kamehameha V in 1864 and remains in the hands of Kauai's Robinson family.

Fewer than 300 people live on the island, and virtually all who do work for the Robinsons, running cattle and sheep, making charcoal from *kiawe* trees and gathering honey. Ni'ihau is the only island in Hawaii where Hawaiian is the primary language.

In Ni'ihau's only village, **Pu'uwai**, there is a grammar school run by three Ni'ihau residents, and children learn English along with the other academic pursuits recommended by the state board of education, including solar-powered computers, as the island has no electricity. The children go to Kauai or to Oahu (usually to the Kamehameha Schools for Hawaiians) for high school and further education, although those who wish to remain on the island may pursue their high school diploma on Ni'ihau.

State education officials and tax officers are allowed on the island, and a couple of doctors make infrequent trips to check on the populace, but otherwise, access is limited to residents and members of the Robinson family. The residents move freely from Ni'ihau to Kauai on the somewhat limited transportation facility, a World War II landing craft,

**The forbidden island of Ni'ihau.**

because there is no airfield on Niʻihau. The only visitors allowed on Niʻihau are those who take a long, expensive helicopter ride to a remote and uninhabited part of the island. The helicopter service was established to provide emergency medical care for the island's residents, and the strictly controlled excursions offered to tourists help offset the operating costs.

The island is politically a part of Kauai County, but the relationship is little more than a paper one. There are virtually no county services, no county roads, no sewers or garbage collection, indeed, no county employees. But Niʻihau residents do vote. They voted Republican long after the Democratic Party gained control of the state government, and while the rest of "modern" Hawaii voted 17-1 in favor of statehood, Niʻihau's Hawaiian voters cast the one dissenting district vote against it.

Niʻihau is a small, arid island – it contains just 73 sq. miles (190 sq. km) compared to Kauai's 553 sq. miles (1,440 sq. km) – but in the center of its

desolation is **Lake Halaliʻi**, the largest (182 acre/73 hectare) natural lake in the Hawaiian Islands.

One of Niʻihau's claims to fame comes in the form of precious garlands that Niʻihau lei-makers make of tiny shells, which wash onto the island's shores. A good Niʻihau shell lei is highly priced in off-Niʻihau jewelry stores and museum shops. It takes hundreds of shells to make one strand, and several strands to make a proper Niʻihau shell lei.

The lei are worn with pride by Hawaii's women to special social gatherings, to be displayed and to be admired. Indeed, at any Kauai gathering worthy of proper *kamaʻaina* patronage, the only adornment of stature equivalent to that of the Niʻihau shell *lei* is another *lei* native to Kauai County: a wreath of *maile* and *mokihana*.

**Scents of old Kauai:** While the fragrant *maile* vine grows on several of the islands, it is Kauai's small-leaved *maile lauliʻi* that is most fragrant. And the anise-scented *mokihana (Pelea anisata)* is found only on Kauai.

*Maile* is a vine that normally grows on the sides of other plants, in the wet areas of the island's mountains. Given a twist, its bark comes loose from the stem and can be pulled free, leaving a supple strand with the leaves still attached. These strands are tied together into lengths of six or more feet. Six or eight lengths are then braided together. The aroma comes some time after the stripping, from the bruised bark.

*Maile* alone can be draped around the neck, or used in place of ribbon-cutting for formal dedications. Instead of being cut, the *maile* is untied. But for wearing, even more prized than *maile* alone is a wreath intertwined with a lei of *mokihana* berries.

These berries, too, are gathered in the mountains above Kauai. They grow on gangly shrubs with waxy leaves that also give off the pleasant scent of anise. The berries are light green and shaped somewhat like small, round dice. The *maile-mokihana* lei is most frequently given to honored visitors, graduates and to the bride and groom at traditional weddings.

**Left and right**, scents of old Kauai.

# INSIGHT GUIDES
# Travel Tips

# Swatch. The others just watch.

seahorse/fall winter 94-95

shockproof
splashproof
priceproof
boreproof
swiss made

swatch+
SCUBA 200

# TRAVEL TIPS

### Getting There
314 By Air
314 By Sea

### Travel Essentials
315 Visas & Passports
315 Money Matters
315 Health
315 What to Wear

### Getting Acquainted
316 Government
316 Economy
316 Geography
317 Population
317 Time Zones
317 Climate
318 Culture & Customs
318 Business Hours
319 Holidays
319 Religious Services

### Communications
319 Media
320 Postal Services
320 Telephone

### Emergencies
320 Security & Crime

### Getting Around
321 Island Hopping
321 Orientation
321 Public Transportation

### Where to Stay
322 Oahu
325 Hawaii
326 Kauai
328 Maui
331 Molokai & Lanai
331 Camping
331 State Parks
331 County Parks

### Food Digest
332 Where to Eat
332 Oahu
333 Hawaii
333 Kauai
333 Maui

### Things to Do
334 Tours & Cruises
334 Around Honolulu
335 Waikiki
335 Elsewhere on Oahu
335 Neighbor Islands
336 Diary of Events

### 338 Nightlife

### Shopping
339 What to Buy
340 Shopping Areas

### Sports
342 Watersports
342 Land Sports

### 343 Language

### Useful Addresses
344 Hawaii Visitors Bureaux
344 Consulates

### 345 Further Reading

### 347 Art/Photo Credits

### 348 Index

# GETTING THERE

*Unless otherwise stated all numbers are preceded by the area code 808. Numbers beginning (800) are all toll-free if dialed in the US.*

## BY AIR

Hawaii is regularly serviced from the North American mainland, from Europe, from the South Pacific, and from Asia. Aircraft landing at **Honolulu International Airport** touch down on the Reef Runaway, completed in 1977 on a shallow reef-lagoon between Honolulu Harbor and Pearl Harbor. Inside the airport complex are murals, sculptures, paintings, weaving, stitcheries and batiks in Hawaiian themes created by top local artists. This airport art display, which breathes cultural life and color onto the terminal's walls and stretching corridors, is a result of a 1967 Hawaii legislative act that designated one percent of all appropriated public works funds for the purchase of works for state buildings throughout Hawaii. Japanese, Hawaiian and Chinese gardens also enhance the terminal's promenade areas.

Some airlines fly direct to neighbor islands, particularly Maui and the Big Island, from the US mainland. If you're traveling on a full-fare round-trip ticket from the US mainland or Canada, inquire about discount tickets that allow travel from Oahu to any of the neighboring islands at a relatively low fare per island stopover. This bargain, designed to serve as an island-hopping incentive, is available in cooperation with Aloha Airlines and Hawaiian Airlines, the two primary inter-island carriers.

**Leaving the airport**: A yellow-brown-and-orange striped bus – TheBus – departs frequently from Honolulu Airport to Waikiki via downtown and Ala Moana Shopping Center. Exact change is required. Passengers are limited to one carry-on bag compact enough to be held on the lap or placed under the seat. No exceptions. If you have more than a small carry-on piece of luggage, forget the bus.

Better to take a taxi into Waikiki and pick up a rental car there. You can rent cars at the airport. But the drive into Waikiki is no fun. It's a messy route, and after a long flight, few people want to negotiate the half-hour drive. A taxi is more relaxing, and you'll get a pleasant earful from the driver.

Airport 24-hour switchboard: Tel: 836-6411
Airport visitor information: Tel: 836-6413

## INTERNATIONAL AIRLINES

**Air New Zealand**: Tel: (800) 262-1234
**American Airlines**: Tel: 833-7600
**Canadian Airlines International**:
Tel: (800) 426-7000
**China Airlines**: Tel: 955-0088
**Continental Airlines**: Tel: 523-0000
**Delta Airlines**: Tel: (800) 221-1212
**Garuda Indonesia**: Tel: (800) 342-7832
**Japan Airlines**: Tel: 521-1441
**Korean Air Lines**: Tel: 923-7302
**Northwest Airlines**: Tel: 955-2255
**Philippine Airlines**: Tel: (800) 435-9725
**Qantas Airways**: Tel: (800) 227-4500
**TWA**: Tel: (800) 221-2000
**United Airlines**: Tel: 547-2211

## INTER-ISLAND AIRLINES

**Air Molokai**: Tel: 521-0090
**Aloha Airlines**: Tel: 836-1111; Maui: 244-9071; Big Island: 935-5771; Kauai: 245-3691; toll free from mainland: (800) 367-5250
**Hawaiian Airlines**: Tel: 537-5100. toll free from other islands: (800) 882-8811; Toll free from mainland: (800) 367-5320.

For information on inter-island travel, *see Getting Around.*

## BY SEA

Calling by ship at Honolulu Harbor in the downtown district of Oahu is still a gracious and romantic way to arrive in the islands. Only a few passenger liners, however, regularly put in at Honolulu these days. Some of these liners are of foreign registration and people cannot legally travel between only two US ports on them. Some lucky souls, of course, arrive by private yacht.

A Wise Man Never Thinks How Far He's Come. He Thinks How Far He Can Still Travel.

FINE CHAMPAGNE
COGNAC
REMY MARTIN
XO
SPECIAL

REMY XO BECAUSE LIFE IS WHAT YOU MAKE IT

# INSIGHT GUIDES

## COLORSET NUMBERS

### North America
160 **A**laska
173 American Southwest
    Atlanta
227 **B**oston
275 **C**alifornia
180 California, Northern
161 California, Southern
237 Canada
184C Chicago
184 Crossing America
243 **F**lorida
240 **H**awaii
275A **L**os Angeles
243A **M**iami
237B **M**ontreal
    **N**ational Parks of
    America: East
    National Parks of
    America: West
269 Native America
100 New England
184E New Orleans
184F New York City
133 New York State
147 **P**acific Northwest
184B Philadelphia
172 **R**ockies
275B **S**an Francisco
184D Seattle
    Southern States
    of America
186 **T**exas
237A **V**ancouver
184C **W**ashington DC

### Latin America and The Caribbean
150 **A**mazon Wildlife
260 Argentina
188 **B**ahamas
292 Barbados
    Belize
217 Bermuda
127 Brazil
260A Buenos Aires
162 **C**aribbean
151 Chile
281 Costa Rica
    Cuba
118 **E**cuador
213 **J**amaica
285 **M**exico
285A Mexico City
249 **P**eru
156 Puerto Rico
127A **R**io de Janeiro
116 **S**outh America
139 **T**rinidad & Tobago
198 **V**enezuela

### Europe
155 **A**lsace
158A Amsterdam
167A Athens
263 Austria
107 **B**altic States
219B Barcelona

187 Bay of Naples
109 Belgium
135A Berlin
178 Brittany
109A Brussels
144A Budapest
213 Burgundy
122 **C**atalonia
141 Channel Islands
135E Cologne
119 Continental Europe
189 Corsica
291 Côte d'Azur
165 Crete
226 Cyprus
114 Czech/Slovak Reps
238 **D**enmark
135B Dresden
142B Dublin
135F Düsseldorf
149 **E**astern Europe
148A Edinburgh
123 **F**inland
209B Florence
154 France
135C Frankfurt
135 **G**ermany
148B Glasgow
279 Gran Canaria
124 Great Britain
167 Greece
166 Greek Islands
135G **H**amburg
144 Hungary
256 **I**celand
142 Ireland
209 Italy
202A **L**isbon
258 Loire Valley
124A London
201 **M**adeira
219A Madrid
157 Mallorca & Ibiza
117 Malta
101A Moscow
135D Munich
158 **N**etherlands
111 Normandy
120 Norway
124B **O**xford
154A **P**aris
115 Poland
202 Portugal
114A Prague
153 Provence
177 **R**hine
209A Rome
101 Russia
130 **S**ardinia
148 Scotland
261 Sicily
264 South Tyrol
219 Spain
220 Spain, Southern
101B St. Petersburg
170 Sweden
232 Switzerland

112 **T**enerife
210 Tuscany
174 **U**mbria
209C **V**enice
263A Vienna
267 **W**ales
183 Waterways of Europe

### Middle East and Africa
268A **C**airo
204 **E**ast African Wildlife
268 Egypt
208 **G**ambia & Senegal
252 **I**srael
236A Istanbul
252A **J**erusalem-Tel Aviv
214 Jordan
270 **K**enya
235 **M**orocco
259 **N**amibia
265 Nile, The
257 **S**outh Africa
113 **T**unisia
236 Turkey
171 Turkish Coast
215 **Y**emen

### Asia/Pacific
287 **A**sia, East
207 Asia, South
262 Asia, South East
194 Asian Wildlife,
    Southeast
272 Australia
206 **B**ali Baru
246A Bangkok
234A Beijing
247B **C**alcutta
234 China
247A **D**elhi, Jaipur, Agra
169 **G**reat Barrier Reef
196 **H**ong Kong
247 **I**ndia
212 India, South
128 Indian Wildlife
143 Indonesia
278 **J**apan
266 Java
203A **K**athmandu
300 Korea
145 **M**alaysia
218 Marine Life in the
    South China Sea
272B Melbourne
211 Myanmar
203 **N**epal
293 New Zealand
205 **P**akistan
222 Philippines
250 **R**ajasthan
159 **S**ingapore
105 Sri Lanka
272 Sydney
175 **T**aiwan
246 Thailand
278A Tokyo
255 **V**ietnam
193 **W**estern Himalaya

# TRAVEL ESSENTIALS

## VISAS & PASSPORTS

Some people forget that Hawaii, like California and New York, is part of the United States. Whatever requirements are necessary for entry to the United States are necessary for Hawaii. Visitors from most foreign countries need to show a valid passport with a US visa. For onward travelers requiring visas for other countries, or for those experiencing problems with their own passports, a listing of foreign consulates in Hawaii is found under *Useful Addresses*.
US Passport Agency: Tel: 541-1919
US Customs: Tel: 836-3613
US Immigration: Tel: 541-1379
Travel immunization information: Tel: 586-4586

## MONEY MATTERS

Hawaii uses standard US currency and coins in all denominations. $1 = 100 cents. All internationally-popular credit cards are accepted most everywhere: American Express, Visa, MasterCard, Discovery, JCB, and to a lesser degree, Diners Club. Most car rental companies require a credit card. Cash machines are everywhere, especially at banks and shopping centers. They accept most bank cards from the mainland and are accessible 24-hours daily.
**Currency Exchange**: Currency conversion is readily available at Honolulu International Airport, in the customs area, and elsewhere at most major branches of banks in Hawaii. Currency exchange is also available at most hotels, although the rate tends to be a little less than at the bank. Normal banking hours are Monday–Thursday 8am–3pm, and Friday 8am–6pm. Some banks open at 8.30am. Note that street money changers are non-existent in Hawaii. Banks are everywhere. In almost every small town or hamlet, on Oahu or on the other islands, there is a Bank of Hawaii branch, or often a First Hawaiian Bank branch.

## HEALTH

Health standards in Hawaii are the same as Europe and North America. Tap water is safe everywhere.
**For foreign visitors**: the US does not have national health insurance. Most hospital care is paid by private insurance, health plans, or out of one's own

pocket. Be sure you're covered before arriving.
Not just "mad dogs and Englishmen" choose to go out in Hawaii's midday sun. Sunbathing is a common sport here. To prevent sunburn, be sure to use a sunscreen (e.g. PABA) when exposing yourself to the intense ultraviolet rays found in these latitudes. Also, tan slowly: take no more than about 30 minutes of direct sun exposure the first day, 40 minutes the second day, and 50 minutes the third day, slowly creating a tolerance for tropical sunlight.
For treatment of sunburn, commercial remedies are available, but locals often rub on the juice of a freshly cut aloe vera cactus plant. Liquid vitamin E also soothes sunburn when applied topically.
**Travel immunization information**: Tel: 586-4586

## WHAT TO WEAR

Dress is cool and casual in Honolulu and even more so beyond the city proper. Light, loose garments are suitable for the summer months. Wear what makes you comfortable. Local Hawaiian-print *muumuu* and aloha shirts are practical all-round garments and are considered an acceptable substitute for continental wear on most occasions. (Just don't wear matching prints with your spouse or partner.) Thongs, flip-flops, slippers, *zoris* – different names for the same thing – are ideal for pacing the pavement and are easy to slip off and on at the beach.
A few exclusive restaurants and nightclubs still require a coat, maybe a tie, and definitely shoes, but they are rare exceptions. Leather sandals and shoes are appropriate for night life. In most island homes, shoes are removed at the entrance.
For the cooler, wetter months, pack a sweater and an umbrella. A parka and heavy jacket are advised for hiking in mountainous areas on Maui, Kauai and particularly on the Big Island.

## ANIMAL & AGRICULTURAL REGULATIONS

Hawaii is rabies-free, snake-free, and poison ivy-free. All incoming animals are placed in quarantine for 120 days at the owner's expense.
**Agricultural Regulations**: Baggage is inspected coming and going through the airport. It is forbidden to import and export fresh fruits and plants, except for coconuts and pineapples. Avocados, bananas, and papayas must first be fumigated at the Plant Quarantine Division at 701 Ilalo Street, and mangoes and lichees must be pitted and peeled before they can be taken to the mainland. Fumigated fruits bound for foreign countries may be purchased at the airport. Most flowers strung in lei may be worn to the mainland. Those restricted outside Hawaii are the rose, gardenia, jade flower, *maunaloa* and all plants in soil.
State Dept of Agriculture: Tel: 948-0145
Animal Quarantine Station: Tel: 483-7171
Plant Quarantine Station: Tel: 541-2951

# GETTING ACQUAINTED

## GOVERNMENT

The structure and hierarchy of Hawaii's local government is simple, actually, although the shenanigans and machinations of some politicians are as dismal as anywhere.

The governor of Hawaii is popularly elected, as are the lieutenant governor, state legislators, and county mayors. The state legislature convenes in January each year, in Honolulu, for a 60-day session. The legislature is comprised of the Senate, with 25 members, and the House of Representatives, with 51 members. For the past several decades, the dominant political party has been the Democratic Party.

The state is divided into four counties, with a mayor for each one: Honolulu, Hawaii (Big Island), Maui, and Kauai. The City and County of Honolulu – the only officially incorporated city in the state – includes Oahu and all islands of the Hawaiian chain not included in one of the three other counties. The County of Maui includes Molokai, Lanai, and the uninhabited island of Kaho'olawe. The County of Kauai includes the privately-owned island of Ni'ihau, with its Hawaiian population of 230.

The last of the 50 states to be admitted to the American union (in 1959), Hawaii has a congressional delegation of four in Washington, DC: two senators and two representatives.

## ECONOMY

For a century, agriculture dominated the economy of Hawaii. Sugar was king of the islands, followed by pineapple. (Both crops are introduced species to the islands.) But after World War II, the structure of Hawaii's economy began a slow shift, and by statehood in 1959, Hawaii was ready to begin a new economic era: tourism. Sugar has in fact been on a steady decline: in 1972, there were 230,000 acres under sugar cultivation; in 1992, there were less than 150,000 acres. That same year, one of the Big Island's largest sugar companies went bankrupt.

The four big industries in Hawaii are, in order, tourism ($9.5 billion); the military ($3.2 billion); sugar ($330 million); pineapples ($220 million).

As tourism is the top money earner, the quality of its hotels is paramount. Of the world's top 100 resorts, according to *Conde Nast's Traveler*, eight are in Hawaii, led by Waikiki's Halekulani Hotel and the Big Island's Mauna Lani Bay Hotel. Oahu, Maui, and Kauai are in the top 10 US destinations, and 13 of Hawaii's resorts were in the top 20 tropical resorts, led by the Halekulani again, in first place. (The huge Japanese investment in Hawaii's economy and real estate during the so-called "bubble economy" of the late 1980s, although routinely criticized, improved the overall quality of Hawaii's hotel infrastructure with needed renovation capital.)

In 1971, there was an average of 41,000 tourists in Hawaii on any given day. In 1991, there were 160,000, with 4.8 million tourists annually from North America, 1.6 million from Asia, 260,000 from Australia and New Zealand, and 210,000 from Europe. In popularity, Oahu is first with tourists, followed by Maui, Kauai, the Big Island, Molokai, and Lanai.

The largest single source of jobs is in the service industry – the hotels and other tourist-related businesses. After that comes retail trade, government, and the self-employed.

Hawaii's economy generates money, but not so much for local residents working in the service sector. Hawaii is 13th in average annual income in the United States, but first in food prices, gas prices, and average price of a home. On the plus side, however, Hawaii is 49th in the number of business failures and in its unemployment rate.

## GEOGRAPHY

Honolulu's location is 21°18'30"N, 157°52'15"W, nearly 1,500 miles (2,400 km) *north* of the equator. Thus, contrary to popular belief, Hawaii is *not* in the South Pacific. (It is part of Polynesia, however, most of which is in fact in the South Pacific.)

The two points in Hawaii farthest apart are Cape Kumukahi, on the east coast of the Big Island, and Kure Atoll, at the northwest end of the Hawaiian archipelago. The antipode of Honolulu – the point on the opposite side of the globe equidistant from Honolulu in all directions – is the country of Botswana, on the continent of Africa. (Hawaii is the only place in the United States with an antipode on land.) The ocean depth of the Kauai Channel, 72 miles (115 km) wide between Oahu and Kauai, is 10,890 ft (3,320 meters). The deepest Hawaiian channel is between Lisianski Island and Hermes Atoll, at 17,400 ft (5,300 meters). The deepest harbor is Honolulu Harbor at 40 ft (12 meters). There are 23 lighthouses in the state.

In comparison with the other American states, Hawaii is 4th in coastline miles, 14th in land owned by the federal government, and 47th in total land area.

Distance in miles (km) from Honolulu to:

| | | |
|---|---|---|
| Hilo | 214 | (342 km) |
| Kailua-Kona | 168 | (269 km) |
| Kahului, Maui | 98 | (157 km) |
| Lanai | 72 | (115 km) |
| Molokai | 54 | (86 km) |

316

| Lihue, Kauai | 103 | (165 km) |
|---|---|---|
| Midway Island | 1,309 | (2,094 km) |
| Kure Atoll | 1,367 | (2,187 km) |

| Botswana (Hawaii's antipode) | 12,417 | (19,867 km) |
|---|---|---|
| Anchorage | 2,781 | (4,450 km) |
| Auckland | 4,393 | (7,029 km) |
| Equator | 1,470 | (2,352 km) |
| Hong Kong | 5,541 | (8,866 km) |
| London | 7,226 | (11,562 km) |
| Los Angeles | 2,557 | (4,091 km) |
| Manila | 5,293 | (8,469 km) |
| New York | 4,959 | (7,934 km) |
| North Pole | 4,740 | (7,584 km) |
| San Francisco | 2,397 | (3,835 km) |
| Tahiti | 2,741 | (4,386 km) |
| Tokyo | 3,847 | (6,155 km) |
| Vancouver | 2,709 | (4,334 km) |

### Island High Points

| | | |
|---|---|---|
| Big Island, Mauna Kea | | 13,796 ft (4,205 meters) |
| Maui | Haleakala | 10,023 (3,055) |
| Kauai | Kawaikini | 5,243 (1,598) |
| Molokai | Kamakou | 4,970 (1,515) |
| Oahu | Ka'ala | 4,020 (1,225) |
| Lanai | Lanaihale | 3,370 (1,027) |
| Kaho'olawe | Puu Moaulanui | 1,483 (452) |
| Ni'ihau | Paniau | 1,281 (390) |
| Kure Atoll | | 20 (6) |

## POPULATION

Details of Hawaii's wide diversity of peoples and cultures are covered in the main text of the book. But for those with a knack for statistics… Compared with the rest of the United States, Hawaii is first in average life expectancy; 2nd in people per household and in the number of marriages per 1,000; 13th in population density; 16th in divorces per 1,000 people; 32nd in percentage of residents below poverty level; 38th in the rate of violent crimes; 47th in the rate of cancer deaths; 49th in infant mortality; last in the percentage of white people.

Population (1990 census)

| | |
|---|---|
| Total population | 1,108,229 |
| Oahu | 836,231 |
| Big Island | 120,317 |
| Maui | 100,504 (inc. Lanai, Molokai) |
| Kauai | 51,177 (inc. Ni'ihau) |

Ethnicity (1990 census)

| | | |
|---|---|---|
| Asian/Pacific Islanders | 685,236 | (61.8 percent) |
| Chinese | 68,804 | (6.2 percent) |
| Filipino | 168,682 | (15.2 percent) |
| Japanese | 247,486 | (22.3 percent) |
| Korean | 24,454 | (2.2 percent) |
| Vietnamese | 5,468 | (0.5 percent) |
| Hawaiian | 138,742 | (2.5 percent) |
| Samoan | 15,034 | (1.4 percent) |
| Other | 16,566 | (1.5 percent) |
| White | 369,616 | (33.4 percent) |
| Black | 27,195 | (2.5 percent) |
| Native American, Eskimo, Aleut | 5,099 | (0.5 percent) |
| Other races | 21,083 | (1.9 percent) |

## TIME ZONES

To find out the time of day: Tel: 983-3211
**North American time differences**:
San Francisco, Pacific Standard Time + 2 hours
Dallas, Central Standard Time + 4
New York, Eastern Standard Time + 5

When the mainland United States sets its clocks forward for Daylight Savings Time, usually from May through October, add an hour to all the above time zones.

**International standard time differences**:

| | | |
|---|---|---|
| Sydney | + | 20 hours |
| Tokyo | + | 19 |
| Bangkok | + | 17 |
| Paris | + | 11 |
| London | + | 10 |
| Mexico City | + | 4 |

## CLIMATE

The seasons are subtle in Hawaii, but they do exist. It just takes time to recognize them. Most of Hawaii experiences balmy 73°F–88°F (23°C–31°C) weather from April through October, and cooler, wetter 65°F–83°F (18°C–28°C) weather during other months. Rarely does the mercury drop below 60°F (15°C), nor higher than 90°F (32°C).

The surrounding sea and northeasterly trade winds are a natural air-conditioning system. Once in a long while, these trade winds stop and rare southerly or westerly winds take over, causing a sticky-humid weather situation from the moisture-rich Kona winds. This mugginess, however, is usually temporary and before long, prevailing Pacific trade winds resume as usual.

Certain areas on each island – usually on the windward side of mountains – receive more rainfall than others. The wettest spot on earth is Mount Waialeale on Kauai, which has been drenched by as much as 486 inches (1,234 cm) of rain in a year. On the other side of the mountains in the rain shadow, annual precipitation can be almost nothing.

In higher places such as Kula and Haleakala on Maui, and Koke'e on Kauai, temperatures range from 48°F to 72°F (9°C–22°C), and in mountainous parts of the Big Island the average temperature drops down to 31°F to 58°F (-1°C–14°C) during the winter, and at night. Snow falls on Mauna Kea (and sometimes Haleakala on Maui) in the winter, so be prepared with warm clothing if you intend to tour these areas.

Sometimes when there is a volcanic eruption on the Big Island, a smoky pall lingers over the islands for a few days, especially in the Kona area. Islanders call this volcanic haze "vog," volcanic smog.

## Flash Floods

In the mountain areas, intense localized rain can cause flash floods – the quick flooding of streams and valleys. If hiking in valleys, take care during heavy rains in the mountains. Flash floods can occur in a very short time, and without warning.

## Hurricanes

Hawaii lies in Pacific storm tracks. Hurricanes are infrequent in Hawaii, but when they do touch the islands, they generally hit hard. Take all warnings seriously. Telephone books contain detailed information, including flood and tidal wave zones for each island, and public shelter locations. Hurricane season is from June through November, with as many as 13 storms forming. In general, Pacific storms do more damage when coming from the south than from other directions. There are several classifications of storms leading up to hurricane status.

*Tropical depressions* are weather fronts of sustained winds less than 40 miles (64 km) per hour.

*Tropical storms* are cyclones with winds between 40 (64 km) and 75 miles (120 km) an hour. A *hurricane* is declared when a tropical cyclone has winds greater than 75 miles (120 km) an hour.

*Hurricane watch*: expect within 36 hours

*Hurricane warning*: expect within 24 hours

*Civil defense sirens*: Listen to the radio/TV for emergency disaster instructions. Secure loose objects, cover windows with boards or tape. Stay indoors during high winds, and evacuate areas that may flood. At all times, evacuation orders by civil authorities must be followed.

## Tsunami

Earthquakes, particularly on the Big Island, sometimes forebode a *tsunami*, the proper term for a seismic or tidal wave. Earthquakes elsewhere, including in Alaska, can send a tsunami to Hawaii. They can occur with little warning or time for preparation.

*Tsunami watch*: tsunami possible, be prepared.

*Tsunami warning*: leave coastal areas immediately. Use the tsunami evacuation maps published in all island telephone directories.

*Civil defense sirens*: Listen to the radio/TV for instructions. If outside of the danger zones indicated in the telephone directory maps, remain there. Near the shore, always head for higher ground.

## Civil Defense Siren Tests

Civil Defense sirens that warn of natural disasters or a now-unlikely nuclear holocaust are tested at 11.45am on the first business day of every month. Related tests are broadcast on all commercial radio stations by the Emergency Broadcast System. For more information, call the Oahu Civil Defense Agency: 523-4121.

**Weather forecasts**

Honolulu: Tel: 833-2849

Oahu: Tel: 836-0121

Maui: Tel: 877-5111

Hawaiian waters: Tel: 836-3921

Surf: Tel: 836-1952

**Civil Defense**

Emergency fire, police, ambulance: Tel: 911

State Civil Defense: Tel: 734-2161

Oahu Civil Defense: Tel: 523-4121

Maui and Molokai Civil Defense: Tel: 243-7285

Big Island Civil Defense: Tel: 935-0031

Kauai Civil Defense: Tel: 241-6336

# CULTURE & CUSTOMS

## Aloha Friday

Friday is usually greeted in the islands with *aloha* attire. On this day, even businessmen doff coats and ties – if they've been wearing them at all during the week, highly unlikely – and don aloha shirts of bright and cheerful Hawaiian floral, *kapa* and other island prints. Ladies often tuck a fragrant plumeria behind their ears or drape a gracious *kukui* nut or flower lei on their shoulders. These are appropriate accessories for their *muumuu*. This is a unique Friday custom that has become *de rigeur* here, even in state, federal and business offices and at public schools.

## Hawaiian Time

Time in the islands is not noticeably defined by the four seasons, and Hawaii's balmy tropical climate tends to warp any rigid schedule. Islanders are lax about time, especially when going on dates and to meetings outside of strictly commercial business circles. Some even consider it rather brash or inconvenient to be too early or punctual to a casual affair. This tendency of being "fashionably late" by 10 minutes or so is commonly referred to as being on "Hawaiian time." If on vacation, time matters not anyway.

## Tipping

Tipping for service is expected in Hawaii. Tips are part of a service worker's overall salary. Skimp on the tip, and she or he is not getting a full salary, important in Hawaii where wages are below par anyway. Generally, airport porters' baggage handling fees run about 50¢ per bag, and taxi drivers get tipped 15 percent plus about 25¢ per bag. A 15 to 20 percent tip at an exclusive restaurant is usual, if you enjoyed the meal, and at other eating establishments, you should tip whatever you feel is fair, typically 15 percent.

## Electricity

Standard US 110–120 volts, 60 cycles AC. Large hotels usually have voltage and plug converters.

# BUSINESS HOURS

People in Hawaii get an early start on the day. Most workers are in their offices by 8am, if not earlier. Often people are at their desks by 7 or 7.30am.

Offices typically open between 8 and 9am, closing between 4.30–5.30pm. Banks open at 8 or 8.30am, closing at 3pm, 6pm on Friday.

## HOLIDAYS

Hawaii observes all the US national holidays, plus two special state holidays – Prince Kuhio Day and Kamehameha Day. On national holidays, all government offices, banks, post offices and most businesses, except shops, will be closed. On state holidays, local government offices are closed, as are banks, but federal offices including post offices are open.
New Year's Day: January 1
Martin Luther King Day: third Monday in January
Presidents' Day: third Monday in February
Prince Kuhio Day: March 26
Good Friday: Friday preceding Easter Sunday
Memorial Day: last Monday in May
King Kamehameha I Day: June 11
Independence Day: July 4
Labor Day: first Monday in September
Veterans' Day: November 11
Thanksgiving Day: fourth Thursday in November
Christmas Day: December 25

## RELIGIOUS SERVICES

**Central Union** (United Church of Christ), 1660 Beretania at Punahou Street, Makiki. Tel: 941-0957.
**Church of Jesus Christ of the Latter Day Saints** (Mormon), 1500 Beretania Street, Makiki. Tel: 941-5693.
**Daijingu Temple** (Shinto), 61 Puiwa Road. Tel: 595-3102.
**First Church of Christ** (Christian Scientist), 1508 Punahou Street, Makiki. Tel: 949-8403.
**First Presbyterian Church**, 1822 Ke'eaumoku at Nehoa Street, Makiki. Tel: 537-3321.
**Friends, Religious Society of** (Quakers), 2416 Oahu Avenue, Moana Valley. Tel: 988-2714.
**Greek Eastern Orthodox Church**, 930 Lunalilo Street. Tel: 521-7220.
**Honpa Hongwanji Mission** (Buddhist), 1727 Pali Highway, Nu'uanu. Tel: 522-9200. Services in both English and Japanese.
**Jehovah's Witness,** 1228 Pensacola Avenue, Makiki. Tel: 531-2990.
**Kawaiahao Church** (Congregational), 957 Punchbowl at King Street, downtown. Tel: 522-1333. Services in Hawaiian and English.
**Korean Buddhist Temple**, 2420 Halelaau Place. Tel: 735-7858.
**Nichiren Shoshu Academy**, 2719 Pali Highway, Nu'uanu. Tel: 595-3517.
**Our Lady of Peace Cathedral** (Roman Catholic), Fort Street Mall at Beretania Street. Tel: 536-7036.
**Prince of Peace Church** (Lutheran), 333 Lewers Street, Waikiki. Tel: 922-6011.
**St Andrew's Cathedral** (US Episcopalian), Corner of Queen Emma and Beretania Streets, Downtown. Tel: 524-2822.
**St Augustine's Church** (Catholic), 130 Ohua Avenue, Waikiki. Tel: 923-7024.
**Seventh Day Adventist Church**, 1313 Nu'uanu Avenue. Tel: 524-1352.
**Temple Emanuel** (Jewish), 2550 Pali Highway, Nu'uanu. Tel: 595-7521.
**Todaiji Hawaii Bekkaku Honzan** (Buddhist), 426 Luakini Street, Nu'uanu. Tel: 595-2083.
**United Methodist**, Wesley Foundation, 20 S. Vineyard. Tel: 536-1864.
**Waikiki Baptist Church**, 424 Kuamoo Street (across Ambassador Hotel). Tel: 955-3525.
**Hare Krishna Temple**, 51 Coelho Way, Nu'uanu. Tel: 595-4913.

# COMMUNICATIONS

## MEDIA

**Television**: There are over ten broadcast TV channels that originate in Hawaii. They include Channels 2 (KHON-NBC); 4 (KITV-ABC); 5 (KFVE); 9 (KGMB-CBS); 11 (KHET-educational); and 13 (KHNL). For broadcasts originating in Honolulu, relay transmitters serve the neighbor islands, and several private cable television companies provide uninterrupted and special television programming by subscription only. Most hotels subscribe to cable.

**Radio**: Honolulu's listeners tune in to some 30 radio stations. Selections range from progressive rock and jazz music stations, to an all-Hawaiian music station (KCCN) and all news. Special programming is scheduled in the Hawaiian, Japanese, Chinese, Korean, Samoan, Tongan, Portuguese and Filipino languages. Check newspaper listings.

**Press**: Hawaii has nine daily newspapers – six in English, one in Japanese, one in Korean and one in Chinese – plus several weekly and semi-weekly papers and numerous magazines. The statewide circulated English dailies are *The Honolulu Advertiser*, a morning newspaper owned by Gannett, and *The Honolulu Star-Bulletin*, an afternoon independent newspaper. Neighbor islands have their own daily newspapers, with circulation restricted to that island. Other newspapers are published by ethnic groups, the military, religious organizations and the tourism and business industries. The Associated Press maintains a bureau in Honolulu to cover Hawaii and the Pacific.

## POSTAL SERVICES

Normal American postal rates apply. From Honolulu, it costs the same to mail a letter to Maui as to New York City.

**Honolulu Main Office** (at the airport): Tel: 423-3930; Window: Monday–Friday 8am–7.30pm, Saturday 8am–2.30pm.

**Waikiki**: 330 Saratoga Road. Tel: 941 1062

Customer information: Tel: 423-3990
24-hour answer line: Tel: 422-7070
Express mail: Tel: 423-3942
Mailing requirements: Tel: 423-3750
Special delivery: Tel: 423-3911

## TELEPHONE

From the middle of the Pacific, you can dial directly to almost anywhere in the world. Because of underwater fiber-optic cables, the quality to both Asia and North America is excellent. On the other hand, the quality of local calls is often dismal. All inter-island calls are toll calls and expensive.

Both inter-island and mainland/international calls are usually discounted in evenings and nights. Inter-island calls, for example, are discounted 35 percent evenings (5–11pm) and 60 percent at night (11pm–8am). Weekends are also discounted.
Same-island calls: dial just the number
Inter-island calls (direct): 1 + number
Inter-island calls (operator assisted): 0 + number
Mainland (direct dial): 1 + area code + number
Mainland (operator assisted): 0 + area code + number
International calls (direct dial): 011 + country/ city codes + number
International calls (operator assisted): 01 + country/city codes + number
**Home-country direct**: Operators in some countries can be called directly from Hawaii by special toll-free 800 numbers. Call 643-1000 for a list of numbers and foreign countries where service is available.
**Directory Assistance**:
Operator assistance: dial 0
Same-island directory assistance: 1 + 411
Inter-island directory: 1 + 555-1212
Mainland directory: 1 + area code + 555-1212
800 toll free directory: 1 + 800 + 555-1212
Military directory assistance: 471-7110
Federal Information Center: (800) 733-5996
Hawaiian Tel consumer line: 643-3377
Time of day: 983-3211

# EMERGENCIES

## SECURITY & CRIME

Hawaii is an exquisite place with a reputation for hospitality and all the good cheer that the word *aloha* implies. However, travelers should be warned that all types of crime – including burglary, robberies, assaults, rapes – occur on the islands, especially with the increasing numbers of visitors and residents. On the whole, however, Honolulu is one of the safest cities in North America.

Follow the usual cautions as when traveling anywhere else. In areas far from population centers, car break-ins and beach thefts of unattended personal property are becoming common, even at popular tourists sites. There have been some reports of locals on one or more neighbor islands extracting modest vehicle protection fees while cars are parked at trail heads.

**Emergency Calls**:
Fire, Police: Tel: 911
Ambulance: Tel: 911
Coast Guard Search and Rescue: Tel: 536-4336 or 541-2450
Food poisoning: Tel: 586-4586

**Other Vital Services** (Oahu):
American Red Cross: Tel: 734-2101
Dental emergency service: Tel: 536-2135
FBI: Tel: 521-1411
Life Guard Service: Tel: 922-3888
Poison Information Center: Tel: 941-4411
Sex Abuse Treatment Center: Tel: 524-7273
Suicide & Crisis Center: Tel: 521-4555
US Secret Service: Tel: 541-1912

**Finding a Physician**: Most of the larger hotels have a physician on call. Other medical services can be obtained at three main hospitals in Honolulu:
**Kaiser-Permanente**, (clinics throughout Hawaii), 1010 Pensacola. Tel: 545-2950.
**Queen's Medical Center**, 1301 Punchbowl. Tel: 538-9011.
**Straub Clinic and Hospital**, 888 South King. Tel: 522-4000.

# GETTING AROUND

## ISLAND HOPPING

Hawaii's two major inter-island carriers are *SS Independence* and *SS Constitution*. These large passenger liners, operated by American Hawaii Cruises, provide trips between the islands, sailing weekly in opposite directions to and from Honolulu. Seven-day voyages as well as 3- and 4-day trips are available. All of the amenities of full-service cruise ships are aboard. Bus excursions are optional and rental cars are also offered in each port for those passengers who want a more leisurely pace. Contact a travel agent for current schedules and prices.

Given that Hawaii is an archipelago of islands with a large number of travelers between them, one might expect numerous options for getting around the islands. Aside from the multi-day cruises described above, however, the only commercial inter-island transportation is by air. There is no inter-island ferry service, except a limited service between Maui and Molokai, mostly for Maui hotel workers living on Molokai.

Fortunately, flights between islands are frequent, typically every hour. There are two primary carriers, Aloha and Hawaiian Airlines, using jets between all major airports. In addition, Aloha Island Air, a subsidiary of Aloha Airlines, uses small prop craft to smaller airports like Princeville on Kauai. Air Molokai offers limited service between Molokai and neighbor islands. You can also charter fixed-wing and helicopter flights from a number of companies, both for sight-seeing and for inter-island travel.

Except for morning and later afternoon commute times, when local workers and businessmen are returning to their home islands, you can usually get a seat on short notice. And as there are frequent flights all day, if one flight is full there is another flight in about half an hour to an hour. However, weekends and holidays are busy times; reserve ahead if possible. Flights are by reservation, but seating is not assigned; if at the end of the line during boarding, you'll get the worst seats with views of nothing. Inter-island flights are short, from 15 to 45 minutes, depending on the route.

Both Aloha and Hawaiian Airlines offer hotel and rental car deals with their flights, again often on very short notice. In addition, the first couple of early morning flights and the last couple of night flights are sometimes discounted.

## ORIENTATION

Hawaiian islanders share a common vernacular for directions, which has nothing to do with cardinal directions or where the sun rises and sets. Rather, it deals with *local* geographical features.

The two most common directional terms are *mauka* and *makai*. *Mauka* means upland or towards the mountains, and *makai* means towards the sea. In the Honolulu area, directions are also given in relation to *Ewa*, a plantation town just west of Pearl Harbor, and to *Diamond Head*, the famous landmark to the east side of Waikiki. Those four orientations – *mauka*, *makai*, *Ewa* and *Diamond Head* – make eminent sense to local people. Say north, south, east or west and you'll receive looks of bewilderment.

## PUBLIC TRANSPORTATION

### BY BUS

Only Oahu has a pragmatic bus system. On the other islands, bus transportation, other than tour buses, is *not* an option. The main office for **TheBus**, the bus transit line that services all of Oahu, is located at 811 Middle Street, near downtown, where good, up-to-date maps and bus schedules are available without charge. Free information and printed schedules are also available at the Ala Moana Shopping Center information booth.

All areas of interest to the traveler, and then some more, are accessible by Honolulu's comprehensive bus system. For information on routes, connections, and other bus-related items, tel: 848-5555 between 5.30am and 10pm daily. No matter where you are and no matter where you want to go, the person who answers will do his or her best – Oahu has a first-rate bus system and the information "helpers" know the island well. There is no limit on distance traveled. A monthly pass is also available.

Customer service: Tel: 848-4500
Schedule and route info: Tel: 848-5555
Lost and found: Tel: 848-4444
Handicapped services: Tel: 841-4322
Handicapped van reservations: Tel: 841-8267

### BY TAXI

Taxi service is available on all islands, but beyond local destinations it becomes cheaper to rent a car. All taxis are metered, although most are available for sightseeing at a fixed rate. Honolulu, of course, has the most taxis, but don't expect to flag one down on the street. If a taxi is required, go to a nearby hotel. Elsewhere on Oahu, call one of these companies:

Aloha State Cab: Tel: 847-3566
Charley's Taxi: Tel: 531-1333
Sida Taxi: Tel: 836-0011

# WHERE TO STAY

Hawaii abounds in accommodations of every persuasion, and usually lots of it. There are four types of places to stay: hotels (including small but classy inns), rental condominiums, bed-and-breakfasts, and camping.

Many of the international luxury hotel chains have resorts in Hawaii. If you can afford them, you'll probably know what you're looking for. But for those on a budget or wanting to visit on an extended stay, the multitudinous offerings of economical and mid-range hotels can be intimidating.

You can take a gamble and book sight unseen, based on price. Another way is to arrive with a confirmed reservation for a day or two, and look for a suitable place. Depending on season, you might be successful, or you might be sleeping on the beach in the rain.

Another option is the resort management companies that manage a string of properties – some offer only hotels, some split between hotels and condominiums, and others offer only condominiums. Most of their properties are quite satisfactory, with quality and amenities usually in direct proportion to the price. Call one of the outfits below and tell them what you're looking for.

If particular about *exact* location, confirm a particular place's location with the property or reservations company. Mailing addresses sometimes don't reflect the actual location of a hotel or condominium. For example, Lahaina is often the mailing post office for places throughout West Maui.

**Aston Hotels & Resorts**, 2255 Kuhio Avenue, 18th Floor, Honolulu 96815. Tel: 931-1400, fax: 922-8785, toll free: (800) 922-7866.
**Colony Resorts**, Worldwide Reservation Center, 11340 Blondo Street, Omaha, NE 68164. fax: (402) 498-9166, toll free: (800) 777-1700.
**Hawaiiana Resorts**, 1270 Ala Moana Boulevard, Honolulu 96814. Tel: 923-8828, fax: 923-3743, toll free: (800) 882-9696.
**Marc Resorts Hawaii**, 2155 Kalakaua Avenue, Suite 706, Honolulu 96815. Tel: 922-9700, fax: 922-2421, toll free: (800) 535-0085.
**Outrigger Hotels**, Denver Reservations Center, 3443 S. Galena Street, Denver, CO 80231. Tel: (303) 369-7777, fax: (303) 369-9403, toll free: (800) 733-7777.

## BED & BREAKFAST

Bed-and-breakfast places were slow to catch on in Hawaii. There is also little regulation or licensing of them, so the standards vary widely. The reservation companies below book for most of the islands.
**A1 Homes and Villas in Paradise**, 150 Hamakua Drive, Box 719, Kailua, HI 96734. Tel: 236-4143, toll free: (800) 282-2736.
**Affordable Paradise Bed & Breakfast**, 362 Kailua Road, Kailua, HI 96734. Tel: 261-1693, toll free: (800) 925-9065.
**All Islands Bed & Breakfast**, 823 Kainui Drive, Kailua, HI 96734. Tel: 263-2342, toll free: (800) 542-0344.
**Bed & Breakfast Honolulu**, 3242 Kaohinani Drive, Honolulu, HI 96817. Tel: 595-7533, toll free: (800) 288-4666.
**Bed & Breakfast Hawaii**, PO Box 449, Kapa'a, HI 96746. Tel: 822-7771, toll free: (800) 733-1632.
**Hawaiian Islands Vacation Rentals**, 1277 Mokulua Drive, Kailua, HI 96734. Tel: 261-7895, toll free: (800) 258-7895.
**Hawaii's Best Bed & Breakfasts**, PO Box 563, Kamuela, HI 96743. Tel: 885-4550, toll free: (800) 262-9912.
**Pacific-Hawaii Bed & Breakfast**, 19 Kai Nani Place, Kailua, HI 96734. Tel: 263-4848, toll free: (800) 999-6026.

The following listings are not comprehensive, and they do not carry endorsements. An establishment not listed – especially in rental condominiums – could be just as satisfactory as those listed. For travelers wanting a more inclusive and comprehensive listing, the Hawaii Visitors Bureau has a booklet, *Accommodation and Car Rental Guide,* which can be requested from them. The listings below come from the booklet.

Prices fluctuate with the seasons and the type of accommodation. An individual hotel can have rooms ranging from $100 to $1,000. For convenience, we have included a relative *price* ranking according to an establishment's normal rate for a standard room or condo. Our pricing notations – $ to $$$$$ – are intended only as a relative guide of a place's cost compared to others. Bargains, discounts, packages and season deals abound and should be pursued through travel agents, airlines, or brokers.

## OAHU

### HOTELS

**Ala Moana Hotel**, 410 Atkinson Drive, Honolulu, HI 96814. Tel: 955-4811, toll free: (800) 367-6025. $$$ Area A – Waikiki. Total units: 1,172. Fully air-conditioned, parking, TV, restaurants, cocktail lounges, swimming pool, shops, meeting rooms.
**Best Western Plaza Airport Hotel**, 3253 N. Nimitz Highway, Honolulu, HI 96819. Tel: 836-3636, toll

free: (800) 327-4570. $$ Area C – Airport. Total units: 274. Fully air-conditioned, parking, TV, restaurant, cocktail lounge, swimming pool, shop, meeting rooms.

**Breakers Hotel**, 250 Beach Walk, Honolulu, HI 96815. Tel: 923-3181, toll free: (800) 426-0494. $$ Area A – Waikiki. Total units: 64. Fully air-conditioned, parking, TV, swimming pool.

**Coconut Plaza**, 450 Lewers Street, Honolulu, HI 96815. Tel: 923-8828, toll free: (800) 882-9696. $$ Area A – Waikiki. Total units: 80. Fully air-conditioned, TV, lounge, restaurant, pool, parking.

**Colony Surf Hotel**, 2895 Kalakaua Avenue, Honolulu, HI 96815. Tel: 923-5751, toll free: (800) 252-7873. $$$+ Area A – Diamond Head, on the beach. Total units: 101. All suites. Parking, TV, restaurant, cocktail lounge; children: 10 years or older.

**Continental Surf**, 2426 Kuhio Avenue, Honolulu, HI 96815. Tel: 538-3652, toll free: (800) 367-5004. $ Area A – Waikiki. Total units: 140. Fully air-conditioned, parking, TV.

**Coral Reef Hotel**, 2299 Kuhio Avenue, Honolulu, HI 96815. Tel: 931-1400, toll free: (800) 922-7866. $$ Area A – Waikiki. Total units: 247. Fully air-conditioned, parking, TV, swimming pool, shops.

**Halekulani**, 2199 Kalia Road, Honolulu, HI 96815. Tel: 923-2311, toll free: (800) 367-2343. $$$$ Area A – Waikiki, on a sand beach. Total units: 456. Fully air-conditioned, parking, TV, restaurants, cocktail lounges, swimming pool, shops, meeting rooms.

**Hawaii Prince Hotel**, 100 Holomoana Street, Honolulu, HI 96815. Tel: 956-1111, toll free: (800) 321-OAHU. $$$$+ Area A – Waikiki, overlooking yacht harbor. Total units: 521. Fully air-conditioned, TV/VCR, pool, shopping, restaurants, health club, parking.

**Hawaiian Regent**, 2552 Kalakaua Avenue, Honolulu, HI 96815. Tel: 922-6611, toll free: (800) 367-5370. $$+ Area A – Waikiki. Total units: 1,346. Fully air-conditioned, parking, TV, restaurants, cocktail lounges, swimming pools, shops, meeting rooms, tennis court.

**Hawaiiana Hotel**, 260 Beach Walk, Honolulu, HI 96815. Tel: 923-3811, toll free: (800) 367-5122. $$ Area A – Waikiki. Total units: 95. Fully air-conditioned, parking, TV, swimming pools.

**Hilton Hawaiian Village**, 2005 Kalia Road, Honolulu, HI 96815. Tel: 949-4321, toll free: (800) HILTONS. $$$$ Area A – Waikiki, on the beach. Total units: 2,542. Fully air-conditioned, parking, TV, restaurants, cocktail lounges, swimming pools, shops, meeting rooms.

**Hyatt Regency Waikiki**, 2424 Kalakaua Avenue, Honolulu, HI 96815. Tel: 923-1234, toll free: (800) 233-1234. $$$$ Area A – Waikiki, across street from beach. Total units: 1,230. Fully air-conditioned, parking, TV, restaurants, cocktail lounges, swimming pool, shops, meeting rooms.

**Ilikai Hotel Nikko**, 1777 Ala Moana, Honolulu, HI 96815. Tel: 949-3811, Toll free: (800) 367-8434 $$$ Area A – Waikiki, on the beach. Hotel units: 800. Fully air-conditioned, parking, TV, restaurants, cocktail lounges, swimming pools, tennis courts, shops, meeting rooms.

**Ilima Hotel**, 445 Nohonani Street, Honolulu, HI 96815. Tel: 923-5200, toll free: (800) 367-8434. $$ Area A – Waikiki. Total units: 99. Fully air-conditioned, parking, TV, swimming pool, restaurant, cocktail lounge.

**Kahala Hilton**, 5000 Kahala Avenue, Honolulu, HI 96816. Tel: 734-2211, toll free: (800) 367-2525. $$$$+ Area A – Kahala, on the beach. Total units: 370. Fully air-conditioned, parking, TV, restaurants, cocktail lounges, swimming pool, tennis court, shops, meeting rooms.

**Laniloa Hotel**, 55-109 Laniloa Street, La'ie, Oahu, HI 96762. Tel: 293-9282, toll free: (800) 526-4562. $+ Area E – La'ie, across road from beach; next to Polynesian Cultural Center. Total units: 48. Fully air-conditioned, parking, TV, swimming pool.

**Malihini Hotel**, 217 Saratoga Road, Honolulu, HI 96815. Tel: 923-9644. $ Area A – Waikiki. Total units: 30; rental units: 28. Partially air-conditioned, TV, shop.

**Manoa Valley Inn** (country-style inn), 2001 Vancouver Drive, Honolulu, HI 96822. Tel: 847-6019, toll free: (800) 634-5115. $$ Area B – in Manoa Valley. Total units: 8. Parking, TV; maid service: daily.

**Miramar at Waikiki**, 2345 Kuhio Avenue, Honolulu, HI 96815. Tel: 922-2077, toll free: (800) 367-2303. $$ Area A – Waikiki. Total units: 357. Fully air-conditioned, parking, TV, restaurants, cocktail lounges, swimming pool, shops, meeting rooms.

**New Otani Kaimana Beach Hotel**, 2863 Kalakaua Avenue, Honolulu, HI 96815. Tel: 923-1555, toll free: (800) 421-8795. $$$ Area A – Diamond Head, on the beach. Total units: 125. Fully air-conditioned, parking, TV, restaurants, cocktail lounge, shops, meeting rooms.

**Outrigger Maile Sky Court**, 2058 Kuhio Avenue, Honolulu, HI 96815. Tel: 947-2828, toll free: (800)

# OAHU

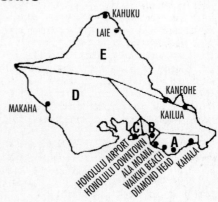

733-7777. $$ Area A – Waikiki. Total units: 596. Air-conditioned, parking, TV, swimming pool.

**Outrigger Reef Hotel**, 2169 Kalia Road, Honolulu, HI 96815. Tel: 923-3111, toll free: (800) 733-7777. $$+ Area A – Waikiki, on the beach. Total units: 885. Fully air-conditioned, parking, TV, restaurants, cocktail lounges, swimming pool, shops, meeting rooms.

**Outrigger Seaside Suite Hotel**, 440 Seaside Avenue, Honolulu, HI 96815. Tel: 922-2383, toll free: (800) 733-7777. $$+ Area A – Waikiki. Total units: 56. Fully air-conditioned, parking, TV.

**Outrigger Surf**, 2280 Kuhio Avenue, Honolulu, HI 96815. Tel: 922-5777, toll free: (800) 733-7777. $+ Area A – Waikiki. Total units: 251. Fully air-conditioned, parking, TV, restaurant, cocktail lounge, swimming pool.

**Pacific Beach Hotel**, 2490 Kalakaua Avenue, Honolulu, HI 96815. Tel: 923-4511, toll free: (800) 367-6060. $$$ Area A – Waikiki. Total units: 832. Fully air-conditioned, parking, TV, restaurants, swimming pool, shops, tennis courts, meeting rooms.

**Pagoda Hotel**, 1525 Rycroft Street, Honolulu, HI 96814. Tel: 923-4511, toll free: (800) 367-6060. $$ Area A – Ala Moana. Total units: 362. Fully air-conditioned, parking, TV, restaurants, cocktail lounge, swimming pools, shops, meeting rooms.

**Park Shore Hotel**, 2586 Kalakaua Avenue, Honolulu, HI 96815. Tel: 923-0411, toll free: (800) 367-2377. $$ Area A – Waikiki. Total units: 227. Fully air-conditioned, parking, TV, cocktail lounge, swimming pool, shopping center.

**Queen Kapiʻolani Hotel**, 150 Kapahulu Avenue, Honolulu, HI 96815. Tel: 531-5235, toll free: (800) 367-5004. $$ Area A – Waikiki. Total units: 315. Fully air-conditioned, parking, TV, restaurant, cocktail lounge, swimming pool, shops, meeting room.

**Royal Grove Hotel**, 151 Uluniu Avenue, Honolulu, HI 96815. Tel: 923-7691. $ Area A – Waikiki. Total units: 85. Partially air-conditioned, TV, pool.

**Royal Hawaiian Hotel**, 2259 Kalakaua Avenue, Honolulu, HI 96815. Tel: 923-7311, toll free: (800) 325-3535. $$$$$ Area A – Waikiki, on the beach. Total units: 526. Fully air-conditioned, parking, TV, restaurants, cocktail lounges, swimming pool, shops, meeting rooms.

**Sheraton Makaha Resort and Country Club**, 84-626 Makaha Valley Road, Waiʻanae, Oahu, HI 96792. Tel: 695-9511, toll free: (800) 325-3535. $$$ Area D – Leeward Oahu. Total units: 185. Fully air-conditioned, parking, TV, restaurants, cocktail lounge, swimming pool, golf course, tennis courts, shops, meeting rooms.

**Sheraton Moana Surfrider**, 2365 Kalakaua Avenue, Honolulu, HI 96815. Tel: 923-2800, toll free: (800) 325-3535. $$$$$ Area A – Waikiki, on the beach. Total units: 790. Parking nearby, TV, restaurants, cocktail lounges, shops, meeting rooms.

**Sheraton Princess Kaiulani Hotel**, 120 Kaiulani Avenue, Honolulu, HI 96815. Tel: 922-5811, toll free: (800) 325-3535. $$$ Area A – Waikiki. Total

units: 1,150. Fully air-conditioned, parking, TV, restaurants, cocktail lounges, swimming pool, shops, meeting rooms.

**Sheraton Waikiki**, 2255 Kalakaua Avenue, Honolulu, HI 96815. Tel: 922-4422, toll free: (800) 325-3535. $$$ Area A – Waikiki, on the beach. Total units: 1,843. Fully air-conditioned, parking, TV, restaurants, cocktail lounges, swimming pools, shops, meeting rooms.

**Turtle Bay Hilton**, 57-091 Kamehameha Highway, Kahuku, HI 96731. Tel: 293-8811, toll free: (800) HILTONS. $$$$ Area E – North Shore, on the beach at Kuilima Point. Total units: 485. Fully air-conditioned, parking, TV, restaurants, cocktail lounges, swimming pool, golf course, tennis courts, shops, meeting rooms.

**Waikiki Circle Hotel**, 2464 Kalakaua Avenue, Honolulu, HI 96815. Tel: 923-1571. $ Area A – Waikiki. Total units: 100. Fully air-conditioned, TV, parking, restaurant, cocktail lounge.

**Waikiki Gateway**, 2070 Kalakaua Avenue, Honolulu, HI 96815. Tel: 955-3741, toll free: (800) 633-8799. $ Area A – Waikiki. Total units: 185. Fully air-conditioned, parking, TV, restaurant, cocktail lounge, swimming pool, shops.

**Waikiki Joy Hotel**, 320 Lewers Street, Honolulu, HI 96815. Tel: 923-2300, toll free: (800) 733-5569. $$+ Area A – Waikiki. Boutique hotel. Total units: 93. Fully air-conditioned, parking, TV, swimming pool, restaurant, cocktail lounge.

**Waikiki Parc Hotel**, 2233 Helumoa Road, Honolulu, HI 96815. Tel: 921-7272, toll free: (800) 422-0450. $$$ Area A – Waikiki. Total units: 298. Fully air-conditioned, parking, TV, restaurants, swimming pool, shops. Economical sister of the Halekulani.

**Waikiki Parkside Hotel**, 1850 Ala Moana Boulevard, Honolulu, HI 96815. Tel: 955-1567, toll free: (800) 237-9666. $$ Area A – Waikiki. Total units: 250. Fully air-conditioned, parking, TV, cocktail lounges, swimming pool.

**Waikiki Prince Hotel**, 2431 Prince Edward Street, Honolulu, HI 96815. Tel: 922-1544. $ Area A – Waikiki. Total units: 30. Partially air-conditioned, parking, TV; maid service: twice weekly.

**Waikiki Resort Hotel**, 2460 Koa Avenue, Honolulu, HI 96815. Tel: 922-4911, toll free: (800) 367-5116. $$ Area A – Waikiki. Total units: 309; rental units: 295. Fully air-conditioned, parking, TV, restaurants, cocktail lounge, swimming pool, shops, meeting room.

**Waikiki Sand Villa Hotel**, 2375 Ala Wai Boulevard, Honolulu, HI 96815. Tel: 922-4744, toll free: (800) 247-1903. $+ Area A – Waikiki. Total units: 220. Fully air-conditioned, parking, TV, restaurant, cocktail lounge, swimming pool.

**Waikikian on the Beach**, 1881 Ala Moana Boulevard, Honolulu, HI 96815. Tel: 931-1400, toll free: (800) 922-7866. $+ Area A – Waikiki, on the beach. Total units: 135. Partially air-conditioned, parking, TV (rental), restaurant, cocktail lounge, swimming pool, shops.

## CONDOMINIUM RENTALS

**Aloha Punawai**, 305 Saratoga Road, Honolulu, HI 96815. Tel: 923-5211. $ Area A – Waikiki. Total units: 19. Limited parking, partial air-conditioning; maid service: twice a week; minimum stay: 3 nights.

**Aston Waikiki Beach Tower**, 2470 Kalakaua Avenue, Honolulu, HI 96815. Tel: 931-1400, toll free: (800) 922-7866. $$$$$ Area A – Waikiki, across from beach. Total units: 140; rental units: 85. Fully air-conditioned, parking, TV, pool, meeting rooms.

**Imperial Hawaii Resort**, 205 Lewers Street, Honolulu, HI 96815. Tel: 923-1827, toll free: (800) 745-7666. $$ Area A – Waikiki. Total units: 277; rental units: 250. Fully air-conditioned, parking, TV, swimming pool, restaurant, shop; maid service.

**Inn on the Park**, 1920 Ala Moana Boulevard, Honolulu, HI 96815. Tel: 931-1400, toll free: (800) 922-7866. $$ Area A – Waikiki. Total units: 238; rental units: 130. Fully air-conditioned, parking, TV, swimming pool, cocktail lounge.

**Lealea Hale**, 2423 Cleghorn Street, Honolulu, HI 96815. Tel: 922-1726. $ Area A – Waikiki. Total units: 30. Partially air-conditioned, parking, TV; minimum stay: 2 days.

**Polynesian Plaza**, 2131 Kalakaua Avenue, Honolulu, HI 96815. Tel: 923-4818. $ Area A – Waikiki. Total units: 47; rental units: 25. Fully air-conditioned, cocktail lounge, restaurant, shops, swimming pool; minimum stay: 7 days.

**Waikiki Grand**, 134 Kapahulu Avenue, Honolulu, HI 96815. Tel: 922-9700, toll free: (800) 535-0085. $$ Area A – Waikiki. Total units: 173; rental units: 103. Fully air-conditioned, parking, TV, swimming pool, restaurant, shop.

**Waikiki Royal Suites**, 255 Beach Walk, Honolulu, HI 96815. Tel: 922-9700, toll free: (800) 535-0085. $$$ Area A – Waikiki. Total units: 47. Fully air-conditioned, parking, TV, shops, restaurant.

**White Sands Waikiki Resort**, 431 Nohonani Street, Honolulu, HI 96815. Tel: 923-7336. $+ Area A – Waikiki. Total units: 78. Fully air-conditioned, parking, TV, swimming pool.

## ·HAWAII

### HOTELS

**Dolphin Bay Hotel**, 333 Iliahi Street, Hilo, HI 96720. Tel: 935-1466. $ Area F, near downtown. Total units: 18. Fans, parking, TV.

**Hawaii Naniloa Hotel**, 93 Banyan Drive, Hilo, HI 96720. Tel: 969-3333, toll free: (800) 367-5360. $$+ Area F – on Hilo Bay. Total units: 325. Fully air-conditioned, parking, TV, restaurants, cocktail lounges, swimming pool, tennis courts, shops.

**Hilo Bay Hotel, Uncle Billy's**, 87 Banyan Drive, Hilo, HI 96720. Tel: 961-5818, toll free: (800) 367-5102. $+ Area F – Hilo. Total units: 145. Fully air-conditioned, parking, TV, swimming pool, restaurant, cocktail lounge, shops.

**Hilo Hawaiian Hotel**, 71 Banyan Drive, Hilo, HI 96720. Tel: 531-5235, toll free: (800) 272-5275. $$ Area F – on Hilo Bay. Total units: 290. Fully air-conditioned, parking, TV, restaurant, cocktail lounge, swimming pool, shops, meeting room.

**Holualoa Inn** (country inn), Mamalahoa Highway, Holualoa, HI 96725. Tel: 324-1121, toll free: (800) 367-5360. $$ Area I. Total units: 4. Parking, swimming pool; minimum stay: 2 nights.

**Hyatt Regency Waikoloa**, One Waikoloa Beach Resort, Waikoloa, HI 96743. Tel: 885-1234, toll free: (800) 233-1234. $$$$$ Area G – oceanfront. Total units: 1,240. Fully air-conditioned, parking, TV, swimming pool, restaurant, cocktail lounge, shop, meeting room, golf course, tennis court; maid service: daily.

**Kamuela Inn**, PO Box 1994, Kamuela, HI 96743. Tel: 885-4243. $$ Area G – Waimea. Total units: 31. Shops, TV, parking.

**Keauhou Beach Hotel**, 78-6740 Alii Drive, Kailua-Kona, HI 96740. Tel: 322-3441, toll free: (800) 367-6025. $$ Area J – on a sand beach. Total units: 310. Fully air-conditioned, parking, TV, restaurant, cocktail lounge, swimming pool, tennis court, shop, meeting room.

**Kilauea Lodge** (country inn), Old Volcano Road, Volcano, HI 96785. Tel: 967-7366. $$ Area I. Total units: 12. Parking, restaurant, cocktail lounge. Fireplaces.

**King Kamehameha Kona Beach Resort**, 75-5660 Palani Road, Kailua-Kona, HI 96740. Tel: 923-4511, toll free: (800) 367-6060. $$$ Area J – on the beach at Kailua. Total units: 460. Fully air-conditioned, parking, TV, restaurants, cocktail lounges, pool, tennis courts, shops, meeting rooms.

**Kona Bay Hotel, Uncle Billy's**, 75-5739 Alii Drive, Kailua-Kona, HI 96740. Tel: 961-5818, toll free: (800) 367-5102. $+ Area J – across from Kailua Bay. Total units: 145. Fully air-conditioned, parking, TV, pool, restaurant, cocktail lounge, shops.

HAWAII

Kona Hilton Resort, 75-5852 Alii Drive, Kailua-Kona, HI 96745. Tel: 329-3111, toll free: (800) HILTONS. $$$ Area J – on Kailua Bay. Total units: 445. Fully air-conditioned, parking, TV, restaurants, cocktail lounges, swimming pool, tennis courts, shops, meeting rooms.

Kona Surf Resort, 78-128 Ehukai Street, Keauhou-Kona, HI 96740. Tel: 322-3411, toll free: (800) 367-8011. $$ Area J – on Keauhou Bay. Total units: 530. Fully air-conditioned, parking, TV, restaurants, cocktail lounges, swimming pools, golf course, tennis courts, shops, meeting rooms.

Kona Village Resort, PO Box 1299, Kaupulehu-Kona, HI 96740. Tel: 325-5555, toll free: (800) 367-5290. $$$$$ Area J – on the beach at Kaupulehu. Total units: 125 (individual *hale,* or bungalows). Parking, restaurant, cocktail lounge, swimming pool, tennis courts, shop, meeting room.

Manago Hotel, PO Box 145, Captain Cook-Kona, HI 96740. Tel: 323-2642. $ Area J. Total units: 64. Parking, restaurant, cocktail lounge. Long-time family-run legend.

Mauna Kea Beach Resort, One Mauna Kea Beach Drive, Kohala Coast, HI 96743. Tel: 882-7222, toll free: (800) 882-6060. $$$$$ Area G – on the Kohala Coast, white sand beach. Total units: 310. Fully air-conditioned, parking, restaurants, cocktail lounge, swimming pool, golf course, tennis courts, shops, meeting rooms.

Mauna Lani Bay Hotel & Bungalows, One Mauna Lani Drive, Kohala Coast, HI 96743. Tel: 885-6622, toll free: (800) 367-2323. $$$$$ Area G – S. Kohala Coast, on a sand beach. Total units: 350. Fully air-conditioned, parking, TV, restaurants, cocktail lounges, swimming pool, tennis courts, golf course, shops, meeting rooms.

Parker Ranch Lodge, PO Box 458, Kamuela, HI 96743. Tel: 885-4100. $$ Area G – Waimea. Total units: 21. Parking, TV, meeting room.

Ritz-Carlton, Mauna Lani, One North Kaniku Drive, Kohala Coast, HI 96743. Tel: 885-2000, toll free: (800) 845-9905. $$$$$ Area G. Total units: 542. Fully air-conditioned, swimming pool, health club, shops, golf, restaurants, parking.

Royal Waikoloan, HC02 Box 5300, Waikoloa, HI 96743. Tel: 885-6789, toll free: (800) 733-7777. $$$ Area G – on a sand beach. Total units: 545. Fully air-conditioned, parking, TV, restaurants, cocktail lounges, swimming pool, tennis courts, golf course, shops, meeting room.

Shirakawa Motel, PO Box 467, Na'alehu, HI 96772. Tel: 929-7462. $ Area H – near South Point. Total units: 13. Parking.

Volcano House, PO Box 53, Hawaii Volcanoes National Park, HI 96718. Tel: 967-7321. $$ Area I – inside national park. Total units: 42. Shop, restaurant, lounge, parking. Also, simple cabins.

Wild Ginger Inn, 100 Puueo Street, Hilo, HI 96720. Tel: 935-5556, toll free: (800) 882-1887. $ Area F, near downtown. Total units: 28. Garden, laundry, parking.

## CONDOMINIUM RENTALS

Aston Royal Sea Cliff Resort, 75-6040 Alii Drive, Kailua-Kona, HI 96740. Tel: 931-1400, toll free: (800) 922-7866. $$+ Area J – Kona, oceanfront. Total units: 148. Fully air-conditioned, parking, TV, swimming pools, tennis court.

Colony's Kanaloa at Kona, 78-261 Manukai Street, Kailua-Kona, HI 96740. Tel: 322-9625, toll free: (800) 777-1700. $$$ Area J – Keauhou oceanfront. Total units: 166. Parking, swimming pools, restaurant, cocktail lounge, tennis courts.

Country Club Hotel, 121 Banyan Drive, Hilo, HI 96720. Tel: 935-7171. $ Area F – on Hilo Bay. Total units: 150; rental units: 60. Partially air-conditioned, parking, some rooms with TV, restaurant, cocktail lounge, swimming pool, meeting room, golf course.

Keauhou Resort Condominiums, 78–7039 Kamehameha III Road, Kailua-Kona, HI 96740. Tel: 322-9122, toll free: (800) 367-5286. $+ Area J – Kona Coast. Total units: 48; rental units: 28. Parking, TV, swimming pools, golf course; maid service: weekly; minimum stay: 5 days.

Kona by the Sea, 75-6106 Alii Drive, Kailua-Kona, HI 96740. Tel: 931-1400, toll free: (800) 922-7866. $$$ Area J – Kailua Bay. Total units: 86; rental units: 78. Fully air-conditioned, TV, swimming pools, restaurant.

Kona Islander Inn, 75-5776 Kuakini, Kailua-Kona, HI 96740. Tel: 931-1400, toll free: (800) 922-7866. $$ Area J – Kailua Bay. Total units: 144; rental units: 58. Fully air-conditioned, parking, TV, swimming pool.

Kona Reef, 75-5888 Alii Drive, Kailua-Kona, HI 96740. Tel: 523-7785, toll free: (800) 367-7040. $$ Area J – Kona oceanfront. Total units: 130; rental units: 45. Fully air-conditioned, parking, TV, swimming pool, restaurant; minimum stay: 2 nights

Seamountain at Punalu'u, PO Box 70, Pahala, HI 96777. Tel: 928-8301, toll free: (800) 488-8301. $$ Area H – Punalu'u, on oceanfront near Black Sand Beach, nr South Point. Total units: 75; rental units: 28. Parking, TV, restaurant, cocktail lounge, swimming pool, tennis courts, golf course, meeting rooms; maid service: weekly; minimum stay: 2 days.

Waikoloa Villas, PO Box 38-3498, Waikoloa, HI 96738. Tel: 922-9700, toll free: (800) 535-0085. $$ Area G – South Kohala. Total units: 104; rental units: 34. Parking, TV, swimming pools, golf course, meeting room; maid service: weekly.

## KAUAI

## HOTELS

Aston Kauai Beachboy Hotel, 484 Kuhio Highway, Kapa'a, Kauai, HI 96746. Tel: 931-1400, toll free: (800) 922-7866. $$ Area L – beach at Wailua. Total units: 24. Fully air-conditioned, parking, TV, restaurant, cocktail lounge, pool, shops, meeting rooms.

**Coco Palms Resort Hotel**, 4-241 Kuhio Highway, Kapa'a, Kauai, HI 96746. Tel: 822-4921, toll free: (800) 338-1338. $$ Area L – across from Wailua Beach. Total units: 390. Fully air-conditioned, parking, TV, restaurants, cocktail lounges, swimming pools, tennis courts, shops, meeting rooms.

**Garden Island Inn**, 3445 Wilcox Road, Lihue, HI 96766. Tel: 245-7227, toll free: (800) 648-0154. $ Area K. Total units: 21. Ceiling fans, TV, refrigerators, parking.

**Hotel Coral Reef**, 1516 Kuhio Highway, Kapa'a, Kauai, HI 96746. Tel: 822-4481, toll free: (800) 843-4659. $ Area L – Waipouli. Total units: 26. Parking, TV.

**Hyatt Regency Kauai Resort & Spa**, 1571 Poipu Road, Koloa, HI 96756. Tel: 742-1234, toll free: (800) 233-1234. $$$$$ Area N. Total units: 600. Fully air-conditioned, TV, shops, swimming pools, health club, golf, tennis, restaurants, parking.

**Islander on the Beach**, 484 Kuhio Highway, Kapa'a, Kauai, HI 96746. Tel: 822-7417, toll free: (800) 847-7417. $$ Area L – on the beach. Total units: 200. Fully air-conditioned, parking, TV, swimming pool, shops.

**Outrigger Kauai Beach**, 4331 Kauai Beach Drive, Lihue, Kauai, HI 96766. Tel: 245-1955, toll free: (800) 733-7777. $$$ Area L – Waipouli, on a sand beach. Total units: 350. Fully air-conditioned, parking, TV, swimming pool, restaurant, cocktail lounge, shop, meeting room, tennis courts.

**Sheraton Kauai**, 2440 Ho'onani Road, Koloa, Kauai, HI 96756. Tel: 742-1661, toll free: (800) 325-3535. $$$$ Area N – on the beach at Poipu. Total units: 450. Fully air-conditioned, parking, TV, restaurants, cocktail lounges, swimming pools, tennis courts, shops, meeting rooms.

**Sheraton Princeville Hotel**, 5520 Kahaku Road, Princeville, Kauai, HI 96722. Tel: 826-9644, toll free: (800) 325-3535. $$$$$ Area M – on Hanalei Bay, oceanfront beach. Total units: 250. Fully air-conditioned, parking, TV, restaurants, cocktail lounges, swimming pool, tennis courts, golf courses, shops, meeting rooms.

**Stouffer's Poipu Beach Resort**, 2251 Poipu Road, Koloa, Kauai, HI 96756. Tel: 742-1681, toll free: (800) 426-4122. $$+ Area N – on the beach at Poipu. Total units: 138. Fully air-conditioned, parking, TV, restaurants, cocktail lounges, swimming pool, tennis courts, shops.

**Stouffer's Waiohai Beach Resort**, 2249 Poipu Road, Koloa, Kauai, HI 96756. Tel: 742-9511, toll free: (800) 426-4122. $$$$ Area N – Poipu, on the beach at Poipu. Total units: 426. Fully air-conditioned, parking, TV, restaurants, cocktail lounges, swimming pools, tennis courts, shops, meeting room.

**Tip Top Motel**, 3173 Akahi Street, Lihue, Kauai, HI 96766. Tel: 245-2333. $ Area K – Lihue. Total units: 34. Fully air-conditioned, parking, restaurant, cocktail lounge, meeting room.

**Waimea Plantation Cottages** (cottages), PO Box 367, Waimea, Kauai, HI 96796. Tel: 338-1625, toll free: (800) 9-WAIMEA. $$ Area N – Waimea. Total units: 50. Parking; maid service: weekly.

**Westin Kauai**, Kalapaki Beach, Lihue, Kauai, HI 96766. Tel: 245-5050, toll free: (800) 228-3000. $$$$ Area K – Nawiliwili, on a sandy beach. Total units: 847. Fully air-conditioned, parking, TV, restaurants, cocktail lounge, swimming pool, tennis courts, golf course, meeting rooms.

## CONDOMINIUM RENTALS

**Garden Isle Cottages**, 2666 Pu'uholo Road, Koloa, Kauai, HI 96756. Tel: 742-6717. $$ Area N – oceanfront. Total units: 13. Parking, TV, swimming pool; no maid service; minimum stay: 2 days.

**Hanalei Bay Resort**, 5380 Honoiki Road, Princeville, Kauai, HI 96714. Tel: 826-6522, toll free: (800) 827-4427. $$$ Area M – Hanalei Bay. Total units: 280; rental units: 85. Parking, swimming pool, restaurant, cocktail lounge, shops, meeting rooms, golf course, tennis court.

**Hanalei Colony Resort**, PO Box 206, Hanalei, Kauai, HI 96714. Tel: 826-6235, toll free: (800) 628-3004. $$$ Area M – on the beach at Ha'ena. Total units: 52; rental units: 47. Parking, swimming pool; maid service: every 3rd day; minimum stay: 3 days.

**Kaha Lani**, 4460 Nehe Road, Lihue, Kauai, HI 96766. Tel: 931-1400, toll free: (800) 922-7866. $$+ Area L – on the beach. Total units: 74; rental units: 65. Ceiling fans, parking, TV, swimming pool, tennis court.

**Kapa'a Sands**, 380 Papaloa Road, Kapa'a, Kauai, HI 96746. Tel: 822-4901, toll free: (800) 222-4901. $$ Area L – oceanfront at Wailua. Total units: 24; rental units: 21. Parking, TV; maid service: on request; minimum stay: 3 days.

**Kiahuna Plantation**, 2253 Poipu Road, Koloa, Kauai, HI 96756. Tel: 742-6411, toll free: (800)

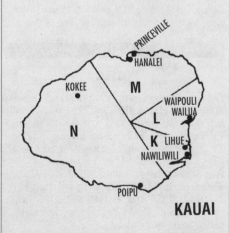

KAUAI

367-7052. $$$$ Area N – on Poipu Beach. Total units: 330; rental units: 307. Parking, restaurant, cocktail lounge, swimming pool, tennis court, golf course, shop; minimum stay: 2 nights.

**Koke'e Lodge** (rustic housekeeping cabins), PO Box 819, Waimea, Kauai, HI 96796. Tel: 335-6061. $ Area N – inside Koke'e State Park. Total units: 12. Parking, restaurant, cocktail lounge, convenience store; no maid service.

**Nihi Kai Villas**, 1870 Hoone Road, Poipu, Kauai, HI 96756 Tel: 742-1412, toll free: (800) 742-1412. $$ Area N – Poipu. Total units: 70; rental units: 32. Parking, TV, swimming pool, tennis court.

**Pali Ke Kua at Princeville**, 5300 Ka Haku Road, Hanalei, Kauai, HI 96714. Tel: 922-9700, toll free: (800) 535-0085. $$ Area M – Princeville, oceanfront. Total units: 98; rental units: 30. Parking, TV, restaurant, cocktail lounge, swimming pool, golf course; maid service: midweek.

**Plantation Hale**, 484 Kuhio Highway, Kapa'a, Kauai, HI 96746. Tel: 822-4941, toll free: (800) 733-7777. $$ Area K – Kapa'a, in coconut plantation. Total units: 153. Fully air-conditioned, parking, TV, restaurants, cocktail lounges, swimming pool, shops.

**Poipu Kapili**, 2221 Kapili Road, Koloa, Kauai, HI 96756. Tel: 742-6449, toll free: (800) 443-7714. $$$ Area N – Poipu Beach. Total units: 60; rental units: 45. Parking, TV, swimming pool, tennis courts; minimum stay: 2 days.

**Poipu Shores Oceanfront Condo**, 1775 Pe'e Road, Koloa, Kauai, HI 96756. Tel: 742-7700, toll free: (800) 869-7959. $$$ Area N – Poipu. Total units: 32. TV, swimming pool, tennis courts; maid service: every other day; minimum stay: 3 days.

**Prince Kuhio Resort**, PO Box 1060, Koloa, Kauai, HI 96756. Tel: 742-1409, toll free: (800) 722-1409. $ Area N. Total units: 65; rental units: 48. Parking, TV, swimming pool; maid service: upon request.

**Whalers Cove**, 2640 Pu'uholo Road, Koloa, Kauai, HI 96756. Tel: 283-9050, toll free: (800) 367-7052. $$$$ Area N. Total units: 38; rental units: 19. Ceiling fans, parking, TV, in-room Jacuzzi, swimming pool; maid service: daily.

## MAUI

### HOTELS

**Embassy Suites Resort**, 104 Ka'anapali Shores Place, Lahaina, Maui, HI 96761. Tel: 661-2000, toll free: (800) GO-2-MAUI. $$$$ Area R – Ka'anapali. Total units: 413. Fully air-conditioned, parking, TV, restaurant, cocktail lounge, swimming pool, shop, meeting room.

**Four Seasons Resort Wailea**, 3900 Wailea Alanui, Wailea, HI 96753. Tel: 874-8000, toll free: (800) 332-3442. $$$$$ Area T. Total units: 380. Fully air-conditioned, TV/VCR, shopping, restaurants, tennis, health spa, parking.

**Grand Hyatt Wailea Resort & Spa**, 3850 Wailea

Alanui Drive, Wailea, HI 96753. Tel: 875-1234, toll free: (800) 233-1234. $$$$$ Area T. Total units: 787. Fully air-conditioned, TV, shopping, restaurants, health club/spa, nightclub, parking.

**Hotel Hana-Maui**, PO Box 9, Hana, Maui, HI 96713. Tel: 248-8211, 536-7522 (Honolulu Direct Line), toll free: (800) 321-HANA. $$$$$ Area Q – Hana Bay. Total units: 96. Parking, restaurant, cocktail lounge, swimming pool, golf course, tennis courts, shop, meeting room.

**Hyatt Regency Maui**, 200 Nohea Kai Drive, Ka'anapali, Maui, HI 96761. Tel: 661-1234, toll free: (800) 233-1234. $$$$+ Area R – oceanfront and sand beach. Total units: 815. Fully air-conditioned, parking, TV, restaurants, cocktail lounges, pool, tennis courts, golf course, shops, meeting rooms.

**Ka'anapali Beach Hotel**, 2525 Ka'anapali Parkway, Lahaina, Maui, HI 96761. Tel: 661-0011, toll free: (800) 657-7700. $$$ Area R – on the beach at Ka'anapali. Total units: 431. Fully air-conditioned, parking, TV, restaurants, cocktail lounges, swimming pool, golf courses, tennis nearby, shops, dinner showroom.

**Kapalua Bay Hotel & Villas**, One Bay Drive, Kapalua, Maui, HI 96761. Tel: 669-5656, toll free: (800) 367-8000. $$$$$ Area R. Total units: 194. Villas: 117. Fully air-conditioned, parking, TV, restaurants, cocktail lounge, swimming pools, tennis courts, golf courses, shops.

**Kea Lani Hotel**, 4100 Wailea Alanui Drive, Wailea, HI 96753. Tel: 875-4100, toll free: (800) 882-4100. $$$$+ Area T. Total units: 450. Fully air-conditioned, TV/VCR, microwave, shops, health spa, golf, tennis, restaurants, parking.

**Kula Lodge** (cottages), RR.1, Box 475, Kula, HI 96790. Tel: 878-2517, toll free: (800) 233-1535. $$ Area S – Upcountry. Total units: 5. Parking, shop, restaurant and lounge.

**Lahaina Hotel**, 127 Lahainaluna Road, Lahaina, HI 96761. Tel: 661-0577, toll free: (800) 669-3444. $$ Area R – downtown Lahaina, near waterfront. Total units: 12. Restored 1860s boutique hotel, antiques, restaurant, parking.

**Maui Beach Hotel**, 170 Ka'ahumanu Avenue, Kahului, Maui, HI 96732. Tel: 531-5235, toll free: (800) 367-5004. $$ Area U – on Kahului beach. Total units: 148. Fully air-conditioned, parking, TV, restaurants, cocktail lounge, swimming pool, shop, meeting room.

**Maui Inter-Continental Wailea**, 3700 Wailea Alanui Drive, Wailea, Maui, HI 96753. Tel: 879-1922, toll free: (800) 367-2960. $$$+ Area T. Total units: 516. Fully air-conditioned, parking, TV, restaurants, cocktail lounge, swimming pools, tennis courts, golf course, shops, meeting rooms.

**Maui Marriott Resort**, 100 Nohea Kai Drive, Lahaina, Maui, HI 96761. Tel: 667-1200, toll free: (800) 228-9290. $$$$ Area R – on the beach. Total units: 720. Fully air-conditioned, parking, TV, restaurants, cocktail lounges, swimming pool, tennis courts, shops, meeting rooms.

**Maui Prince Hotel**, 5400 Makena Alanui Road, Kihei, Maui, HI 96753. Tel: 874-1111, toll free: (800) 321-MAUI. $$$$+ Area T – Makena. Total units: 310. Fully air-conditioned, parking, TV, restaurants, cocktail lounge, swimming pools, tennis courts, golf course, shops, meeting room.

**Mauian Hotel**, 5441 Honoapiilani Road, Lahaina, Maui, HI 96761. Tel: 669-6205, toll free: (800) 367-5034. $$ Area R – Napili, across beach. Total units: 44. Ceiling fans, parking, swimming pool; maid service: every 3rd day.

**Plantation Inn**, 174 Lahainaluna Road, Lahaina, HI 96761. Tel: 667-9225, toll free: (800) 433-6815. $$ Area R – downtown Lahaina. Total units: 24. Fully air-conditioned, TV/VCR, restaurant, swimming pool, parking.

**Ritz-Carlton Kapalua**, One Ritz-Carlton Drive, Kapalua, HI 96761. Tel: 669-6200, toll free: (800) 241-3333. $$$$$ Area R. Total units: 550. Fully air-conditioned, TV, shops, swimming pool, health club, golf, tennis, restaurants, parking.

**Royal Lahaina Hotel**, 2780 Kekaa Drive, Lahaina, Maui, HI 96761. Tel: 661-3611, toll free: (800) 447-6925. $$$ Area R – on the beach at Ka'anapali. Total units: 520. Fully air-conditioned, parking, TV, restaurants, cocktail lounges, tennis courts, golf courses, shops, meeting rooms.

**Sheraton Maui Hotel**, 2605 Ka'anapali Parkway, Lahaina, Maui, HI 96761. Tel: 661-0031, toll free: (800) 325-3535. $$$+ Area R – on the beach at Ka'anapali. Total units: 492. Fully air-conditioned, parking, TV, restaurants, cocktail lounges, swimming pools, tennis courts, golf course, shops, meeting rooms.

**Stouffer's Wailea Beach**, 3550 Wailea Alanui Drive, Wailea, Maui, HI 96753. Tel: 879-4900, toll free: (800) 992-4532. $$$$ Area T – on the beach at Wailea. Total units: 347. Fully air-conditioned, parking, TV, restaurants, cocktail lounge, swimming pool, tennis courts, golf course, shops, meeting rooms.

**Westin Maui**, 2365 Ka'anapali Parkway, Lahaina, Maui, HI 96761. Tel: 667-2525, toll free: (800) 228-3000. $$$$ Area R – Ka'anapali, on the beach. Total units: 762. Fully air-conditioned, parking, TV, restaurants, cocktail lounge, swimming pools, tennis courts, golf course, shop, meeting rooms.

## CONDOMINIUM RENTALS

**Aston Ka'anapali Shores**, 3445 Lower Honoapiilani Highway, Lahaina, Maui, HI 96761. Tel: 931-1400, toll free: (800) 922-7866. $$+ Area R – on the beach. Total units: 463; rental units: 440. Fully air-conditioned, parking, TV, restaurant, cocktail lounge, swimming pool, tennis courts, shop.

**Aston Kamaole Sands**, 2695 S. Kihei Road, Kihei, Maui, HI 96753. Tel: 931-1400, toll free: (800) 922-7866. $$ Area T – Kihei, across from beach. Total units: 334; rental units: 440. Parking, TV, swimming pool, tennis courts.

**Hale Kai**, 3691 Honoapiilani Road, Lahaina, Maui, HI 96761. Tel: 669-6333, toll free: (800) 446-7307. $$ Area R – oceanfront. Total units: 40. Parking, TV, swimming pool; maid service: on request; minimum stay: 3 days.

**Hololani Resort Condominium**, 4401 Honoapiilani Road, Lahaina, Maui, HI 96761. Tel: 669-8021, toll free: (800) 367-5032. $$+ Area R – oceanfront. Total units: 62; rental units: 25. Ceiling fans, parking, TV, swimming pool; maid service: weekly.

**Hono Kai Resort**, RR Box 389, Wailuku, Maui, HI 96793. Tel: 244-7012, toll free: (800) 367-6084. $+ Area T – Ma'alaea Bay, on a sand beach. Total units: 45; rental units: 30. Partially air-conditioned, parking, TV, swimming pool; maid service: on request; minimum stay: 5 days.

**Honokeana Cove**, 5255 Lower Honoapiilani Road, Lahaina, Maui, HI 96761. Tel: 669-6441, toll free: (800) 237-4948. $$ Area R – on the oceanfront at Honokeana. Total units: 38; rental units: 31. Parking, TV, swimming pool; maid service: weekly; minimum stay: 3 days.

**Ka'anapali Ali'i**, 50 Nohea Kai Drive, Ka'anapali, Maui, HI 96761. Tel: 667-1400, toll free: (800) 642-6284. $$$$ Area R. Total units: 264; rental units: 208. Fully air-conditioned, parking, TV, swimming pools, tennis courts, golf course.

**Ka'anapali Royal**, 2560 Kekaa Drive, Lahaina, Maui, HI 96761. Tel: 523-7785, toll free: (800) 367-7040. $$$ Area R – Ka'anapali. Total units: 105; rental units: 15. Fully air-conditioned, parking, TV, restaurant, swimming pool, tennis court, golf course; minimum stay: 2 nights.

**Kahana Villa**, 4242 Lower Honoapiilani Highway, Lahaina, Maui, HI 96761. Tel: 922-9700, toll free: (800) 535-0085. $$ Area R – 50 feet to beach. Total units: 100; rental units: 61. Ceiling fans, parking, TV, restaurant, cocktail lounge, swimming pool, tennis court, shop.

**Kaleialoha Condominium**, 3785 Honoapiilani High-

**MAUI**

way, Lahaina, Maui, HI 96761. Tel: 669-8197, toll free: (800) 222-8688. $$ Area R – oceanfront. Total units: 67; rental units: 30. Parking, TV, swimming pool; maid service: none; minimum stay: 3 nights.
**Kapalua Ridge Villas**, 100 Ridge Road, Kapalua, Maui, HI 96761. Tel: 669-9696, toll free: (800) 326-MAUI. $$ Area R. Total units: 161. Rental units: 70. Parking, TV, restaurants, cocktail lounge, swimming pool, tennis courts, golf courses, shops; maid service: on request; minimum stay: 5 nights.
**Kihei Beach Resort**, 36 S. Kihei Road, Kihei, Maui, HI 96753. Tel: 879-2744, toll free: (800) 367-6034. $$ Area T – on the beach. Total units: 54; rental units: 36. Fully air-conditioned, parking, TV, swimming pool; minimum stay: 3 days.
**Kihei Kai**, 61 N. Kihei Road, Kihei, Maui, HI 96753. Tel: 879-2357, toll free: (800) 735-2357. $ Area T – on the beach at Kihei. Total units: 24; rental units: 20. Fully air-conditioned, parking, TV, swimming pool; minimum stay: 4 days.
**Kulakane**, 3741 Lower Honoapiilani Road, Lahaina, Maui, HI 96761. Tel: 669-6119, toll free: (800) 367-6088. $$ Area R – oceanfront at Honokowai. Total units: 36. Parking, TV, swimming pool; maid service: on request; minimum stay: 3 days.
**Lahaina Shores Beach Resort**, 475 Front Street, Lahaina, Maui, HI 96761. Tel: 667-1400, toll free: (800) 642-6284. $$ Area R – on a sand beach. Total units: 199; rental units: 127. Fully air-conditioned, parking, TV, swimming pool, tennis court.
**Luana Kai**, 940 S. Kihei Road, Kihei, Maui, HI 96753. Tel: 879-1268, toll free: (800) 669-1127. $$ Area T. Parking, TV, swimming pool, tennis court; maid service: every 3rd day.
**Makani A Kai**, RR 1 Box 389, Ma'alaea Village, Maui, HI 96793. Tel: 244-5627, toll free: (800) 367-6084. $$ Area T – on the beach at Ma'alaea. Total units: 24; rental units: 16. Partially air-conditioned, parking, TV, swimming pools; maid service: on request; minimum stay: 5 days.
**Mana Kai Maui**, 2960 S. Kihei Road, Kihei, Maui, HI 96753. Tel: 879-1561, toll free: (800) 525-2025. $$ Area T – on sand beach. Total units: 98; rental units: 67. Parking, TV, swimming pool, restaurant, cocktail lounge, meeting room.
**Maui Eldorado Resort**, Ka'anapali Beach, Lahaina, Maui, HI 96761. Tel: 971-1700, toll free: (800) 535-0085. $$$ Area R. Total units: 204; rental units: 109. Fully air-conditioned, parking, TV, swimming pool, golf course, shop.
**Maui Kai**, 106 Ka'anapali Shores, Lahaina, Maui, HI 96761. Tel: 667-3500, Toll free: (800) 367-5635. $$ Area R – on the beach at Ka'anapali. Total units: 80; rental units: 60. Fully air-conditioned, parking, TV, swimming pool; maid service: twice weekly; minimum stay: 2 nights.
**Maui Lu Resort**, 575 S. Kihei Road, Kihei, Maui, HI 96753. Tel: 931-1400, toll free: (800) 922-7866. $$ Area T – on the beach. Total units: 156; rental units: 129. Fully air-conditioned, parking, TV, restaurant, cocktail lounge, pool, tennis courts, shops.

**Maui Vista**, 2191 Kihei Road, Kihei, Maui, HI 96753. Tel: 931-1400, toll free: (800) 922-7866. $$ Area T. Total units: 279; rental units: 90. Fully air-conditioned, parking, swimming pools, tennis courts; maid service: daily.
**Nani Kai Hale**, 73 N. Kihei Road, Kihei, Maui, HI 96753. Tel: 879-9120, toll free: (800) 367-6032. $ Area T – on a sand beach. Total units: 46; rental units: 31. Parking, TV, swimming pool; no maid service; minimum stay: 3 days.
**Napili Kai Beach Club**, 5900 Honoapiilani Road, Lahaina, Maui, HI 96761. Tel: 669-6271, toll free: (800) 367-5030. $$$$ Area R – on Napili Bay. Total units: 162. Partially air-conditioned, parking, TV, restaurant, cocktail lounge, swimming pools, tennis courts, shops, meeting rooms.
**Napili Point**, 5295 Honoapiilani Highway, Lahaina, Maui, HI 96761. Tel: 669-9222, toll free: (800) 669-6252. $$$ Area R – Napili oceanfront. Total units: 110; rental units: 100. Parking, TV, swimming pools.
**Napili Sunset**, 46 Hui Drive, Lahaina, Maui, HI 96761. Tel: 669-8083, toll free: (800) 447-9229. $$ Area R – on a sand beach. Total units: 42; rental units: 41. Parking, TV, swimming pool; minimum stay: 3 nights.
**Napili Surf Beach Resort**, 50 Napili Place, Napili Bay, Maui, HI 96761. Tel: 669-8002, toll free: (800) 541-0638. $$ Area R – on the beach at Napili Bay. Total units: 53. Parking, TV, swimming pool; maid service: daily; minimum stay: 5 days.
**Napili Village**, 5425 Honoapiilani Highway, Lahaina, Maui, HI 96761. Tel: 669-6228, toll free: (800) 336-2185. $+ Area R – Napili, Napili Bay. Total units: 28. Parking, swimming pool, shop.
**Noelani Condominium Resort**, 4095 Lower Honoapiilani Road, Lahaina, Maui, HI 96761. Tel: 367-6030, toll free: (800) 367-6030. $$ Area R – Lahaina. Total units: 50; rental units: 41. Parking, TV, swimming pools; maid service: midweek.
**Paki Maui**, 3615 Lower Honoapiilani Highway, Lahaina, Maui, HI 96761. Tel: 922-9700, toll free: (800) 535-0085. $$$ Area R – on a sand beach. Total units: 110; rental units: 77. Parking, TV, swimming pool, tennis courts, meeting room.
**Papakea Resort**, 3543 Honoapiilani Highway, Lahaina, Maui, HI 96761. Tel: 669-4848, toll free: (800) 367-7052. $$$ Area R – on the beach at Honokowai. Total units: 364; rental units: 114. Ceiling fans, parking, TV, pools, tennis courts.
**Polo Beach Club**, 3750 Wailea Alanui Drive, Wailea, Maui, HI 96753. Tel: 879-1595, toll free: (800) 367-5246. $$$$ Area T. Total units: 71; rental units: 40. Fully air-conditioned, parking, TV, swimming pool; maid service: daily.
**Polynesian Shores**, 3975 Honoapiilani Way, Lahaina, Maui, HI 96761. Tel: 669-6065, Toll free: (800) 433-MAUI. $$ Area R – on the beach at Mahinahina. Total units: 52; rental units: 35. Parking, TV, swimming pool; maid service: on request; minimum stay: 3 days.

**Sands of Kahana**, 4299 Honoapiilani Highway, Lahaina, Maui, HI 96761. Tel: 669-0400. $$$ Area R – on the beach. Total units: 196; rental units: 129. Parking, TV, restaurant, cocktail lounge, swimming pool, tennis court, meeting room.

**Whaler at Ka'anapali Beach**, 2481 Ka'anapali Parkway, Lahaina, Maui, HI 96761. Tel: 661-4861, toll free: (800) 367-7052. $$$$ Area R – on a sand beach. Total units: 360; rental units: 161. Fully air-conditioned, parking, TV, swimming pool, tennis courts, golf course, shop, meeting room; minimum stay: 2 days.

## MOLOKAI & LANAI

**Colony's Kaluakoi Hotel & Golf Club** (Hotel – Molokai), PO Box 1977, Maunaloa, Molokai, HI 96770. Tel: 552-2555, toll free: (800) 777-1700. $$+ On Kepuhi Beach. Total units: 170. Parking, TV, restaurants, cocktail lounge, pool, tennis courts, golf course, shops, meeting rooms.

**Ke Nani Kai**, (Condominium – Molokai), PO Box 126, Maunaloa, Molokai, HI 96770. Tel: 552-2761, toll free: (800) 888-2791. $$$ Oceanfront. Total units: 120; rental units: 45. Parking, TV, swimming pool, tennis courts, golf course; minimum stay is at least 2 nights.

**Molokai Shores** (Condominium – Molokai), Star Route, Kaunakakai, Molokai, HI 96748. Tel: 922-9700, toll free: (800) 535-0085. $$ On the beach. Total units: 100; rental units: 39. Parking, TV, swimming pool, shop.

**Pau Hana Inn** (Cottage-type inn – Molokai), PO Box 860, Kaunakakai, Molokai, HI 96748. Tel: 553-5342, 531-4004 (Honolulu Direct Line), toll free: (800) 367-8047. $ On the oceanfront at Kaunakakai. Total units: 39. Parking, restaurant, cocktail lounge, swimming pool.

**Manele Bay Hotel** (Hotel – Lanai), PO Box 774, Lanai City, HI 96763. Tel: 565-3800, toll free: (800) 223-7637. $$$$$ On the beach. Total units: 250. Fully air-conditioned, TV, shops, swimming pool, health club, restaurant, tennis, Jacuzzi, parking.

**The Lodge at Ko'ele** (Hotel – Lanai), PO Box 774, Lanai City, HI 96763. Tel: 565-3800, toll free: (800) 321-4666. $$$$$ In the highlands. Total units: 102. Partially air-conditioned, TV/VCR, pool, shop, golf, tennis, restaurants, parking.

## CAMPING

Campgrounds are run by the National Park Service, the state of Hawaii, and the four island counties. *Plan camp outings ahead of time.* Campsites are popular. Conditions and rates vary, so refer to current maps, brochures and proper agencies for information. To make reservations, call or write to the following agencies:

**Haleakala National Park**, PO Box 369, Makawao, Maui, HI 96768.

Park headquarters: Tel: 572-9306

Cabin & camping information: Tel: 572-9177
General information/recorded: Tel: 572-7749
Haleakala weather forecast: Tel: 871-5054

There are two drive-in campgrounds near the summit, and one in Kipahulu, at 'Ohe'o Pools near Hana. For the two near the crater, permits are required, issued on arrival at the park. Sites are first come, first serve. In Haleakala Crater itself, there are 3 cabins available, accessible by hiking and assigned by lottery reservations. It is recommended that applications be made three months in advance.

**Hawaii Volcanoes National Park** PO Box 53, Hawaii Volcanoes National Park, HI 96718 Tel: 967-7311. There are three drive-in campgrounds, no permits required, first come, first served. There are also privately-operated cabins (rustic, utilitarian and without windows) available at inflated prices at the Namakani Paio campground; arrangements and payment of the fee is at the Volcano House hotel, in the park. Bedding is provided.

## STATE PARKS

There are over 60 state parks throughout the major islands. Some are well developed, others primitive and rustic. Many have simple cabins available for rent. Some of the state parks are real gems. Permits required, no fees for camping.

Camping permits: Tel: 587-0300
Hiking: Tel: 587-0166
Fishing licenses: Tel: 587-0077

**Regional Offices**

**Big Island**: Department of Land and Natural Resources, Division of State Parks, PO Box 936, Hilo, Hawaii 96720. Tel: 933-4200.

**Kauai**: Department of Land and Natural Resources, Division of State Parks, 3060 Eiwa, #306, Lihue, Kauai, Hawaii 96766. Tel: 241-3444.

**Koke'e State Park** (housekeeping cabins), Manager, Koke'e Lodge, PO Box 819, Waimea, Kauai, Hawaii 96796. Tel: 335-6061.

**Maui** (includes Molokai): Department of Land and Natural Resources, Division of State Parks, 54 High Street, Wailuku, Maui, Hawaii 96793. Tel: 243-5354.

**Oahu**: Department of Land and Natural Resources, Division of State Parks, PO Box 621, Honolulu, Hawaii 96809. Tel: 587-0300.

## COUNTY PARKS

**County of Hawaii** (Big Island): Department of Parks and Recreation, 25 Aupuni Street, Hilo, Hawaii 96720. Tel: 961-8311. 13 county beach parks, tent and vehicle camping. Permits and fees required.

**City and County of Honolulu**: Department of Parks and Recreation, 650 South King Street, Honolulu, Hawaii 96813. Tel: 523-4525. 13 beach parks, tent and vehicle camping. Permits required, no fee.

**County of Kauai**: Department of Parks and Recreation, 4193 Hardy Street, Lihue, Kauai 96766. Tel: 241-6670. Seven county parks, beach and inland. Permits and fees required.

**County of Maui** (includes Molokai): Department of Parks and Recreation, 1580 Kaahumanu Avenue, Wailuki, Maui, Hawaii 96793. Tel: 243-7389. Two county parks, inland. Permits and fees required. On Molokai: seven parks, permits and fees required.

# FOOD DIGEST

## WHERE TO EAT

If trying to squeeze into that swim suit, you should've planned ahead. Forget about dieting while in Hawaii. There are simply too many restaurants in the islands – tens of hundreds – to ignore a good meal amidst Hawaii's sensuality. And because of the stiff competition, almost every restaurant is decent, if not good. Indeed, it's difficult to find a bad or even unsatisfactory meal in the islands.

This listing is intended to make the traveler's transition to island life a little easier, but it is anything but comprehensive. Exclusion from this list indicates nothing about an establishment's quality or cuisine; there are just too many to list. For a more comprehensive listing, a copy of the Visitors Bureau *Entertainment and Dining Guide* includes everything from luaus to fast-food joints.

One problem in describing Hawaii's restaurants – and it's a delightful problem – is that chefs here enjoy experimenting, adding a little Asian to Continental, or Italian to Pacific. The results are excellent, including the highly regarded "Pacific Rim" cuisine gaining popularity and international respect. So, when you go to an Italian restaurant, you might find touches of Asian cuisine; in a Continental restaurant, embellishments from the Pacific region are likely. Now get out and eat.

These price listings are broad guides for relative costs of an average meal, and have nothing to do with subjective evaluations of quality or menu offerings.

$ = less than $20; $$ = $20 to $40; $$$ = more than $40. Breakfast: B; lunch: L; dinner: D.

## OAHU

**A Little Bit of Saigon,**1160 Maunakea Street, Chinatown. Tel: 528-3663. Vietnamese. Basic place with a solid following and good food. $ LD

**Andy's** (aka **Manoa Health Market**), 2904 East Manoa Road, Honolulu, Manoa Valley. Tel: 988-6161. Vegetarian. Family-run, simple seating with diverse menu, bakery. $ BL

**Buzz's Steak House**, 413 Kawailoa Road, Lanikai (near Kailua). Tel: 261-4661. American. Local steak and seafood place, island ingredients. $-$$ LD

**Cafe Brio**, Manoa Marketplace, Honolulu, Manoa Valley. Tel: 988-5555. Pacific Rim. Pasta, with unique twists. Loyal following. Popular. $$ LD

**Compadres**, Ward Centre, 1200 Ala Moana Blvd. Honolulu. Tel: 523-1307. Mexican. Popular upscale local hangout, lively. $-$$ BLD

**Dynasty II**, Ward Warehouse, 1050 Ala Moana Blvd. Honolulu. Tel: 531-0208. Chinese. Overlooking Kewalo Basin; Peking duck, shark's fin soup. $$ LD

**Garden Cafe**, Honolulu Academy of Arts, 900 South Beretania Street, Honolulu. Tel: 532-8734. Contemporary cuisine. Casual open-air café at the art gallery. $ L

**Hala Terrace**, Kahala Hilton, 5000 Kahala Avenue, Honolulu. Tel: 734-2211. American. Oceanfront, with nightly show by favorite local entertainers. $$ BLD

**Horatio's**, Ward Warehouse, 1050 Ala Moana Blvd. Honolulu. Tel: 521-5002. Contemporary. Seafood, pasta, beef – popular with local professionals. $$ LD

**Jameson's by the Sea**, Kamehameha Highway, Hale'iwa, North Shore. Tel: 637-4336. American. Lots of seafood, sunset views. $+ LD

**Maile Restaurant**, Kahala Hilton, 5000 Kahala Avenue, Honolulu. Tel: 734-2211. Continental. Touches of Pacific, Asia in menu. Jacket required. $$$+ D

**Orson's**, Ward Warehouse, 1050 Ala Moana Blvd. Honolulu. Tel: 521-5681. Seafood. Overlooking Kewalo Basin, local favorite. $$ LD

**Pagoda Restaurant**, Pagoda Hotel, 1525 Rycroft Street, Honolulu. Tel: 941-6611. Continental/Japanese. Popular local restaurant, with waterfall and oriental fishponds. $-$$ BLD

**Rose City Diner**, Restaurant Row, 500 Ala Moana Blvd. Honolulu. Tel: 525-ROSE. American. 1950s theme, lots of nostalgia. $+ BLD

**Roy's Restaurant**, 6600 Kalanianaole Highway, Hawaii Kai. Tel: 396-7697. Contemporary. Nouvelle cuisine with global flourishes. $$ LD

## WAIKIKI

**Bali by the Sea**, Hilton Hawaiian Village, 2005 Kalia Road. Tel: 941-BALI. Continental. Open-air, upscale with touches of Pacific and Asia on menu. $$-$$$ BLD

**Banyan Veranda**, Sheraton Moana Surfrider, 2365 Kalakaua Avenue. Tel: 922-3111. American/Continental. Breakfast buffets in historic beach front courtyard. $$ B

**Caffélatte**, 339 Saratoga Road. Tel: 924-1414. Italian. Family-run, small and classy, open-air tables at quiet *Ewa* end of Waikiki. $+ D

**Ciao Mein**, Hyatt Regency Waikiki, 2424 Kalakaua Avenue. Tel: 923-1234. Chinese/Italian. Upscale, blending of East and West. Indoor/outdoor. $$+ D
**Duke's Canoe Club**, Outrigger Waikiki Hotel, 2335 Kalakaua Avenue. Tel: 922-2268. American. Casual, trendy steak-and-seafood place. $–$$ BLD
**Hau Tree Lanai**, New Otani Kaimana Beach Hotel, 2863 Kalakaua Avenue. Tel: 921-7066. American. On the beach, outside where Stevenson once sat. $–$$ BLD
**Kacho**, Waikiki Parc Hotel, 2233 Helumoa Road. Tel: 921-7272. Japanese. Definitely authentic Kaiseki-style cuisine and setting. $$$ BLD
**Keo's Thai Cuisine**, 625 Kapahulu Avenue, near Waikiki. Tel: 737-8240. Thai. Lively, popular with locals and celebrities. Also at Ward Centre. $$ LD
**La Mer**, Halekulani Hotel, 2199 Kalia Road. Tel: 923-2311. French. Very upscale, with touches of the Pacific in menu. Jacket required. $$$+ D
**Miyako Restaurant**, New Otani Kaimana Beach Hotel, 2863 Kalakaua Avenue. Tel: 921-7079. Japanese. Traditional setting with authentic cuisines, ocean views. $$ D
**Orchids**, Halekulani Hotel, 2199 Kalia Road. Tel: 923-2311. Contemporary. Open air to the beach, upscale. $$+ BLD
**Parc Cafe**, Waikiki Parc Hotel, 2233 Helumoa Road. Tel: 921-7272. Asian/Pacific. Changing gourmet buffets, entree quality with unique offerings. $–$$ BLD
**Prince Court**, Hawaii Prince Hotel, 100 Holomoana Street. Tel: 956-1111. Regional. Emphasis on local ingredients, blending East and West. $$+ BLD

## HAWAII

**Aloha Theater Cafe**, Highway 11, Kainaliu/Kona. Tel: 322-3383. Contemporary. In an old theater building. Diverse menu with terrace seating. $ BLD
**Café Pesto**, 308 Kamehameha Avenue, Hilo. Tel: 969-6640. Italian. Traditional and nouveaux, popular. Espresso. Also in Kohala, tel: 882-1071. $–$$ LD
**Canoe House**, Mauna Lani Bay Hotel, South Kohala. Tel: 885-6622. Pacific Rim. Open-air views of the Pacific Ocean and Kohala sunset. $$–$$$ D
**Holuakoa Cafe**, 76-5900 Mamalahoa Hwy. Holualoa (above Kailua-Kona). Tel: 322-2233. Contemporary. Easy-going espresso bar, light simple meals. Quiet artist town. $ BLD
**Jameson's by the Sea**, 77-6452 Alii Drive, Kailua-Kona. Tel: 329-3195. American. On the waterfront, with fresh local fish, salmon. $–$$ LD
**Jaspers**, 110 Kalakaua Street, Hilo. Tel: 969-6686. Contemporary. Casual, open air, for espresso or solid meal. $ BLD
**Kilauea Lodge**, Old Volcano Road, Volcano Village. Tel: 967-7366. Continental. Spacious country dining, casual but upscale. $$+ D
**Lehua's Bar & Grill**, 90 Kamehameha Avenue, Hilo. Tel: 935-8055. American. Live jazz music, active night scene. $$ LD

**Manago Hotel**, Captain Cook, Kona. Tel: 323-2642. American. Casual fundamentals in family-run hotel. $ BLD
**Merriman's**, Opelo Plaza, Highway 19, Waimea. Tel: 885-6822. Regional. Renowned chef Peter Merriman's Hawaiian-and-Pacific menu. $$–$$$ LD
**Reuben's**, 336 Kamehameha Avenue, Hilo. Tel: 961-2552. Mexican. Family-run place just like down south. Immense servings. $ LD
**Roussels**, 60 Keawe Street, Hilo. Tel: 935-5111. French Creole. Good Cajun. $$–$$$ LD
**Sibu Cafe**, 75-5695 Alii Drive, Kona. Tel: 329-1112. Casual, known for Indonesian variations. $ LD

## KAUAI

**A Pacific Cafe**, 4138 Kuhio Highway, Kapa'a. Tel: 822-0013. Asian, Pacific Rim. Upscale, easy-going. Consistently praised by critics. $$ LD
**Brennecke's Beach Broiler**, 2100 Ho'one Road, Po'ipu Beach. Tel: 742-7588. American. Seriously casual, steak and seafood on the beach. $–$$ LD
**Cafe Hanalei**, Princeville Hotel, Princeville, North Shore. Tel: 826-9644. Contemporary. Overlooking Hanalei Bay, upscale but casual. $$ BLD
**Casa di Amici**, Kilauea Lighthouse Road, Kilauea. Tel: 828-1388. Italian. A real gem in an unexpected place, intimate music in evenings. Behind in the same rustic complex are the equally delightful **Kilauea Bakery** and **Pau Hana Pizza**. $–$$ LD
**Gaylord's at Kilohana**, 3-2087 Kaumualii Highway, Puhi, near Lihu'e. Tel: 245-9593. Continental. In restored 1935 plantation estate, outside seating. $$+ LD
**International Museum & Cafe**, 9875 Waimea Road, Waimea. Tel: 338-0403. Contemporary. Spacious old building with worldly artifacts. $ LD
**Kun Ja's**, 4252 Rice Street, Lihu'e. Tel: 245-8792. Korean. Traditional Korean cuisine in simple surroundings. $ LD
**La Cascata**, Princeville Hotel, Princeville, North Shore. Tel: 826-9644. Italian. Mediterranean cuisine with sunset views over Hanalei Bay. $$$ D
**Sinaloa Mexican Restaurant**, 1-3959 Kaumualii Highway, Hanapepe. Tel: 335-0006. Mexican. Good solid Mexican food in old sugar town. $ LD

## MAUI

**Alex's Hole in the Wall**, Wahie Lane, Lahaina. Tel: 661-3197. Italian. Funky and small, downtown off Front Street. $+ LD
**Avalon Restaurant & Bar**, 844 Front Street, Lahaina. Tel: 667-5559. Asian and Pacific. Outdoors in busy courtyard. $–$$ LD
**Casanova Italian Restaurant**, 1188 Makawao Ave, Makawao. Tel: 572-0220. Italian. Popular local hangout, views of Makawao street life. Deli. $ LD
**Cheeseburger in Paradise**, 811 Front Street, Lahaina. Tel: 661-4855. American. On the waterfront, on the scene. Live music and cheeseburgers. $ LD

**David Paul's Lahaina Grill**, Lahaina Hotel, 127 Lahainaluna Road, Lahaina. Tel: 667-5117. Pacific Rim. Part of restored historic Lahaina Hotel. Casual, sophisticated. $$ LD

**Gerard's**, Plantation Inn, 174 Lahainaluna Road, Lahaina. Tel: 661-8939. French. Outdoors or inside the restored plantation home. $$–$$$ LD

**Hakone**, Maui Prince Hotel, 5400 Makena Alanui, Makena/Wailea. Tel: 874-1111. Japanese. High-class, with authentic food and ambiance. $$+ D

**Hard Rock Cafe**, 900 Front Street, Lahaina. Tel: 667-7400. American. Loud like all Hard Rock cafes. Outside seating. $+ LD

**Longhi's**, 888 Front Street, Lahaina. Tel: 667-2286. Continental. Walking/talking menus, people watching, celebrities. $$ BLD

**Mama's Fish House**, 799 Poho Place, On main highway near Pa'ia. Tel: 579-8488. Seafood/Hawaiian. Overlooks cove, consistently a local favorite. $$ LD

**Pacific Grill**, Four Seasons Resort, 3900 Wailea Alanui, Wailea. Tel: 874-8000. Pacific Rim. Outside seating, menu mixes East and West. $$ BL

**Saeng's Thai Cuisine**, 2119 Vineyard Street, Downtown Wailuku. Tel: 244-1567. Thai. Pleasant setting and friendly. Garden setting. $+ LD

**Seasons**, Four Seasons Resort, 3900 Wailea Alanui, Wailea. Tel: 874-8000. Regional. Mixed Pacific and Asian cuisine. Classy and upscale. $$$ D

**Siam Thai Cuisine**, 123 North Market Street, Wailuku. Tel: 244-3817. Thai. A long-time favorite, basic diner ambiance. $+ LD

**Sound of the Falls**, Westin Maui, Ka'anapali Resort, Tel: 667-2525, Continental. Open-air elegance, waterfalls, ocean views, upscale. $$–$$$ D

**Swan Court**, Hyatt Regency Maui, Ka'anapali Resort. Tel: 667-4420. Continental. Top-10 romantic restaurant, says "Lifestyles of the Rich and Famous." $$$ BLD

# THINGS TO DO

## TOURS & CRUISES

Beyond peeking out at paradise from behind tinted tour bus windows, you can dip in and out of fantasy settings on scores of advertised glider, helicopter and small-prop plane tours, off-shore dinner and sunset-booze cruises, catamaran and glass-bottom boat rides, and even deep-sea fishing craft. All such tours are advertised in the media. Provided below are some points of interest on Oahu. All are accessible by TheBus.

For more information about these tours and about other places of interest, consult the numerous visitors' publications available free everywhere, the daily newspapers' entertainment and community calendar sections, or call the Hawaii Visitors Bureau on 924-0266.

## DOWNTOWN HONOLULU & ENVIRONS

**'Iolani Palace**: The palace is located in downtown Honolulu with an entrance from King Street; Tel: 522-0832. Tours are scheduled Wednesday–Saturday from 9am–2.15pm. They take about 45 minutes. Admission: free. No children under 5.

**Mission Houses Museum**: 553 S. King Street; Tel: 531-0481. Open: daily 9am–4pm, Sunday noon–4pm. Closed: Monday, Easter, Thanksgiving, Christmas and New Year's Day. Admission; children under 5 free. Admission to the Museum includes a guided tour lasting about 45 minutes through the historic houses.

**Bishop Museum & Planetarium**: 1525 Bernice Street, Kalihi; Tel: (museum) 847-3511. Open: 9am–5pm daily except Christmas. Admission: free. Planetarium Show at 11am and 2pm, and 7pm Friday and Saturday. Admission: free.

**Aloha Tower**: Pier 9 at Honolulu Harbor; 10th floor observation deck open from 8am–9pm daily. Admission free. The Maritime Center and Museum (9th Floor) is open Monday–Friday from 10am–4.30pm.

**Hawaii Maritime Center**: Pier 7 downtown, adjacent to Aloha Tower; Tel: 536-6373. Kalakaua Boathouse features museum exhibits; admission includes tour of *The Falls of Clyde*, a restored four-masted, fully rigged sailing ship; *Hokule'a,* a replica of an ancient Polynesian canoe world-famous for its expeditions to Tahiti over the past two decades, is tied up nearby. Open: 9am–5pm. Admission fee; free for children under 6.

**Queen Emma Summer Palace**: 2913 Pali Highway, Nu'uanu Valley; Tel: 595-3167. Open: 9am–4pm daily. Admission fee.

**Foster Botanic Garden**: 180 N. Vineyard Boulevard (entrance on Vineyard Boulevard at Nu'uanu Stream); Tel: 522-7066. Open: 9am–4pm daily. There is an admission fee.

**Honolulu Academy of Arts**: 900 S. Beretania Street, *mauka* of Thomas Square; Tel: 532-8701. Open: Tuesday–Saturday, 10am–4.30 p.m; and Sunday, 1pm–5 p.m; closed Monday. Admission free.

**The Contemporary Museum**: 2411 Makiki Heights Drive. Located on a beautiful historic estate overlooking Honolulu, the museum has several galleries featuring changing exhibits of contemporary art. There is also a permanent pavilion housing works by artist David Hockney, a sculpture garden, gift shop and cafe. Tel: 526-1322. Entrance to the galleries is for members only but the introductory membership is not expensive. The museum is open Tuesday–Saturday, 10am–4 p.m; Sunday, noon–4 p.m; closed Monday.

**National Memorial Cemetery of the Pacific**: In Punchbowl Crater, top of Puowaina Drive; Tel: 546-3190. Open: September 30–March 1, 8am–5.30pm daily; March 2–September 29, 8am–6.30pm daily; Memorial day, 7am–7pm. Admission free.

**Royal Mausoleum**: 2261 Nu'uanu Avenue, Nu'uanu Valley; Tel: 536-7602. Open: Monday–Friday, 8am–4.30pm, closed holidays; advance reservations requested for groups. Admission free.

**USS Arizona Memorial Cruise**: At Pearl Harbor, conducted by the National Park Service on shuttle boats operated by the US Navy; Tel: 422-0561. Open: Tuesday–Sunday, 9am–3pm, except on rainy or windy days. Admission free, but on a first-come first-served basis. Not admitted: children under 6, barefooted and swimsuit-clad visitors. Half-hour shuttle ride and tour of the memorial conducted by a National Park Service guide. (Commercial Pearl Harbor boat tours that cruise by the *USS Arizona* Memorial leave from Kewalo Basin daily, but passengers on these tours are not permitted to board the Memorial. Advance reservations can be made at Waikiki hotel travel desks.)

**USS Bowfin/Pacific Submarine Museum**: At Pearl Harbor, near Arizona Memorial; Tel: 423-1341. Restored World War II submarine and museum. Open: 8am–5pm daily. Admission; free for children under 6.

**Paradise Park**: 3737 Manoa Road, Manoa Valley; Tel: 988-0233. Open: 9.30am–4pm weekdays, until 5pm weekends. Admission fee.

**Harold L. Lyon Arboretum**: 3860 Manoa Road, Manoa Valley; Tel: 988-7378. Open: 9am–3pm daily except Sunday and holidays. Admission free although it is limited to a few visitors only, so do make advance reservations.

## IN WAIKIKI

**Kapi'olani Park**: At the foot of Diamond Head across from Queen's Surf Beach. Features a special 1.8 mile jogging course, soccer field, driving range, archery cove, tennis courts, picnic tables, aquarium, amphitheater, zoo, and bandstand.

**Honolulu Zoo**: *Diamond Head* end of Kalakaua Avenue in the Kapiolani Park complex. Tel: 971-7171. Open: 8.30am–4pm daily. Special shows during the summer at 6pm on Wednesday. Admission for ages 12 and above.

**Kodak Hula Show**: Off Monsarrat Avenue near the Waikiki Shell amphitheater; show times 10am Tuesday, Wednesday, Thursday; and 10am Friday during the summer. Admission for ages 12 and above.

**Waikiki Aquarium**: 2777 Kalakaua Avenue, opposite Kapiolani Park; Tel: 923-4725. Open: 9am–5pm daily. Admission; youths under 15 free.

**US Army Museum at Fort DeRussy**: Diamond Head of the Hilton Hawaiian Village and inside Battery Randolph; Tel: 438-2821. Open: 10am–4.30pm Tuesday through Sunday. Admission free.

## ELSEWHERE ON OAHU

**Sea Life Park**: At Makapu'u Point; Tel: 259-7933. Open: 9.30am–5pm daily, Fridays until 10pm. Admission fee.

**Senator Fong's Plantation & Gardens**: 47-285 Pulama Road north of Kane'ohe on the Windward Side. Tours cover an area of 725 acres (295 hectares). Open: 10am–4pm. Admission; children under 5 free.

**Byodo-In Temple**: 47-200 Kahekili Highway on Windward Oahu; Tel: 239-8811. Open: 8am–4.30pm daily. Admission fee. Replica of a 900-year old Buddhist Temple at Kyoto, Japan.

**Polynesian Cultural Center**: At La'ie on Oahu's North Shore; Tel: 923-2911. Open: daily 12.30-9pm daily except Sunday. Call for show times. Admission fee. Complete package including dinner, and the Polynesian Show is also available.

**Waimea Valley** (a.k.a. **Waimea Falls Park**): 59-864 Kam Highway, at Waimea on Oahu's North Shore. Tel: 638-8511. Arboretum, picnic sites, waterfall trail hike. Open: 10am–5.30pm daily. Admission.

## NEIGHBOR ISLANDS

Most commercial and historical activities are centered on Oahu, as it is the island with the best-developed tourism industry and the state's largest population. The neighbor islands rely more on their geography and resorts to attract and satisfy visitors, something they do quite well. But there are several museums on the neighbor islands that are worthwhile visits, both for the knowledge they add about Hawaii, past and contemporary, and for their intrinsic uniqueness.

## MAUI

**Alexander & Baldwin Sugar Museum**: Pu'unene, near Kahului Airport. Tel: 871-8058. Daily 9.30am–4.30pm. An under-rated museum that not only displays the history and processing of sugar, but also the cultural and ethnic lifestyles of Hawaii's early plantation workers.

**Whalers Museum**: Whalers Village Shopping Complex, Ka'anapali Resort. Tel: 661-5992. Daily 9.30am–10pm. A well-presented exhibit of whaling and early life in Lahaina and Maui.

## HAWAII

**Kamuela Museum**: Junction of Routes 19 and 250, Waimea. Tel: 885-4724. Daily 8am–5pm. An amazing and valuable collection with no apparent theme – like a discriminating collector's attic. Ancient Hawaiian to Viet Cong.

**Lyman Museum and Mission House**: 276 Haili Street, Hilo. Tel: 935-5021. Monday–Saturday 9am–5pm, Sunday 1–4pm. Restored 1800s missionary house, with an adjacent museum that includes superb shell and mineral collections.

**Parker Ranch Visitor Center & Historic Homes**: Waimea. Tel: 885-7655. Daily 9am–5pm; historic homes Tuesday–Saturday 10am–5pm. Museum of the Big Island's Parker family, owner of the largest ranch in Hawaii. Includes the art collection of current family head, Richard Smart.

## KAUAI

**Kauai Museum**: 4428 Rice Street, Lihu'e. Tel: 245-6931. Weekdays 9am–4.30pm, Saturday 9am–1pm. This former library contains lots of natural and people history in a compact space.

## DIARY OF EVENTS

### JANUARY

**Hula Bowl**: An annual football classic featuring East and West college all-stars in a head-on tumble at the Aloha Stadium; usually first Saturday, with name rock band concert afterward.

**State Legislature Opening**: Annual Legislative session is initiated on the third Wednesday of January with a colorful ceremony: *lei* presentations, Hawaiian music, hula and informal speeches.

**Chinese New Year**: Celebrated on the day of the second new moon after the winter solstice (around mid to late January) for 15 days. Clanging cymbals, pounding drums, rounds of fire-crackers and traditional lion dances chase bad spirits out of homes and shops in Chinatown, downtown Honolulu, clearing the way for a *Kung Hee Fat Choi* (Prosperous New Year).

**Narcissus Festival**: Five weeks of various Chinese shows, displays and events coinciding with Chinese New Year; topped with the coronation of the New Year's Chinese Narcissus Queen. Into February.

### FEBRUARY

**Punahou Carnival**: Largest and most popular school carnival in the state, taking place in early February. Fruit jams, jellies and other homemade local foods on sale; Manoa Valley, Honolulu.

**Buffalo's Big Board Surfing Classic**: Buffalo Keaulana, a "classic" himself, sponsors this annual fun-test for longboard riders at Makaha, on the Wai'anae Coast, where he and at least one of his sons are lifeguards. Entertainment and crafts demonstrations. Date varies according to surf condition.

### MARCH

**Girls' Day (Hinamatsuri) Dolls Festival**: Japanese customarily honor young girls on the third of March with a gift of a doll for their heirloom collections. Department stores usually host intricate doll displays.

**Cherry Blossom Festival**: An 11-week Japanese festival of cultural demonstrations including flower arrangement, tea ceremony, martial arts, and an annual Cherry Blossom Queen contest.

**Polo Season opens**: Early March; matches are held on Sundays at the Mokuleia Polo Field on Oahu's North Shore.

**Kamehameha Schools Song Festival**: A Friday evening in the month; a Hawaiian choral singing competition between classes for Hawaiian and part-Hawaiian youths is staged at the Blaisdell International Center; admission free.

**Kuhio Day**: March 26 is a state holiday honoring the birthday of Prince Jonah Kuhio Kalanianaole. Celebrated with parades, memorial services at the Nu'uanu Royal Mausoleum, and ceremonies at Kawaiahao Church downtown. A special Prince Kuhio festival takes place on the weekend closest to his birthday on the island of Kauai, his birthplace.

**Kona Stampede**: Two days of hooting *paniolo*, Hawaiian cowboy rodeo events; in the Honaunau Arena, Honaunau, Big Island.

### APRIL

**Merrie Monarch Festival**: Four to five days of fun and pageantry – costume, mustache and sideburns contest, parade, pageant and flower show; a celebration in honor of King David Kalakaua, the hula competition is the state's finest and most popular. In Hilo on the Big Island.

**Buddha's Birthday (Wesak)**: Celebrated largely by Japanese Buddhists with tea ceremonies and traditional singing and dancing on the Sunday closest to April 8. Blaisdell Concert Hall.

**Carole Kai Bed Race**: Fund-raising craziness with teams pushing decorated beds down Kalakaua Avenue in Waikiki; Front Street in Lahaina and the Kukui Grove Center in Lihue.

**Easter**: Sunrise services held at the former leprosy colony of Kalaupapa, Molokai; and at the National Memorial Cemetery of the Pacific, Punchbowl Crater, Honolulu. Consult local papers for details.

# MAY

**Lei Day**: "May Day is Lei Day in Hawaii. Garlands of flowers everywhere..." goes a popular hula melody. On May 1 every spring, people celebrate May Day island style – dressed in cheerful, printed *muumuu* and *aloha* shirts, lots of lei and smiles. Students (particularly in the elementary level) throughout the islands perform multi-ethnic dances and songs in full costume (usually on the first workday of the month) and welcome visitors to attend their shows. Much happens at the Waikiki Shell at Kapiolani Park, including a lei-making contest, sunset hula show and the coronation of a Lei Day Queen. Every elementary school in the state has a May Day program and if you have kids, this is a must; just pick a school and blend with the crowd.

**Boys' Day**: Long colorful paper or cloth carp are strung up on May 5 outside Japanese homes to honor boys in the family – so that they may pursue their goals like the strong-spirited carp that fights upstream currents.

**Honoka‘a Rodeo**: sponsored by the Hawaii Saddle Club, Honoka‘a, Big Island.

**Fiesta Filipina**: Month-long series of Filipino music and dance performances, handicraft exhibitions, and the selection of a Miss Filipiniana Hawaii, Honolulu.

# JUNE

**Kamehameha Day**: In commemoration of Kamehameha I, the great king who united the islands; Kamehameha's gold statue in front of the Judiciary Building in downtown Honolulu is draped with 40-foot long lei. On June 11 there is a gala parade down Kalakaua Avenue, complete with floats and elegant *pa‘u* horseback riders wearing colors and flowers representative of their home islands.

**King Kamehameha Traditional Hula & Chant Contest**: The most "traditional" (ancient) hula and the only chant contest in the islands, usually held at Brigham Young University at La‘ie, Oahu.

# JULY

**Fourth of July**: Independence Day is celebrated at the Parker Ranch Rodeo & Horse Races: Paniolo Park, Waimea, Big Island, affiliated with the 139,000-acre Parker Ranch, and the largest privately owned ranch in the US. Also, Makawao Statewide Rodeo, on Maui, is one of Hawaii's most popular July Fourth celebrations and rodeo.

**Transpacific Yacht Races**: Single hullcraft race on odd-number years; multi-hulls on even-number years; setting off from San Pedro, California on July 4 and racing until they cross a Diamond Head finish line

some 9 to 25 days later. Conventional yachts race from Victoria, British Columbia, to Lahaina, Maui, on even number years. Also, two other competitions – the "Around-the-State Yacht Race" and "Little Transpac" – follow the Transpacific Yacht Race.

**Prince Lot Hula Festival**: Another "authentic" hula event – no contest, but a demonstration in the relaxing Moanalua Gardens setting on Oahu not far from the airport.

**Japanese Bon Odori Dance Festival**: Japanese Buddhists dress in simple cotton *kimono* and *yukata* honor deceased ancestors in this lively dance under *shoji* paper lanterns and around a tower supporting a spirited drum beater and vocalists. Temples throughout the islands advertise these dances (around 7.30pm to midnight) throughout July and August; outsiders are invited to join. The season ends with the Floating Lanterns Festival at the Hale‘iwa Jodo Mission where candlelit hexagonal lanterns on a lotus base are set afloat at a nearby beach.

**Samoan Flag Raising Day**: Lots of Samoan singing, dancing and athletic competitions and a *kava* root-drinking ceremony, Honolulu. Check Oahu newspapers for the date.

**Kapalua Wine Symposium**: Chamber music by some of America's finest artists, with wine and cheese tastings and other formal and semi-formal events; Kapalua Bay Hotel, Maui.

# AUGUST

**Japanese Bon Odori Festival**: Continuing from the month of July.

**Queen Lili‘uokalani Keiki Hula Competition**: "Keiki" means children in Hawaii, with island stage mothers in abundant supply. The music and island "style" are great. The competition includes ancient and contemporary hula.

**50th State Fair**: Hawaiian quilt-making contests, local musicians, and a rainbow of ethnic dances, produce and livestock shows, food booths, carnival rides and commercial booth displays and specially scheduled entertainment; usually at the Aloha Stadium.

**Hawaiian International Billfish Tournament**: Around July through August; giant marlin are caught during this 10-day tournament at Kailua-Kona on the Big Island.

# SEPTEMBER

**Labor Day Rodeo**: On the island of Kauai; check newspapers for details.

**Labor Day Fishing Tournament**: On Maui; check newspapers for details.

**Na Mele o Maui**: Five-day festival of Hawaiian music, dance, arts, crafts, cultural displays, canoe races and luaus; Maui.

**Aloha Week**: Hawaiian-style festivities, including coronation of a Hawaiian Royal Court at ‘Iolani Palace, flower parade from downtown to Waikiki, Aloha and Monarchy Ball, and an exhibit of shells from international shores sponsored by the Hawaiian Malacological Society; Honolulu and on neighboring islands.

## OCTOBER

**Maui County Fair**: Early October at Kahului. Check local newspaper for announcements.
**Shinto Thanksgiving Festival**: Celebrated in early October on a Sunday afternoon by Japanese people at Daijingu Temple, 61 Puiwa Road, Nuuanu Valley, Oahu.
**Molokai-to-Oahu Canoe Race**: International paddling competition; race runs from Hale o Lono Harbor, Molokai, to Waikiki; greet the winner about noon at the Fort DeRussy beachfront.
**Ironman World Triathlon Championship**: A 2.4-mile open-ocean swim, followed by a 112-mile bike ride and a full 26-mile marathon is the order of the Kailua-Kona day.

## NOVEMBER

**Kona Coffee Festival**: Four-day festivities in mid-November; includes judging of coffee recipes, Kona coffee farm tours, and local parade and pageantry; Kailua, Big Island. See papers for announcements.
**Mission Houses Museum Christmas Fair**: Handicraft fair in late November features over 50 of Hawaii's finest craftspeople; a special display in the 1831 Chamberlain House, and free entertainment.
**Na Mele O Maui Festival**: Several Ka'anapali hotels participate in a celebration of Hawaiian music and dance; Maui.
**Surfing Contests**: November through February are the Big Surf months on Oahu's North Shore. Several world championship contests are scheduled each year, dates determined by the condition of the surf. The surf here at this time is regarded as the world's best, and the world's best surfers are on the beach, waiting for the perfect break. Check local newspapers for day-by-day announcements.
**Hawaii International Film Festival**: Films, emphasizing those from Asia, are shown in theaters around Honolulu, with sponsorship by the East-West Center.

## DECEMBER

**Honolulu Marathon**: At the crack of dawn one morning every December, thousands of runners from all over the world set off from the Aloha Tower on a 26-mile, 385-yard AAU-certified marathon course along Oahu's south shore. The marathon ends at Kapiolani Park Bandstand.
**Pearl Harbor Day**: In memory of those who were killed during the Japanese bombing of Oahu on December 7, 1941, a memorial service is held at the *USS Arizona* Memorial.
**Bodhi Day**: Japanese day of Enlightenment on the first Sunday of the month; ceremonies at Buddhist temples around the islands.

**Kamehameha Schools Christmas Song Festival**: Sung in Hawaiian and English by this Hawaiian school's glee club accompanied by the school's orchestra; Blaisdell Center; also televised.
**Mission Houses Museum Candlelight Tour**: A tour through the old-fashioned Christmas-decorated abodes of early Christian missionaries; choral singing and hosts in old-style missionary attire add to the holiday ambiance.
**Kawaiahao Church Midnight Service**: A candlelit Christmas Eve service in this old coral church: the choir sings in both Hawaiian and English.

# NIGHTLIFE

It goes without saying that Waikiki leads the islands with night life. One can't leave a Waikiki hotel without tripping over or stumbling into some sort of night scene. In fact, one needn't leave the hotel at all; most hotels, in Waikiki and elsewhere in the islands, offer live music of some sort, and many have dinner shows or hot discos popular with both locals and visitors.

On the neighbor islands, however, night life is mostly restricted to resort hotels. On Maui, a vigorous night scene is found in Lahaina and all along Ka'anapali Beach. On the Big Island, downtown Kona does a fair job of sustaining some night activity. On Kauai, well, the island goes to bed early.

For Hawaiian music, check newspaper listings for shows by some of Hawaii's classic musicians. Venues are usually at hotels, but sometimes local lounges carry headliners. Most hotel staff have excellent knowledge about Hawaiian musicians. Let them know your taste, whether commercial or traditional. There's probably a show for you.

As night life by definition comes and goes and changes, there's little reason to offer a listing of specific places – especially for Waikiki, about as practical as a nightlife listing for Las Vegas. If you're looking for a particular style or activity, hotel staff are the best source of information, as are the newspapers.

A unique form of Hawaiian night life that usually begins at sundown is the luau, traditionally a feast, a celebration of life. There is a wide range of luau offerings and styles, from the Hollywood-tinsel "Polynesian" revue with drums, fire gymnastics, and shimmering hula dancers, to some quite authentic presentations, mostly on the neighbor islands. Whatever type you choose, it's usually worth the $50 or so per person, which includes copious amounts of food and a satisfying show of varying authenticity.

# SHOPPING

Cosmopolitan residents and visitors shop for a variety of international goods and domestic creations in shops throughout the islands, but Hawaii has its own distinct goods. Items range from Polynesian kitsch tiki gods with olivine stone eyes to fine Ni'ihau shell lei that may cost as much as $2,500 for four strands.

**Chinese preserves**: Introduced by the Chinese, these preserves have become a favorite snack treat in Hawaii and are craved by those truly accustomed to local tastes. Plums, cherries, mangoes, olives, apricots, lemons and limes are dried and salted or preserved in sweet-sour pickled plums known as "crack seed." Shops specializing in these pickled seeds can be found in major suburban shopping areas and downtown.

**Clothes, print textiles, patterns**: Hawaii has its own fashions, the *muumuu* and *aloha* shirt. The first *muumuu*, designed and introduced by the early missionaries, was a loose, lengthy, high-necked, long-sleeved shroud. Because of variations in its style, *muumuu* has come to refer to just about any casual smock, long or short, made of Hawaiian print fabric. The *aloha* shirt was first marketed in the 1930s by a Chinese tailor in Honolulu. It is a simple button-front shirt with short sleeves made of Hawaiian print textiles. *Muumuus* and *aloha* shirts are sold and worn everywhere. Some island occasions, such as wedding receptions and dinner parties, specify "*aloha* attire" as the preferred dressing mode.

**Coral jewelry**: As with shells, forget coral souvenirs. Coral is a delicate yet essential component in the ocean ecosystem, especially in reef communities. Hawaii's reefs are young and fragile; taking coral is unsound. If imported, it is usually harvested in a similarly brutal manner as shells in the Philippines.

**Dried gourds**: Called *ipu* in Hawaiian, the large tan bottle gourd is hollowed-out and dried and used as a drum and as a receptacle for food, water, and paraphernalia. A smaller dark gourd is used to make hula instruments. The *ipu* is also attractive as a hanging flower pot.

**Feather hat bands**: The iridescent hues of the feathers of birds such as the pheasant and peacock are worn as hat bands by properly attired locals.

**Hawaiian instruments**: Popular Hawaiian hula instruments include the *ipu* drum, *puili* (slashed percussive bamboo sticks), *uliuli* (a feather-topped gourd rattle filled with seeds) and *iliili* (small smooth stones used like castanets in a set of four). There are also the *hano* (nose flute) and ukulele. All are available at island hula supply shops and some music stores.

**Jellies, jams and preserves**: Local tropical fruits such as guava, *poha*, mango, *lilikoi* passion fruit, papaya and coconut are made into luscious spreads unlike any you'll taste anywhere else on earth.

**Kona coffee**: Hawaii's own homegrown and roasted coffee beans are produced at Kona on the only commercial coffee plantations in the United States. This Big Island product is accorded a gourmet status in international coffee-drinking circles. Stay away from the blends, which require only 10 percent Kona beans. The Kona coffee plants originally came from Rio de Janeiro in the early 1800s. It takes 500 pounds (230 kg) of coffee beans to make 100 pounds (45 kg) of processed coffee.

**Kukui nut and seed lei**: The tradition of stringing and wearing the brown and black-and-white *kukui* nuts, commonly called candlenuts, is still very popular. *Koa* seed lei are also appealing, but most of those are strung in the Philippines.

**Macadamia nuts**: Delicious roasted and eaten plain or chocolate-covered, this rich nut is true gourmet fare. Macadamia nut products are grown and packaged in Hawaii.

**Ni'ihau shell lei**: Privately owned by the wealthy Robinson family of Kauai, Ni'ihau island is used mostly for ranching. Small, rare shells are washed up onto its beaches, where some of the 200-plus residents will gather and string them into lei or necklaces. There is a beautiful range of delicate, subtle colors. The lei are very expensive, and found only in upscale shops, especially on Kauai.

**Perfumes and colognes**: Select your favorite fragrance from a large variety of bottled tropical flowers such as gardenia, *pikake*, ginger and others.

**Photographs of old Hawaii**: Peer into Hawaii's past. Leaf through the photo albums at the State of Hawaii Archives (tel: 548-2355), downtown off South King Street on the 'Iolani Palace grounds. The Archives are open Monday–Friday 7.45am– 4.30pm. Copies are available for a dollar and up and take a few days for printing. Or visit the Bishop Museum's Photographic Collection (tel: 847-3511), by far the largest in the state with more than 500,000 images. Here, copies are more expensive, but the choice is greater.

**Plants**: Exotic hibiscus, anthurium, bamboo, orchid, *ti* and bird of paradise plants (and their seeds) are potted in sterile peat moss and agriculturally inspected. (Warning: Be sure they were inspected by the Agricultural Inspection Board before attempting to take them on to the mainland.) Some sellers will ship these pre-fumigated.

**Scrimshaw**: This Pacific art came into its own in the 1800s when bored sailors on whaling vessels scratched pictures on whale teeth. Nowadays, a number of non-endangered materials are used, such as fossilized walrus tusk. Traditionally, scrimshaw was the engraving of a polished bone or ivory surface with a sharp, pointed tool. Ink was then spread over the surface and absorbed only in the engraved lines. The result was a cross between an etching and a tattoo. Predictably, Maui is a good place to look at and purchase scrimshaw, particularly in West Maui.

**Sea shells**: Forget these. A souvenir whose time has passed. Shells taken locally deprive sea life of shelter. More importantly, many if not most of the sea shells sold in Hawaii actually come from places like the Philippines, where coral reefs are dynamited and sea floors massively dredged for the shells.

**Surfboards**: Custom-made fiberglass surfboards can be adapted to your height, weight and personal taste in design by some of the world's finest shapers.

**Tapa**: *Tapa* (bark cloth), properly called *kapa*, is made into popular items – wallhangings, place mats, bags, hats, etc. – but the *tapa* for sale is not actually Hawaiian *kapa*, but a related fabric made in Samoa and Tonga. Real Hawaiian *kapa* became extinct during the 19th century.

**Wood**: Monkeypod, *koa* and *milo* are three popular island woods used in the making of furniture, calabashes (large ceremonial bowls) and other fine wood creations. *Koa* and rosewood are also used to make quality guitars and ukuleles. Note that there is increasing opposition to the use of *koa* for souvenirs and furniture. Unique to Hawaii, its supply is now limited.

**Woven goods**: *Lauhala* (pandanus), coconut frond and fiber baskets and hats are popular. Rattan baskets of a finer weave are used to carry school books as well as hula instruments.

## SHOPPING AREAS

### OAHU

Listing a detailed shopping and tour guide to Oahu alone would be almost as exhausting as actually shopping at each and every one of those stores and attractions. Waikiki itself is flooded with shops, arcades, marketplaces and other amusements running up and down streets and narrow lanes and rising some 30 stories above street level.

Free weekly publications available everywhere advertise some of the myriad shopping and tour options available. Also, the Hawaii Visitors Bureau at 2270 Kalakaua Avenue, 7th floor, has all the brochures and information you may want.

### IN WAIKIKI

**International Market Place**: 2330 Kalakaua Avenue, across from the Sheraton Moana Surfrider, in the heart of Waikiki. Open: daily 9am–11pm. This is probably one of the most cluttered tourist markets in the world; merchants pay thousands of dollars just to have a tiny stall for display of what sometimes appears to be little more than an endless array of gold jewelry and tourist items made in various Third World countries. Nonetheless, the spectacular banyan tree in the center of this 5-acre market and the eye-popping variety of shops and people (both shoppers and sellers) make it worth a visit. A food court is at the rear of the market.

**Kuhio Mall**: Located behind the International Market Place on Kuhio Avenue, between Seaside and Kaiulani Avenues. Open: daily 10am–10pm. You can wander from one into the other and not even notice, although the tempo seems a bit quieter here.

**King's Village**: 131 Kaiulani Avenue, a block *mauka* of Kalakaua Avenue, behind the Hyatt Regency. Open: daily 9am–11pm. This rambling, split-level commercial complex takes its theme from the 19th century, right down to a changing of the Hawaiian King's Guard nightly at 6.15pm.

**Hyatt Regency Shopping Center**: Located on the first three floors of the Hyatt Regency Hotel, 2424 Kalakaua Avenue. The first of the spectacular resort hotels designed and built by developer Chris Hemmeter, known for his "fantasy resorts" on Maui, Kauai and the Big Island. Shops are pricey, but worth at least a look. Visit the café on the first level, next to a cascading, three-story waterfall.

**Royal Hawaiian Shopping Center**: Stretches for three blocks along Kalakaua Avenue, fronting the Waikiki Sheraton and Royal Hawaiian hotels, and offering a wide variety of shops and restaurants on three levels. Virtually everything you can imagine is sold here, in small shops and larger department stores, from junk food to your very own condominium. Open: daily 9am–10pm except Sunday, when shops close an hour earlier.

**Rainbow Bazaar**: 2005 Kalia Road, on the grounds of the Hilton Hawaiian Village, the largest hotel in Hawaii. Open: daily 9am–11pm. More fun than most malls, because you're outdoors almost all of the time. The hotel has been given a $100-million facelift, and the good mix of shops and restaurants (from the "affordable" to the very expensive) remains, most of them scattered over several acres stretching to the beach.

### AROUND THE ISLAND

**Downtown Honolulu**: On Bishop Street. Named after the islands' first banker (Charles Bishop) and today the financial center of Hawaii. All the major banks are here, along with many of the airlines, and a wide range of restaurants and shops. Noontime Friday there are free concerts at Bishop Square, a good time to mingle with the dressed-up working crowd. Remember that Friday is "Aloha Friday" when everyone wears *aloha* shirts and *muumuus*. Open roughly: 8am–5pm.

**Chinatown**: Adjacent to Downtown and by far the

most interesting shopping area in the islands. Asian immigration has changed the look, smell and taste of this old neighborhood, but the open market ambiance is the same. Watch noodles being made, take your ailments to an acupuncturist's or herbal shop, choose between more than 30 ethnic restaurants, or visit more than a dozen fine art galleries on side streets from Hotel Street. At night, a small section of Hotel Street retains its sailors-on-liberty flavor, with strip joints, porn parlors and bars that should not be entered alone.

**Ala Moana Center**: The largest mall in the state and one of the largest in the world – about 200 stores including 21 eating places covering 50 open-air acres across from Ala Moana Park. Open: Monday–Saturday 9.30am–9 p.m, Sunday 10am–5pm. Services include a post office and a Hawaii Visitors' Bureau booth, and free island entertainment is scheduled regularly on a canopied stage.

**Ward Center**: 1200 Ala Moana Boulevard, just a few blocks from Ala Moana Center on Ala Moana Boulevard. Open: weekdays 10am–9p.m, Saturday 10am–5p.m, Sunday 11am–4pm. This center is mostly upscale, with several popular but semi-expensive restaurants and gourmet shops. Good night life.

**Ward Warehouse**: This is not a warehouse at all, but a two-level complex of affordable restaurants and shops, featuring almost 70 shops. Same hours as the nearby Ward Center, although there are a few shops that open earlier, including a curbside coffee bar.

**Pearl Ridge Shopping Center**: 98-211 Pali Momi, in Pearl City. A massive mall in two "phases," divided by a watercress farm whose owner refused to sell his land to the developer. (A nice reminder that Hawaii's motto says the land is perpetuated in "righteousness.") The two sections are connected by a monorail and everything you could possibly want is here. The crowd is decidedly more "local" – that is, Asian and Pacific Islander – here than at Ala Moana. Open: weekdays 10am–9p.m, Saturday 10am–5.30pm.

**Kahala Mall**: In the Kahala residential district just east (or Koko Head) of Diamond Head and Waikiki, home of the designer pizza and a movie complex. Many of the shoppers tend to be upscale, as are many of the prices. Openings are staggered, beginning at 8.30am Most shops are closed by 9pm, although the supermarkets are open 24 hours.

## NEIGHBOR ISLANDS

While Oahu is shopping central for most of the Pacific, the neighboring islands of Maui, the Big Island and Kauai offer delightful places to find both the frivolous and the essential, or at least the thought-to-be essential.

## MAUI

For those heading to Maui, Kahului is the focus of urban commerce, but don't overlook the street shopping of historic Wailuku, just above Kahului, and of Makawao and Pa'ia, towards Upcountry. As nearly everybody visiting Maui stays in either the Wailea or Ka'anapali resorts, those two areas are rich with shopping wonders, mostly within the expansive hotel resorts. Lahaina, of course, lives off both shopping and eating, and rambling its streets yields a whale of cash-and-credit card opportunities.

**Whalers Village,** Ka'anapali Resort, West Maui. Tel: 661-3417. Over 50 shops, whaling museum, 40-foot sperm whale skeleton. Popular restaurants on the beach. Outdoors. Open: daily 9.30am–10pm.

**Kapalua Shops,** Kapalua Bay Hotel and Villas, Kapalua, West Maui. Tel: 669-0244. Small with upscale shops, clothing to antiques. Open: Monday–Saturday 8am–9pm, Sunday 8am–5pm.

**Lahaina Cannery Mall,** 1221 Honoapiilani Highway. Tel: 661-5304. West Maui's most comprehensive indoor shopping mall, north end of Lahaina. Open: daily 9.30am–9.30pm.

## HAWAII

On the Big Island, the commercial centers of Hilo and Kona are the obvious choices. Historic downtown Hilo is small, compact and undergoing a revival, and is good for quiet walking and browsing. Kona's waterfront thrives on tourism, and the offerings range – with an emphasis on low-end souvenirs – from T-shirts and postcards to some-times-dubious art. The resort hotels of Kohala – Mauna Lani, Waikoloa, Mauna Kea – have what those with gold cards are looking for.

**Prince Kuhio Plaza,** 111 East Puainako Street, Hilo. Tel: 959-3555. Largest enclosed mall on the Big Island. Open: Monday–Wednesday and Saturday 9.30am–5.30pm, Thursday and Friday 9.30am–9pm, Sunday 10am–4pm.

**Parker Square Shopping Mall,** Route 19, Waimea. Small center with specialty shops, restaurants. Open: daily 9am–5pm. There are also a number of commercial strip malls in Waimea for the usual stuff.

## KAUAI

In keeping with its personality, Kauai's shopping is lower-key than the other islands, but pleasurable and often unique. Commercial shopping centers are Lihu'e – including the Po'ipu, Koloa, and Kapa'a areas – and Princeville and Hanalei on the north shore. Kauai's shopping tends to be decentralized, with small but high-quality pockets of stores.

**Kilohana,** Route 50, 1.4 mi north of Lihu'e. Tel: 245-5608. Plantation estate with high-quality retail shops, galleries. Open: daily 9am.

**Coconut Marketplace,** On main highway, near Kapa'a. Tel: 822-3641. Standard open-air shopping mall with 70 assorted shops. Open: daily 9am–9pm. **Kukui Grove,** Highway 50, near Lihuʻe. Tel: 245-7784. Large standard enclosed shopping mall, Kauai's largest.

# SPORTS

## WATERSPORTS

An island archipelago in the Pacific, Hawaii is obviously a watersports place, with windsurfing, scuba diving, fishing, kayaking and yachting the more obvious options. Every hotel in the state, regardless of size or price, can make arrangements for any of these activities, including lessons. One advantage in booking arrangements this way is that the hotel has a stake in the satisfaction of you, its guest. If concerned about quality, go to one of the high-end luxury hotels and make arrangements through their activities desk. The price may be five or ten percent higher, but those hotels have international reputations to maintain, and so they won't send guests out with questionable activity operators. At least that's the theory, and it usually works well.

## WINDSURFING

Hawaii has world-class windsurfing, especially at Kailua Beach on Oahu and Hoʻokipa Beach on Maui. In fact, both these locations are the sites of international World Cup competitions. Most of the watersport desks at resort hotels offer lessons to both guests and non-guests. Check around for prices, and for an instructor you're comfortable with – you'll be out there with him or her in full view of everyone on the beach, and the less stress the better.

## SCUBA DIVING

While the diving in Hawaii is not equal to that in Fiji or Palau, it is quite good and often unique, especially around the Big Island, which is too young for a decent coral reef but which has lots of interesting underwater lava formations. The waters are usually warm, although in winter a full wetsuit is needed. Diving excursions and lessons are available on all the main islands.

There are scores of dive shops and operators in Hawaii, and the problem for the visitor is finding a trip that will assure a quality dive. On Oahu,

especially in the Waikiki area, a number of dive operators treat their dive trips like a factory process, and the experience is thoroughly unrewarding, especially for the experienced diver. Some dive shops cater to Japanese tourists, and Western divers may not find their style of diving particularly satisfying.

The activities desks of the larger luxury hotels usually have a long-term working relationship with a single dive operator, and most of them maintain high standards in their dives. Again, the prices may be cheaper elsewhere, but so too the experience.

If you're looking for diving lessons leading to certification, make sure the dive instructor is PADI or NAUI certified. Depending on the schedule used for instruction, it can take two to five days to complete the lessons. Again, hotel activity desks can set you up with lessons.

## FISHING

There's not much in the way of lake or river fishing, as there's not much in the way of lakes or rivers in Hawaii. But the big game fishing... Now that's another story. Hawaii is world-famous for big game fishing, especially off the Kona Coast of the Big Island. In fact, there's a world-class competition there every year.

It's all done by charter boats, most of which are located in Kona Harbor or at another harbor up near the Kona airport. Book a charter through a hotel activities desk, or go to the harbors and check out the boats and skippers in person.

## YACHTING & KAYAKING

Oddly enough, few people think of taking a yacht trip through the islands. It is pricey, perhaps, but the experience is unmatched. There are several yachts available for charters, complete with meals and captain. They can be customized for big game fishing or scuba diving, or general holiday sloth. Most of them seem to be based on the Big Island, so check there, or with hotel activity desks.

Kayaking is gaining popularity in the islands. River kayaking is limited mostly to Kauai, especially on the Hanalei River. Ocean kayaking is found everywhere there's an ocean, and that's everywhere in Hawaii. Popular excursions include the Na Pali Coast of Kauai, and the coast of Molokai.

Ocean kayaking in Hawaii requires skill, or the use of an experienced guide/instructor. Don't rent a kayak and push out into the ocean if you're not experienced. The channels between the islands are rough and tricky, and you'll end up a statistic.

## LAND SPORTS

Hawaii is not usually thought of as a place for hiking, but the islands have hundreds of miles of trails, some for short afternoon hikes, others for backpacking.

There are several state parks that have extensive hiking trails. Check with the state parks office for both information and for camping permits. Names and addresses can be found in the *Accommodation* section of Travel Tips.

Both Haleakala National Park on Maui and Hawaii Volcanoes National Park on the Big Island are hiking wonderlands, offering both day hikes and overnight camping hikes. Both park headquarters have maps and trail listings available, and they can be requested in advance by mail.

# LANGUAGE

In its development, the Hawaiian language has acquired several interesting grammatical complications and a sound system known for its complex vowel combinations and small number of consonants. Hawaiian has eight consonants, each roughly equivalent in pronunciation to their equivalent letter symbols in English, with the exception of *w* and the glottal stop: '.

| h | *hula* | (Hawaiian dance) |
| k | *kai* | (sea) |
| l | *lani* | (heaven) |
| m | *manu* | (bird) |
| n | *niho* | (tooth) |
| p | *pua* | (flower) |
| w | *wa'a* | (canoe) |
| ' | *'ala* | (fragrance) |

The symbol *w* varies in pronunciation among Hawaiians between a *w* and *v* sound. To English speakers this *w* symbol often sounds like an English *v* after a stressed vowel as in the place names Hale'iwa. At the beginning of a word or after an unstressed vowel the *w* symbol sounds like an English *w* as in the place names Waikiki and Wahiawa.

Meanwhile, the consonant symbolized ' – called the *'okina* in Hawaiian – represents a glottal stop. The glottal stop indicates a stop-start-again pronunciation. It is common to Hawaiian, but is also found in several dialects of English such as in the Cockney pronunciation of a little bottle of beer (which comes out a *li'l bo 'l a beer*) and the American English pronunciation of button (bu'n) and cotton (co'n).

The five Hawaiian vowels come in both short and long duration forms. Long duration vowels are marked by a bar termed the *kahako* in Hawaiian (and macron in English) and sometimes differ from short vowels in quality as well as duration.

Pronunciation of vowels is similar to Spanish or Japanese: no sloppy or lazy sounds as found in English.

| a as in father | *nana* (look) |
| e as in hay | *nene* (goose) |
| i as in beet | *wiwi* (skinny) |
| o as in boat | *lolo* (paralyzed) |
| u as in boot | *pupu* (hors d'oeuvre) |

If you would like more *kokua* (help) with the rudimentary Hawaiian language you'll be learning, refer to three key books on the subject: *Spoken Hawaiian*, by Samuel Elbert; *Let's Speak Hawaiian*, by Dorothy Kahananui and A. Anthony; and *The Hawaiian Dictionary*, by Samuel Elbert and Mary Kawena Pukui.

## Word List

| *ali'i* | ancient Hawaiian royalty, nobility |
| *aloha* | love, greetings, farewell |
| *'Ewa* | towards 'Ewa |
| *haole* | technically all foreigners, mainly now those of Caucasian ancestry |
| *hapa* | half, part |
| *hapa-haole* | part Caucasian |
| *heiau* | traditional Hawaiian place of worship, a temple |
| *imu* | cooking oven in ground |
| *kama'aina* | island-born or longtime resident of Hawaii |
| *kanaka* | a man, person, especially a native Hawaiian |
| *kane* | a man, husband |
| *keiki* | a child, children |
| *kokua* | help, assistance |
| *lanai* | porch, balcony, verandah |
| *lauhala* | pandanus leaf, for weaving |
| *lu'au* | traditional feast |
| *mahalo* | thank you |
| *makai* | towards the ocean |
| *malihini* | a newcomer or visitor to the islands |
| *mana* | spiritual power |
| *mauka* | towards the mountains |
| *mauna* | mountain |
| *Mele Kalikimaka* | Merry Christmas |
| *ohana* | family, inc. extended family |
| *'okole* | rear end, butt |
| *'ono* | delicious, tasty |
| *pakalolo* | marijuana |
| *pali* | cliff |
| *paniolo* | a cowboy |
| *pau* | finished, completed |
| *pau hana* | end of work |
| *poi* | food paste made from taro roots |
| *puka* | hole, opening |
| *pupu* | hors d'oeuvres |
| *shaka* | slang for an island hand greeting |
| *wahine* | a woman, wife |
| *wikiwiki* | quick, fast |

# USEFUL ADDRESSES

Hawaii Visitors Bureau: Tel: 924-0266
State Tourism Office: Tel: 586-2550

Honolulu International Airport visitor information:
Tel: 836-6413

Bus customer service: Tel: 848-4500
Bus schedule and route info: Tel: 848-5555
Bus lost and found: Tel: 848-4444

Governor's Office: Tel: 586-0034
Honolulu Mayor's Office: Tel: 523-4141
Consumer Protection/Complaints: Tel: 587-3222
Police (Honolulu) lost and found: Tel: 529-3283
Veterans Center: Tel: 541-1764

University of Hawaii: Tel: 956-8111
UH Bookstore: Tel: 956-6884
UH Library recorded info: Tel: 956-7204
UH Library reference desk: Tel: 956-7214

State Dept of Agriculture: Tel: 948-0145
Animal Quarantine Station: Tel: 483-7171
Plant Quarantine Station: Tel: 541-2951

US Passport Agency: Tel: 541-1919
US Customs/24 hour: Tel: 836-3613
US Immigration: Tel: 541-1379

Weather forecasts:
  Honolulu: Tel: 833-2849
  Oahu: Tel: 836-0121
  Hawaiian waters: Tel: 836-3921
  Surf: Tel: 836-1952, 531-7873

Time: Tel: 983-3211

Neal S. Blaisdell Center (ticket office): Tel: 521-2911
Honolulu Symphony (ticket office): Tel: 537-6191
Aloha Stadium (ticket office): Tel: 486-9300
Waikiki Shell (ticket office): Tel: 521-2911

Hawaii State Library: Tel: 586-3500
Telephone reference service: Tel: 586-3621
Circulation desk: Tel: 586-3505
Waikiki-Kapahulu Branch: Tel: 732-2777

## HAWAII VISITORS BUREAUX

**Hawaii**: Waikiki Business Plaza, 7th Floor, 2270 Kalakaua Avenue, Honolulu 96815. Tel: 924-0266; Big Island/Hilo: Tel: 961-5797; Big Island/Kailua-Kona: Tel: 329-7787; Kauai: Tel: 245-3971; Maui: Tel: 871-8691.

**North America**: 205-1624 56th Street, Delta, BC V4L 2B1. Tel: (604) 943-8555, fax: (604) 943-8555; Central Plaza, 3440 Wilshire Boulevard, #610, Los Angeles, CA 90010. Tel: (213) 385-5301, fax: (213) 385-2513; 180 North Michigan Avenue, #2210, Chicago, IL 60601. Tel: (312) 236-0632, fax: (312) 236-9781; Empire State Building, #808, 350 Fifth Avenue, New York, NY 10118. Tel: (212) 947-0717, fax: (212) 947-0725.

**Australia**: c/o Walshes World, 92 Pitt Street 8F, Sydney, NSW 2000. Tel: 2 235-0194, fax: 2 221-8297.

**New Zealand**: c/o Walshes World, 87 Queen Street, 2F Dingwall Building, Auckland 1. Tel: 9 379-3708, fax: 9 309-0725.

**Singapore**: c/o Pacific Leisure, No. 3 Seah Street, #01-04 0718. Tel: 338-1612, fax: 338-9620.

**United Kingdom**: 14, The Green, Richmond TW9 1PX. Tel: 81 332-6969, fax: 81 332-7001.

**Germany**: c/o Hans Regh Associates, Postfach 930247, Ginnheimer Landstrasse 1, D-6000 Frankfurt/Main 90. Tel: 69 70-4013, fax: 69 70-4043.

## CONSULATES

American Samoa Office: Tel: 545-7451
Australia: Tel: 524-5050
Austria: Tel: 923-8585
Belgium: Tel: 533-6900
China: Tel: 595-6347
Finland: Tel: 737-8788
France: Tel: 599-4458
Germany: Tel: 946-3819
Italy: Tel: 739-3979
Japan: Tel: 536-2226
Korea: Tel: 595-6109
Marshall Islands Office: Tel: 942-4422
Republic of Nauru: Tel: 842-4201
The Netherlands: Tel: 537-1100
Philippines: Tel: 595-6316
Sweden: Tel: 528-4777
Switzerland: Tel: 737-5297
Royal Thai: Tel: 524-3888
Tonga Government Office: Tel: 537-9525.

# FURTHER READING

*The 1993 Almanac of Hawaii*, by Anthony Michael Oliver. Mutual Publishing, Honolulu, 1993. Compact bundle of information, including people, education, government, land, sports, and business.

*A Voyage to the Pacific Ocean, 1776–1780*, by Captain James Cook and James King. London: 1784, 3 vols. The first and still one of the best guidebooks about Hawaii and the Pacific. The official account of Cook's voyages, including the discovery of Hawaii.

*Arts and Crafts of Hawaii*, by Sir Peter Buck. Bishop Museum, 1957.

*Atlas of Hawaii*, University of Hawaii Press, 1983. 2nd edition. The definitive reference for diverse information about the islands, and everything a geographer – amateur or professional – needs.

*The Beaches of Oahu*, 1977; *The Beaches of Maui County*, 1980; *The Beaches of the Big Island*, 1985; *The Beaches of Kauai*, 1990, by John R.K. Clark. University Press of Hawaii. Informative and detailed guides to Hawaii's shorelines.

*The Betrayal of Lili'uokalani*, by Helena G. Allen. Glendale: Clark, 1982. All-important biography of Hawaii's last queen.

*Born in Paradise*, by Armine Von Tempski. Duell, 1940. One of the best, if not the best, look at old Hawaii ranch life on the island of Maui.

*Chanting the Universe*, by John Charlot. Honolulu: Emphasis International, 1983. An examination of Hawaiian culture through its poetry and chants.

*Discovery*, by Bishop Museum Press. Honolulu: 1993. A superb collection of essays and photographs addressing ancient and contemporary Hawaii, as well as the future.

*Hawaii: A Literary Chronicle*, by W. Storrs Lee. Funk and Wagnalls, 1967. A collection of Hawaii impressions penned by prominent visiting authors of the late 18th and 19th centuries.

*Hawaii Recalls: Selling Romance to America*, by Ann Ellett Brown and Gary Gienza De Soto. Honolulu: Editions Limited, 1982. Nostalgic images of the Isles, 1910–50.

*Hawaii's Birds*, by Hawaii Audubon Society. Honolulu, 1981 A local birdwatcher's bible.

*Hawaii's Story by Hawaii's Queen*, by Queen Lili'uokalani of the Hawaiian Islands. Boston: Lothrop, Lee & Shepard Co., 1898; and Ruthland, Vermont & Tokyo: Charles E. Tuttle, 1990.

Queen Lili'uokalani's memoirs.

*Hawaiian Antiquities (Moolelo Hawaii)*, by David Malo. Bishop Museum Press, 1951.

*The Hawaiian Canoe*, by Tommy Holmes. Kauai: Editions Limited, 1981. A definitive study.

*Hawaiian Hiking Trails*, by Craig Chisholm. The Touchstone Press, 1977. A must for backpackers and nature-seekers.

*The Hawaiian Kingdom*, by Ralph Simpson Kuykendall. 3 vol. University Press of Hawaii, 1938–67. Considered to be the most important historical work about Hawaii during the 19th century.

*Hawaiian Legends*, by William Hyde Rice. Bishop Museum Press, 1977. Attractive reprint of a 1923 classic, with new photographs by Boone Morrison.

*Hawaiian Music and Musicians*, by George S. Kanahele. University Press of Hawaii, 1979. An encyclopedia of Hawaii's musical heritage.

*Hawaiian Mythology*, by Martha Warren Beckwith. New Haven: Yale University Press, 1940; and University Press of Hawaii, 1970. Definitive and comprehensive.

*Hawaiian Petroglyphs*, by J. Halley Cox with Edward Stasack. Bishop Museum, 1970.

*Hawaiian Yesterdays*, by Ray Jerome Baker. Honolulu: Mutual Publishing, 1982. Edited by Robert E. Van Dyke with text by Ronn Ronck. A wonderful collection of historic photographs by Hawaii's pioneer cameraman.

*History Makers of Hawaii*, by A. Grove Day. Mutual Publishing, 1984. A biographical dictionary of the people who shaped Hawaii from ancient times to the present.

*Holy Man*, by Gavan Daws. New York: Harper and Row, 1973. An entertaining and scholarly biography of Father Damien. Molokai's leper priest.

*Images of the Hula*, by Boone Morrison and Malcolm Chun. Volcano, Summit Press, 1983. Contemporary photographs of the *hula* with lively commentary.

*Ka Poe'e Kahiko, the People of Old*, by Samuel Manaiakalani Kamakau. Bishop Museum, 1964; and *Ruling Chiefs of Hawaii*. Honolulu: Kamehameha Schools, 1961. Important memoirs by a 19th-century Hawaiian historian.

*Kaawa*, University Press of Hawaii, 1972; *Molokai*, World Publishing Company, 1963; *The Return of Lono*, University Press of Hawaii, 1971; *A Walk Around Old Honolulu*, Kapa, 1976; *The Stone of Kannon*, University Press of Hawaii, 1979; and *The Water of Kane*, University Press of Hawaii, 1980, by Oswald Bushnell. Important works by a much-esteemed local man-of-letters.

*Ku Kanaka (Stand Tall): A Search for Hawaiian Values*, by George S. Kanahele. University Press of Hawaii, 1986.

*The Kumulipo, a Hawaiian Creation Chant*, by Kumulipo. Edited with commentary by Martha Warren Beckwith. Chicago: University of Chicago Press, 1951.

*Mark Twain's Letters from Hawaii*, by Mark Twain (pseudonym for Samuel Langhorne Clemens). New York: Appleton-Century, 1966. Twain's look at Hawaii in the 1860s, published as dispatches in the *Sacramento Union* newspaper.

*Na Mele o Hawaii Nei*, by Samuel Elbert. University Press of Hawaii, 1970. A review of favorite Hawaiian folk songs.

*Oceanwatcher, An Above-Water Guide to Hawaii's Marine Animals*, by Susan Scott. Honolulu: Green Turtle Press, 1988. *Plants and Animals of Hawaii*. Honolulu, Bess Press, 1991. *Exploring Hanauma Bay*. Honolulu: University of Hawaii Press, 1993. A set of books essential for the traveler curious about Hawaii's natural wildlife, above and below water.

*Pau Hana*, by Ronald Takaki. Honolulu: University of Hawaii Press, 1983. A history of plantation life and labor in Hawaii.

*Place Names of Hawaii*. University Press of Hawaii, 1966; *Nana I Ke Kumi (Look to the Source)*. Hui Hanai: Honolulu, 1972; *The English-Hawaiian Dictionary*. University Press of Hawaii, 1964; and *The Hawaiian-English Dictionary*. University Press of Hawaii, 1965, by Mary Kawena Pukui (Wiggin). Basic Hawaiian reference books by an esteemed Hawaiian scholar.

*Russia's Hawaiian Adventure, 1815–1817*, by Richard A. Pierce. Berkeley, California: University of California, 1965. The curious story about how a German physician working for the Russian-American Company tried to overthrow and claim Hawaii for Tzarist Russia.

*Shoal of Time*, by Gavan Daws. New York: Macmillan, 1968. Hawaiian history from Cook's arrival to the 1960s; very enjoyable reading, true to scholarly sources.

*Six Months in the Sandwich Islands*, by Isabella Luch Bishop (Bird). Tokyo: Charles E. Tuttle, 1974. Comments by a traveling English lady who visited Hawaii in 1873.

*Travels in Hawaii*, by Robert Louis Stevenson. University Press of Hawaii, 1973.

*Unwritten Literature of Hawaii*, by Nathaniel Emerson. Tuttle, 1965. A scholarly look at the hula and ancient Hawaiian chants.

*Volcanoes in the Sea*, by Gordon A. MacDonald. University of Hawaii Press, Second Ed., 1983. A historical and scientific look at Hawaii's spectacular volcanoes.

Mutual Publishing, Honolulu. In addition to a number of fine contemporary books about Hawaii, Mutual publishes a large collection of paperback reprints of Hawaii and Pacific literature, from Jack London to the obscure.

# ART/PHOTO CREDITS

# INDEX

## A

*ae'o* bird 196
Affandi 189
agriculture 63–64, 222, 306
'Ahihi-Kina'u Natural Area Reserve 224
Ahu'ena 281
'Ahuimanu Valley 195
*ahupua'a* 72
'Aiea 203
*'aina* 71
'Ainamoana State Recreation Area 165
air transport 61, 64
Akaka, Daniel K. 86
'Akaka Falls 270
*akialoa* bird 297
Ala Moana 187
Ala Moana Beach Park 165
Ala Moana Boulevard 159, 163
Ala Moana Shopping Center 165
Ala Wai Bridge 165
Ala Wai Canal 165, 167
Ala Wai Yacht Harbor 160, 165, 167
Alaka'i Swamp 297–298
Albert, Prince 184
Alekoko Fishpond 302
Alexander and Baldwin 59
*ali'i* 75, 100, 105, 147, 150, 234
Ali'iolani Hale 149
Allerton, John Gregg 301
aloha 21
*Aloha 'Oe* 59, 73, 101, 159, 194
Aloha Stadium 203, 204
Aloha Tower 159–160 , 162
Aloha Week 250
alphabet 107–108
alpine zones 128
American Civil War 47, 202, 230
American Factors 59
American football 93
Americans of Japanese ancestry (AJAs) 62, 88–89
Anahola Mountains 298
'Anaeho'omalu 279
anchialine pools 279
Anderson, Ruthadell 176
annexation 52, 54–55, 59, 63, 67, 100
Annexation Club 54
*apapane* bird 105, 176, 299
*Apollo 11* 204
aquaculture 195, 198, 246–247, 278, 306, 307
Armed Forces YMCA 156
atolls 128, 135
'Au'au Channel 229
*aumakua* 25, 73

*auwana hula* 102
Awa'awapuhi 306
'Awehi Trail 259
axis deer 117, 250

## B

Babe Ruth 183
Bachman Hall 189
Bailey, Edward 227
Bailey House 227
Baker, John Timoteo 148
Baker, Ray Jerome 105
Baldwin, Dwight 233
Baldwin House 233
ballet 152
Banyan Courtyard 170
Banyan Drive 268
Banyan Tree 233
Banzai Pipeline 121, 122, 209
Barking Sands Beach 300
barrier reefs 128
baseball 183
Battery Randolph 173
Bayonet Constitution 53, 54
beach art 176
beaches
    Banzai Pipeline 209
    Barking Sands 300
    Brennecke's 307
    Fort DeRussy 166
    Green Sand 285
    Hamoa 239
    Hapuna 278
    Ho'okipa 221
    Kahala 190
    Kalapaki 307
    Kauapea 305
    Kauai 301–302
    Ka'anapali 217, 227, 228
    Ke'e 295, 302
    Kualoa 194
    Kuhio 166, 167, 169
    Makua 210
    Mauna Kea 278
    Po'ipu 304, 307
    Queen's Surf 166, 175
    Sandy 191, 193
    Sans Souci 166, 169
    Shipwreck 25, 258
    Sunset 122, 209
    Waikiki 59, 61, 122, 167–176
    Wailua 308
    Waimanalo 193
    Wai'anapanapa State 240
Bellows Air Force Station 194
Benjamin Parker Elementary School 195
Berger, Heinrich 99–100
"Big Five" 59–60, 63, 157, 255, 304
Big Island, the 135, 161, 162, 217, 265–289
Biggers, Earl Derr (*Charlie Chan*) 88, 173
Bingham, Reverend Hiram 45, 150, 187
Bird, Isabella 267
birds 25, 31, 105, 175–176, 188, 193, 194, 196, 211, 224, 227, 240, 297–298, 299
Birth Stones of Kukaniloko 204
birthplace of Kamehameha the Great, Lapakahi 277
Bishop, Charles Reed 157, 181

Bishop, Princess Bernice Pauahi 182
Bishop Hall 181
Bishop Square 157
Black Rock 234
Blount, James H 54–55
Blue Hawaii
   film 101
   song 191
Boiling Pots 268
braquinho 94, 100
Brennecke's Beach 307
Brewer, C. 59
Brick Palace 231
Brigham Young University 197
Bronte, Emory 247
Brooke, Rupert 170
Brown, Captain William 161
Brownlee, Edward M 176
Buck, Sir Peter (*Vikings of the Pacific*) 26
Buddhism 82, 90, 158, 182, 221
Buffalo's Longboard Contest 209
Byodo-In Temple 195, 197
Byron, Lord George 45

# C

calderas 127
California Gold Rush 47, 229
Campbell, James 234
candlenut tree 130
canoeing 168
Cape Kina'u 224
Cape Kumukahi 269
Cariaga, Roman 90
Carnegie, Andrew 152
*Carthaginian II* 231
Cartwright, Alexander Joy 183
Castle and Cooke 59, 255
Catholicism 46, 48, 82, 91, 94, 156
cattle 117, 196, 222, 223, 240, 249, 309
Caucasians 82, 93–94
Cave of Kane 210
Center for Korean Studies 189
Central Hawaii 267–273
cereus 188
*cha-lang-a-lang* music 102
Chain of Craters Road 288
Chamberlain House 152
Chaminade University 189
charcoal 309
*Charlie Chan* 88, 173
Charlot, Jean 176, 187, 189
Chief Kalanimoku 45
Chinaman's Hat 196
Chinatown 87–88, 157
Chinese 48, 59, 82, 87–88, 115, 158, 276, 303
churches
   Cathedral of Our Lady of Peace, Honolulu 156
   Central Union, Manoa 187
   Church of the Holy Ghost, Maui 222
   Hau'ula 193
   Huialoha 222, 240
   Kalua'aha 248
   Kaulanapueo 236
   Kaumakapili 181
   Kawaiaha'o 149–150, 151, 183
   Ka'ahumanu 227
   Moku'aikaua 282

Our Lady of Sorrows, Kalua'aha 247
Palapala Ho'omau 239
Saint Andrew's Cathedral, Honolulu 151, 155
St Benedict's, Kona 283
St Gabriel's, Maui 237
St Joseph's, Maui 224
St Joseph's, Kamalo 247, 251
St Peter and Paul, Oahu 199
St Peter's, Kona 281
St Philomena, Molokai 252
Siloama, Molokai 252
Cleveland, President Grover 54–55
*Club Hubba Hubba* 158
*Club Lanai* 258, 259
cockfighting 91, 271
Coconut Plantation Marketplace 308
coconuts 116, 246
coffee 130
communications 59
constitution 229
Cook, Captain James 25, 27, 28, 31, 35–38, 74, 75, 93, 121, 130, 148–149, 161, 219, 265, 282, 283, 297, 299–300
Coral House, Honolulu 152
coral reefs 127–128, 150, 151, 152, 156, 208
Coronation Stand, 'Iolani Palace 147
cost of living 82
Courts of the Missing, Honolulu 186
Crater Rim Road 287
Crosby, Bing 101
Crouching Lion, Oahu 197
Crowningburg, Amalu Samuel 86
cuisine 115–117

# D

dance 99–102
Davies, Theo H. 59
Davis, Isaac 42–43
Daws, Gavan 111
defense 63
Del Monte 246, 248, 251
Democratic Party 63, 310
Diamond Head 143, 159, 165, 167, 168, 169, 173–174, 187, 189
Dillingham Air Field 200
diving 195
Dole, James D. 59, 205, 255, 258
Dole, Sanford B. 54–55, 59, 67, 205
Dole Pineapple Company 162–163, 246, 249, 255
Dole Pineapple Pavilion 205
dolphins 129
Dominis, John Owen 154–155
Dong Ji Hoi 92
doubletalk 101
Duke Kahanamoku Beach 166
Duke Paoa Kahanamoku 168, 183

# E

East Manoa Road 188
East Rift 286
East-West Center 189
ecosystems 128, 135
Edith Kanakaole Stadium 102
Edwards, Webley 171
*Elsie's Club Polynesian* 145, 158
employment 82

Escobar, Marisol 154
ethnic mix 81–82
European diseases 36, 85
'Ewa 143, 207
'Ewa Beach Park 207
Eyck, Anthony Ten 154–155

## F

Fagan, Paul 238
*Falls of Clyde* 160, 163, 181
Farrington Highway 208
Fasi, Frank 65
Father Damien 154, 156, 245, 247, 251–252, 283
fauna 130
featherwork 31, 76, 105, 297
Federal Post Office Building, Honolulu 157
Fern Grotto 308
Filipino Federation and Labor Union 90
Filipino Higher Wages Movement 60
Filipinos 48, 82, 90–91, 207, 255, 303
fishing 116–117, 195, 246–247, 306–307
flag 153–154
flora 127–130, 301
flowers 222, 306
Fon, Ho 88
food 91, 115–117
Ford Island 204
foreign investment 64–66
forests 128
Fornander, Abraham 28
Fort DeRussy Beach 166
Fort Elizabeth 300
Fort Street Mall, Honolulu 156
Foster Botanic Gardens 158
442nd Regimental Combat Team 62, 89
Frame House, Honolulu 151
Franck, Harry A. 90
Fraser, Juliette May 195
Front Street, Lahaina 230
fruit 116
Fuchs, Lawrence H. 47, 89

## G

Gandhi, Mohandas K. 176
Garden of the Gods 259
Germans 48, 303
giant telescopes, Mauna Kea 272
Gibson, Walter Murray 255, 258
Giddings, Evelyn 187
golf 190, 210, 234, 250, 308
Gould, Thomas B. 148–149
government workers 82
Grant, President Ulysses S. 52
Great Mahele 47
Great Wall 283
guava 130, 306
guitars 100, 115

## H

*hala* 188
Halawa Bay 246
Halawa Valley 248, 249, 276
Hale Ho'ike'ike 227
Hale o Lono 250
Hale Pa'ahao 233

Haleakala 135, 217, 219–221
Haleakala Crater 224, 240
Haleakala Highway 221
Haleakala National Park 217, 220, 239
Halema'uma'u 286
Hale'iwa 200
Hale'iwa Jodo Mission 200
Halona Blowhole 191
Halulu 257
Hamakua 270
Hamakua Coast 269, 276
Hamoa Beach 239
Hana 238
Hana Airport 237
Hana Bay 236, 238
Hana Coast 217, 236–240
Hana Highway 236, 237
Hana Ranch 238
Hanakapi'ai 305
Hanakoa 305
Hanalei Bay 308
Hanapepe 60, 300
Hanapepe Salt Makers Group 300
Hanauma Bay 143, 191
Hansen's disease 245, 252
haole 42, 47, 53, 59, 60, 93, 111, 150, 161, 182, 183
*hapa-haole* song 101, 245
Hapuna Beach State Park 278
Hasegawa General Store 239
Hau'ula 197
*Hawaii*, James Michener 81,155, 210, 251
"*Hawaii Calls*" 171
Hawaii Government Employees Union 86
Hawaii Institute of Marine Biology 195
Hawaii Kai 64, 190
Hawaii Maritime Center 160
Hawaii Pono'i 100
Hawaii State Library 152
Hawaii Volcanoes National Park 268, 285, 286
Hawaiian Airlines 61
Hawaiian bat 129
Hawaiian gods 74
Hawaiian Hall 181
Hawaiian Homes Act **1920** 186
Hawaiian International Billfish Tournament 282
Hawaiian Islands National Wildlife Refuge 211
Hawaiian language 46, 86
Hawaiian League 53
Hawaiian Mission Children's Society 152
Hawaiian Open PGA Golf Tournament 190
Hawaiian Pineapple Company 205
Hawaiian rights 224
Hawaiian Volcano Observatory 287
Hawi 275
Ha'ena 302
Ha'ena State Beach Park 304, 305
Ha'upu Mountains 298
Healing Stones 204
*heiau* 30, 43, 45, 200, 208, 209, 247, 248, 257
Helena Pt Townsend 258
Hemmeter, Chris 64, 156, 279, 307
Herbert, Allen 166
Heuck, Theodore 183
He'eia Fishpond 195
hibiscus 129
Hickam Air Force Base 204
Hilo 62, 267
Hilo Bay 267

Hilo Harbor 268
Hilo Hattie 101
Hilton Hawaiian Village 176
historical downtown district, Hilo 267
history 25–31, 35–38, 42–49, 52–55, 59–67
Hi'iaka 99
Hi'ilawe Falls 269, 271
*HMS Discovery* 35–38
*HMS Resolution* 35–38, 149
Ho, Don 86, 101, 102
hoary bat 27, 176
Hokule'a 160
holua slides 174, 245
Holualoa 281
Holy Ghost festivals 94
Honaunau Bay 283
Honoapi'ilani Highway 227
Honokane 277
Honoka'a 270
Honokohau 234
Honokowai 234
Honoloi'i 269
Honolulu 21, 45, 64, 65, 82, 88, 143–165, 181–191
Honolulu Academy of Arts 155
Honolulu Hale 152
Honolulu Harbor 159, 161
Honolulu Marathon 176
Honolulu waterfront 160
Honolulu Zoo 175
Honomu 270
Honopu 306
Honouliuli 207
Honpa Hongwanji Mission 183
Hotel Street 157
hotels
    Coco Palms 302
    Colony's Kaluako'i Hotel and Golf Resort 250
    Halekulani 172–173
    Hana, Maui 238
    Hawaii Naniloa 268
    Hawaiian Prince 165
    Hotel Lanai 256
    Hyatt Regency Maui 234
    Hyatt Regency Waikiki 169
    Hyatt Regency Waikoloa 279
    Kahala Hilton 190
    Kapalua Bay Hotel and Villas 234
    Kilauea Lodge 285
    King Kamehameha 281–282
    Kona Hilton 282
    Lahaina 234
    Lodge at Ko'ele 256
    Manele Bay 256
    Maui Marriott 234
    Mauna Lani Bay Hotel and Bungalows 278
    Moana 166, 170
    New Otani Kaimana Beach 166
    Ritz-Carlton 234, 278
    Royal Hawaiian Hotel 171–172
    Royal Waikoloan 279
    Sheraton Maui 234
    Sheraton Moana Surfrider 170–171
    Sheraton Waikiki 172
    Turtle Bay Hilton Resort and Country Club 199
    Westin Kauai 307
    Westin Maui 234
Ho'okio Gulch 258
Ho'okipa Beach 221

Ho'olehua Airport 245
Hsing Chung Hui 88
Hualalai 280
Huelo 236
hula 31, 43, 46, 49, 74, 76, 85, 99, 100, 101–102, 173, 174, 200, 251, 302
Hula Bowl 203
Hule'ia River 307
Hulihe'e Palace 282
Hulop'e Bay 257
Hurricane Iniki 297, 301, 303, 304, 307, 308

**I**

'Iao Needle 227
'Iao Stream 227
'Iao Valley 217, 227
'Iao Valley State Park 227
Ii, John Papa 28
Iliau Nature Loop 299
'Ili'ili'iopae Heiau 248
'Iolani Barracks 147
'Iolani Palace 52, 53, 55, 67, 102, 143, 145–146, 148, 155, 181, 183
immigrant labor 48, 59–60, 85–94, 87, 88–89, 90, 222, 234, 255, 259, 303
Inter-Island Airways 61
inter-racial marriages 81–82, 85
International Market Place 169
internment 89
*iwa* bird 196
Iwilei 162–163, 205
*i'iwi* bird 105, 299

**J**

Jack-and-Stripes flag 153–154
Japanese 48, 59, 61–62, 82, 88–90, 115, 255, 259, 267, 277, 303,
Japanese-Americans 62, 88–89
Japanese investment 64–66
Jefferson Hall 189
Jodo Mission Buddhist Cultural Park 234
Johnson, President Lyndon 191

**K**

*Ka Hoku O Hawai'i* 108
Ka Lae 285
Ka Lahui Hawaii 67
Kahala 181, 190
Kahala Beach 190
Kahaloa 167
Kahana 234
Kahana Bay 197
Kahanu Garden 238
Kahe 207
Kahe Point Beach Park 208
*kahiko hula* 102
Kaho'olawe 224, 254
Kahuku 198
Kahuku Sugar Mill 198
Kahului 227, 62
Kahuna Falls 270
*kahuna* 302
Kaiaka Bay 200
Kaiko'o 267
Kailua 64, 185, 194

351

Kailua Bay 194, 281
Kailua Beach Park 194
Kailua-Kona 44, 162, 280
Kaimuki 189
Kaiser, Henry J 190
Kaiser Estate 190
Kaiwi Channel 250
Kalahaku Overlook 220
Kalahuipua'a 278
Kalakaua, King 52–54, 88–89, 100, 102, 145–146,
    147, 148, 160, 166, 175, 181, 268
Kalakaua 90, 183
Kalakaua Avenue 167
Kalalau 305–306
Kalalau Valley Lookout 299
Kalalau Valley 306
Kalalea Heiau 285
Kalaniana'ole Highway 190, 191
Kalanikaula 248
Kalanikupule 161
Kalaniopu'u, King 37
Kalapaki Beach 307
Kalapana 268
Kalapana Village 288
Kalaupapa 154, 251
Kalaupapa National Historical Park 252
Kalaupapa Overlook 251
Kalaupapa Peninsula 245, 251, 252
Kalawao 252
Kalihi 181
Kaliuwa'a Falls 197
Kaluanui Stream 197
Kalua'aha 247
Kamakahonu 281
Kamakau, Samuel M. 28, 35, 38, 75
Kamakou 247
Kamakou Preserve 245
Kamalo 247
Kamamalu, Queen 147
Kamapua'a 208
Kamehameha canoe landing 278
Kamehameha Day 148, 175
Kamehameha dynasty 42–49, 181
Kamehameha Heights 182
Kamehameha I (the Great) 42–44, 74, 82, 148–149,
    153, 162, 172, 181, 183, 209, 227, 228, 231, 234,
    238, 247, 254, 258, 265, 277, 281, 288–289, 295
Kamehameha II 30, 43, 44, 45, 99, 147, 162, 183
Kamehameha III 46–48, 150, 162, 183, 229, 233,
    234, 272
Kamehameha IV 48–49, 87, 150, 183, 184
Kamehameha V 49, 99, 149, 183, 309
Kamehameha V Highway 246
Kamehameha Schools 181–182
Kamehameha Statue 148–149, 150, 276
Kamoa Wind Farm 285
Kamohoali'i 210
Kamuela 275
Kanaha Pond 227
kanaka maoli 71, 73, 75, 76
Kanakaole, Aunty Edith 76
Kanaloa 74
Kana'ina, Charles 151
Kana'ina Building 147
Kane 74
Kaneana 210
Kaneohe 194
Kaneohe Bay 181

Kanepu'u Forest 259
Kane'aki Heiau 209
Kane'ilio Point 208
Kane'ohe 64, 185
Kane'ohe Bay 195
Kane'ohe Marine Corps Air Station 194
Kaohikaipu Island 193
kapa 28, 31, 37, 73, 220
Kapaemahu 168
Kapalua Resort 234
Kapa'au 275
Kapena Falls 183
Kapi'olani, Chiefess 46
Kapi'olani, Queen 53, 147
Kapi'olani Park 174, 175, 176
kapu 28–29, 30, 44–45, 46, 63, 72, 75, 99, 148, 153,
    166, 238, 247
Kapuaiwa Coconut Grove 246
Kapuni 167
Karawina, Erica 187
Kauai 35–36 , 43, 44, 60, 64, 66, 128, 135, 209,
    295–310
Kauapea Beach 305
Kauhako 245
Kauhako Crater 252
Kauhi 197
Kauikeaouli 228
Kauiki Hill 236
Kauiki Lighthouse 237
Kaulakahi Channel 309
Kaule o Nanahoa 251
Kaulula'au 254
Kaumahia State Park 236
Kaumakani 303
Kaumalapau 255
Kaumalapau Harbor 256
Kaumuali'i, King 43, 300
Kaunakakai 245–246, 248
Kaunolu Bay 254, 256
Kaunolu Village 257
Kaupe 183
Kaupo 223, 224
Kaupo Gap 224, 240
Kaupo Ranch 240
Kaupo Store 240
Kau'uiki Hill 238
Kawaihae 275
Kawaikini 295
Kawaikini Peak 295
Kawamoto, Genshiro 65
Kawananakoa, Abigail 171
Kawananakoa, Edward Keliiahonui 86, 146
Kawananakoa, Kapi'olani 146
Kawananakoa, Kekaulike 147
Kawananakoa, Poomaikelani 146
Kawela 247
Ka'ahumanu, Queen 44–45, 46, 48, 187, 188, 238
Ka'ahupahau 207
Ka'alaneo 254
Ka'anapali Resort 234
Ka'awali'i 270
Ka'ena Point 200, 210, 211
Ka'ena Point Satellite Tracking Station 210
Ka'u 285
Ka'u Desert 289
Ka'upulehu 280
Ke Au Hou 108
Ke Kumu Hawaii 107

Keahole (Kona) Airport 280
Kealakekua Bay 36, 37, 38, 42, 283
Kealia 303
Kealohi Point 195
Keanakolu 270
Keaulana, Buffalo 209
Keauokalani, Kepelino 28, 121
Keawa'ula Bay 210
Keck Observatory 272
Kekaha 298, 303
Kennedy, Jacqueline 191
Kennedy, President John F. 271
Keokea 222
Keomuku 258
Keomuku Village 258
Keoua 43
Kepaniwai Heritage Gardens 227
Kepuhi Bay 250
Kepuhi Point 209
Kewalo Basin 163
Ke'anae 236
Ke'anae Arboretum 237
Ke'anae Peninsula 236
kiawe tree 250, 278, 299, 309
Kihei 228
Kilauea 74, 127, 265, 268, 303
Kilauea Iki Crater 27, 285, 288
Kilauea Visitor Center 287
Kilauea Volcano 286
kim chee 91
King, James 42, 121
Kinohi 167
Kipahulu 239
Kipahulu Sugar Mill 239
Kipahulu Valley 220, 240
Kipahulu Village 239
kipuka 289
Kipuka Puaulu 289
Kipuka 'Ainahou Nene Sanctuary 273
Ko 'olina Resort 207
koa tree 128, 129, 153, 166, 182, 184, 187, 240, 251
Kodak Hula Show 174–175
Kohala Ditch 277
Kohala Mountains 275
Kohala Tong Wo Society Building 276
Kohala 275, 276
Koko Crater 191
Koko Head 191, 193
Kok'e 298
Kok'e Lodge 298
Kolekole Pass 205
Koloa 303
Kona 275
Kona Gold 282
Kona Village Resort 280
Koreans 48, 59, 82, 91–92, 115, 303,
Kotzebue, Otto von 28
Ko'ele 258
Ko'olau Mountains 158, 181, 186, 187, 193, 199
Ku 30, 74
Kualapu'u 251
Kualoa Ranch 196
Kualoa Regional Park 196
Kuhio Avenue 167
Kukailimoku 42, 74, 209
Kukui Grove Shopping Mall 304
Kukui Trail 299
kukui tree 130, 248, 299

Kukuiho'olua Islet 198
Kula 222
Kula onions 116, 222, 246
Kure Atoll 143
Kuykendall, Ralph 89
Ku'ilioloa 208
Ku'ilioloa Heiau 208
Kwan Yin Temple 158, 159

# L

La Pérouse Bay 223
labor movements 60–61, 62, 63, 64, 86, 90
Lahaina Harbor 228
Lahaina Restoration Foundation 231
Lahaina Ka'anapali & Pacific Railroad 162, 228–229, 230, 234
Lahainaluna High School 229
Laka 74, 99, 251
Lake Halali'i 310
Lake Wai'au 271
Lanai 66, 85, 135, 245, 254–259
Lanai City 256
Lanai Company 257
Lana'ihale 257
land ownership 47, 66–67, 71–72, 86, 93
Langdon, Robert 38
language 107–108, 111
Lanikai 194
Lanikaula 248
Lapakahi State Historical Park 277
laulau 115
Laupahoehoe 270
Laupahoehoe Natural Area Reserve 270
Lava Tree State Monument 269
lava trees 268
Lawa'i Kai 301
Lawa'i Valley 301
La'ie 197
La'ie Point 198
Ledyard, John 36
Lee, Kui 102
Leeward Islands 211
lei 29, 73, 76, 105, 148, 304, 310,
Leilehua Plain 205
leprosy 154, 245, 251–252
Liholiho, Kamehameha II 43, 44, 150, 228–229
Lihu'e 303, 307
Likeke Hale 151
Lili'uokalani, Queen Lydia 54–55, 59, 66–67, 73, 90, 100–101, 145–146, 154–155, 175, 181, 183, 194
Lili'uokalani, statue 153
Lili'uokalani Gardens 159, 268
Liloa 148
Limahuli 301
Limahuli Stream 304
limu 207
Lindbergh, Charles 239
Lisianski Island 211
Lohiau's hula platform 302
London, Jack 121, 172, 252
Lono 36, 74, 209
Lo'ihi 127, 135, 287
lua 99
Luahine, Iolani 102
luakini 30, 288
luau 115, 117, 197, 207
Lumaha'i 308–309

Lunalilo, King William 49, 52, 150, 151, 183
Lunalilo Freeway 202
Lyman Mission House and Museum 267
Lyon Arboretum 188

# M

M. Matsumoto Store 200
Magic Island 165
Mahie Point 196
Mahukona 276
*maile* 73, 310
*mai'a* 74
Makaha 207, 208
Makaha Historical Society 209
Makaha International Surfing Championships 209
Makaha Stream 209
Makaha Valley 209
*makahiki* 36–37, 74
*makai* 143
Makai Research Pier 193
Makakilo 64, 208
Makanalua 245
Makapu'u Beach Park 193
Makapu'u Point 193
Makawao 221–222
Makena 223, 228
Makiki 187
Makiki Heights 186
Makua and Waikahalulu Falls 159
Malo, David 28, 29, 229–230
Malu'uluolele Park 233
*mana* 72, 75–76, 248
Manana Island 193
Manele Boat Harbor 257
Manifest Destiny 55
Manoa 187
Manoa Chinese Cemetery 188
Manoa Falls 188
Manoa Road 188
Manoa Valley 187
Mantojuki Mission 221
marijuana 64, 282
marine life 128
Marquesas Islands 25–26, 66, 107
Martin, Liko 207
Matson Navigation Company 171
Mauan Kamakou 245
Maugham, William Somerset 81, 82, 163
Maui 36, 42, 44, 64, 66, 135, 161, 162, 208, 217–240, 269
*mauka* 143
Maulua 270
Mauna Kea 36, 265, 268, 271, 272, 273
Mauna Kea adze quarry 272
Mauna Kea Beach Resort 278
Mauna Loa 36, 127, 128, 245, 265, 268, 273, 285, 289
Maunaiki footprints 289
Maunakea Marketplace 158
Maunalei Sugar Company 258
Maunaloa 249
Maunaloa Highway 249
Maunaulu 286
Maunawili 194
Mausoleum of King Lunalilo 151
Ma'alaea 228
Ma'alaea Bay 228

Ma'ili 207
McAllister, J. Gilbert 208
McKinley, President William 55, 59
Melville, Herman 230
Menehune Ditch 302
Menehune Fishpond 302, 307
menehune 26, 189, 248, 302
Merchant Street 157
Merry Monarch Festival 102, 268
Metcalfe, Simon 87
Michener, James, *Hawaii* 81, 155, 210, 251
Midway Islands 143, 211
Mililani 64
Miloli'i 283, 306
Mission Houses 151
Mission Memorial Building 152
missionaries 45, 46, 66, 85, 99, 100, 102, 107–108, 122, 150, 151, 156, 157, 182, 187, 197, 219, 229, 233, 248, 255, 304
*moa* 298
Moanalua Gardens Foundation 202
Moanalua Valley 202
Moa'ula Falls 249
Mokapu Peninsula 194
Mokoli'i 196
Moku 247
Mokualai Islet 198
Mokuho'oniki Island 248
Mokule'ia Polo Farm 200
Mokuolo'e (Coconut Island) 194
Moku'aweoweo 273
Moli'i Fishpond 196
Molokai 44, 61, 66, 85, 128, 135, 154, 245–252
Molokai Ka Hula Piko 251
Molokai Ranch Wildlife Park 250
Molokai Ranch 249–250
Molokai-to-Oahu canoe race 250
Molokini Island 224
monarchy 49, 54, 55
monk seals 27, 129, 135, 176, 211
Montagu, John, Earl of Sandwich 35
Mormon Temple 197
Mormons 197, 255
Mo'ili'ili 189
Mo'okini Heiau 277
Munro, George C. 258
Munro Trail 257
Murdock, David 255
museums
    Alexander & Baldwin Sugar 227–228
    Baldwin House 233
    Bernice Pauahi Bishop 74, 143, 181, 184, 209, 211
    *Carthaginian II* 231
    Contemporary 187
    Eva Parker Woods Cottage 278
    Grove Farm Homestead 304
    Hale Ho'ike'ike 227
    Hawaii Maritime Center 160
    Jaggar 287
    Kamuela 275
    Kauai 303, 304
    Kok'e 298
    Lyman Mission House and Museum 267
    US Army 173
    USS Bowfin Submarine Museum and Park 203–204
    Wo Hing Society Temple 234
music 99–102
M'ili'ili 187

## N

Na Pali 297
Na Pali Coast 128, 295, 305
Naha 259
Nahiku 237
Nankuli 207
Napeahi, Aunty Abby 86
Napili 234
Napili Bay 234
National Memorial Cemetery of the Pacific 186
National Park Service 209
Nature Conservancy Office 245
Nawiliwili 62
Nawiliwili Harbor 302, 307
Necker 211
News Building 150
Nguyen Van Thieu 191
Nihoa 211
Nimitz Highway 159, 162
niu 74
Niuli'i 276
Ni'ihau 44, 63, 66, 85, 108, 295, 309–310
North Kohala 270, 275
North Kona 280
North Shore 199
Norwegians 48
Numila 303
Nu'alolo-kai 306
Nu'alolo-aina 306
Nu'uanu 182
Nu'uanu Pali Drive 185
Nu'uanu Pali Lookout 185
Nu'uanu Stream 158
Nu'uanu Valley Park 184
Nu'uanu Valley 161, 174

## O

Oahu Cemetery 183
Oahu Market 158
Oahu 35, 43, 43, 44, 61–62, 65, 66, 82, 122, 135, 143, 148, 161, 167, 193–200, 202–210
obsidian glass 281
'Ohe'o Gulch 239
'ohia tree 240, 297, 298, 299
ohia-lehua tree 128, 129
'olapa tree 297
Old Judiciary Building 149
Olmsted, Frederick Law, Pulling Teeth 231
olo surfboards 166
Olomana 194
Oneali'i Park 246
One'ula 207
onions 116, 222, 246
Onomea Bay 269
oral tradition 28, 38, 74, 75, 107, 150, 167, 183, 208, 302
orchids 130, 196
Ossipoff, Vladimir 187
Outrigger Canoe Club 122
outrigger canoeing 85, 165, 250
o'o'a'a bird 297

## P – Q

Pacific Missile Range Facility 300
Pacific Plate 127–128
Pacific Tropical Botanical Garden 301
Pahinui, Gabby 101, 194
Pahoa 268
Pailolo Channel 248
palapala 151
Palawai 255
Palawai Basin 255
Pala'au State Park 251
Pali Coast 249
Pali Highway 183, 185, 194
palu 85
Panama-Pacific International Exposition 1915 101
paniolo 220
Papa 71, 73
Papaenaena Heiau 174
Papakolea 186
papaya 130, 306
Papa'aloa 270
Papa'ikou 269
Papohaku Beach Park 250
Paradise Park 188
Park Chung Hee 191
Parker, John Palmer 275
Parker Ranch 275
Pauoa Bay 278
Pa'ao 75
Pa'auhau 270
Pa'auilo 270
Pa'ia 221, 222
Peace Corps 271
Pearl City 203, 207
Pearl Harbor 52, 53, 55, 61, 63, 88, 89, 93, 143, 145, 172, 173, 187, 195, 202, 203, 207
Pele 43, 46, 74, 105, 174, 189, 197, 210, 271, 281, 302
Pelekunu Valley 249, 251
people 81–82, 85–94
Pepe'ekeo 269
petroglyphs 25, 183, 202, 278, 279
Philippines 59
pidgin 111, 145
piko ma'i 73
piko po'o 73
piko stone 303
piko waena 72
Pineapple Variety Garden 205
pineapples 59, 94, 116, 130, 205, 245–246, 248, 249, 251, 255–256
Pioneer Inn, Maui 231
Pioneer Mill, Maui 234
Pi'ilanihale Heiau 238
plantation era 269
plover 25
Pohakuho'ohanau 303
Pohakuloa 273
poi 115
Poka'i Bay 208
poke 115
Polihale 200
Polihale Beach Park 305
politics 59–60
Poli'ahu 271
Pololu Valley Lookout 276
Polynesian Cultural Center, Oahu 197–198

Polynesian settlers 25–26, 27, 28, 74, 129, 160, 176
population 64, 82, 85
Portuguese 25, 48, 59, 94, 115, 222, 275, 303
Po'ipu 307
Preis, Alfred 203
Presley, Elvis 191, 203
Prince Kuhio Kalaniana'ole Federal Building 163
Princeville 308
property ownership 64–65, 67, 72, 93
Protestantism 82
Puako petroglyph field 279
Puako Village 279
Pua'aka'a State Park 237
Puerto Ricans 48, 59, 94, 303
Puhi 303
Pukalani 221
Punahou School 187–188
Punchbowl 185, 187
Punchbowl Crater 185
Puohookamoa Falls 236
Purvis, Edward 94
Pu'u Keka'a 234
Pu'u Kukui 217
Pu'u o Hoku Ranch 248
Pu'u Ula'ula 221
Pu'uhonua 'O Honaunau 71
Pu'uhonoa 'O Honaunau National Historical Park 29, 283
Pu'ukohola 277
Pu'unene 228
Pu'uomahuka 200
Pu'uomahuka Heiau State Monument 199
Pu'uwai 309
Pu'uwa'awa'a 281
Pu'u'Kukui 227
Pu'u'ualaka'a State Park 187
Pyle, Ernest Taylor 186
Queen Emma 43, 52, 87, 249, 301
Queen Emma's Summer Palace 183
Quirios, Pedro Fernandez de 25

# R

Rabbit Island 193
rain forests 128, 239, 245
Rainbow Falls 268
Rainbow Tower 176
rainfall 217, 227, 239, 297, 298, 308, 309
Red Hill 289
religion 82
Republican Party 59, 63, 310
Rhee, Dr Syngman 92
Rice, William Harrison 304
Rice, William Hyde 304
Richards House 233
Riou, E. Jeux Haviens 122
Robinson family 63, 309
rodeo 194, 221
Roosevelt, President Franklin D. 62, 203
Rosenthal, Bernard 157
Round Top Drive 186
Rowe, Thomas 149
Rowen, Chad 194
Royal Burial Ground and Tomb, 'Iolani Palace 147
Royal Hawaiian Band 102, 147, 159
Royal Mausoleum, Nu'uanu 151
Royal Mausoleum, Honolulu 183
rubber 237

# S

Sacred Falls 197
Saddle, the 272
Saddle Road 272
Salamanca, Lazaro 90
salt ponds, Hanapepe 300
Samoans 82, 92–93
Sand Island 145
sandalwood boat, Molokai 250
sandalwood 44, 46, 64, 75, 87, 250, 282
Sandwich Islands 35
Sanji Pagoda 183
Schofield Barracks 204
Science City, Maui 221
Sea Life Park, Oahu 193
Seaman's Hospital, Maui 234
seamounts 127
service industry 82
Seven Pools of Kipahulu 239
shave ice 200
Sheffer, Dr Anton 300
Sheppard, Eugenia 187
Sheraton Makaha Resort 209
Shinto 82, 90
shipping 63
silverswords 128, 219, 220–221
slack key 100
Sliding Sands Trail 219
Smart, Richard 86
Smith, Ernest 247
snakes 175
snorkeling 195
Soto Zen Mission of Hawaii 182
South Kohala 277
South Pacific 309
South Point 285
Southwest Rift 286
sovereignty movement 67, 86, 150, 224
Spaniards 38, 48, 303
Spanish-speaking cowboys (paniolo) 275
Spouting Horn 307
Spreckels, Claus 53
State Archives Building, Honolulu 147
State Capitol Building, Honolulu 149, 152
statehood 63
Statewide Center for Students with Hearing and Visual Impairments 176
Steaming Bluff 287
steel guitar 100
Stevens, John B. 54
Stevenson, Robert Louis 52, 166, 245
stone fort, Lahaina 233
Stones of Kapaemahu 167
sugar 28, 47–48, 52, 55, 59, 63–64, 66, 87, 90, 94, 100, 101, 130, 157, 196, 198, 200, 207, 221–222, 223, 227–228, 234, 258, 259, 267, 270, 276, 298, 300, 303, 306
Suisan Fish Market 268
sumo wrestling 93, 194
Sun Disc 157
surfing 31, 85, 121–122, 168, 199, 209, 210, 239
Sweet Leilani 101

## T

Tahiti 26–27, 66, 74, 75, 107, 129, 146, 167, 197
"talking story" 73, 75
Tamashiro's Market 181
Tantalus 186
Tantalus Drive 186
Tantalus-Round Top 185
*taro* 28, 71–72, 74, 76, 115, 166, 195, 200, 236, 306
tattooing 31
Taylor, Howard 304
Taylor, Samuel and Mary 240
Taylor Camp 304–305
Tedeschi Winery 223
Tern Island 211
Territorial Hotel Company 171
Thomas Square 155
Thompson, Pete 86
Thurston, Lorrin A. 54
Thurston Lava Tube 288
*ti* 28, 115, 147, 174, 189, 200, 204, 249
Tonga 146
*Tora! Tora! Tora!* 205
tourism 61, 64, 167, 307
Tracks 208
traditions 71–76
Transpac Regatta 161
Transpacific Yacht Race 165
Trask, David 86
Tripler, General Charles Stuart 202
Tripler Army Medical Center 202
Turtle Bay Hilton Resort and Country Club 199
Twain, Mark 49, 121, 219, 230, 245
*Two Jacks Bar* 158

## U

*'uala* 74
ukulele 94, 100, 102, 115
*'ulu* 74
'Ulupalakua Ranch 222
unions 60–63
United States 52, 67, 92, 100, 101, 181, 224
United States Navy 224
University of Hawaii at Manoa 188–189, 190, 195, 221
Upcountry 221–224
'Upolu Point 277
Upside Down Falls 185
US Pacific fleet 203
*USS Arizona* Memorial 203
*USS Boston* 54
*USS Utah* 204
Uwekahuna 287

## V

Valley of the Temples Memorial Park 195
Vancouver, George 28, 44, 87, 153, 200
Veuster, Joseph de (*Father Damien*) 154, 156, 245, 247, 251–252, 283
Victoria, Queen of England 184
Vietnam War 186
Volcano, Big Island 285
Volcano Art Center, Big Island 285
Volcano House, Big Island 285
volcanoes 127, 189, 219, 227, 245, 265, 268, 271, 273, 285, 286

## W–Y

Wahiawa 204
Wahiawa Botanic Garden 204
Wai'alae Country Club 190
Wai'ale'ale 295
Wai'anae 207
Wai'anae Coast 200, 207
Wai'anae Mountains 187, 205, 207
Wai'anapanapa State Park 238
Waiahole Valley 196
Waialua 200, 248
Waianuenue Avenue 267
Waihe'e, Governor John 67, 86
Waikane Valley 196
Waikiki 21, 63, 65, 145, 161, 163, 165, 167–176, 187
Waikiki Shell amphitheater 174
*Waikiki Wedding* 101
Waikoloa Resort 279
Waikolu Lookout 251
Wailea 223, 228
Wailua 237, 302
Wailua Beach 308
Wailua Falls 239
Wailua River 308
Wailua Valley 249
Wailuku 227
Wailuku River 267
Wailuku River State Park 268
Waimanalo 194
Waimanu Valley 271, 277
Waimea 275, 298, 300, 303
Waimea Bay 122, 199
Waimea Canyon 295, 299
Waimea Falls Park 200
Waimoku Falls 239
Wainiha Bay 305
Waipahu 207
Waipi'o Valley 21, 89, 269, 270
Waipuhia Valley Falls 185
Wakea 71, 73
War Memorial Natatorium 175
Ward Centre 165
Ward Warehouse 165
warfare 30, 75
Washington Place 154
water sports 195
waterfront, Lahaina 230
*wauke* 28
West Maui Mountains 227
whales 46–47, 48, 64, 94, 129, 162, 228–230, 232, 233
Wheeler Army Air Field 205
Wi'ale'ale 297
Wilcox, George N 304
*wiliwili* tree 167, 299
Wimea River 299
windsurfing 194, 221
Wizard Stones 167
Wo Hing Society Temple 234
World War I 93, 186
World War II 59, 61–63, 88, 92, 94, 172, 186, 203, 254, 271
Yatsen, Dr Sun 88, 276
Yokohama Bay 210
Young, John 42–43, 184
YMCA, Armed Forces 156
YWCA, Honolulu 156

A
B
C
D
F
G
H
I
J
a
b
c
d
e
f
g
h
i
j
k

# INSIGHT GUIDES

## COLORSET NUMBERS

**North America**
160 Alaska
173 American Southwest
 Atlanta
227 Boston
275 California
180 California, Northern
161 California, Southern
237 Canada
184C Chicago
184 Crossing America
243 Florida
240 Hawaii
275A Los Angeles
243A Miami
237B Montreal
 National Parks of
 America: East
 National Parks of
 America: West
269 Native America
100 New England
184E New Orleans
184F New York City
133 New York State
147 Pacific Northwest
184B Philadelphia
172 Rockies
275B San Francisco
184D Seattle
 Southern States
 of America
186 Texas
237A Vancouver
184C Washington DC

**Latin America and
The Caribbean**
150 Amazon Wildlife
260 Argentina
188 Bahamas
292 Barbados
 Belize
217 Bermuda
127 Brazil
260A Buenos Aires
162 Caribbean
151 Chile
281 Costa Rica
 Cuba
118 Ecuador
213 Jamaica
285 Mexico
285A Mexico City
249 Peru
156 Puerto Rico
127A Rio de Janeiro
116 South America
139 Trinidad & Tobago
198 Venezuela

**Europe**
155 Alsace
158A Amsterdam
167A Athens
263 Austria
107 Baltic States
219B Barcelona

187 Bay of Naples
109 Belgium
135A Berlin
178 Brittany
109A Brussels
144A Budapest
213 Burgundy
122 Catalonia
141 Channel Islands
135E Cologne
119 Continental Europe
189 Corsica
291 Côte d'Azur
165 Crete
226 Cyprus
114 Czech/Slovak Reps
238 Denmark
135B Dresden
142B Dublin
135F Düsseldorf
149 Eastern Europe
148A Edinburgh
123 Finland
209B Florence
154 France
135C Frankfurt
135 Germany
148B Glasgow
279 Gran Canaria
124 Great Britain
167 Greece
166 Greek Islands
135G Hamburg
144 Hungary
256 Iceland
142 Ireland
209 Italy
202A Lisbon
258 Loire Valley
124A London
201 Madeira
219A Madrid
157 Mallorca & Ibiza
117 Malta
101A Moscow
135D Munich
158 Netherlands
111 Normandy
120 Norway
124B Oxford
154A Paris
115 Poland
202 Portugal
114A Prague
153 Provence
177 Rhine
209A Rome
101 Russia
130 Sardinia
148 Scotland
261 Sicily
264 South Tyrol
219 Spain
220 Spain, Southern
101B St. Petersburg
170 Sweden
232 Switzerland

112 Tenerife
210 Tuscany
174 Umbria
209C Venice
263A Vienna
267 Wales
183 Waterways of Europe

**Middle East and Africa**
268A Cairo
204 East African Wildlife
268 Egypt
208 Gambia & Senegal
252 Israel
236A Istanbul
252A Jerusalem-Tel Aviv
214 Jordan
270 Kenya
235 Morocco
259 Namibia
265 Nile, The
257 South Africa
113 Tunisia
236 Turkey
171 Turkish Coast
215 Yemen

**Asia/Pacific**
287 Asia, East
207 Asia, South
262 Asia, South East
194 Asian Wildlife,
 Southeast
272 Australia
206 Bali Baru
246A Bangkok
234A Beijing
247B Calcutta
234 China
247A Delhi, Jaipur, Agra
169 Great Barrier Reef
196 Hong Kong
247 India
212 India, South
128 Indian Wildlife
143 Indonesia
278 Japan
266 Java
203A Kathmandu
300 Korea
145 Malaysia
218 Marine Life in the
 South China Sea
272B Melbourne
211 Myanmar
203 Nepal
293 New Zealand
205 Pakistan
222 Philippines
250 Rajasthan
159 Singapore
105 Sri Lanka
272 Sydney
175 Taiwan
246 Thailand
278A Tokyo
255 Vietnam
193 Western Himalaya

# INSIGHT *Pocket* GUIDES

**EXISTING & FORTHCOMING TITLES:**

| North America | Corsica | Middle East and Africa |
|---|---|---|
| Atlanta | Costa Blanca | Istanbul |
| Boston | Costa Brava | Kenya |
| British Coumbia | Cote d'Azur | Maldives |
| Florida | Crete | Morocco |
| Florida Keys | Denmark | Seychelles |
| Hawaii | Florence | Tunisia |
| Miami | Gran Canaria | Turkish Coast |
| Montreal | Hungary | **Asia/Pacific** |
| New York City | Ibiza | Bali |
| North California | Ireland | Bali Birdwalks |
| Quebec | Lisbon | Bangkok |
| San Francisco | Loire Valley | Beijing |
| South California | London | Bhutan |
| Toronto | Madrid | Canton |
| **Latin America and** | Mallorca | Chiang Mai |
| **The Caribbean** | Malta | Fiji |
| Bahamas | Marbella | Hong Kong |
| Baja | Milan | Jakarta |
| Belize | Moscow | Kathmandu, |
| Bermuda | Munich | Bikes & Hikes |
| Jamaica | Oslo/Bergen | Kuala Lumpur |
| Mexico City | Paris | Macau |
| Puerto Rico | Prague | Malacca |
| US Virgin Islands | Provence | Nepal |
| Yucatan Peninsula | Rhodes | New Delhi |
| **Europe** | Rome | New Zealand |
| Aegean Islands | Sardinia | Penang |
| Algarve | Scotland | Phuket |
| Alsace | Seville | Sabah |
| Athens | Sicily | Sikkim |
| Barcelona | Southeast England | Singapore |
| Bavaria | St Petersburg | Sri Lanka |
| Berlin | Tenerife | Sydney |
| Brittany | Tuscany | Thailand |
| Brussels | Venice | Tibet |
| Budapest | Vienna | Yogyakarta |

● ● ● ● ● ● ● ● ● ● ● ● ● ● ● ● ● ● ● ● ● ● ● ● ●

*United States:* **Houghton Mifflin Company, Boston MA 02108**
**Tel: (800) 2253362  Fax: (800) 4589501**

*Canada:* **Thomas Allen & Son, 390 Steelcase Road East**
**Markham, Ontario L3R 1G2**
**Tel: (416) 4759126  Fax: (416) 4756747**

*Great Britain:* **GeoCenter UK, Hampshire RG22 4BJ**
**Tel: (256) 817987  Fax: (256) 817988**

*Worldwide:* **Höfer Communications Singapore 2262**
**Tel: (65) 8612755  Fax: (65) 8616438**

**66** I was first drawn to the Insight Guides by the excellent "Nepal" volume. I can think of no book which so effectively captures the essence of a country. Out of these pages leaped the Nepal I know – the captivating charm of a people and their culture. I've since discovered and enjoyed the entire Insight Guide Series. Each volume deals with a country or city in the same sensitive depth, which is nowhere more evident than in the superb photography. **99**

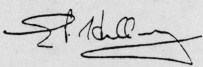

*Sir Edmund Hillary*